The Brethren
During the Age
of World War

The Brethren During the Age of World War

The Church of the Brethren Encounter with Modernization, 1914-1950

A Source Book

Stephen L. Longenecker

Brethren Press

The Brethren During the Age of World War
The Church of the Brethren Encounter with Modernization, 1914-1950
A Source Book

Edited by Julie Garber

Copyright © 2006 by Stephen L. Longenecker
Published by Brethren Press®. Brethren Press is a program of the Church
of the Brethren General Board, 1451 Dundee Avenue, Elgin, IL 60120.

ISBN-13: 978-0-87178-075-1
ISBN-10: 0-87178-075-5

Library of Congress Control Number: 2006924215

10 09 08 07 06   5 4 3 2 1

Printed in the United States of America

*This book is one of several Brethren Press publications displaying the
mark of the 300th anniversary of the Brethren (1708-2008). It represents
the theme "Surrendered to God, Transformed by Christ, Empowered by
the Spirit."*

To
Donald F. Durnbaugh
and
Carol, Lew, and Ada

About the author
Stephen L. Longenecker (Johns Hopkins, Ph. D.) is professor of history and chair of the Department of History and Political Science at Bridgewater College in Virginia. His most recent publication is *Shenandoah Religion: Outsiders and the Mainstream, 1716-1865* (Baylor University Press, 2002).

CONTENTS

FOREWORD

I first encountered the Church of the Brethren source book series as an undergraduate toiling on a term paper. Since then, I have used these volumes as a graduate student (as did my advisor) and then as a researcher. Considering my long familiarity with these volumes, I was deeply flattered when the Church of the Brethren Historical Committee commissioned me to add a fifth volume to the series.

Admittedly, my treatment of history in this book is more interpretive than that of other authors in the series. In part, this reflects my idiosyncrasies as a scholar. Perhaps I could have kept my thoughts to myself and waited for another scholar to come along to produce a monograph. But the small and overworked family of Brethren historians is unlikely in the foreseeable future to write another major work on this period; therefore, some innovation with the genre seems acceptable.

Modernization forms the theme and organizational framework for this book. During what historians call the "early modern" period, between the Renaissance and the French Revolution, nations, science, capitalism, humanism, and rationalism replaced medieval systems. In the following period—the nineteenth century—individualism, competition, secularism, and industrialization added their weight to modernization. Gradually, but inexorably, merit and competition displaced birth and rank as status determinants, science competed with religion as a source of truth, and individualism overcame community. By 1914 many of the great changes crafted by these trends were in position, leaving American society increasingly diverse, urban, bureaucratic, industrial, technological, professional, non-Protestant, consumer-driven, and class-oriented.[1]

During the age of world war, Americans sometimes felt the sting of modernization's short-term impact and other times struggled to accept its long-term consequences. World War I, for example, was the first global conflict between modern, industrialized nation-states, and it quickly mobilized their societies, including public opinion and manpower, more fully than ever before. Following the war, however, American society strained under the load of the long-term consequences of modernization. Women during the twenties showed greater independence, the economy created new anxieties, youth developed their own subculture, popular culture became more secular, and Americans contemplated their nation's role in international affairs. In the thirties the modern economy stunned America with the Great Depression, and in the last decade of this book, modern war returned, bigger and even worse than before, with a national draft, a managed economy, broad taxation, and catastrophic human consequences. Indeed, between 1914 and 1950 modernization demonstrated striking aptitude for surprising Americans with innovative ways to transform lives.[2]

Likewise, the first half of the twentieth century meant great change for the Brethren, much of it flowing from modernization. The world wars challenged pacifist Brethren with military conscription, positioning nonviolent Brethren to face hostile and occasionally aggressive public opinion. In the end the state pressured the church into submission on conscription. Throughout the Second World War, including the years before and immediately after, the contemporary shift from overseas mission to overseas service accelerated.

In the relatively brief period between the two global conflicts, the Brethren strained to adapt to the continuing consequences of modernization. During the Great Depression, for example, the modern industrial economy at its worst ravaged the finances of Brethren individuals and organizations, demonstrating the increasingly close tie between Brethren and the economy. On the other hand, many Brethren resisted some aspects of modernization in society. The growing secularization of popular values, exemplified by movies, the youth cult, and jazz, alarmed most Brethren, and the denomination enlisted in the great crusade to ban alcohol.

As Brethren fought some elements of modernization in the popular culture, they absorbed others. Their leadership became more professional, their denominational structure more bureaucratized, and their women more independent. Individualism grew among the rank and file. As brothers and sisters made more religious decisions by themselves without guidance from the faith community, discipline declined, most noticeably regarding dress. Many of these adjustments to modernization divided the fellowship along lines similar to those of the larger society. Conservatives lamented individualism's impact on unity within the faith community and on nonconformity to the mainstream, both core Brethren values. Likewise, defenders of the old Brethren order lamented the professionalization of the ministry and the growing numbers of independent young women in the denomination. They detested new trends that applied professionalization, specialization, and the scientific method to biblical interpretation; to many traditionalists this movement did not promise progress but, instead, jeopardized the core of the faith.

Some Brethren found spiritual kinship with fundamentalism, a movement often called "anti-modernist," which girded its loins to protect traditional faith. Many Brethren agreed with fundamentalists about preserving orthodox biblical interpretation and opposing secular trends in popular culture, but fewer joined the movement, whose militancy they disliked. Still, the impact of modernization on Old Order Brethrenism and old time Protestantism was similar enough that in 1926 a small group of conservatives left the denomination to create the Dunkard Brethren. Throughout the remainder of the period of this book, other Old Orders, fundamentalists, and traditionalists threatened to abandon the Church of the Brethren. To be sure, modern war, the modern economy, and the modernization of society had a profound impact on the Brethren during the age of world war.

○ℛ

Seven chapters describe the Brethren encounter with modernization during the age of world war. The Introduction places the Brethren in American society prior to World War I. Chapter I, "The World at War: America at Peace," describes the period between the outbreak of war in Europe and the American decision to enter it; this chapter highlights denominational issues unrelated to the conflict. Chapter II, "World War I: America Joins the Conflict," discusses the war directly. The next three chapters cover the Twenties. Chapter III, "The Twenties: Change," explores changes within the denomination during this period, and Chapter IV, "The Twenties: Conflict," documents the Brethren reaction to shifts in the larger society. Chapter V, "The Twenties: Division," explains tension within the fellowship created by these changes, including the Dunkard Brethren schism. Chapter VI, "The Thirties: Economic and International Crises," describes the Brethren during the Great Depression and their response to a growing predicament in foreign relations. The twenties receive more space in this volume than the thirties because Americans struggled especially hard during the Jazz Age with the consequences of modernization and because social and religious trends in the thirties were basically a continuation of trends developed during the previous twenties. During the thirties the Depression overwhelmed everything else until the end of the decade when war clouds dominated. Chapter VII, "World War Again," describes the Brethren during World War II, and, finally, Chapter VIII, "Postwar Recovery: The Greatest Generation?" concludes the era of world war. In truth, the period from 1945 to 1950 is both the end of an era and the beginning of another, which includes the Cold War, civil rights, Billy Graham, Normal Vincent Peale, baby boomers, feminism, and Vietnam. The last chapter, however, focuses only on the setting of the world war period. To begin a new era is the task of the next source book.

Documents that record the story of Brethren and modernization during this period come from a variety of sources. By definition, source books chronicle top-down, institutional history, and, therefore, major denominational decisions, including the deliberation and actions of Annual Conference. But the denominational story also involves long-term trends and the faith journeys of thousands of men and women. The beliefs of an anonymous sister in Ohio often reveal as much about the Brethren past as those of an Annual Conference moderator. Thus, *Brethren During the Age of World War* also contains a view from the bottom up with interviews, letters, and diaries that shed light on the Brethren rank and file.

CR

Several comments about editorial decisions are appropriate. Generally, the excerpts have been reproduced verbatim. On occasion, I have tinkered with punctuation to make the text more readable. Some issues of the denominational periodical, *The Gospel Messenger,* oddly combine a comma and a dash,—like this,—but I have removed them, except this pair to show what they looked like. Also, it was popular among Brethren to identify themselves only by their initials rather than by their given and/or middle names. Hence, Daniel Webster Kurtz usually called himself "D. W. Kurtz." I have maintained the customary usage ("D. W.") in the text, but the footnotes include the full name for the benefit of researchers.

Several colleagues and friends contributed to this project. Donald Durnbaugh, Kenneth Kreider, William Kostlevy, Kenneth Shaffer, and Anna Speicher read drafts of the manuscript, caught numerous errors, and offered valuable suggestions. Publisher Wendy McFadden also provided a very helpful critique and Nancy Klemm labored tirelessly copyediting and managing the details of production. She and Ken Shaffer also assisted with the selection of photographs. My skillful and highly professional editor, Julie Garber, appreciably polished the manuscript by unearthing small errors buried within its text and asking big, thoughtful thematic questions. I leaned heavily on Rick Fogarty, my friend and colleague at Bridgewater College, for advice on European history. I am also indebted to many librarians, including the staffs at the University of Virginia, Elizabethtown College, Juniata College, and Bridgewater. I am especially indebted to Ken Shaffer at the Brethren Historical Library and Archives in Elgin, Illinois, and to Mike Ours and Robert Tout at Bridgewater. Lisa Houff, the faculty secretary for my building, provided indispensable clerical assistance. Interviews with Harry Badorf, George Daniel Baughman, Esther Fry, Monroe Good, Mary Greenawalt, Earl Heckman, Urban and Alma Moyers Long, Julia and Roy Longenecker, Dorothy and Ray Summy, Stanley Wampler, and Naomi West were both pleasurable and highly beneficial.

One of the dedications is to the memory of Donald F. Durnbaugh. The more I became acquainted with Don, the more I appreciated him. He particularly supported this project; he read the drafts promptly, and to say that he read them carefully is an understatement. Additionally, Don's prolific body of scholarship made my task lighter and more pleasurable. His *European Origins of the Brethren*[3] began this series, and his subsequent research on the denomination blazed a well-marked trail for all who have come after him. Even a cursory glance at this book's footnotes reveals just how much I stand on his shoulders. On a very personal level, I deeply enjoyed my conversations with him about this project. Therefore, early on I decided to dedicate the book to Don, but I never told him. He had protested a modest mention deep inside the footnotes of his postwar work in Austria, and I feared he would object to the larger honor. Instead, I planned to inform him of the dedication at the last minute, but, sadly, I waited too long. Donald Durnbaugh died unexpectedly just before publication of this book. All of us who study Brethren history will miss him deeply.

I also dedicate this volume to my family with thanks once again for their support. I have dedicated other works to them, but that was a generation ago when Carol and Lew, my children, were in elementary school. Now they are grown and building careers. Repeating words of my appreciation for them feels timely. My wife, Ada, of course, has endured my professional obligations without complaint all these years, and the dedication of a second book to her is small compensation for all she has given me.

NOTES

1. Thomas J. Schlereth, *Victorian America: Transformations in Everyday Life, 1876-1915* (New York: Harper Collins, 1991), 300.
2. Paul S. Fass, *The Damned and the Beautiful: American Youth in the 1920s* (New York: Oxford University Press, 1977), 4-5; Nancy MacLean, *Behind the Mask of Chivalry: The Making of the Second Ku Klux Klan* (New York: Oxford University Press, 1994), 23-51; Maury Klein, *Rainbow's End: The Crash of 1929* (New York: Oxford University Press, 2001), xvii-xviii, 271-74; David M. Kennedy, *Freedom from Fear: The American People in the Depression and War, 1929-1945* (New York: Oxford University Press, 1999), 619-37, 644-47.
3. Donald F. Durnbaugh, *European Origins of the Brethren: A Source Book on the Beginnings of the Church of the Brethren in the Early Eighteenth Century* (Elgin, Ill.: Brethren Press, 1958).

The Church of the Brethren, 1708-1914

On June 28, 1914, a Serbian nationalist assassinated Franz Ferdinand, the Austro-Hungarian archduke, and his wife, Sophie, during an official visit to Sarajevo, Bosnia-Herzegovina. This political murder ignited a chain of events that closed the Victorian era and opened a lengthy period of global conflict. As the "lamps went out all over Europe," in the well-known words of the British ambassador to Russia, the world entered an age of war that lasted until 1945, interrupted only by a twenty-one-year breathing period.[1]

LATE VICTORIAN AMERICA

Until the lamps went out in the United States, adjustment to industrialization preoccupied the country. Late nineteenth-century American society had undergone intense industrial expansion, sometimes called the Age of Big Business, with an especially difficult last decade that included a depression, labor violence, an agrarian revolt, and a war. Thus, in the first decade and a half of the new century, the consequences of a more heavily industrialized society were still new, and many Americans spent much of this period accommodating to these changes. Optimism, with encouragement from religion, abounded even as modernization continued to rework society.

Some aspects of industrialization appealed to turn-of-the-century Americans. After the steep depression of the 1890s, prosperity returned, and the economy approached full employment. Income improved from a median annual industrial wage of $418 in 1900 to approximately $880 in 1915. Agriculture, too, entered flush times, enjoying a rare "golden age" in which market forces favored it; between 1900 and 1910 farm prices rose nearly fifty percent.[2]

New technology accompanied economic growth and changed life in ways large and small. In particular, electricity quickened industrialization and raised the standard of living. Installment plans allowed consumers up to two years to pay for the costs of wiring their homes and buying appliances; many new electrical gadgets, including fans, flatirons, stoves, sewing machines, and clothes washers, enhanced the daily lives of women. Other innovations were similarly impressive. New canning methods and refrigerated railroad cars expanded the fare on middle-class tables. Fresh peas, for example, became available regardless of the season, and between 1909 and 1920, grapefruits, shipped north in refrigerated boxcars, rose in consumption from under one pound to over five pounds annually per capita. Processed foods, such as canned soup and Jell-O products, shortened family meal preparation. In 1904 King Camp Gillette manufactured 12.4 million razor blades, a new product that contributed to the decline of the full beard. A Texas oil gusher (1901), Orville and Wilbur Wright's airplane (1903), and Henry Ford's Model T automobile (1908) foreshadowed the early stages of a transportation revolution. From Jell-O to smooth-shaven men to the Model T, technology promised change.[3]

For middle-class consumers, the new technology and improving economy also meant more abundance. Rural free delivery (1896), parcel post (1913), and catalogues brought consumerism to the rural countryside. In 1910 an estimated 10 million Americans purchased goods through the mail. In 1906 Congress authorized messages on the address side of postcards, and their popularity soared. That year Americans mailed 770.5 million of the little communiqués, and in 1909 correspondents dropped 968 million of them into mailboxes. One company alone printed 3 million cards per day. In 1900 George Eastman's cheapest handheld Kodak camera, the Brownie, sold for a dollar. In the 1890s soda fountains began serving ice cream sundaes, and hungry Americans first bit into ice cream cones at the 1904 St. Louis Exposition. Life improved for consumers with a little cash.[4]

Many Americans also had more time to pursue the new technology and the growing list of available consumer goods. By 1914 the average work week in manufacturing was fifty hours, and white-collar workers toiled nine-hour days Monday through Friday and a half day on Saturday. Increased wages and leisure time hours led to the rise of mass entertainment, especially in urban areas. Ballparks, for example, often occupied strategic space beside trolley lines; amusement parks, such as Coney

Island, grew up at the end of those lines. Trolley ridership on weekends and holidays was significantly greater than on workdays as city dwellers gladly paid the nickel fare to flee their neighborhoods. Around 1910 dancing became a national craze as dance halls, school proms, and lodge cotillions proliferated. Movies, usually fifteen to twenty minutes long, supplanted nickelodeons, and phonographs edged aside band concerts as a popular form of entertainment. As record sales increased, the middle class listened more and played and sang less. Ragtime became popular, especially after Irving Berlin's *Alexander's Ragtime Band* appeared in 1911. Many listened to ragtime and other music on a Victrola, which transformed a bulky phonograph into an attractive piece of furniture fit for any middle-class home. More than ever, Americans had leisure time and enjoyed it.[5]

Technology, prosperity, and amusement were relatively easy adjustments, but other changes brought by industrialization were more difficult. Despite the unprecedented bounty of the period, tremendous economic inequality persisted. As the recovery proceeded, big business consolidated, and between 1897 and 1904 some three thousand corporations reorganized into three hundred larger concerns. The most conspicuous merger combined the nation's largest steelmakers, which earned more income than the federal government. So top-heavy was the economy that the greatest four percent of American firms generated fifty-seven percent of the nation's industrial production, and seventy Americans held one-sixteenth of the nation's wealth.

At the lowest rungs in the social ladder, racism heavily restrained minorities. Lynching terrorized African Americans, and in the South tenant farmers, both black and white, labored in conditions that approached serfdom. In the American Southwest, Mexican Americans who lost their ranches due to drought, crop loss, and a new tax structure joined more recent Mexican immigrants to become a permanent migrant labor force. Though the rising economic tide lifted all boats, some boats rode the waves much lower than others.[6]

Urbanization, a trend hardly new but more prominent than ever, perplexed Americans. Cityscapes portrayed contrast, a mixture of technology, prosperity, diversity, and poverty. By 1900 trolleys, another late nineteenth-century innovation, had replaced horse cars, freeing thoroughfares of animal waste (ten pounds per horse per day) and dead animals, which rotted where they fell. Webs of trolley tracks, like spokes of a wheel, pulled shoppers, theatergoers, workers, and businessmen downtown—few lines went crosswise. For the middle class, turn-of-the-century urban centers became a stunning cluster of theaters, restaurants, lobster palaces, and department stores blazing with light at all hours, thanks to electricity. Other aspects of urban life, however, troubled the middle class. Typically, just a few blocks from the glowing oases of middle-class amusement, working-class neighborhoods bent under the burden of poverty. These areas were overcrowded, poorly ventilated, dirty, disease-ridden, and plagued with crime. Sewers clogged, garbage rotted in tenement air shafts and courtyards, and dead horses decayed in the streets. (Trolleys did not replace private horse-drawn carts, so dead horses, therefore, remained a problem.) One Manhattan neighborhood had 986 residents per acre. Urban utilities struggled to keep pace, lagging behind the consumer and transportation revolutions. New York City, for example, deposited daily five hundred million gallons of raw sewage into surrounding waterways, while Baltimore and New Orleans had no sewage systems at all. Many who lived in working-class districts were recent immigrants, who flooded into the country at the heaviest rate in American history and added to the complexity of urban life. Between 1900 and 1910, approximately one million immigrants, mostly non-Protestants, entered annually. In 1910 three-fifths of the residents of the nation's twelve largest cities were recent immigrants from Europe or their children. Urban America, then, presented a paradox: dirty but dazzling, amusing but depressing, rich but poor.[7]

Laborers in America's expanding industry created another uncomfortable corollary to industrialization. In the struggle between labor and management, capital still held most of the cards. Child labor, for example, was commonplace. In 1913 one-fifth of all children supported themselves through employment. When reformers persuaded states to regulate child labor, legislation typically restricted only children ages eleven and under from working ten-hour days. Furthermore, conditions for labor were frequently difficult. In the South mill hands worked sixty-hour weeks for some of the lowest wages in the nation. Often entire families labored at the same mill. The industrial workplace was also dangerous. In 1913 a national survey revealed that 25,000 had died while laboring and 700,000 suffered serious injury. The Triangle Shirtwaist factory fire in New York in 1911, which claimed the lives of 150 Jewish and Italian immigrant women, became a tragic symbol of the hazards faced by labor. The doomed workers were trapped on the top floor, because management locked the doors to prevent employee theft and fraternization with union organizers. Although many immigrants reported that conditions in America were better than in the old country and wages for skilled labor improved, on balance a significant gap remained between the middle and laboring classes in living and working conditions. With its dismal urban poverty and a David/Goliath battle with management, labor's problems were part and parcel of industrialization.[8]

Thus, increased technology, growing consumer opportunities, and more leisure time were obvious benefits of industrialization, but other consequences of the modernizing economy, such as big business, urbanization, industrial poverty, and an exploited working class, were troublesome. Many turn-of-the-century Americans, however, confidently attacked their anxieties about society, and a broad movement, usually called Progressivism, arose to help society adjust to the uncomfortable by-products of recent economic growth.

Aside from its focus on the consequences of industrialization, especially urbanization, Progressivism was otherwise so fragmented and diverse that it defies easy definition. Some Progressives simply worked for government to provide more effective services or to grow more efficient by using experts, such as city planners, public health officials, housing officers, community development advisors, and social scientists. Other Progressives, particularly women, were social reformers who aided the working class by establishing settlement houses and advocating women's suffrage and birth control. Moral reformers promoted antiprostitution legislation and campaigned for Prohibition, which they believed liberated the working classes from their alcoholic albatross, freed politics of the baneful influence of saloons, and accelerated assimilation of immigrants into the American mainstream. In education Progressives encouraged the growth of public education and its professionalization. The political wing of Progressivism declared war on urban machines and endorsed city managers, primary elections, ballot reform, initiatives, referenda, and recalls. Perhaps most famous for attacking monopolies, including utilities and railroads, Progressives were often cast as liberal idealists, though sometimes their trust-busting was merely an attempt to restore order in a chaotic marketplace. From city managers to birth control to the regulation of utilities, all that held this broad movement together was a desire to adjust to an industrialized society.[9]

Progressives enjoyed mixed success. On one hand, they failed to eliminate poverty or transform society. Nevertheless, Progressivism left a string of individual reforms, and it elected three men from two parties to the White House: Theodore Roosevelt (R), William Howard Taft (R), and Woodrow Wilson (D). Progressives amended the U. S. Constitution four times, securing the graduated federal income tax (1913), the direct election of United States senators (1913), Prohibition (1919), and women's suffrage (1920). Prior to the Progressive amendments, changes to the Constitution had only come in two brief spurts—the Founders era

(Amendments 1-12) and Reconstruction (Amendments 13-15)—so the Progressive period was only the third time in 125 years that the Constitution was amended, which suggests the importance of this movement. Finally, the Progressive legacy left the growing conviction that government had a larger role to play in the lives of individuals, whether cleaning city streets, managing natural resources, regulating the economy, or banning alcoholic beverages.[10]

Religion during the Progressive era mirrored developments in the larger society. Overseas mission, for example, came hand-in-glove with the expansion of American influence around the world. As imperialists worked for the growth of American economic and political power, missionaries spread the gospel and American culture in new lands. Between 1890 and 1905, the number of American missionaries to China doubled, and by 1919 they again increased twofold. In addition to their traditional message of salvation, turn-of-the-century missionaries added lessons on health, education, and employment, further widening the influence of American culture. In the 1890s cooperation between the United States government and overseas mission grew especially close, and many Protestant mission boards viewed the U. S. victory over Catholic Spain as a special opportunity to convert and civilize heathens in dark lands. After 1900 popular opinion shifted toward an informal cultural and economic empire rather than a messy, formal one with political boundaries, but imperialists still understood religion's ability to support the American empire.[11]

Most conspicuously, religion contributed to the middle-class motivation to solve social problems. At the heart of this reform impulse was liberal theology with its insistence that Christianity accommodate to the modern age. Liberals fondly modernized their faith by stripping it of what they considered archaic myths and leaving behind the core truth. They achieved this through the historical-critical approach to biblical study, sometimes called "higher criticism," which applied modern knowledge, including literary analysis, archeology, history, linguistics, and the scientific method, to the study of the scriptures. An optimistic view of human nature added to the liberal readiness to face social problems. According to liberals, humans could improve themselves and society, and even the kingdom of God was within reach without waiting for Christ's second coming. Liberals also emphasized the humanity of Jesus rather than his divinity and often considered Jesus as a role model rather than a divine presence who atoned for human sin. This suggested that humans were not depraved but, instead, could aspire to imitate Jesus. Finally, liberals believed in a loving, forgiving, fatherlike God active in human life, and they downplayed God as a distant, stern judge, yet another uplifting concept. In short, accommodation to modernity, optimism about human nature, Jesus as exemplar, and a loving, active God became the building blocks of liberalism and belonged to the intellectual foundation of Progressive reform.[12]

Most liberals enrolled in the Social Gospel movement, which applied religion to social problems and taught that society sins as do individuals. This practical theology emerged in the 1890s when liberal seminaries concluded that Old Testament prophets and Jesus spoke about society as much as they spoke about the individual. Rather than conversion and evangelicalism, religion was about human relationships. In the next decade, the Social Gospel became more widespread, especially after the publication of Walter Rauschenbusch's *Christianity and the Social Crisis* in 1907.[13] The sin of socio-economic injustice stemming from industrialization particularly concerned followers of this system, and in practice they sought to educate middle-class Protestants about the problems of urban labor and the causes of industrial conflict. The assumption that the Social Gospel was an antidote to the growing socialist movement added to its appeal.[14]

Many mainline fellowships became active in social issues. Social workers equipped the poor, including recent immigrants, for self-improvement through household economy, better hygiene, and literacy and English language instruction. Institutional churches, drawing inspiration from British and African American examples, opened buildings with a wide variety of services, including kindergartens, day nurseries, reading rooms, assembly halls, club rooms, gymnasiums with showers, legal aid, employment services, sewing classes, and educational facilities. Temple University in Philadelphia was the outgrowth of one of these multi-faceted churches. The movement also gave attention to political reform. Many Social Gospelers concluded that urban machines harmed the interests of labor, and, therefore, they battled political corruption and championed Progressive political reforms. With its liberal optimism about human betterment and emphasis on reform and democracy, the Social Gospel functioned as the religious version of Progressivism.[15]

Conservatives, as well, sought to change cities, denying liberals and the Social Gospel movement a monopoly on reform. Many conservatives who preached the traditional theology of sin and salvation also enthusiastically battled vice, closed brothels, operated institutional churches, and fought gambling, political corruption, and, especially, alcohol. Conservatives, however, maintained their traditional evangelical message about a changed heart, which distinguished these reformers from

Social Gospel adherents. The Salvation Army, for example, ran missions in urban areas with a strongly evangelical viewpoint. Although many conservatives later became fundamentalists who de-emphasized social reform, in the first decade of the twentieth century they yielded little ground to liberals in their desire to fix social ills resulting from an industrialized society.[16]

Turn-of-the-century religion also contributed to American diversity. Protestantism continued to spawn new denominations, as it had throughout its existence in North America. Holiness groups, who believed that the sanctified are inwardly pure, enjoyed greater acceptance and in 1895 added the Church of the Nazarene to their fold. Pentecostals, a related movement known for intensely spiritual worship, gained momentum from the 1906 Azusa Street revivals in Los Angeles. Several Pentecostal denominations, including the Pentecostal Holiness Church (1911) and the Assemblies of God (1914), began during this period. Recent immigrants added to the American religious quilt, including diversity within their own traditions unknown in Europe. American Catholicism, for example, included Irish, German, Italian, Polish, Mexican, and other subgroups, each with its distinctive version of the Roman Church. American Judaism divided into the Orthodox, who were usually recent arrivals from Eastern Europe, and Reformed, generally well-assimilated German Americans. Eastern Orthodox Christianity subdivided into at least fifteen groups based on nationalities, all at this point nominally under the leadership of the Russian Church because it first brought Orthodoxy to the U. S. (After the Russian Revolution, the various ethnic Orthodox faiths went their own way.) Religion undoubtedly added to America's pluralism.[17]

Doctrinal conflict between liberal and conservative Protestants, primarily over biblical interpretation, formed another piece in the mosaic of American religion. As liberals accommodated religion to the present age, conservatives increasingly focused on the last days. Premillenialism became increasingly vital for them, and late in the nineteenth century Cyrus I. Scofield developed a popular, detailed chronology of the end times that circulated widely in his *Scofield Reference Bible,* published in 1909. Bible conferences and so-called prophetic conferences, which studied end-times thought exclusively, attracted conservatives from various denominations. Related to the end-times interest was the growing conviction in biblical literalism, the polar opposite of liberal myth-busting. Bible schools further energized the growing conservative movement. These institutions trained leaders for the ministry and the mission field but placed less emphasis on formal educational requirements than seminaries. The best known was the Moody Bible Institute, opened in 1889 but unnamed until 1900, founded by famed revivalist Dwight L. Moody, who desired trained, conservative pastors to help with urban evangelical efforts. Another well-known Bible school, the Bible Institute of Los Angeles (BIOLA), began in 1907.[18]

Late Victorian Americans, then, spent the first decade and a half of the twentieth century adjusting to what industrialization had wrought, including gadgets, trinkets, overcrowded cities, and unequal distribution of wealth and power. Sometimes religion likewise acclimated itself to the age, in the case of liberalism and the Social Gospel, and at other times, particularly through diversity, it inadvertently contributed to the social changes faced by all Americans.

THE CHURCH OF THE BRETHREN IN LATE VICTORIAN AMERICA

For the Church of the Brethren, the question was how much of late Victorian America to accept. Separation from the sinful world, along with unity within the fellowship, had always been bedrock Brethrenism. By 1900 much of that tradition lingered, but enough had been lost to alarm conservative Brethren. Turn-of-the-century Brethren wondered whether they could be more mainstream and resemble other Protestants but still remain faithful.

The tradition that late Victorian Brethren inherited, maintained, and debated was two centuries old. It began in 1708 when Alexander Mack and seven others baptized themselves in a German river; the movement flourished and evolved in North America, where it moved in its first generation.

Theologically, several streams of thought contributed to the birth of this system. One inspiration was Pietism, a broad movement that stressed a personal relationship between believers and God. Rejecting predestination, Pietists believed that every individual could freely choose to accept Christ and allow divine forgiveness to lift the weight of sin from them. They understood that those who gave themselves to Christ were spiritually reborn, or, as Alexander Mack said, they "walk[ed] in the newness of life."[19] The intimacy of this relationship often evoked emotion, and converts and worshipers often fell under the Spirit. Moreover, this free-will conversion process and religion of the heart empowered laypeople with the ability to determine their eternal destiny without the aid of intermediaries, such as church hierarchy or clergy. In sum, Pietists found God near rather than distant.

Pietism's radical wing took religious individualism a step further by determining that any form of organized religion, even the church, impeded the relationship between believers and God. In this spirit, Mack concluded that the laws of God were "written in his heart" and that all believers "hear the inner word of life," which encourages them to "true obedience."[20] Implying that the heart was the final source of authority, the denominational founder urged individuals to "listen to their inner voice."[21] Undoubtedly, Pietism offered the first Brethren confidence in their ability to interpret scripture, regardless of how unusual their conclusions might be.

Mack and his followers, however, decided that neglecting the church, especially as taught by Radical Pietists, was unscriptural; therefore, to restore the faith community to what the Brethren considered its place, they turned to Anabaptism. Like Anabaptists, early Brethren were restorationist, i.e., they desired to restore the early New Testament church, and to achieve this they repeatedly stressed biblical obedience.[22] Simply put, according to Mack, "God demands absolute obedience from all of His creatures."[23] True faith generated "works of obedience," and "fruits" distinguished the faithful.[24] In practice, the fruits of the new birth meant nonconformity to the world, including plainness, refusal to swear oaths, and nonviolence, practices that often placed the Brethren at odds with political authorities. Minority status seemed synonymous with faithfulness.[25]

As these outsiders gathered in their church, maintaining its unity and purity was vital. The faith community defined the fruits of the new birth, and those who did not yield to that understanding, those who threatened the fellowship's harmony, had to go. To this end, Mack endorsed a particularly harsh form of excommunication, the ban, which prohibited social interaction with the excluded brother or sister, even if that person was a family member or spouse. Mack claimed that excommunication was necessary "so that the entire body or church is not contaminated"; without it "the devil and his leaven of wickedness would soon contaminate the good," and Christ's church would not exist. The early Brethren, then, were a community of nonconformists to society who craved like-mindedness in their own community.[26]

Rituals within the Brethren fellowship, based on their independent interpretation of scripture, reinforced *outsiderness* and identity. For example, the Brethren were certain that 1 Corinthians 11:20 described the event in the upper room as a "supper" rather than a "morning or noon meal," and so they demanded that this "love feast" occur only in the evening. Likewise, because Jesus washed the feet of the disciples prior to the meal, celebrations of the Lord's Supper always included feetwashing.[27] For direction on the proper form of baptism, Brethren studied Matthew 3:13—the baptism of Jesus—and determined that the entire person should be immersed three times, once each for "God the Father, God the Son, and God the Holy Spirit," because Jesus "commanded that baptism should be performed in these three most exalted names." Moreover, the example of Jesus also taught that symbolic baptism was wrong; this ceremony was only for believers and "certainly not children."[28] Love feast and mode of baptism, then, became distinctive practices and high priorities in the early Brethren universe.

By the early nineteenth century, the outlines of Brethrenism became more fully defined. While most nineteenth-century Brethren practices and rituals emerged during the fellowship's first century, the movement became clearer as the Brethren entered their second hundred years. Undoubtedly, separation from the larger society and maintaining the purity of the fellowship remained the pillars of their system.

Even the buildings in which Brethren met reinforced outsiderness. Although eighteenth-century Brethren generally worshiped in private homes, the Germantown, Pennsylvania, congregation built the denomination's first meetinghouse in 1770, and in the next century church buildings became more widespread. Plainness dominated Brethren meetinghouses, which were without rented pews, raised pulpits, decorations, steeples, or communion rails, all commonplace in most Protestant buildings. Instead, preachers merely sat behind a table on a slightly raised platform before the worshipers, who were on benches, segregated by gender.[29]

Leadership also reflected the unorthodox Brethren way of doing things. The Brethren relied on three levels or degrees of ministry, all selected by the membership in congregational council and serving without pay. Exhorters, the first degree, were typically young and just beginning as spiritual leaders; ministers were more mature and had passed through the exhorter stage; elders were still older, more experienced ministers who supervised one or more congregations. All of these voluntary "free ministers" were self-trained or guided by informal mentors rather than being seminary graduates, and congregations rather than a bishop or council of ministers ordained them. Unordained deacons and deaconesses assisted ministers, directed support for the poor, and visited the membership prior to love feast.[30]

Rituals and practices further emphasized the faith community's distinctive understanding of biblical obedience. Nonswearing, nonresistance, and trine immersion baptism (mentioned earlier) continued. Brothers and sisters exchanged a holy kiss with members of the same gender at love feast and as a greeting at worship. Additionally, ministers anointed and laid hands on those with life-threatening illnesses, and they also laid hands on the baptized and on preachers ordained to a high level of ministry. Each of these practices reinforced Brethren identity and separated it from the Protestant mainstream. Love feast, the Brethren's most cherished ritual, was also distinctive, at least in the form they used, and emphasized unity among the faithful. Deacon visits prior to the service assured that congregational harmony prevailed and that members were at peace with one another. If not, the congregation resolved differences or else postponed the service until it could restore peace. The ritual itself embodied the kind of Brethren literalism discerned by the community. A preparation service on Saturday afternoon preceded the love feast, which always occurred in the evening. The order of the service adhered to the biblical text—worshipers first washed each other's feet, then ate a meal in silence, and concluded the event with communion. On the following day, a lengthy service would end this high point of the religious year.

On the denominational level, Annual Meetings increasingly added weight to early nineteenth-century Brethren unity and nonconformity. By the 1790s annual denominational gatherings had become customary, and by the mid-nineteenth century, they evolved into greater formality and resembled a legislative branch of the fellowship. Congregations sent one or two delegates, and decision-making was by consensus. In 1866 the meeting tinkered with its procedure, leaving all members with the right to attend and speak, but only elders and elected delegates made decisions. A Standing Committee of elders, organized at the beginning of Annual Meeting, prepared the agenda and presented the delegate body with recommendations on the agenda items. Standing Committee elected its own officers, including the moderator, who also presided over the yearly meeting. Despite this increased formality and structure, the annual gathering remained remarkably egalitarian with its floor open to all members, delegates democratically selected by congregations, and decisions by consensus as it laid down the guidelines for Brethren resistance to sin.[31]

Matters came before the Annual Meeting in the form of succinct questions, called "queries," and the delegates' response was similarly concise, rarely more than a sentence or two. In 1827, for example, the minutes note that the question "whether a brother holding an office in the church may distill ardent spirits was considered," and that the delegates concluded that "it is not becoming for any brother to do so, much less a brother in office." Or, in 1849, a query asked, "Whether brethren can be allowed to have their likeness or profile taken?" The meeting responded, "Considered, as not advisable."[32]

Concerning two important trends in the popular culture—revivalism and consumerism—early nineteenth-century Brethren managed a remarkable degree of unity and nonconformity. During this period camp-meeting-style revivalism swept the nation. Methodists led the charge; by 1810 their growth rate exceeded that of every state and major territory in the Union. But revivalism's popularity was hardly limited to one denomination, and the new burst of enthusiastic religion touched most traditions. Of course, born-again, warm religion was deeply embedded in the Brethren Pietist heritage, and in the denomination's second century, undoubtedly, it still appealed to many Brethren. Tears and "spiritual joy" sometimes accompanied worship, and worshipers sang about anguish, tears, rapture, sweet joy, boundless bliss, and "songs of loudest praise." Undoubtedly, the Pietist influence persisted.[33]

Yet Annual Meetings rejected the strong emotionalism of early nineteenth-century revivalism. They disapproved of attendance at camp meetings and prohibited practices, such as prayer with uplifted hands or the anxious bench (designated seats for those desiring conversion), associated with the movement. One annual gathering urged that worship take place "in the order of the house of God," a criticism of the alleged disorder of camp meetings. Instead of sudden conversions that stressed relief from sin, which camp meetings relished, Brethren wanted a sober decision that reflected on obedience to the scriptures and obligation to the faith community, which put them squarely at odds with popular religion.[34]

Yearly Meeting also drew numerous lines against an economic revolution that burst upon early nineteenth-century America. Usually termed the "market revolution," this broad transformation of society included significant improvements in transportation and communications and increased consumerism and leisure time. The newly acquired ability of many Americans to purchase a wide range of store-bought goods, including stoves, nails, umbrellas, garden seed, and Valentine's Day cards, particularly threatened Brethren plainness and separation from the mainstream. Yearly Meeting responded to this potentially overwhelming tide of worldliness by erecting new boundaries against it. The annual gathering banned, for example, sleigh bells, property insurance, carpets, and worldly furniture. Because the market revolution made fashion available to middling rural families, Yearly Meeting gave special attention to clothing and appearance. It prohibited stylish caps and fashionable bonnets, and when hoop skirts became popular, they, too, were off-limits. Brethren men similarly rejected fashion. Trendy men wore their hair in a classical look in tight curls, but Brethren brothers parted their hair on top of the head and combed it straight down or back. They also wore beards, untrimmed, but when facial hair became fashionable, the Annual Meeting criticized those who trimmed it "in conformity to the fashion of the world." When mustaches achieved popularity, the Brethren vetoed them unless worn with a beard. Moreover, the annual gathering specifically authorized excommunication for those who did not conform in clothing. These strong limits on consumption placed the Brethren on the fringes of popular culture.[35]

By mid-century general agreement over distinctive ritual and practices, including resistance to popular religion and popular culture, clearly separated Brethren from the mainstream. When a preacher of another denomination termed the Dunkers in Virginia "odd people," John Kline, a minister, replied that he hoped that his fellow brethren would "always be odd," reflecting his determination that faithfulness required nonconformity.[36]

After the Civil War, nonconformity became more difficult for the Brethren and unity more elusive. Many Brethren increasingly resembled other American Protestants, but some Brethren still fought to preserve what they often called the "old order" or "ancient order" of the church.

Higher education, for example, became an option for Brethren youth, as it was for many small town and rural Protestants. Although a few denominations, especially Presbyterians, had established small colleges prior to the Civil War, American higher education exploded after 1865. Academies and colleges, however, were controversial for the Brethren. In 1853 Annual Meeting ruled against educational institutions, but just five years later it refused to block efforts by individual Brethren to create them. Opponents of higher education argued that it led young people astray by encouraging vanity, worldliness, and abandonment of simplicity. Critics also portrayed advanced education as a backdoor attempt to introduce paid pastors by first creating Bible departments in colleges and then establishing seminaries, which would inflict "hireling" pastors upon the fellowship. Supporters of higher education countered that young people needed an education, and if they had to get it somewhere else, they would eventually leave the Brethren fold. But Brethren schools, they asserted, would educate young people with the denomination's values.

Education-minded Brethren forged ahead. In the 1860s several Brethren initiated educational ventures, but these were short-lived, and in 1876 the first successful enterprise emerged from an academy in Huntingdon, Pennsylvania. In 1879 the institution renamed itself the Brethren's Normal School, but some complained about an unauthorized use of the denominational name, so the institution became Juniata

College. Other Brethren colleges, all founded during this period, were Ashland (Ohio, 1879), Mt. Morris (Illinois, 1879), Bridgewater (Virginia, 1880; originally Spring Creek Normal School), McPherson (Kansas, 1888), La Verne (California, 1891; originally Lordsburg College), Manchester (North Manchester, Indiana, 1895; a United Brethren school in financial straits taken over by Brethren), and Elizabethtown (Pennsylvania, 1899). These new educational institutions were all private ventures that anticipated profits for investors.[37]

Acceptance of Sunday schools and revivals further cast the Brethren in the mainstream Protestant image. Between 1857 and 1871, Annual Meeting considered Sunday schools five times, approving them in 1870 if "conducted according to order and by consent of the church." In 1871 the assembly cautioned that "where the establishing of Sunday-schools would cause trouble or division, brethren had better desist from introducing them." Some took this to mean that a small minority of irreconcilables could block a congregational majority who wanted Sunday schools, so in 1879 the Annual Meeting counseled the "small minority to yield to the majority for the sake of peace." Additionally, Annual Meeting instructed the majority not to "overrule the minority in a way that shows no regard for their feelings." Although delegates consistently approved of Sunday schools, the frequency of this item on the agenda suggests that some Brethren remained determined opponents of this method.[38]

Likewise, revivals were no longer forbidden fruit. In 1858 Annual Meeting refused to condemn protracted meetings, and in 1867 it praised "the desire to have the gospel spread," but did not mention revivals or protracted meetings. In 1871 delegates blessed taking the gospel into areas where there were no Brethren, and in 1874 the meeting ruled that elders had the right to shut down protracted meetings if not conducted appropriately, inferring that under some circumstances these events were acceptable. By 1887 Annual Meeting had fully reversed itself from its previous opposition to revivals and now advised congregations to hold them annually.[39]

Signs of other changes appeared on the Brethren horizon. In 1866 Yearly Meeting took a step toward paid pastors by permitting pay for the support of ministers' families, though disallowing a "stated salary," and in 1882 delegates endorsed donations to ministers for expenses.[40]

Missions also crept into the picture. In 1866 Annual Meeting granted districts permission to create mission boards, which several did. The first to carry the Brethren gospel overseas was Christian Hope, a Danish immigrant who in 1876 returned to his native land with his wife, Mary Katherine Nielsen Hope. Two elders and their wives followed the next year, all sent by the district of Northern Illinois rather than the Annual Meeting. (The Brethren effort in Denmark and later Sweden endured until 1947 but without sinking extensive roots into Scandinavian soil.)[41]

Unity on dress became increasingly challenging. Although Annual Meeting maintained consistency on garb, refusing to relax traditional taboos on jewelry, certain styles of hair and clothing, hats and bonnets for women, and so on, evidence mounted that the Brethren grassroots grew more restive on dress. In 1871 delegates heard that some sisters wore hats to love feast, and they denounced elders and ministers who tolerated this as "transgressors." In 1880 the gathering refused a request to accept "modest hats." But the following year it acknowledged inconsistency within the fellowship regarding hats and called for greater attention to all areas of the dress question.[42] Altering the old Brethren lines of nonconformity on dress appealed to many.

As Brethren edged into the mainstream, unity suffered. Some members, centered in the Miami Valley of Ohio and called Old Orders, adopted an uncompromising position with creeping assimilation, specifically opposing higher education, Sunday schools, revival meetings, salaried pastors, missions, and loss of uniformity in dress. After Standing Committee and Annual Meeting rebuffed their attempts to purge the denomination of alleged growing worldliness, disaffected traditionalists left the denomination in 1881 to organize the Old German Baptist Brethren. Old Order elders visited congregations seeking converts while those opposing the separation, called Conservatives, similarly called on local fellowships to discourage the Old Order movement. Congregations with majorities for one side expelled their opponents, and in a few cases Conservatives changed locks or took legal action to prevent Old Orders from using meetinghouses even if they had a majority within the congregation.[43]

Others thought that the Brethren needed more, not less, mainstream Protestantism. These Progressives, the converse of Old Orders, demanded financial support and higher education for ministers, Sunday schools, revival meetings, missions, and greater individual choice in dress, though still preferring plainness over fashion. Progressives welcomed revivalism and believed that preserving traditional Brethrenism was much less important than saving souls. In 1882 Henry Holsinger, their leader, and his supporters departed the denomination and organized the Brethren Church at a convention in Ashland, Ohio. Left in the middle, retaining the name German Baptist Brethren, were the so-called Conservatives, who willingly applied new methods, such as revivalism, to win souls for the ancient order.[44] Thus, in two successive Annual Meetings the Brethren suffered schism over unity and nonconformity.

Despite the departure of its most progressive wing, between 1900 and 1914 the German Baptist Brethren continued to journey into mainstream Protestantism. Although many of their distinctive practices and rituals remained intact, significant changes made the Brethren less nonconformist than they had been.

In 1905 Bethany Bible School opened its doors and evolved into the first Brethren seminary. The project's organizers established their institution on Chicago's south side to counter the popularity of Moody's Bible School with Brethren students. The curriculum stressed Bible study rather than theology and also included mission or service work in the city. The school started in a house with twelve students, but within three years 150 enrolled, most of whom were Bible School rather than seminary students. Soon Bethany purchased a city block and in 1908 began erecting buildings. That same year the denomination recognized Bethany Bible School, and in 1925 Annual Conference assumed control over it.[45]

Mission work was another major step into Late Victorian Protestantism. Although reformers since the antebellum period had praised the cause of urban mission, Brethren remained aloof from this impulse until the late nineteenth century. By 1900, however, the mission efforts of Brethren in Philadelphia led to several new congregations, and Brethren in Baltimore instituted work with orphans. Mission efforts in Brooklyn, New York, beginning with Sunday schools for children and visitations through the neighborhood, resulted in a congregation comprised chiefly of Italian immigrants. In Chicago the Hasting Street Mission benefitted from the interest of students at the Bethany Bible School across the street. On Christmas 1901, Sunday school workers gave the children pocketbooks, each with a new nickel in it. (Nickels bought a variety of popular items, including chewing gum, soda pop, candy bars, admission to nickelodeons, and trolley fare.) They could keep the pocketbook, but the children were to use their coin to earn money for donations at Easter. They performed a variety of odd jobs and turned in twenty-five dollars. To be sure, domestic mission now belonged to Brethrenism.[46]

Brethren were just as fervent over foreign mission. After Christian Hope and the others went to Denmark, the Brethren overseas mission movement languished. In 1880 Yearly Meeting created the Domestic and Foreign Mission Board, but four years later its treasury held a meager $8.69. Then Wilbur B. Stover, a fiery young preacher, caught mission fever. Sporting a necktie under his plain coat and a fashionable mustache with his trimmed beard, Stover was a tireless preacher who spread zeal for mission wherever he went. He struck a Brethren chord, and in 1894 Annual Meeting sent him and his wife, Mary Emmert Stover, ages twenty-eight and twenty-two respectively, to India, where they stayed for twenty-six years. Scores of orphans, whom the Stovers and others fed, housed, clothed, and raised, became the core of a successful mission church. In 1945 the Brethren in India could point to twenty-two congregations with a total of eight thousand members as evidence that the seed planted by the Stovers had borne much fruit.

Brethren missionaries to other lands had more mixed success. Attempts to start congregations in Smyrna, Turkey (1895), and Geneva, Switzerland (1899), demonstrated growing interest in overseas mission, but they failed. Efforts in China were more rewarding. In 1908 Brethren sent five missionaries to Shansi province, North China, and in 1916 a smaller effort began in Kwangtung province in South China. Before the Communist revolution permanently closed the Chinese mission field, approximately one hundred Brethren preachers, educators, medical missionaries, and agricultural specialists served there.[47]

In addition to mission, many Brethren enlisted in the Social Gospel movement. Its concern for the elderly and orphans, in particular, became a new cause. Between 1883 and 1910, Brethren built fourteen homes for the elderly and for orphans, sometimes putting both in the same building. The Honey Creek Orphans' and Old Folks' Home (1886) near Sulphur Springs, Indiana, one of the first of these, adopted this pattern.[48]

Peace concerns also received a higher priority, and Brethren now carried their message directly to political authorities. In 1902 Annual Meeting petitioned the king of Denmark on behalf of young men who were converted by Brethren missionaries but persecuted by the Danish government for conscientious objection to military service. In 1909 the yearly gathering complained to the United States Congress about increased military spending. In 1911 Annual Meeting created a Peace Committee to assist conscientious objectors and to distribute peace literature. Although the new agency received no budget, delegates nevertheless authorized it to "use every lawful gospel means" to achieve "peaceful settlements of difficulties when such may arise between governments or societies."[49] Undoubtedly, the Brethren had turned a new, activist leaf.

Many individual Brethren also became more like the Protestant mainstream, especially regarding dress. After unsuccessful attempts in 1898 and 1909 to provide clarity on dress codes, in 1911 Annual

Meeting dropped conformity in garb as a denomination-wide test of membership. Congregations remained free to set standards on dress, but now they did it without backing from the Yearly Meeting. Instead, the denominational body counseled "love and forbearance" toward those who "do not fully conform" so long as they avoided "unbecoming fashions" and their lifestyle reflected their faith. The meeting added that brothers and sisters with "an arbitrary spirit" who followed "foolish fashions" still deserved discipline, but most congregations ignored this. Increasingly, individuals could define dress standards by themselves.[50]

As numerous Brethren accepted higher education, a seminary, missions, and diversity in dress, Progressives simultaneously redefined several concepts near the center of Brethrenism. In particular, noncreedalism and no force in religion underwent revision. Brethren had always considered themselves noncreedal, meaning that they opposed prescribed statements that could lead to dead formalism, and they had always rejected "force in religion," which they identified as state religion and persecution. Now Progressives revised these principles and touted them as arguments for diversity and individualism. Discipline, they claimed, violated no force in religion, and guidelines adopted by Annual Meeting contradicted noncreedalism. According to Progressives, noncreedalism and no force in religion resulted from individual conscience rather than Annual Meeting minutes and their enforcement.

Similarly, rhetoric shifted to stress simplicity instead of plainness. Plain Brethren dressed in noticeably distinct garb approved by Annual Meeting with cuts and styles peculiar to the Brethren. Men, for example, wore collarless coats, and capes concealed the female figure. Simplicity, however, allowed for modesty and practicality and avoidance of costly or outlandish fads, a less demanding and less nonconformist standard. Brothers and sisters who were simple rather than plain could look more like the mainstream so long as they avoided overdoing it. Old traditions took on new definitions.[51]

Lastly, in 1908 the denomination modified its name to reflect the aspirations of its mission enthusiasts and its assimilation into the American mainstream. Until 1836 the Brethren had no official name; then the Annual Meeting accepted "Fraternity of German Baptists," and in 1871 the meeting adopted "German Baptist Brethren." But at the turn of the twentieth century, home mission activists complained that "German" was misleading and others said the same about "Baptist." After debating various alternatives for several years, including "Dunker Brethren" and "New Testament Church," Annual Meeting accepted "Church of the Brethren" as its new appellation in the bicentennial year, 1908.

Thus, as the Church of the Brethren entered its third century, its mission/Social Gospel/progressive wing appeared ascendant. The Honey Creek Orphans' and Old Folks' Home, Wilbur Stover, Bethany Theological Seminary, Brethren colleges, the 1911 dress decision, and recast traditions all indicate that this was a religious society undergoing transformation.

Yet much of the tradition remained. Although Brethren might shift emphasis from plainness to simplicity and give greater latitude to individualism, elders still guided brothers and sisters in their daily walk, and most congregations selected ministers from the laity. Many members dressed plainly, practiced nonswearing and nonviolence, and washed feet. Much had survived. In the next historical period, the age of world war, modernization would place new pressures on what remained of the Brethren's ancient order.

NOTES

1. The British ambassador to St. Petersburg was Sir Edward Grey. I first encountered his quotable thoughts on the impending war in Barbara W. Tuchman, *The Guns of August* (New York: The MacMillan Company, 1962), 122.

2. George Donelson Moss, *America in the Twentieth Century,* 4th ed. (Upper Saddle River, N.J.: Prentice Hall, 2000), 43-44.

3. David A. Horowitz and Peter N. Carroll, *On the Edge: The U.S. in the 20th Century,* 2nd ed. (Belmont, Cal.: West/Wadsworth Publishing, 1998), 11-12; Sean Dennis Cashman, *America in the Age of the Titans: The Progressive Era and World War I* (New York: New York University, 1988), 16-18, 32-34, 37-38; David Nasaw, *Children of the City: At Work and At Play* (New York: Oxford University Press, 1985), 14-15; Thomas J. Schlereth, *Victorian America: Transformations in Everyday Life, 1876-1915* (New York: Harper Collins, 1991), 163-65.

4. Schlereth, *Victorian America,* 153-57, 181, 198, 230.

5. Horowitz and Carroll, *On the Edge,* 29-31; Kenneth T. Jackson, *Crabgrass Frontier: The Suburbanization of the United States* (New York: Oxford University Press, 1985), 112-13; Moss, *America in the Twentieth Century,* 46-47; Schlereth, *Victorian America,* 193.

6. W. Fitzhugh Brundage, *Lynching in the New South: Georgia and Virginia, 1880-1930* (Urbana: University of Illinois Press, 1993), 2-3; Cashman, *America in the Age of the Titans,* 40-43; Horowitz and Carroll, *On the Edge,* 10, 33-34.

7. Horowitz and Carroll, *On the Edge,* 14-15, 27-28; Jackson, *Crabgrass Frontier,* 113-14; Moss, *America in the Twentieth Century,* 45; Nasaw, *Children of the City,* 1-16.

8. Horowitz and Carroll, *On the Edge,* 32-34; Cashman, *America in the Age of the Titans,* 202.

9. Cashman, *America in the Age of the Titans,* 49-50, 52-56, 139; Horowitz and Carroll, *On the Edge,* 46-52, 65-67; Moss, *America in the Twentieth Century,* 49-51, 58-63.

10. Cashman, *America in the Age of the Titans,* 46; Moss, *America in the Twentieth Century,* 77-78.

11. Jane Hunter, *The Gospel of Gentility: American Women Missionaries in Turn-of-the-Century China* (New Haven, Ct.: Yale University Press, 1984), 5-11; Martin E. Marty, *Modern American Religion, Volume 1: The Irony of It All, 1893-1919* (Chicago: University of Chicago Press, 1986), 307-10; Heather A. Warren, *Theologians of a New World Order: Reinhold Niebuhr and the Christian Realists, 1920-1940* (New York: Oxford University Press, 1997), 11.

12. Winthrop S. Hudson and John Corrigan, *Religion in America: An Historical Account of the Development of American Religious Life,* 6th ed. (Upper Saddle River, N. J.: Prentice Hall, 1999), 256-66; Ferenc Morton Szasz, *The Divided Mind of Protestant America, 1880-1930* (Tuscaloosa: The

University of Alabama Press, 1982), 15-41, 68-70; Warren, *Theologians of a New World Order,* 9-10.

13. Walter Rauschenbusch, *Christianity and the Social Crisis* (New York: Macmillan Company, 1907).
14. Hudson and Corrigan, *Religion in America,* 303-6; Winthrop S. Hudson, ed., *Walter Rauschenbusch: Selected Writings* (Mahwah, N. J.: Paulist Press, 1984), 33-37; Szasz, *The Divided Mind of Protestant America,* 45-48; Warren, *Theologians of a New World Order,* 10.
15. Szasz, *The Divided Mind of Protestant America,* 49-50; Warren, *Theologians of a New World Order,* 9.
16. Szasz, *The Divided Mind of Protestant America,* 56-67.
17. Hudson and Corrigan, *Religion in America,* 317-35.
18. Szasz, *The Divided Mind of Protestant America,* 73-78.
19. Alexander Mack, "Rights and Ordinances," *European Origins of the Brethren,* compiled and translated by Donald F. Durnbaugh (Elgin, Ill.: Brethren Press, 1958) 369.
20. Mack, "Rights and Ordinances," 385, 386.
21. Alexander Mack, "Basic Questions," *European Origins of the Brethren,* compiled and translated by Donald F. Durnbaugh (Elgin, Ill.: Brethren Press, 1958) 327.
22. Mack, "Basic Questions," 340, 343.
23. Mack, "Rights and Ordinances," 355.
24. Mack, "Basic Questions," 327, 336.
25. Mack, "Basic Questions," 329.
26. "The devil and his leaven . . ." in Mack, "Basic Questions," 336; "So that the entire body . . ." in Mack, "Basic Questions," 370. See also 367-69, 370, 381, 393-94, 399-40.
27. Mack, "Rights and Ordinances," 363-64.
28. "God the father . . ." in Mack, "Rights and Ordinances," 350; "certainly not for children" in Mack, "Rights and Ordinances," 351. See also Mack, "Rights and Ordinances," 361; Mack, "Basic Questions," 329, 331, 335.
29. Donald F. Durnbaugh, *Fruit of the Vine: A History of the Brethren, 1708-1995* (Elgin, Ill.: Brethren Press, 1997), 104-08.
30. Durnbaugh, *Fruit of the Vine,* 110-13; Morgan Edwards, *Materials Towards a History of the Baptists in Pennsylvania both British and German* (1770), in Donald F. Durnbaugh, ed., *The Brethren in Colonial America* (Elgin, Ill.: Brethren Press, 1967), 175.
31. Durnbaugh, *Fruit of the Vine,* 211-14.
32. *Minutes of the Annual Meetings of the Church of the Brethren: Containing All Available Minutes from 1778 to 1909* (Elgin, Ill.: Brethren Publishing House, 1909), 51, 107.
33. "spiritual joy" in Benjamin Funk, *Life and Labors of Elder John Kline, The Martyr Missionary* (Elgin, Ill.: Brethren Publishing House, 1900), 123, 205; "songs of loudest praise" in "Come Thou Fount" in *A Choice Selection of Hymns from Various Authors, Recommended for the Worship of God* (Poland,

Ohio: Henry Kurtz, publisher, 1852), No. 46; Stephen L. Longenecker, "Emotionalism Among Early American Anabaptists," *The Dilemma of Anabaptist Piety: Strengthening or Straining the Bonds of Community,* edited by Stephen Longenecker (Bridgewater, Va.: Forum for Religious Studies, Bridgewater College, 1997), 61-67.

34. Longenecker, "Emotionalism Among Early American Anabaptists," 61-67; Stephen L. Longenecker, *Shenandoah Religion: Outsiders and the Mainstream, 1716-1865* (Waco, Tex.: Baylor University Press, 2002), 66, 75-76; *Minutes of the Annual Meetings 1778-1909,* 75, 81 98, 104, 151.

35. *Classified Minutes of the Annual Meetings of the Brethren: A History of the General Councils of the Church from 1778 to 1885* (Mt. Morris, Ill. and Huntingdon, Pa.: The Brethren's Publishing Company, 1886), 254-56, 261-62; Longenecker, *Shenandoah Religion,* 107-08; *Minutes of the Annual Meetings 1778 to 1909,* 26, 27, 40, 46-47, 53, 58, 70, 85, 90-91, 94-95, 135, 145, 207, 209.

36. "odd people" in Funk, *Life and Labors of Elder John Kline,* 378.

37. Carl F. Bowman, *Brethren Society: The Cultural Transformation of a "Peculiar People"* (Baltimore, Md.: The Johns Hopkins University Press, 1995), 99-100; Durnbaugh, *Fruit of the Vine,* 243-64.

38. Roger E. Sappington, *The Brethren in Industrial America* (Elgin, Ill.: Brethren Press, 1985), 211-14; *Minutes of the Annual Meetings 1778-1909,* 163, 205, 210, 271, 290, 295-96, 366-67.

39. Sappington, *The Brethren in Industrial America,* 219-21; *Minutes of the Annual Meetings 1778-1909,* 174, 265-66, 293, 319, 466.

40. Sappington, *The Brethren in Industrial America,* 222-23; *Minutes of the Annual Meetings 1778-1909,* 257.

41. Durnbaugh, *Fruit of the Vine,* 354-56; Sappington, *The Brethren in Industrial America,* 116-32.

42. Sappington, *The Brethren in Industrial America,* 94-102; *Minutes of the Annual Meetings 1778-1909,* 349-50, 376, 399.

43. "doctrines and principles" from Samuel Murray, George V. Siler, and Samuel Kinsey, "The Brethren's Reasons for Producing and Adopting the Resolutions of August 24th (1883), in Sappington, *The Brethren in Industrial America,* 362; Durnbaugh, *Fruit of the Vine,* 291-301.

44. Carl Bowman, *Brethren Society,* 126-27; Durnbaugh, *Fruit of the Vine,* 301-15.

45. Durnbaugh, *Fruit of the Vine,* 395-98; Sappington, *The Brethren in Industrial America,* 132-49.

46. Durnbaugh, *Fruit of the Vine,* 353-54; Sappington, *The Brethren in Industrial America,* 34-41.

47. Durnbaugh, *Fruit of the Vine,* 345-63.

48. Durnbaugh, *Fruit of the Vine,* 374-76.

49. Durnbaugh, *Fruit of the Vine,* 373; *Full Report of the Proceedings of the Brethren's Annual Meeting, 1902* (Elgin, Ill.: Brethren Publishing House, 1902), 127; *Full Report, 1909,* 103-6; *Full Report, 1911,* 149-60.

50. Durnbaugh, *Fruit of the Vine,* 387-89; *Full Report, 1911,* 91-93.

51. Carl Bowman, *Brethren Society,* 356-58; Durnbaugh, *Fruit of the Vine,* 389-92.

PART I
World War I

I. THE WORLD AT WAR
America at Peace

On October 23, 1913, Raymond and Laura Cottrell, medical doctors, husband and wife, boarded a train in North Manchester, Indiana, to begin their journey to the mission field in India. Like all missionaries, they left behind family and friends, not knowing when, if ever, they would see them again. A wave of emotion swept over those who witnessed the event, as one of them reported.

> Last evening at 6:00 o'clock the train pulled away from us with Bro. and Sister Cottrell aboard. The College Volunteer Band, a number of the friends of theirs, and also the near relatives of Raymond's were at the station to bid them farewell and to wish them God speed. After they had made the round to all of us with the farewell, we all sang "Blest be the tie that binds," "In the sweet bye and bye," and then as the train was approaching, we sang, "God be with you till we meet again." It was a noble way in which the mother gave up her boy for the cause of Christ, and as well Raymond was very happy in the separation because of the calling he feels from his blessed Master to the needy fields of India.
>
> . . . As I stepped on the train with their suitcases, I could not but feel that we would like to be one of their number. I know this, that there were some impressions made at the station that will never leave the minds of those who witnessed the home leaving and leaving of loved ones.[1]

The Cottrells' story was indeed heartening. Laura and Raymond met as employees at the Brethren Publishing House in Elgin, Illinois, and married. Soon they decided to become missionaries. Laura Cottrell recalled the moment.

> Strange it is that both of us had thought of doing mission work of some kind, but had said little to each other. One evening at prayer meeting the topic for discussion was of a missionary nature. Our hearts were touched as never before, and on the way home we spoke of it. That night we gave ourselves to Him, and oh! the joy of full surrender! We have given ourselves to go wherever He leads.[2]

Raymond and Laura Cottrell, medical missionaries in Bulsar, India, from 1913 to 1949. *Photo courtesy of the Brethren Historical Library and Archives (BHLA), Elgin, Illinois.*

After a year at Bethany Bible School, the Cottrells attended the American Medical Missionary College in Battle Creek, Michigan, under the leadership of John Harvey Kellogg, who had established a wellness program that included a center for training missionaries. (Kellogg recommended strict dietary discipline, which included the now famous Corn Flakes® developed by his brother, William K. Kellogg.) After the Cottrells spent one year at Battle Creek, Kellogg's medical school merged with the University of Illinois, and they transferred to the new institution. In 1912 Laura and Raymond graduated, and sixteen months later they bid farewell to friends and family on the Indiana train platform.[3]

Laura and Raymond Cottrell left North Manchester at the end of an era. Within months of their arrival in India, World War I began in Europe, but because the U. S. entered the war almost three years after its start, America's Victorian Age closed gradually rather than abruptly. Yet, as armies marched in Europe, Victorianism in America undoubtedly entered its twilight.

The Gospel Messenger announced the assassination of Austro-Hungarian Archduke Franz Ferdinand and his wife, Sophie, in balanced prose. The denominational periodical condemned the violent deed but also noted that Austrian policy, especially its 1908 annexation of Bosnia and Herzegovina, had contributed significantly to regional tensions.

June 28 Archduke Francis Ferdinand, nephew of Emperor Francis Joseph, and heir to the Austrian throne, and the Duchess of Hohenberg, his morganatic wife, were assassinated at Sarayevo, the capital of Bosnia. The first missile of destruction—a bomb—was warded off by the archduke before it had a chance to explode. Later on, two pistol shots, aimed at the royal couple by a Bosnian student, proved fatal. The tragic occurrence is but a sequence of Austria's annexation of Bosnia and Herzegovina in 1908, against the loud protest of Servia as well as Bosnia. As both of these countries are represented by the persons implicated in the assassination, the inference seems to be clear that the forcible seizure of 1908 is being resented by the Slavic part of Austria's complex population, and that it found expression in the deplorable act of assassination. For such violence there is no excuse, though it must be regretted that Austria's unlawful seizure should have so aroused the wild frenzy of the Slavs as to lead to the tragedy in which the royal pair were so foully slain.[4]

For another two and a half years the United States proclaimed neutrality from the global bloodletting, in word if not deed, and as Europeans slaughtered one another, American life at first changed little. Between Sarajevo and the American declaration of war in April 1917, President Woodrow Wilson advocated another round of progressive reform that included workers' compensation, child welfare legislation, and an eight-hour workday for federal workers. Overseas Wilson stressed the Open Door Policy in China and intervened freely in Latin America, both time-worn objectives of American diplomacy. At the instance that war broke out in Europe, the president was mourning the death of his wife, and formulation of his policy fell to Secretary of State Robert Lansing, but soon the conflict claimed a higher priority on the Wilsonian agenda. When in 1915 a German submarine sank the British passenger ship, the *Lusitania,* with the loss of 128 American lives, Wilson demanded that Germany limit its use of submarines (which it did until early in 1917), and in 1916 he attempted to mediate the conflict. In Wilson's 1916 campaign for re-election, the slogan "He Kept Us Out of War" was critical to his victory, although progressive politics, not foreign policy, put pivotal California in the president's column. The European war, therefore, evolved into a grave foreign policy problem but without displacing politics as usual.[5]

Likewise, for the Brethren new questions related to the war coexisted with familiar patterns of congregational life and with older issues that had perplexed the denomination for years. To be sure, World War I marked a fresh phase of modernization, but prior to U. S. entry in the war, the denomination struggled with the gradual version of modernization that had confronted Victorian Brethren.

DISCIPLINE, DRESS, AND THE MINISTRY

Before the United States sent its soldiers "over there," the war had minimal impact on daily and denominational routines. When Brethren attended Sunday services or Annual Meeting, they worshiped and debated much as they had before the assassin's bullets struck. Women's societies, for example, remained active by sewing and raising money for missions and charities. This 1915 report of the Sugar Creek, Indiana, congregation is typical.

> SUGAR CREEK, IND.—Following is our report for the year ending Dec. 14, 1915: We held eleven meetings, with an average attendance of fifteen. We knotted seven comforters, quilted five quilts, made eleven garments, sewed seven pounds of carpet-rags, pieced and joined one quilt, made and sold sixteen prayer-coverings, sold three comforters and two quilts. We donated two comforters and some clothing to the Home at Mexico, Ind. During the year we received $112.50, which includes free-will offerings, donations and four sale dinners. We paid out during the year $79.50. Out of this we repapered our church, which cost $39.35. We gave $5 for home missions. Dec. 14 we reorganized, with Sister Carrie Neff, President; Sister Harriet Sherfahn, Vice-

President; the writer, Secretary-Treasurer,—Manerva Kitch, R. D. 2, South Whitley, Ind., Feb. 3.[6]

Additionally, many congregations practiced love feast as they always had. One correspondent to *The Gospel Messenger* exhorted Brethren to redouble their efforts toward self-examination, traditionally a vital part of the service.

> The weekly visitor—the MESSENGER of Sept. 16—came to us with over two hundred communion announcements. To us it appears that the church is still wide-awake in its duty of looking after its members relative to the love and peace existing among them. It is customary for the different congregations to have the visit paid to each member preceding the love feast in their several congregations. This, then, brings to our mind the thought of self-examination which, we are inclined to believe, is sometimes neglected. We remember that the first exercise of the evening, preceding the communion service, is the subject of self-examination. This being the custom, the cause would be helped much by making this a daily work.
>
> Our bankers make it their business to count up all their several accounts of that day's work, in order to ascertain their standing. It is customary, you know, to have read the eleventh chapter of First Corinthians. In the twenty-eighth verse we have this language: "Let a man examine himself, and so let him eat of that bread, and drink of that cup," etc. This self-examination is not only to look at ourselves, but also to set ourselves right before God and men, and to remove obstacles that might be a hindrance to the cause of Christ. As we are weak mortals, we often make mistakes. May God, in his mercy, help us to be more zealous in our calling![7]

Despite strong threads of continuity on the congregational level, modernization nevertheless touched many fellowships. The swift appearance of automobiles, for example, required Brethren to think about how this amazing technology fit into their religious behavior. Adaline Hohf Beery had little trouble picturing the Son of Man behind the wheel, a liberal image of Jesus as a role model who adapted to the modern age.

If Jesus were going down town, I think he would have a cheery "Hello!" for everybody—bricklayer, bank cashier, ragamuffin, doctor, coal-heaver, shoe-dealer, junk-man, schoolboy, editor, blacksmith! And if he had an automobile—big as they make 'em—he would never go bowling along the avenue by himself, but it would be piled full of youngsters bubbling over with glee, or a bunch of stoop-shouldered, begrimed day-laborers, with lunch done up in newspaper, who would otherwise have to walk a mile and a half to work. And if Jesus were a woman, he would send his daughter or housemaid to take care of some children while he took their mother, a tired little dressmaker, out for a spin into the delicious country air. And he wouldn't forget, either, that the physical exhilaration isn't everything, but the personal contact of soul with soul. . . .

Dear Jesus, we are glad there are so many people we have a chance to be kind to, and that *You* are one of the family![8]

The mission field, too, felt the influence of modernization, particularly in the form of increased educational expectations for missionaries. The Cottrells with their medical degrees exemplified this trend, but Adam Ebey, an older missionary to India, ran afoul of it. In 1917 Ebey, who had studied at Manchester College but never earned a degree, came home from India for a furlough but had trouble returning. He feared that his lack of formal education prevented resumption of his work, and Ebey poured out his frustration to Galen B. Royer, secretary to the General Mission Board. The correspondence also reveals the financial sacrifices that were part of the missionary life.

We should have been glad to know whether we may return to India if health permit. When we had the talk on April 1, you intimated that we would be barred from going because we did not have enough literary training. On that ground we have been thinking, perhaps, the Board would not send us out again. It would not be fair to us, so we think, to be told next December that the Board has no further use for us, go and shift for yourselves. Next winter will be a harder winter than the past one has been. We have been imposing on Alice's folks. It will mean some money to set up housekeeping. We do not feel it best for the folks nor for our children to stay here much longer. If we are to remain unsettled for an indefinite time, we should get to ourselves. We have been cramped and crowded here, but we have gotten along. Father

King is old and does not like the noise and play of the children. We have held them in all winter. It is not fair to them. They must have some room for exercise. We think we should have a place to stay where we will not need to crush the spirit out of the little ones all the time or annoy the older people. Were we told that because of the lack of literary training we would not be returned to the field, we could invest a little money in the necessary household fixtures and get to ourselves, but it seems the Board does not think of those things. We left our bedding, etc., in India, but if we are not wanted any longer, we should like to know it before another cold winter is upon us. We are not situated as some other missionaries are.

Our expense is running up. In India we were able to get along fairly well, even keeping our bullocks at our own expense. True, for the sickness and death of our six children we spent of personal money some Three Hundred Dollars, never asking the Committee for it. But we do not have a very large fund to draw on any more. Have a few hundred dollars left by my parents, but I am loath to use that just yet. This is not said to complain. It is a plain statement. I think you can see the position we are in and why we should like to have a definite answer. I am now fifty years old and cannot expect to get very much of a position in life. But if the worst comes to the worst we shall try to get along some way. We are not ready to become subjects of charity.

Further, there has been a good deal of talk in India among the missionaries about the educational qualifications. Some very cutting things have been said about those who do not have degrees. I suppose some of them have written to you leading to your remarks about our lack of training.

There is just one thing we should like to know at present—Is our lack of literary training in the way of our return to the field?[9]

Royer confirmed that education now received a higher priority for missionaries, but he maintained that in Ebey's case poor health was all that stood between him and another term in the mission field.

The field Committee have expressed a desire for your return. You refer to my statement about the literary qualifications being changed to what they were when you went out. That is true. But you took a further meaning that is not meant in what I said when you took that statement to mean that on that ground you would not go back. Such a thot [sic] could not be sustained for did not the Board send Sister Zigler back last fall and her preparation is not any greater if as great as yours. Your knowledge of the country and language more than compensates for your lack of literary training at this stage of your life and our work. It is a fact, however, that were you to apply today with the standards as they are and your attainments as they were when you went out, it is all together probable that you would not be sent. That, however, has no bearing on the case now.

The thing that bothers the Board, the doctors on the field, the doctors at home, is your ailment. That still remains as a problem, for one time you report better, another time worse. That is why the Board deferred the decision. Had they decided at this meeting on the grounds of your physical condition they would have declined your return.

. . . I may be thoroughly wrong but I believe the thing for you to do for a few months is to do some physical work. Is there not a brother near you who will let you work on the farm and pay you according to your work? You go at the work first gently and then stronger and stronger as opportunity opens. There is nothing that restores vigor and health as bodily exercise that brings gain. There is nothing that will restore the nerves and bring back the pink of health as judicious labor. . . .

Try a couple of months of prudent physical work and see what will be the result if I may suggest this.[10]

Eventually, Alice and Adam Ebey continued their mission in India, serving a total of thirty-one years from 1900 until 1931. Alice went back to India for another two years, 1945-47.[11]

Another persistent Brethren pattern, uninterrupted by Sarajevo, were the debates over discipline and separation from the mainstream, interrelated controversies that also felt modernity's sway. Conservatives favored denominational standards that upheld discipline for those who violated the traditional order, and they fought a rear-guard action against individualism and loss of nonconformity—both consequences of modernity—that increasingly won approval at Annual Meetings and within congregations. I. J. Rosenberger, a prominent conservative and popular evangelist, published in *The Gospel Messenger* a vigorous defense of discipline and unity that included excommunication.

There is a growing sentiment that the present and pressing need of the church is more teaching. Discipline is discouraged and expulsion is criticised [sic]. This, I affirm, is due to the environment of our churches, and the natural trend to seek the path of least resistance. I maintain that *the government of the church is growing lax.* I shall assume that this fact is admitted.

1. Government Implies Restraint and Discipline—Where there is no restraint there is no discipline and, of course, no government. It was said of Christ: "The government shall be upon his shoulders"; i.e., at hand, ready for use. Christ says of the offender: "If he neglect to hear the church, let him be unto thee as an heathen man and a publican." Here is discipline authorized in the church, with a tribunal, an executive and a penalty, with the assurance that heaven will ratify the verdict of men—the church. These are essentials of government. Paul says: "Is it so, that there is not a wise man among you? no, not one that shall be able to judge between his brethren?" Hence men sat in judgment in the church in Paul's day, because the church had a government. And all governments have men who sit in judgment, and judge the right or wrong, and render verdicts.

2. Men Rule in the Church—Christ says: "If they neglect to hear the church," etc. "To hear" means to obey; this implies a ruling. And Christ affixes a penalty if the offender refuse to be ruled or governed. This is government in the executive. Paul says: "Remember them which have the rule over you, who have spoken unto you the Word of God. . . . Obey them that have the rule over you, and submit yourselves: for they watch for your souls. . . . Let elders that rule well be counted worthy of double honour." These texts show that the church in Christ's time and Paul's day had officials that ruled, leaving no room for cavil or doubt on this question.

3. Expelling Members—Christ says of the offending member: "If he neglect to hear the church, let him be unto thee as an heathen man and a publican." Here Christ authorizes expulsion of the offender for refusing to be governed. The church at Corinth retained a fornicator in fellowship, and Paul writes them thus: "In the name of our Lord Jesus Christ, when ye are gathered together, . . . deliver such an one unto Satan for the destruction of the flesh, that the spirit may be saved." Mark Paul's clear logic: "Deliver such an one to Satan, that the spirit may be saved." When the penalty has been meted out, then is the guilty free. Then "the spirit may be saved." This is true in our civil code, and in the Divine as well. At the close of this chapter Paul gives general directions that cover all future cases, thus: "I wrote unto you in an epistle not to company with fornicators. . . . If any man that is called a brother be a fornicator. . . . Therefore put away from among yourselves that wicked person." In the foregoing Paul authorizes expulsion in the name of the Lord Jesus Christ. This must be apparent to candid minds. Paul says of Hymenaeus and Alexander: "Whom I have delivered unto Satan, that they may learn not to blaspheme." This is expulsion, clear and strong; in fact it sounds like avoidance. The lack of the church, along these lines, is today making lamentable growth.

. . . The function of rules or laws is to protect the normal— the faithful—and to restrain the abnormal or unfaithful. Reforms and normal conditions are wrought by rule or law, followed by teaching, restraint and discipline. We need to discriminate between the things that need to be *taught*, and the things that need only to be *told*. A boy only needs to be *told* to water the horses. Seekers hungering after God's righteousness only need to be *told not to wear gold*.[12]

The tide ran strongly against Rosenberger and his fellow conservatives. In 1915 traditionalists suffered another setback when Annual Meeting voted to forgive repentant fornicators, repealing a long-standing policy against allowing those who committed this sin to return to the fellowship, even if they confessed. Conservatives, stressing literalism, argued in vain that fornication was the most foul of iniquities and that 1 Corinthians denies forgiveness for those who committed this sin.

It has been well said that this is an exceedingly grave sin, perhaps the greatest sin. . . . [I]n view of the fact that it is a hard matter to determine the penitence of the sinner, that it takes time to manifest a reformed life, that it is an exceedingly dangerous sin to our social life, and that it is growing in prevalence, I think we ought to have some further safeguard.[13]

———————

In the early church—I am speaking of the time of the old church fathers—they tell us that for the sin of adultery or fornication the individual was disowned— the shortest time was one year. We often restore them inside of a day or less. Now it is urged that we receive them simply by showing penitence.[14]

Progressives, however, carried the day by emphasizing the power of confession and unlimited forgiveness.

Now, brethren, how can we, in the name of Heaven, refuse to forgive a penitent sinner? Who dare say, "I will not forgive" when a person is penitent? And the question before us asks only that forgiveness be granted where they come in penitence and beg it and ask it, and that that penitence is satisfactory to the church; then forgive. Who of us dare refuse to forgive in such a case?[15]

Frustrated conservatives also challenged the 1911 dress decision, which had removed plain dress as a requirement for membership. Congregations could discipline for dress if they chose, but they were not obligated to do so, leading to assorted standards across the denomination. According to traditionalists, this weakened both nonconformity and unity, and in 1915 they specifically asked Annual Meeting to clarify the appropriateness of neckties, which the 1911 decision omitted from the list of forbidden adornments. The delegates' response maintained the status quo.

The letter of the dress decision of 1911 does not forbid the wearing of the necktie, but we urgently advise our brethren to refrain from wearing neckties and other unnecessary articles of adornment.[16]

Conservatives further proposed a study committee with instructions to encourage unity on dress and discipline. They complained that the growing respect for individual conscience eroded the scriptural call for unanimity.

What we now have on this question [of dress] does not lead us to harmony. We are considerably divided on this question. . . . We are strictly congregational, in many instances—not only congregational but more than congregational. For instance, in one congregation, of which you may be the overseer [i.e., elder in charge], you desire to maintain a certain form of church government, and you expect those that come to you to subscribe, in some degree, or to some extent, to these conditions. But they have decided that they would rather not conform or, at least, not subscribe to any form of government. Just over the way is a congregation where, possibly, they are not making an effort to have members subscribe to a form of government, or to any conditions. Then those dissenting ones decide to go over to that other congregation and unite with it, or to be baptized in the congregation, and then come back and live in your congregation, in defiance of your form of government or your effort to maintain a form of government.[17]

———

That is where we feel the thing needs to be remedied—that there may be better understanding and more union, as the scripture refers to, in carrying out the principles for which the Brethren stand. Personal ideas are being carried into effect, contrary to the rulings of our brotherhood. It is the individual man, carrying out his wishes in preference to following the decisions of our Brotherhood. . . . The scripture says we should all work by the same rule, all speak the same thing, and be joined together in the same mind and same judgment. But when I set up my judgment against established church practices, which some other brother sanctions, you see where we are. It is not the same judgment; it is not walking by the same rule. I would like to have a committee look forward to so remedying this thing, that it will help us all to respect, as pastors, as ministers, as elders, the decision that is laid down for us to walk by.[18]

Progressives, weary of the seemingly endless discussion of dress, countered that the 1911 decision was more than adequate.

The history of the dress question in the Church of the Brethren is a long one. It has been a problem ever since I have been in the church—now fifty-three years. At one time I counted some seventy or eighty decisions which we have had published on this vexed question. . . . [I]f every minister in the Church of the Brethren would go home from this Conference, resolved that in spirit and in letter he will carry out the decision we now have, we have all we need.[19]

Moreover, the thought of disciplining other brothers and sisters affronted progressives.

Let us take what we have and carry it out. It is an aggressive, positive decision. There is such a thing as putting people on the wrong
track, and having a positive decision which permits some cases, but
that is better than to say, "You must not, you must not, you must
not," and having no regard paid to our decisions at all. The very
fact is, that when you tell a man or a woman, "You must not,"
there is an instinctive resentment. But when you place before
them something to reach forward to, you are in a position to lead
them to a higher life. Let us not sacrifice what we already have, by
an attempt to get something else. Let us use the good in it and
reach forward to something better.[20]

Conservatives lost this argument over dress, discipline, and unity.
The 1915 Annual Meeting, dominated by progressives, rejected their
call to create a policy "so that all may walk by the same rule." Instead, a
majority of the Brethren were satisfied to allow brothers and sisters to
choose their own modest dress.[21] In 1916 and 1918 the annual gatherings
again considered fashionable men's neckwear, but both times refused to
change policy.[22] The conservative counter-attack on the 1911 dress decision and the individualism of that policy floundered.

Conservatives also drew a line against recommendations that all
ministers meet ambitious educational levels. In 1915 a committee report
suggested that preachers obtain a high school diploma, complete two
years of Bible training, presumably at one of the Brethren colleges, and
then finish a two-year reading course.[23] Conservatives pounced on this
as unscriptural and insulting to the many current preachers—uneducat-
ed, unpaid free ministers—who fell short of these standards. Anti-intel-
lectualism contributed to the conservative worldview; the "more scholarly, the less spiritual" was their refrain.

It says here [in the committee report] that "the minister shall be
able and apt to teach." Good, fine. "He should have a literary
course equivalent at least to a high school course and to a two
years' Bible course, followed by a two years' reading course."
Brethren, what is in this? Can you see it? I believe you can. Now,
let us get at it. I want to get at it plainly. Dutchmen, you know, do
that. This says that the brother who has not had a high school education or the equivalent of that is not qualified for the ministry, and
therefore should not be elected, but if he should be, then before
he is permitted to operate, he must go to that place and the
church shall see that he goes there. That says so. That is the real

substance of it. Brethren, I wonder what we are thinking about. In the name of reason, where are our heads? Look here. A great statesman long ago said, "We have no way of judging the future but by the past." True, true; more truth than fiction. Let us judge the future church on the line of ministers in that sense, and what do we find? Did not Paul, in the days that are gone by, use men who did not have high school education in the ministry successfully? Did not Paul take hold of men and use them for the uplift of people efficiently and earnestly, give God's Word to the people and save many souls? He did. You dare not deny it. He did, and he is doing it today. I will tell you what is the matter, brethren. If God could use the men in days gone by who did not have high school education in the ministry, or the equivalent, successfully, in the ministry, I want to know, today, by what system of logic or reasoning can you conclude that hereafter a man is not qualified to preach unless he has that. Brethren, if you pass this section as it is, you virtually by that act say that 65 percent, at least, of the preachers of the Church of the Brethren today have not got education, and I tell you it is humiliating. God took our fathers in the days gone by, who did not have the qualifications that you set forth here, and he had his Spirit in their hearts, and they preached the Word with power, and I contend that it is highly wrong to decide that God can not use such men. I contend that a man who is filled with the Holy Ghost can preach the Word successfully. We know men and women work to let the Holy Ghost move them, and I feel sorry if this thing would pass as it stands. The Holy Ghost enabled men in days gone by to do the work successfully, and they can do it in the future, and I tell you there is such a thing as preaching the Gospel from the head and not from the heart, and I find that churches all over the country, the more scholarly and the more learned they become, the less spiritual they become, and I tell you again, I think you ought to vote this thing solemnly down unless it is modified, and I should like to see it buried so deep that it will be beyond the possibilities of resurrection forever.[24]

Another opponent of high educational standards contended that they would worsen the shortage of preachers and that intellectualism meant "farewell to spirituality."

The fact is that all over the Brotherhood there is a dearth of ministers, and we don't have enough to fill the demands of today, and
if you will pass this paper how many ministers will you elect in the
next ten years? I will tell you, you will not elect very many, not very
many. . . . Passing along the street the other day I heard a person
remark in reference to the services. He said, "We are starving,"
and on inquiry I find they belonged to other churches in that city,
where they have the most intellectual qualifications of the whole
city preaching to those men, and yet they say "We are starving."
Why? Too much intellectuality and not enough spirituality, and I say
to you that when we make that the standard of the Brethren
Church, I say farewell to spirituality. God help us to stop and think
upon this question before we make it binding upon us to require
that qualification in our Brotherhood.[25]

Yet another cited the spiritual dangers of an educated ministry.

As I look about at our aged, grey-haired fathers, I thank God it was
their preaching that made me what I am. You watch for yourself,
and you look around in our churches where we have got education, where we get more brains than spirituality, and see what we
get. Brethren, be careful what you do.[26]

Facing opposition, the committee rewrote its recommendations to
encourage but not require education.

Mental and educational: I Tim. 3:2; 2 Tim. 2:15; 3:15-17. The
scriptures cited exhort every minister to make the preparation that
will insure an efficiency approved of God. While we do not fix a
standard of educational qualifications, we do encourage College
and Biblical training: when necessary, the church should assist in
obtaining it. To those elected to the ministry, who can not reason-
ably acquire said training, we recommend a Home Study Course,
arranged by the Educational Board, the books to be secured
through the Gish Committee.* Those ministers who can not avail
themselves of these advantages, but who are rendering faithful

---

*The Gish Book Fund was endowed by James R. and Barbara Kindig Gish to provide
missionaries and preachers with books at discounted prices. See "Gish Fund Books," *The
Brethren Encyclopedia,* I:551.

service notwithstanding, are hereby encouraged to continue their
faithful labors, and the church should give them her fullest support.[27]

In 1917 progressives vanquished guardians of the Old Order once
more when the Brethren approved changes in the ministry. One modification in the levels of clergy threatened tradition only modestly. After
wrangling with the issue for several years, the Annual Conference
removed the three stages of ministry—exhorter, minister, and elder—
and replaced them with two degrees: minister and elder.

> 1. There shall be two degrees in the ministry, to be known as
> ministers and elders. All ministers who, at the time of the adoption
> of this report, are serving in the first and second degrees, shall be
> designated as ministers.
> 2. The duties of the minister are to preach the Word, to
> administer baptism, to serve the communion in the absence of an
> elder or at his request; to solemnize marriage—in brief, to assist
> the elder faithfully in the general work of the ministry (Eph. 4:11,
> 12; 2 Tim. 4:1-5).
> 3. The duties of the elder, in addition to the foregoing duties
> of the minister, are to feed the flock, to preside over council meet-
> ings, especially when official members are on trial, to anoint the
> sick, to have oversight and general management of the church;
> training the young ministers in his charge and apportioning the
> work among them according to their experience and ability—in
> brief, to be a faithful shepherd to the flock, guarding their souls as
> one who must give an account, and be willing to serve in any
> capacity authorized by the church (Acts 20:28; 1 Tim. 5:17; Titus
> 1:5; James 5:14).
> 4. When the minister proves himself faithful and efficient in his
> office, he shall be ordained elder; and, when ordained, he shall
> pledge himself to live and labor in harmony with the accepted stan-
> dards of the church in faith, doctrine, and practice (1 Tim. 5:22;
> Titus 1:5; 1 Peter 5:3).[28]

The 1917 Annual Conference also signaled growing professionalization of the ministry. In the long run, this trend reflected a significant
departure from past Brethren practice and was more controversial and
more disappointing to conservatives than the changes in the levels of
ministry. On one hand, Brethren still spoke warmly of the free ministry:

2. Ministers who are financially able should be encouraged to preach the Gospel without money and without price, as it has been the practice of the Brethren from their beginning.[29]

But now the Brethren also blessed full-time professional ministers.

4. Churches that feel the need of pastors, giving all of their time, are at liberty to secure them, giving them a reasonable support, where it can be done with the approval of the majority of the members in councils.[30]

A further revision to the ministry allowed individuals to volunteer themselves for the pulpit rather than awaiting the congregation to tap them. This would be in addition to other methods of selecting preachers currently used: election by majority and election by plurality. (Election by majority required ballots until one candidate had more than half of the votes, and election by plurality allowed selection of the candidate with the most votes, whether a majority or not, a method that traditionalists opposed because it lacked unity.) According to the guidelines adopted by Annual Conference, those who believed that God called them to the ministry could step forward, conferring upon individualism a respected position beside community in the selection of leadership.

A young man who feels called of the Lord to the ministry, but who has not been chosen, may speak freely to his elder or one of the ministers on the subject, also the Ministerial Board, hereinafter provided, and after special prayer with him and an examination of his faith, the elder may submit the matter to the church for consideration, and the church after due consideration, may set him apart as a minister, by the common charge, if two-thirds of the members in council favor it. This action shall be considered as an election.[31]

Conservatives preferred the traditional method in which the Holy Spirit selected ministers by speaking to the body of believers. Conservative elders disliked their role in the new process, especially the obligation to reject unqualified candidates, and they doubted that the innovation possessed scriptural justification. S. H. Hertzler informed meeting delegates that "there is no elder in the Brotherhood that wants to assume that responsibility of telling a young man who feels called to preach, whether he may or not,"[32] and L. W. Teeter suspected that the least qualified candidates would volunteer and the most qualified would not.

> I am not in favor of a young brother expressing himself to the minister or to the elder as to his feeling, and how he is burdened, and how he is impressed that he ought to be a minister of God. I put that all into the hands of the Eternal Godhead. Let them all join together to bring about the conditions, and if a certain brother is to be chosen let God adjust all the matters and let us wait until the adjustment appears to be made all round. I would like that better than simply to have a young man tell what he thinks about himself. Some young brother might want to preach, and he would not be ready to know the extent of the office. I will have to pass judgment on him and disapprove of his request because he, in my mind, would not at all fill the measure, for all I know. While there might be proper brethren to speak to you their mind, they are generally backward [i.e., reticent] and have nothing to say, leaving it to the Lord, and others who are not so well adapted, or not at all adapted to the ministry, and they are often most apt to speak and do speak, and the judgment then on the matter is left to you. It puts me in an unfavorable position later. I would have to say "No," to a brother who comes up to me, and yet I have no evidence that it is justifiable. If we had Scriptural evidence about that, then I would be satisfied. If this Committee will put in that section, at the proper place, citations of Scripture directly on the point, not inferential, but directly, it will please me wonderfully well, and I know it will please God and please the Holy Spirit.[33]

Supporters of ministerial reform countered that the different election methods merely reflected reality. Procedure, they claimed, varied within the denomination; permitting young men to offer themselves was practical because it allowed those with the call to begin their labor sooner. Furthermore, missionaries volunteered and that worked; why not a similar method for pastors?

> Yesterday we had over here fifteen young brethren and sisters that were offering their lives to go to India and China. Others were here after the completion of their first period, for their furlough, but, my brethren, suppose you write back to the church where they came from and find out when those people were called by

the church to be missionaries, will you? We have got them, and because we have been willing to follow the way that God has led, Bro. Stover has gone to India, and we are getting missionaries. If this form had been in vogue, that a young man might have spoken to some one of his call to the ministry, I would not have fooled a lot of my time away in teaching school and in doing some other things. I would have gone to the ministry when the Lord told me to go, and so would a lot of you. I believe in the church calling the men to the ministry, but I don't believe any minister will do much who is called by the church if he is not also called by the Lord, and this provides for it. . . . I know there are inconsistencies in it [the report]. You know why—because our Brotherhood is not a unit in the way it calls its ministers. That is why, and the Committee has wisely recognized differences in opinion, and has tried to give us the various forms that are recognized and being used today, so we could all get together on it.[34]

Finally, in 1917 Annual Conference revised the ministry by creating District Ministerial Boards, whose duties included assisting congregations with the election and placement of ministers.

(3.) To encourage the election of ministers, as suitable young men develop; and if they are not called to conduct such elections and the ordination of elders, they should be represented, if practicable, at such time and places by at least one of their number. . . .

(5.) To cooperate with churches in securing elders and pastors, and in severing these relations; also with elders, ministers, and pastors in changing location. The ministerial Boards, however, shall not be intrusive, acting with arbitrary authority; they shall be helpful.

(6.) To keep a record of the churches that desire elders and pastors, and also the names of elders, ministers, and pastors who desire change of location and work.

(7.) To cooperate with the Ministerial Boards and the District Mission Boards in securing workers to cover the Districts, and also with the General Mission Board in securing workers for the world field.

(8.) To make annual reports to their respective District Meetings of the work done and the needs of the Districts, with such recommendations as seem good.[35]

The ministerial reforms passed despite heavy opposition. Just prior to voting, conservatives still hoped to speak, but the Acting Moderator, D. M. Garver, recognized a motion to vote. Garver then ruled that the proposal "only requires a majority," rather than two-thirds approval. Finally, after asking delegates to vote by standing, he ignored calls for a count, believing that he observed a visual majority, and he moved to the next item on the agenda. Garver's procedural rulings could not have pleased conservatives.[36]

Thus, conservative frustration mounted. The denomination was less inclined than ever to discipline members; diversity rather than unity gained momentum, especially regarding dress and the method of electing ministers, and individualism advanced at the cost of community, again particularly regarding garb and the ministry. Traditional free ministers now shared the preachers bench with salaried professionals, and although the Annual Conference had not approved mandatory educational standards, the Brethren smiled more broadly than ever on those with formal learning, as Adam Ebey feared. Individualism, diversity, education, and professionalism all marched in the vanguard of modernity.

MARTIN GROVE BRUMBAUGH

Perhaps the most modern Dunker during this period was Martin Grove Brumbaugh. Born in Huntingdon County, Pennsylvania, Brumbaugh was a minister, the first member of the Church of the Brethren to earn a doctorate of philosophy, a professor at the University of Pennsylvania, two-time president of Juniata College, the first commissioner of education in Puerto Rico, the superintendent of schools in Philadelphia, and governor of Pennsylvania. He had wide interests; his University of Pennsylvania dissertation was on the poet John Donne, and he authored the first history of the Church of the Brethren. Perhaps his greatest talent was public speaking, and by his thirties he enjoyed a national reputation as an orator on innovative pedagogy, his primary field.

Easily the best-known, most publicly successful member of the denomination during his lifetime, Brumbaugh evoked mixed feelings among his fellow Brethren. Progressives outwardly admired him for his achievement, and progressive congregations who cast aside plain meetinghouses for larger, more fashionable facilities often invited Brumbaugh as the dedication speaker. Conservatives, however, quietly criticized him for an apparent violation of a 1912 Annual Meeting position that discouraged office holding. Some also disapproved of Brumbaugh's lifestyle. He consorted with the Masons, hobnobbed with the rich and famous (Annie Oakley, John Wanamaker, and William Howard Taft), owned a summer home in Maine, played golf avidly, smoked cigars, and, according to rumors, worked on Sundays. Finally, Brumbaugh's nonviolence departed from orthodox Brethrenism. He suffered the bad luck to serve in the governor's mansion during World War I. He used his influence to assist conscientious objectors, but otherwise his pacifism resembled Woodrow Wilson's as much as Alexander Mack's. When preaching before Brethren congregations, especially before and after the war, he denounced armed conflict in principle, but as governor he sanctioned the Great War as a holy war and the last war. Largely as a consequence of his fast-paced brand of Brethrenism, Brumbaugh never held a major denominational office.[37]

Martin Grove Brumbaugh, Brethren minister and wartime governor of Pennsylvania. *Photo courtesy of BHLA.*

Typical of Brumbaugh's ambiguous image was his dedication of a Billy Sunday tabernacle in Philadelphia. Sunday's tabernacles were temporary, wooden structures that had seating for thousands, replaced tents, and allowed revivals to continue into the winter. On one hand, Governor-elect Brumbaugh's participation in the dedication of this novel building accentuated his success and signaled his approval of revivalistic religion, which enjoyed nearly unanimous support among the Brethren. But

Brumbaugh's appearance as a public officeholder on the platform in Sunday's tabernacle seems out of character for a plain, humble Brethren. Furthermore, Billy Sunday was a controversial figure. A former professional baseball player, he was a super-patriot who mixed the gospel with American foreign policy and was a flamboyant preacher who treasured applause. Many, but not all, Brethren welcomed the efforts of this famous revivalist, and Brumbaugh's time in Sunday's spotlight, though described by an approving eyewitness for *The Gospel Messenger,* nevertheless appears out of character for the Brethren.[38]

> It was our privilege to attend the dedication services of the Billy Sunday tabernacle on the last night of the old year, 1914. The immense structure is intended to seat about twenty thousand people—saying nothing of the standing room for thousands more. We shall never forget the thrill that came over us as we looked out over the thousands of people. Back of the pulpit, on a gradual elevation of seats, sat a choir of three thousand or more trained singers, who fairly made the tabernacle quiver as they sang.
>
> The tabernacle itself is a wooden structure, costing several thousand dollars. It must be seen and studied to be admired and appreciated. It is simply wonderful in its arrangement and acoustic properties.
>
> On Sunday, Jan. 3, was the opening of the tabernacle for the evangelistic services which are to continue for not less than nine weeks, Billy Sunday doing the preaching. At the first service the building was crowded, and thousands turned away. So wonderful is the organization of the tabernacle meetings, reaching out and embracing nearly all the evangelical churches of Philadelphia, and such a magnetic hold has Billy Sunday on the people that, were the capacity of the tabernacle twice as large as it is, it would still be too small for the crowds who come to hear the speaker. We are not an admirer nor a believer in Billy Sunday's methods, as a preacher of the Gospel of the Nazarene, yet we frankly admit that it takes more than a psychologist to interpret the secret of his power over the great mass of people who want to hear him, and are influenced by him.
>
> The first speech of the dedication services was by Mayor [Rudolph] Blankenburg, the genial old man with a young heart, who has the welfare of rich and poor, learned and unlearned, at heart, and who has a warm handshake and a kind word for one and all. The Mayor spoke of the pleasure it gave him to take part in the dedication of the greatest tabernacle for religious services he ever

saw. In concluding his appeals to the people, he referred to the need of a better city government, a growing civic righteousness, higher ideals of life, and an humble walking with God by one and all, closing with these words: "When I was a boy and left home for this country, my father, who was a preacher, laid his hands on my head and gave me his blessing, saying: 'My son, walk with God.' That," said the Mayor, "I have been trying to do ever since." Then, suddenly, the Mayor turned towards the Governor-elect, M. G. Brumbaugh, and said, "There is our next Governor, one of Philadelphia's productions—a man that Philadelphia and the State ought to feel proud of—a scholar, a teacher, a Christian gentleman, a man who walks with God."

The next speaker, Dr. M. G. Brumbaugh, then was announced. If space would permit, I should like to make mention of the many good things he said—things that were an honor and a credit to the Church of the Brethren. Never did I feel more proud of the principles of our people than I did after the masterly address of Bro. Brumbaugh. Let the whole church pray for him that he may be used by God for better government! One thing that the Doctor said and emphasized particularly, I shall never forget: "The man who does not begin the day with daily prayer, is not even a good citizen." Then, after speaking of graft, misrule, debasing shows, and reproving and rebuking the popular sins of society, and wrong-doing in general, he said, with wonderful effect, these words, which we quote as nearly correct as possible. "I hope you will pray tonight that you may always be ruled by such men as our honorable Mayor—men who walk with God." Then came the close of his masterly address, which greatly thrilled the tabernacle audience: "In the midst of light is the beautiful. In the midst of the beautiful is the good. In the midst of the good is God. Find the center, my brother; find the center, my sister."[39]

Politically, Brumbaugh was a Progressive Republican much like Theodore Roosevelt and William Howard Taft. His support for workmen's compensation and child labor laws, regulation of businesses, and reliance on experts rather than political appointees placed him firmly in this tradition. Brumbaugh described his political goals in an article that appeared in *The Outlook*, a popular current events periodical.

In the executive chair at Harrisburg, Pennsylvania, sits a Governor who, it is said, has not met Senator Boies Penrose, the so-called political leader of the State, since he was inaugurated, and this in a Commonwealth where, in the belief of the country at large, practical politics has its real abiding-place. This Governor, in the face of hidebound conservatism, has put on his State's statute-books legislation whose avowed object is social betterment in communities in which the living and working conditions of the industrial element in the past have provoked country-wide criticism.

Martin Grove Brumbaugh, LL.D., schoolmaster by profession, is the latter-day exemplification of the scholar in politics. His career is an anomaly—a teacher, a preacher, an educator known the country over, he has shown himself a master-hand in politics. He has been able to adapt himself to the conditions of active political work; has lived every minute up to his highest moral and religious beliefs; and now, in the first year of his four-year term as Governor of Pennsylvania, sees progressive reforms adopted with equanimity by an old boss-ridden Eastern State, and has marked out a plan of campaign which insures further legislation looking to the betterment of living conditions in the country's greatest industrial commonwealth.

How did the schoolmaster get into politics? How has he reconciled his conservative moral ideals with working political conditions? The country thinks the condition is an anomaly; how does Governor Brumbaugh view it? These were some of the questions which recently were put to the executive of Pennsylvania.

I met the Governor in his home city of Philadelphia, where for many years, up to the time he was inaugurated in January last, he was Superintendent of the Public Schools. As it grew dark he looked out over the crowds of workers hurrying to their homes and said, thoughtfully:

"It's a good old State and I love it. I want to set it right."

The Governor speaks with feeling. He is more than six feet tall, massive in frame, with a strong, intellectual face framed in iron-gray hair. Piercing black eyes under overhanging brows are his distinctive physical feature. His natural mode of thinking is deeply religious. A few words sum up his scheme of government.

"A politician is a good sport," he said, with a happy twinkle from under those great shaggy eyebrows. "He knows when to heed the will of the people. The leaders in the Legislature helped me to get my bills through. I talked it over with them, and they are sensible men and we agreed on things.

"I had to hold a tight hand on the purse strings, however. I sent for the leaders one day and told them that we were planning to spend more money than we would have. My hint was not taken, however, and I had to veto bills carrying appropriations of $7,000,000."

. . . An illustration of the new spirit that pervades Pennsylvania is found in the inaugural address that Governor Brumbaugh made in January last in the Capitol at Harrisburg—the Capitol of fraud memory.

"In assuming the duties of the office to which you have elected me," he said, "I am humbled and steadied by the greatness of the obligation imposed and the abiding conviction that I can do my duty only when aided and guided by the Divine. In His name and for His people I enter upon this new field of endeavor."

And Martin Brumbaugh meant every word of that statement. What did he accomplish? Summed up in the first session of the Legislature under his administration these bills were passed:

1. A Workmen's Compensation Law, which goes into effect on January 1, 1916. This measure is wide in its application and follows the line of progressive thought.

2. A Child Labor Law, which marks out a new path in this reform. The striking features of this law were the ideas of Governor Brumbaugh.

3. Legislation taking the Roads Department of the State entirely out of politics and putting it in the hands of men who are practical road builders, and supporting these men with expert road engineers. The Road Department formerly was a rich political plum.

4. A law establishing in the Department of Labor and Industry a system of regulation of employers seeking employees and of employees seeking work, and a retirement pension for old, faithful employees.

5. A law requiring counties to establish schools for the care of girls under the jurisdiction of the courts.

6. A law establishing a tax on the mining of anthracite and bituminous coal to raise revenue.

7. A consolidation and reorganization of the whole Agricultural Department to carry out the idea thus voiced in the

Governor's inaugural Message: "The funds for the advancement of our agricultural interests ought to express themselves much more largely in wheat and corn and potatoes, and less in clerical and other forms of routine service. Let us legislate for the farmer rather than the office-holder."

8. An amendment to the anthracite code making the mine-owners responsible for their foremen, who formerly, under a kink in the statutes, were held to be agents of the State. . . .

For years local option has been a live question in Pennsylvania. Governor Brumbaugh lost in his great fight last winter on this issue, but he is not yet "licked."

"Local option has had a setback," he remarked, grimly. "They had the cards stacked against me. Many members of the Legislature were elected on a saloon platform, and of course under those conditions I lost. But there will be other legislatures.

"If the people want saloons let them have them, but let the people decide the question. The courts and the Legislature have no right to block the will of the people. In our State the county courts grant the liquor licenses, and in the past judges in many cases were not elected with the idea in mind whether they would hold the scales of justice evenly, but whether they would vote for a saloon license. That was the scandal of the situation. The country districts in most cases are natural dry territory and the cities wet. What I was fighting for was to let the people decide for themselves. The idea has got to win out in the end. If you believe in your democracy, you have got to trust the people.

"I believe in the people. If I have any secret of success, that is it. The people have a perfect right to know and shall know what I stand for. When I took charge of the schools here in Philadelphia they were starved. I called the parents of the various districts to meetings in the schools and I put the case before them plainly. 'Do you want to send your children to such school-houses as these?' I said. I went from district to district. I had 200,000 parents organized as a Home and School Association—and we got the appropriations that we needed to bring about decent conditions.

"About that time a wise old-time politician said, 'You can't beat him in the school business. He can talk for nothing to the parents of the community in the school-houses, and we have to hire a band and a hall.' That is what I do," the Governor said, "take my case direct to the people."

Governor Brumbaugh then turned to his constructive ideas for the future.

"This State loses each year," he said, "$125,000,000 from sickness and death due to preventable illness. Where can the State better employ its energies than in preventing this awful waste?

"I want to get the best sanitary and civil engineering talent that can be engaged, put this talent at the disposal of the people of the State, and I want to see that we have such housing conditions that that terrible waste will be stopped. I want to arrange matters so that the farmer who is going to build a new pig-sty or a chicken-coop can drop a postal card to the Capitol and an engineer will go to his farm and tell him where to put his new building so that the refuse will not drain into the well and give his family typhoid fever. Not alone will the farmer benefit, for I think that the problem of housing conditions is one of the great problems of the day. I would have the houses in our industrial centers constructed on sanitary lines and at the same time have an eye for the aesthetic, for with proper advice the house-holder will construct along good lines and the farmer will place his outbuildings so that nature shall not be shocked.

"At the same time we shall save the lives of the countless babies who now are lost because of ignorance. Leave out of the calculation the sentimental side of it. Is it worthwhile for the State to save $125,000,000 a year which now is thrown away through ignorance and neglect?

"Let us ignore the anguish of parents and the whole senti-mental side of it. I think it is worth while.

"My whole idea is to make it easier to live and to live right.

"Then we are going to stop loose legislation. I believe that we are over-lawed. Why, at the first session of the Legislature we repealed many measures, and a committee is now at work with the idea that at the next session we will repeal as many as one thousand laws now on the books. Soon after I was inaugurated I sent for the Attorney-General and instructed him to go over every bill in the Legislature and see that it was in proper shape, so that if passed it would be upheld by the courts.

"We are going to stop that waste of energy, and we will pass laws that will stay on the books and remove that scandal of government by the courts, for that is what it amounts to under conditions that have prevailed."

Governor Brumbaugh is a Dunkard in religious belief. He is the first man of his faith ever to be elected a Governor of any State of the Union. He took no oath of office, but, according to his religion, affirmed simply. He is today a devout follower of the religion of his fathers.

"I came to America in 1754," the Governor continued, with emphasis. "I am a Pennsylvania German and am proud of it. But put the emphasis on the Pennsylvania. We are the people who, along with the Quakers and the Scotch-Irish, developed this commonwealth. We are not hyphenated Americans.

"There is only one nation for the people who live here. If we are not Americans, we are nothing. That is all there is to it.

"I love this old State as devotedly as I can, and I want to make it so clean and sweet and wholesome that its children will thank God that they were born in Pennsylvania."

Such are the views of the chief executive of a State which has produced some of the most notorious political scandals of modern times. Can Governor Brumbaugh set it right?[40]

Brumbaugh pushed the limits of Brethren progressivism, probably avoiding discipline only because he held membership in the Philadelphia First Church of the Brethren, among the most liberal in the denomination.[41] Some Brethren embraced him while others held him at arm's length, which illustrates the difficulty they had determining how standoffish to be with the world. Educated, urbanized, politicized, and cosmopolitan, Brumbaugh was modern, and he exemplified modernity's power to complicate the relationship between the Brethren and the mainstream.

BRETHREN AND THE WAR

As the Church of the Brethren debated individualism, professionalization, unity, discipline, and a brother in the governor's chair, it could not ignore developments across the Atlantic. Although these questions about the Brethren order demonstrate the distance of the European bloodbath from America's heartland, between Sarajevo and American entry into the war in 1917, Brethren responded to a clash with "no parallel in modern history," as *The Gospel Messenger* pointed out, in ways both customary and exceptional.

The Gospel Messenger perceptively expected a costly conflict, but like most observers, its predictions of a short war sadly erred.

> Outside of the vast military campaign of the great Napoleon, the present European conflict has no parallel in modern history. The French commander covered practically the same territory involved in the present struggle, but since his time there has been a large increase of population, soldiers are more skillfully trained, and armament in general is far more effective. With the long range of present-day rifles and cannon, armies may fight each other at considerable distance, doing even more deadly work than in the days of old. It is this very destructiveness of modern military equipment that leads a noted military expert to venture the opinion that the pending struggle will be sharp, decisive and of comparatively short duration, exceeding any previous encounter in savage destructiveness.[42]

> Army and navy experts maintain that the daily expense of the European war, for all the forces engaged therein, runs to fully $50,000,000 per day—exclusive of the loss of property and other items of value. The greatest loss of all—the thousands of men killed—can not be computed nor replaced. When the great struggle is ended there will be a shortage of men everywhere—on the farms, in the shops, in commercial establishments and so on. When it is further considered that, for the last thirteen years, the cost of maintenance of the armies and navies of the countries at war, as well as the cost of naval construction, has exceeded $20,000,000,000, some idea may be gained of the crushing expense attached to the destructive agencies of war.[43]

In the early days of the Great War, Brethren mixed their peace-witness-as-usual theme with soft expressions of patriotism. Thus, the same issue of *The Gospel Messenger* that carried news of the assassination at Sarajevo encouraged an alternative Brethren celebration of the Fourth of July.

> While, in response to incessant agitation from year to year, there has been commendable progress in the more rational observance of the nation's chief holiday, much remains still to be accomplished.

Strange as it may seem, New York, Chicago, and other large cities have really made more progress along this line than smaller cities and country districts. *The Journal of the American Medical Society,* in its recent compilation, states that since 1903 a total of 41,280 persons were maimed and killed in celebrating Independence Day. The year 1908, with its gruesome record of 5,623 killed and injured, started the first real effort for a sane Fourth, and last year's record showed but 1,163 accidents. But even this smaller number is altogether unjustified. Why not adopt, for the fitting observance of the day, the altogether appropriate practice of many congregations of our Church of the Brethren—to meet in some shady spot in God's great outdoors for the discussion of missionary or other topics—questions that undoubtedly conduce to the moral up-building of those in attendance, and in a wider sense to the real welfare of the nation?[44]

Many Brethren claimed that their form of nonviolent patriotism, as articulated by an editorial in *The Gospel Messenger*, was superior to the more popular variety that went to war. At this point, nationalism and religion had little conflict. Because America remained at peace, jingoists did not browbeat pacifists for weakening national security, and because conscription was absent, Brethren patriotism did not tempt young men to abandon nonresistance. Thus, *The Gospel Messenger* proposed that contributions to the nation-state could coexist with religion.

There is a tendency, nowadays, to instill in the minds of children and young people such a close association between the ideas of patriotism and fighting for one's country, that a large part of the real spirit of patriotism—and that, too, the most essential—is totally ignored or overlooked. Is it not true, after all, that the real patriot is he who maintains the highest standards of honor, purity and justice for his country's laws, its rulers, and its highest interests? Be it remembered that the true patriot is he who is ever willing to sacrifice his time and strength and property to remove the evils threatening society in general, as well as the commonwealth. When history completes the record of men's lives, and posterity pronounces the verdict, it will be exalted moral worth, after all, that will shine most brilliantly, and that will constitute the real essence of true patriotism.[45]

Likewise, in 1917, just days after the United States declared war on Germany, D. W. Kurtz, an educator and preacher at the First Church of the Brethren in Philadelphia, described a "constructive patriotism" that rejected war and popular expressions of patriotism. Kurtz opted instead for a Social Gospel interpretation of national loyalty with majoritarian democracy, environmental conservation, productivity, and social reform.

What shall the pacifist do in this war? This question was raised at the National Educational Association. The teachers of America have been told so often, the last ten years, to get rid of the war-spirit, and teach history properly, not to promote a narrow nationalism, but a broad, humanitarian inter-nationalism. Now we are in a world-war, and the question comes: What shall the teacher do?

I was glad for the sentiment of the teachers—we hate war, it is wrong, and horrible; we shall continue to do all we can against militarism and the war-spirit. The United States is in the war "to make democracy safe" and future peace possible. But the great problem of the teacher is to teach true patriotism—constructive patriotism.

Love of country does not mean only to salute the flag, sing a patriotic song, and shout for war. Patriotism means to build up our country so as to make it strong, and durable, and good; to conserve all that is valuable, so as to make the nation a fit place in which a free people may live. To be patriotic is to be, first of all, a law-abiding citizen. America is full of law-breakers—people who are so individualistic that they want to do as they please, regardless of law and order and the common good. One of the most important duties of the public school is to teach obedience to law, and respect for authority, and cheerful acquiescence in the rule of the majority. This is the basis of government in a democracy. The very idea of government involves the obedience of the people to law, so that order may obtain instead of anarchy. Freedom is not license; and individualism becomes anarchy unless tempered by the social conscience of the brotherhood of man.

Constructive patriotism prepares men for efficient service in building up the nation in its industries, agriculture, and the development of the resources. No more patriotic thing can be done than to educate our youth so that they become producers, and not only consumers; that they add to the sum total of human values, instead of becoming a drag and a parasite to society. Hence our schools should teach the vocations in such a way as to fit our children to work and earn an honest living. Prosperity is a great factor for honesty and public order.

Constructive patriotism conserves the health and life of human beings. Over 3,000,000 people in the United States are sick all the time. Most of this is unnecessary. Sickness is not an individual affair, but a social menace and loss. It is the business of the nation to conserve the health of its people, and all that hygiene, public sanitation, pure foods, and proper living can do for human efficiency and happiness, are patriotic services of the highest order. We should erect monuments to our physicians that promote sanitation rather than to our generals.

Constructive patriotism conserves the life of the people, and does away with intemperance and accidents due to selfishness and carelessness, whereby thousands of lives are lost annually.

The conservation of our land, the soil, the timber and mines, the gas and oil, the food products, and all the material resources that contribute to human needs is a patriotic act. The teachers, 700,000 strong, can do an incalculable amount of good by informing themselves of the facts of waste, and the methods of conservation, and impressing upon the minds of *Young America* that true patriotism is conservation of these blessings.

Above all other services is the patriotic act of conserving and creating ideals of the true and good and beautiful that make life worth living. After all, nothing has value save the human soul, and the soul is lost that is not in tune with God. The ideals that brought the Pilgrims to New England, the Quakers to Pennsylvania, and the persecuted people of Europe to free America—these ideals, as they are purified and ennobled by a larger vision of the Truth— must be maintained. Let each parent, or teacher, who instills the ideals of true religion and morality into the hearts of the children, know that this is supreme patriotism.

The pacifist has much to do. The only way that we can get rid of war is to displace it by inculcating a truer philosophy of life into future generations. This is no time for lamenting, for sadness and pessimism, but for heroic deeds of constructive work, to prepare the children of today for a better civilization of tomorrow.[46]

Because the United States remained officially neutral, Brethren could urge American avoidance of the war without compromising their loyalty. Hence, the 1915 Annual Meeting, the first gathering after the outbreak of hostilities, counseled President Woodrow Wilson to avoid involvement in the European fight. Its statement, drafted by the denominational Peace Committee, judged the Great War as "the most terrible war of all the ages."

> Whereas, The Church of the Brethren is holding its Annual Conference this year at a time when more than one-half of the world's population is engaged in the most terrible war of the ages, thus threatening the peace and happiness of the whole human race; Therefore Be It Resolved,
>
> First, That we do regard this as a most opportune time to express our abhorrence of war, with all of its train of evils.
>
> Second, That we do not consider this a fitting time for our government to increase her armaments and thereby arouse the suspicion of other nations. We hereby pray and beseech all who are in authority to resist the influence of militarism in our land.
>
> Third, We stand for peaceful pursuits and pray that our President and his cabinet shall earnestly endeavor to keep this country out of the throes of war.
>
> Fourth, We look with profound sorrow upon this war of wars, but prophesy that God will turn the wrath of man to praise him by giving to the whole world a higher conception of human brotherhood and the doctrine of peace and good will towards all men.
>
> Fifth, We express the hope that the day may not be far distant when all of our prayers for peace may be gloriously answered in the name of our Great Prince of Peace![47]

As Brethren maintained their peace witness, they nonetheless concluded that the war had at least one benefit: Christian conquest of Jerusalem. Like most Christians, the editor of *The Gospel Messenger* praised British troops for victories over the Ottoman Turks, thereby ending Moslem rule of the Holy Lands.

> No event in modern history has caused so much universal interest and joy among professed Christians, the world over, as the confirmed report that the Holy City has been taken by the British troops, that the unspeakable Turk has been driven out, and that the English have entered the city in triumph. . . .

It is said that the Allies will, when a treaty of peace is made and signed, stipulate, in the strongest possible terms, that the Moslems shall be prohibited from ever entering or possessing Jerusalem again. It is most sincerely hoped that this will be one of the results of the present war. . . .

To Christians the driving out of the Moslems means the rescue of the holy places from the curse of Turkish rule.[48]

The vast suffering of the Great War encouraged Brethren to think harder about the physical needs of those overseas, another new perspective for Brethrenism. True, Brethren mission at home and abroad ministered to the body as well as the soul, but mission philosophy stressed conversion. The war, however, drew attention to pain, hunger, and disease. Thus, at a time when humanitarian foreign aid did not exist, the denominational Peace Committee called for the United States to spend its money on relief for victims, "without respect to race, religion or nationality," rather than armaments, anticipating a new role for the national government.

First. Since the present agitation for military preparedness is contrary to the spirit and teaching of our Lord Jesus Christ, therefore, we, your Peace Committee, suggest that the Church of the Brethren place herself on record again at this time and express our abhorrence of war, with all of its train of evils. It is our sober judgment that all "military preparedness" in the end is futile, in that it does not prevent war, but makes war increasingly possible, and thus hopelessly postponing the goal of international peace and good will.

Second. We recommend that all our congregations and colleges at once organize local Peace Committees and become active in distributing "peace literature," which may be had free for the asking, by addressing the Chairman of the National Peace Committee, 664 44th Street, Brooklyn, New York. (Inclose [sic] postage for information.)

Third. Since many of our sister nations with whom we have ties of friendship are now suffering to an unprecedented degree through this world war, and Whereas, the Christian sympathy of our land is now profoundly stirred in behalf of afflicted humanity in the war zones. Therefore, Be It

Resolved, That this Conference recommend to the President and Congress of the United States, that we do believe this to be an opportune time for our Government to take a great step towards international peace, by making an appropriation out of the national funds (worthy of this great and providentially blessed country of ours), to be applied to the relief of suffering humanity throughout the war zones, without respect to race, religion or nationality.

Since God has so richly blessed our land with great abundance, we believe that our Government should take this Christlike act as an initiative step towards the ending of all war, and the bringing in of the Reign of Peace, and Good will Towards All Men. May "Righteousness exalt our nation" (Prov. 14:34).[49]

The plight of civilians also caught the Brethren eye. Brethren were especially concerned about Armenians; the Turks rounded up and shot thousands of Armenian men and drove hundreds of thousands of their women, children, and old men over the mountains into Cicilia and Syria. By September 1915 more than one million Armenians had died, and Brethren congregations collected for the survivors.[50]

A good mother was teaching her two little girls the prayer that Jesus told us to pray. They were quite small, and did not catch all the words correctly, for in repeating it they said, "Give us this day our 'jelly bread.' " We all like good things, and want God to keep our supply coming. We often sacrifice much to get the things we like. Can we imagine having nothing to eat but roots, and the bark of trees?

Our Sunday-school superintendent called our attention, on a recent Sunday, to the appeal for starving Armenians, as published on the last page of *The Sunday School Times*, and urged us to bring an offering for them the following Sunday. Our pastor also spoke of it and asked us to deny ourselves of some things that we can readily do without, in order to have something to give to these suffering people.

I suggest less candy, less ice cream, less pie and cake, less coffee, no tobacco, no cigarettes for a whole week, or for many weeks, for that matter. This would bring such an offering as would please the Lord, and feed the starving multitude. Will we not share our jelly bread with them? Distance need not hinder. They are our neighbors. Then think of loving them.

> Can we claim to love them while we let them starve? Can we claim to love God and let our brothers and sisters starve? I am so glad for the offerings being taken for them. God is using us to help spread his truth. Let us surrender to him and show our love for him by helping them![51]

No cigarettes, less candy, fewer armaments, and federal tax dollars for international relief: the Great War had already widened Brethren horizons. The Church of the Brethren responded to human tragedy by contributing for relief without an accompanying payoff in mission, unprecedented for the church, and they urged the federal government to undertake overseas aid, unprecedented for the government. But when the Brethren professed peace, they maintained tradition, albeit with a nod toward patriotism.

"God Be with You"

"God be with you till we meet again." So sang those on the North Manchester station platform as they bid farewell to Laura and Raymond Cottrell.

> By His counsels guide, uphold you,
> With His sheep securely fold you;
> God be with you till we meet again.

This hymn, in all its sentimental simplicity, was the perfect selection for the occasion as the two young medical doctors began their lives as missionaries. But this prayer for God's protection "when life's perils thick confound you," as the third verse notes, fit the denomination just as comfortably as it did the pair of idealistic, young missionaries. With the split between progressives and conservatives widening yearly, when would these two viewpoints ever meet again, and with war approaching, what perils might soon confound the Brethren? Perhaps those on the station platform, in addition to praying for the Cottrells, could just as well have been praying for God's protection in the coming days.

> [Refrain] Till we meet, till we meet,
> Till we meet at Jesus' feet;
> Till we meet, till we meet,
> God be with you till we meet again.[52]

NOTES

1. Harvey A. Brubaker to J. H. B. Williams (October 24, 1913), Brethren Historical Library and Archives (BHLA), Elgin, Ill., Missionary Personel/Correspondence, Box 48, File "Drs. A. R. and Laura Cottrell, 1910-1938." Williams edited *The Missionary Visitor,* a periodical that promoted mission work.

2. Olive Miller, "Laura M. Cottrell, M. D.; A. Raymond Cottrell, M. D.," *The Missionary Visitor* (October, 1913): 323.

3. Miller, "Laura M. Cottrell," 322-24.

4. "Royalty Assassinated," *The Gospel Messenger* (July 4, 1914): 417.

5. Sean Dennis Cashman, *America in the Age of the Titans: The Progressive Era and World War I* (New York: New York University Press, 1988), 461, 469-79; Walter LaFeber, *The American Age: United States Foreign Policy at Home and Abroad since 1750* (New York: W. W. Norton, 1989), 268-80

6. *Full Report of the Proceedings of the Brethren's Annual Meeting, 1916* (Elgin, Ill.: Brethren Publishing House, 1916), 142.

7. Jesse K. Brumbaugh, "Our Communion," *The Gospel Messenger* (October 14, 1916): 662.

8. Adaline Hohf Beery, "Shall We Know Each Other Here?" *The Gospel Messenger* (October 28, 1916): 692.

9. Adam Ebey to Galen B. Royer (April 25, 1917), BHLA, Missionary Personnel/Correspondence, Box 49, File "Adam/Alice Ebey."

10. Royer to Ebey (April 27, 1917).

11. "Adam Ebey" and "Alice King Ebey," *The Brethren Encyclopedia,* 3 vols., edited by Donald F. Durnbaugh (Philadelphia, Pa., and Oak Brook, Ill.: The Brethren Encyclopedia, Inc., 1983), I:418.

12. Isaac J. Rosenberger, "Government and Teaching in the Church," *The Gospel Messenger* (October 7, 1916): 643, 644.

13. *Full Report, 1915*, Paul Mohler speaking, 159-60.

14. *Full Report, 1915*, Samuel N. McCann speaking, 158.

15. *Full Report, 1915*, Daniel W. Kurtz speaking, 158-59.

16. *Full Report, 1915*, answer by Standing Committee, 169.

17. *Full Report, 1915*, Tobias S. Fike speaking, 175-76.

18. *Full Report, 1915*, Jacob H. Beer speaking, 178.

19. *Full Report, 1915*, Daniel L. Miller speaking, 176.

20. *Full Report, 1915*, Daniel L. Mohler speaking, 177.

21. *Full Report, 1915*, 175-79.

22. *Full Report, 1916*, 88-89; *Full Report, 1918*, 85-88.

23. *Full Report, 1915*, 83.

24. *Full Report, 1916*, Reuben Shroyer speaking, 45-46.

25. *Full Report, 1916*, Samuel F. Sanger speaking, 46.

26. *Full Report, 1916*, Frank McCoy speaking, 51.

27. *Full Report, 1917*, 40.

28. *Full Report, 1917*, 40-41. See also Carl F. Bowman, *Brethren Society: The Cultural Transformation of a "Peculiar People,"* (Baltimore, Md.: The Johns Hopkins University Press, 1995), 232-38.

29. *Full Report, 1917*, 41.

30. *Full Report, 1917*, 41.

31. *Full Report, 1917*, 40

32. *Full Report, 1917*, Samuel H. Hertzler speaking, 42.

33. *Full Report, 1917*, Lewis W. Teeter speaking, 46-47.

34. *Full Report, 1917*, John E. Miller speaking, 48-49.

35. *Full Report, 1917*, 41.

36. *Full Report, 1917*, 49-50. See also Bowman, *Brethren Society,* 232-38.

37. Earl C. Kaylor, Jr., *Martin Grove Brumbaugh: A Pennsylvanian's Odyssey from Sainted Schoolman to Bedeviled World War I Governor, 1862-1930* (Madison and Teaneck, N.J.: Fairleigh Dickinson University Press, 1996), 59-61, 65-67, 71, 84, 95-100, 125, 198-99, 206-7, 291-92, 299, 312-13, 315, 321, 324-25; Bowman, *Brethren Society,* 245-51.

38. Lyle W. Dorsett, *Billy Sunday and the Redemption of Urban America* (Grand Rapids, Mich.: William F. Eerdmans Publishing Company, 1991), 2-3, 65-67.

39. J. T. Myers, "Dedication of the Billy Sunday Tabernacle, Philadelphia, Pa.," *The Gospel Messenger* (January 23, 1915): 51.

40. Charles Phillips Cooper, "Progress and Reaction in Pennsylvania: A Personal Interview with Governor Brumbaugh," *The Outlook* (December 29, 1915): 1045-49.

41. Bowman, *Brethren Society,* 250-51.

42. "The Extent of the Conflict," *The Gospel Messenger* (August 29, 1914): 545.

43. "Fifty Million Dollars a Day," *The Gospel Messenger* (August 15, 1914): 513.

44. "Why Not a 'Sane' Fourth of July?" *The Gospel Messenger* (July 4, 1914): 417.

45. "True Patriotism," *The Gospel Messenger* (August 29, 1914): 545.

46. [Dwight W. Kurtz], "Constructive Patriotism," *The Gospel Messenger* (August 18,1917): 514.

47. *Full Report, 1915*, 188. The Annual Meeting approved a similar resolution, 192.

48. "Jerusalem Captured—The Moslem Driven Out," *The Gospel Messenger* (January 12, 1918): 17.

49. "Report of the Peace Committee," *Full Report, 1916,* 121-22.

50. Martin Gilbert, *The First World War: A Complete History* (New York: Henry Holt, 1994), 142-43, 166-67.

51. Eleanor J. Brumbaugh, "Our Jelly Bread," *The Gospel Messenger* (November 11, 1916): 724.

52. Jeremiah Rankin, "God Be with You till We Meet Again," No. 600, *The Brethren Hymnal: A Collection of Psalms, Hymns and Spiritual Songs* (Elgin, Ill.: Brethren Publishing House, 1901).

II. WORLD WAR I
America Joins the Conflict

The Great War was the first conflict in which the world's industrialized nation-states marshaled all of their impressive resources for a struggle to the death against each other. Modern governments had arisen during the nineteenth century and now flexed their considerable muscle, including a dominant executive branch, to conscript men, manage the economy, and control public opinion. Birthrates, literacy rates, and the health of citizens became matters of national security. Military officers, less aristocratic and more professional, remained heroes but now also functioned as engineers and managers. Railroads sped the largest, best equipped armies in history into the field more quickly than ever, and industrialization, which had grown impressively in the decades just before the war, turned the battlefield into a "factory of death," in the words of one scholar, characterized by machine guns, barbed wire, and millions of artillery shells. Just as significantly, modern warfare touched the home front more directly than ever. In "industrial warfare" civilians equaled soldiers in importance, as many heavily taxed, cold, hungry, sick, and homeless Europeans soon learned. The destructive powers of modern warfare were unrivaled, and the Grim Reaper cut a wide swath among soldiers and civilians alike.[1]

Although biblical nonviolence was incompatible with industrial warfare, modern war, at least this one, had no place for those seeking a place on the sidelines. As an unpopular minority, Brethren pacifists suddenly found themselves further outside the mainstream than many of them wished. Furthermore, denominational leaders who encouraged nonresistance and young men who took their advice quickly came into conflict with their government. In short, for the Brethren the war meant a clash with both unofficial and official opinion.

One Hundred Percent Americanism

Modern nation-states at war considered the Brethren version of patriotism, which emphasized reform-minded citizenship in place of militarism (described in the previous chapter), as sand in the gears of their war machines, and they possessed the power to suppress this dissent. As early as 1915 Woodrow Wilson had determined that if war came, German Americans were likely sources of opposition and that "such creatures of passion, disloyalty, and anarchy must be crushed out. The hand of our power should close over them at once." Once the war began, Wilson followed through, urging Congress to pass two laws, the Espionage Act (1917) and the Sedition Act (1918), which gave the federal government authority to restrict free speech. Despite this, many of the most ardent patriots concluded that government action lacked the nerve to shape public thought as the times required. Impressed with the staggering demands of total war, a significant segment of public opinion determined that nothing short of total commitment was acceptable. Any deviation from unqualified support, anything less than one hundred percent Americanism, was dangerous, and on that assumption so-called one hundred percenters mobilized support. They made it their business to know what their neighbors thought and did. With evangelical fervor they organized drives and pledge-signings. Four-Minute Men, usually polished community leaders, delivered crisp pep talks between films to the ten million Americans who visited theaters every week. But one hundred percenters believed in coercion as much as persuasion. In the summer of 1918, federal agents, augmented by local law authorities and vigilantes, conducted well-publicized sweeps that publicly embarrassed young men on city streets who were not in uniform, especially those of apparent working class background. On other occasions mobs burned books or destroyed musical instruments belonging to German immigrants or forced them to kiss the American flag in public. In the worst instances, vigilantes flogged, tarred and feathered, or lynched. Pressure on dissenters was intense.[2]

Additionally, to ensure one hundred percent loyalty, the government actively spied on potential critics. The Military Intelligence Division of the army and the Bureau of Investigation, a predecessor of the Federal Bureau of Investigation, assumed responsibility for this, although almost every executive agency, including the Postal Service, the Department of the Treasury (Secret Service), and immigration agencies, had an office devoted to investigations of suspected unfaithful Americans. The government also encouraged private groups to contribute to the hunt for subversives. The American Protective League, consisting of 300,000 businessmen, professionals, and upper-middle-class citizens, conducted over three million inquiries into disloyalty and shared its findings with the government.[3]

One hundred percent Americanism did not overlook the Brethren. Indiana Normal College dismissed a Latin professor, whom it had employed for twenty years, in part because his wife was Brethren. J. A. Robinson, a pastor in Des Moines, Iowa, suffered indictment under the Espionage Act, but his case was dropped. Authorities charged several Brethren with treason for obstructing the draft. Kennesaw Mountain Landis, a federal judge and future commissioner of major league baseball, sentenced David Gerdes, an Illinois pastor, to ten years at Leavenworth for discouraging people from buying Liberty Bonds and for "attacking the activities of the Red Cross." He was released after ten months.[4] Kermit Eby remembered the harassment that his family's German heritage and pacifism attracted in St. Joseph County, Indiana.

> Our home community in Indiana consisted of first- and second-generation Germans. They were typical hard-working, law-abiding Americans. I learned to speak Pennsylvania Dutch as my first language. As a boy I was rocked to sleep by a grandmother who spoke English only when necessary. The first sermons that I am able to remember were preached in German by my grandfather.
>
> I was in high school when the United States entered the war. To this day I recall the mental struggles forced on me by the war. Our church grew out of the struggle of the religious wars in Europe. One of its primary teachings was that of no participation in war—absolute pacifism. Several of our neighbor boys were drafted but refused combatant service. One of my uncles, a college graduate, refused even non-combatant service. The call of "slacker" still rings in my ears.
>
> My great-grandmother died during the war. The pressure of the "patriotic" groups was so great that it was impossible to preach her funeral in German. Temporarily, at least, God was English-speaking. On several occasions our church house was smeared with yellow paint because of our German background. Of course, German was dropped from the curriculum of our high school.

The propaganda stories were the hardest blow of all. How could the Germans kill babies and mutilate women? All the Germans I knew were kindly, neighborly souls willing to help out whenever sickness or death came. Finally, I decided that all good Germans came to the United States and all bad ones stayed in Germany![5]

Public opinion even expected children to be one hundred percenters. Nora Berkebile, a Brethren woman in Bellefontaine, Ohio, recounted the "ridicule for their faith" that "her little boys" endured.

The other day the school superintendent came to the school and advocated military training. He said it is only a question of time until it will be compulsory in the common schools. We have an excellent teacher, who is doing splendid work, and we do not blame her in the least, but at the insistence of the superintendent she said the boys should drill. A young brother, the oldest boy in school, was appointed captain. This was on Friday. On Monday he returned to school and said he could not be captain, or drill, because it is against the rules of the church.

One of the boys spoke up, as boys will, and said: "Awh! that old church of yours down there is full of beans." Another young brother stepped up then and said to the one who would not be captain: "I wish it were, don't you?" He answered: "Yes, I do; beans are high."

Naturally they were left alone that day on the military training question. Our little boys, even, are being called upon, you see, to bear ridicule for their faith. And, mothers and fathers, let us teach them to be firm. May we so instruct them that they may have the peace principle so firmly rooted and grounded within them that they may meet the jeers and taunts of schoolmates without getting angry and that, when they grow older, they may be ready to meet death, if necessary, for their faith.

Far rather would I see my boy shot down before my eyes, because he is true to his faith, than to see him go where he would shoot some other mother's son, and lose his own soul because he is a murderer.

But there may be some mother and father who have taught these lessons to their sons and they have gone of their own free will to fight the enemy. Blame those parents? Never! My heart goes out in sympathy for them. Their hearts are breaking and they are bearing enough without our censure. Were I in their place, I think I could only pray: "Oh, Lord, bring my son back in safety. Help him to see the evil of shedding the blood of another." More than for his safe return, I think I should pray that he be kept from sin—kept from taking the life of another.

We do not know what our little boys may have to meet in years to come, but we can, at least, use our influence to keep military training out of our schools. People seem to be going wild on the question—so wild that, in their efforts to appear patriotic, they advocate for this country the very thing for which the United States says she is fighting Germany.

Let us keep cool, let us be patient and kind! Let us, if reviled, revile not again, but let us dare to be men like Daniel! When school authorities undertake to force our boys to drill, forbid it, for the Government does not yet demand that of us, and we need not do it.[6]

Pacifism, quite simply, was incongruous with one hundred percent Americanism. This translated into prosecution for a few Brethren and persecution for many.

THE DRAFT

War fervor struck draft-age Brethren men especially hard. The Wilson administration decided to satisfy its needs for manpower by conscription, that is by relying on the power and authority of the state rather than volunteerism, but the president and his advisors worried about public support for the draft. After all, in the nation's last major conflict, the Spanish-American War (1898), the army had depended on volunteers raised by local celebrities, exemplified by Teddy Roosevelt's Rough Riders. And in America's last conscription, during the Civil War, loopholes and class bias had plagued the system. The needs of modern warfare were not compatible with the localist and individualized approach, which characterized raising manpower in both previous wars. There would be no Rough Riders in Flanders Fields. Even though local draft boards, comprised of local leaders, still did the dirty work of actually dunning individuals for the service, partly preserving past practice, Big Brother stood just behind them. All men between the ages of eighteen and forty-five were eligible. In the end conscription went much better than the government expected. By the end of the war 24 million men had registered with 4 million selected and 2.8 million inducted.[7]

Several factors made military conscription difficult for the Brethren. For the first time, Brethren answered a draft with individual conscience rather than the instruction of the church. The Brethren precedent, set during the Civil War, was denial of church membership for young men who entered military service, whether through enlistment or conscription. But by 1917 individual decision played a larger role in church life, whether the issue was garb, the ministry, or military service, and, therefore, a consistent approach to conscription was difficult. Moreover, the inclination of many Brethren to appear patriotic diluted the peace position by confusing the boundary between the nation and faith. Finally, the denomination was ill prepared to deal with the draft; like much about the First World War, few had foreseen the nature of conscription in a modern nation-state at war.

On the other side, the government appeared equally surprised by its conscientious objector problem; thus, acquiring CO status from this large, bureaucratized apparatus was difficult. Even before the Selective Service bill passed, representatives of the peace churches and peace activists, such as Jane Addams and Roger Baldwin, visited Washington seeking exemptions for pacifists. The administration, led by Secretary of War Newton Baker, appeared willing to excuse members of recognized peace churches but not individuals unaffiliated with these fellowships or those whose motivations were political rather than religious. Secretary Baker also opposed assigning COs to church-operated alternative service, preferring to keep them in noncombative military roles.[8] As Baker explained to President Wilson, he wanted to draft COs first and then identify them after they arrived in camp.

> It does not seem to me that it would be wise now to designate this work of reconstruction as the sort of noncombatant service contemplated for religious objectors, chiefly for the reason that any definition of that sort of work at this time may have the effect of encouraging further "conscientious" objecting. On the whole subject my belief is that we ought to proceed with the draft, and after the conscientious objectors have gotten into the camps and have made known their inability to proceed with military work, their number will be ascertained and a suitable work evolved for them.[9]

Baker's draft-first/ascertain-later approach became policy. As the first draftees arrived in camp, official policy treated objectors kindly but segregated them from the rest of the camp. Baker hoped that isolation would create a sense of rejection and motivate pacifists to cooperate. From the government's viewpoint, this succeeded, and most who originally claimed conscientious objector status eventually served. The most famous of these was Sgt. Alvin York. Approximately two-thirds of those who remained COs accepted noncombatant roles, such as ambulance drivers and medics, and others consented to government-designated civilian jobs. Among the Brethren a few received assignments to the Farm Furlough project, which provided labor to farmers caught shorthanded by the war, and their wages went to the army or the Red Cross. Four Brethren served with the Friends Ambulance Unit in France.[10]

Many of the fifteen hundred who absolutely refused any form of military service paid a high price for their conscience. Most went to prison, some suffered torture or other forms of harassment, and a few died as a result of their treatment. Five hundred objectors received lengthy prison sentences, and seventeen were sentenced to death although no one suffered execution. Within two years of the war's end, all had been released, and the shortness of American participation in the war undoubtedly spared objectors from even more difficulty.[11]

Despite their success in subduing objectors, government officials were deeply suspicious of them. After Secretary Newton Baker met with COs at Camp Meade, Maryland, he relayed to President Wilson (October 1, 1917) that he considered them "simple-minded"; only two, he said, were "normal mentally." Although Baker's letter did not mention Brethren COs specifically, several were there at the time of his visit.

A large part of my time yesterday was spent with the conscientious objectors. Out of 18,000 there appeared up to last night 27 such objectors. One of them had watched the recruits playing football and baseball, and after two days of separation from the life of the place, he withdrew his objection and joined his company. The remaining 26 are still segregated, receiving considerate treatment but living apart from the rest of the camp. I will send you a complete classification of them later. Nine of them are Old Amish; two, New Amish; three Friends. Then a number of them belong to sects of which I had never heard before; one being "a Brother of God"; another a member of "The Assembly of God"; one was a Russian-born Jew who claimed to be an international Socialist and who, I think, is simply lazy and obstinate, without the least comprehension of International Socialism. For the most part they seem well-disposed, simple-minded young people who have been

imprisoned in a narrow environment and really have no comprehension of the world outside of their own rural and peculiar community. Only two of those with whom I talked seemed quite normal mentally.

Of course, it is too soon to speculate on the problem because
we do not yet know how large the number will turn out to be
either at Camp Meade, or elsewhere; but if it gets no worse than
it is at Camp Meade, I am pretty sure that no harm will come in
allowing these people to stay at the camps, separated from the life
of the camp but close enough to come gradually to understand.
The effect of that, I think, quite certainly would be that a substantial number of them would withdraw their objection and make fairly good soldiers.[12]

Baker's system, then, often worked on Brethren young men.
Brethren leadership had not anticipated the possibility that many young
members of the fellowship would become noncombatants, and they disagreed over compatibility of this trend with the denomination's traditional position on nonresistance. Some believed that military service in
any form violated the "Gospel of Peace," and the growing numbers of
uniformed Brethren alarmed them. They urged the denomination to stiff-
en its resolve and defy the government, whatever the cost.

WE, as Christians, who have been called by God to teach and practice the Gospel of peace on earth and good-will towards men, *can
not willingly* enter into anything that would help war in any way
(Matt. 26:52a). We will only contribute to war when we can not
help ourselves (Rom. 12:17, 18), as from necessity of circumstances—such as buying our daily bread at the high war prices; or
when *forced* by the Government (Rom. 13:1) to pay war taxes or
buy revenue stamps, or to go to the Training Camps to enter noncombatant service. The Government can take our money and
property from us, but we dare not give our services in any way that
will help war, except when forced to, and only then in the things in
which we can work with a *good motive* (Titus 3:1; 1 Cor. 10:31).

It seems to me that perhaps the most important thing we can
do, who are drafted, is to pray that the choice be left with us,
where we feel we can serve God and our fellow-man best. But if
the Government steps in, it becomes a question that each of us
must finally decide between ourselves and God, as to just where

we will draw the line, and in what service we can enter with a right motive and clear conscience before our God. And so, my brother, we can not answer this question for each other, but God will give to each of us the answer if we ask him (John 14:26).

Whatever happens, we must not do evil. God commands us to obey the Government (Rom. 13:1; Titus 3:1). The Government is in authority over us, but God is also, and he is the Supreme Commander both over man and Government. God never gives a Government the right to command a man to disobey any of his laws. But if our Government should dare—as many have in the past—to do so, what must we do? "We must obey God rather than men"—just as Christ always did, and as the apostles did (Acts 5:29), and as thousands have done, who, in the face of Government, have stood true to their God, even to a martyr's death.[13]

Those opposed to military service, whether combatant or noncombatant, charged that many Brethren draftees accepted conscription because the denomination neglected nonresistance. They complained that ministers who counseled draftees to accept noncombatant service undermined the commitment of conscientious objectors.[14] Perhaps more would follow their fellowship's traditional teaching on peace if they heard more about it.

In the Nov. 24 issue of the *The Gospel Messenger* I was very much interested in Bro. Alfred Eckroth's article, written in Camp Meade, Md. He says: "Many of our brethren never reach the Segregation Camp, simply because they have not been properly indoctrinated as to our principles, and have neglected to contemplate the matter sufficiently. Therefore, after arriving at the Camp, they have been influenced, step by step, and finally have fallen in line with the soldiers. Our brethren therefore, whether or not within the draft age limit, should be taught the Bible doctrines of nonresistance."

Ah, how our hearts should rejoice when we see these young soldiers of the cross standing firm, and willing to meet death, if need be, for their faith! How sad we are if some have not the courage to stand for the right, but perhaps theirs is not the greater sin, for if their spiritual leaders did not teach them as they should, something may be demanded of them.[15]

Others, however, considered noncombatant service within acceptable limits. H. C. Early, moderator of the 1918 Annual Conference, urged recruits to comply as much as possible. He hoped that nonresistant young men would accept noncombatant assignments with the military and cooperate with the government.

> . . . I have not come to the point where I can recommend to our young men to refuse noncombatant service and take the consequences. My judgment is that they should obey the Government as far as it can be done without violence to their conscience.[16]

D. L. Miller, a highly influential denominational figure, also endorsed noncombatant service. He was a past president of Mt. Morris College and between 1893 and 1913 president of its board. He traveled the world, unusual for this time, published books about his overseas journeys, and gave popular lantern slide talks about them. Twice he was moderator of Annual Meeting, and served frequently on the committees and boards of the yearly gathering. Since 1891 Miller had been editor-in-chief of *The Gospel Messenger,* and the words of this well-regarded elder must have carried considerable weight.[17]

> How far one may go in serving the Government, at this time, without violating the Gospel doctrine of peace, is one of the important problems to be solved. . . . President Wilson has placed hospital work and caring for the suffering wounded as noncombatant service. As to whether we can engage in this service may result in a difference of opinion. If it is simply caring for the sick and wounded, feeding the hungry and clothing the naked, it is fully in accord with the teachings of Jesus. It is always right, and not only right but our duty, to help suffering, no matter how the suffering has been brought about. When Jesus commended the good Samaritan because he cared for the naked, wounded man by the wayside, he did not favor the robber. The care for the suffering, caused by the war, is not favoring war. So it seems to the writer.[18]

Although this was the first Brethren generation to face a draft without congregational discipline hanging over its head, state coercion and denominational uncertainty appeared more influential in shaping the Brethren response to national conscription. Conscientious objection in a modern nation-state at war was a new and unpleasant experience for a

333

33

33

historic peace church undergoing change itself, and denominational leadership wondered about their next steps.

Brethren in Military Camps

Information from military camps added to the confusion of many Brethren over their religious society and the draft. Young Brethren men in these camps and the ministers who assisted them reported that many Brethren accepted service, that coercion was commonplace, and that conscientious objectors were adrift.

According to Elmer Frick, a draftee in a camp in Ohio, most of his fellow Brethren there, presumably noncombatants, had agreed to wear uniforms although authorities did not require it. He added that the remaining COs suffered mistreatment. He asked for guidance from the denomination.

> I think that we, as a church, should see to it that our young brethren are given the proper papers which they have need of, before coming to Camp. Some of our people have only their church certificate, while some have certificate and form No. 143, and some others have form No. 174. The latter, as I understand, with church certificate, is correct.
>
> One of our brethren is over in the brigade yet. He says that they refuse to recognize his papers, that he has been roughly treated and that he has been forced to drill. Quite a number of our people have accepted the uniform, but we are not required to wear it. Only three or four have refused the uniform entirely.
>
> All we need to do is to show firmly where we stand and that we also have our papers to show that the church stands back of us if we live faithful to the Gospel of Christ.
>
> We often are asked questions which seemingly are hard to answer, regarding our faith, and we have to be careful in all things, so that the light of Christ can shine through us. We have been deprived of our ministers, through some unknown cause, for three weeks, and we are anxiously waiting to know how the church is going to stand on the questions pertaining to war. Whatever is done, we ask that the church may stand unitedly.
>
> One of the Mennonite boys is in a guard-house at present, with the charge of being a "leader" against him.[19]

As Frick noted, harassment could be severe, evidenced in the accounts of Kenneth Long and Roy Peters:

> They carried me a few rods to the end of the tents and started with their fun. I don't know how long they tossed me up or how high. And I don't know how many had hold of the blanket. But I was told that all took a hold that there was room for. I held to the edge of the blanket a few times with my right hand and I suppose that had a tendency to throw me on the ground. They might of did it on purpose and left me fall on the ground for all I know. I noticed that my arm was broken and I told them that it was. They picked me up and took me to the tent, and called an ambulance. They took me first to the infirmary and then to the hospital. It happened about eight in the evening of the 20th of September. . . . That is about as good as I can tell you about it by writing. I received very good attention since I have been at the hospital.[20]

> My turn came. The captain stood there beside a large pile of uniforms; he ordered me to take up mine. I refused to touch it; he ordered me the second time to pick it up, at the same time menacing me with his automatic. Again I refused; he then ordered me under arrest. It was not 7:30 P.M. I was confined to the barracks until 10 A.M. the following day. Meanwhile, a corporal brought in my uniform and other army equipment and threw them down on my bunk.
>
> Next day at 10 A.M. I was released. The Sergeant then ordered me to come with him to the bath house. There was no one else present except him and me. He ordered me to put on the army uniform. I refused. He then proceeded to strip off my civilian clothing and then to dress me up in a new uniform; he forgot to button me up properly as a sudden inspiration struck him to take away all my own clothes and let me finish the buttoning myself.
>
> They couldn't say now that of my own free will I had donned the uniform; but against my will they forced the uniform on me and required me to wear it, or else go without any clothes. This was all done in direct opposition to Secretary of War Baker's order.
>
> After they had gotten the uniform on me, I was then ordered to go and work in the kitchen. I went to the kitchen and worked there all afternoon.

Saturday, March 23. Company ordered out for drill exercises in afternoon. I stepped out of the line and stayed until the lieutenant caught sight of me. He ordered me back into line; I went. He then gave the command "forward march." I remained behind standing still, lieutenant watching me closely, commanded "company halt," caught me by the shoulder and shoved me up into line, told me to stay there. He ordered "company march." I stood still as before, he came back exasperated and wanted to know what was wrong with me. I explained to him my status in brief. He ordered me to quarters. I complied with his order most willingly.[21]

One Brethren, who was spared severe persecution, nevertheless, warned of difficulties for would-be COs who arrived in camp without appropriate documentation.

We get the "Messenger" every week, and all seem to enjoy reading it very much, and especially the pieces from other camps. Our conditions are fairly good—as well as we could expect under the circumstances. We do not get passes to go home, but we should not grumble at that. We should be truly thankful to our Father in heaven that we, as his followers, have been spared, and blessed with conditions as good as they are. We have religious services two or three times a day, and take exercise every day, if the weather is not too rough.

There are about sixty-four in the Detention Camp here. We have been quarantined since about the first of December for measles and mumps. Some are away now at the hospital. We are visited by the ministering brethren of different denominations. Bro. D. A. Montgomery* was with us Jan. 22 and 23, and gave us three good sermons. We would be glad if more of the ministering brethren could visit us.

Let us, as a church, look into the future, as well as the present, and may we take Christ as our Leader and Guide in all things.

We want to tell the brethren that may have to come to Camp as we have, to be sure to get a church certificate and also an exemption paper from their Local Board. You will find them both

---

*David A. Montgomery was an Old Order German Baptist elder from Oak Hill, Virginia. See "David A. Montgomery," *The Brethren Encyclopedia,* III:1719.

to be very important after you enter Camp. Don't give them up to any one but hold on to them.

Our officers came in last week and asked us to show both papers. Some few did not have both, and we don't know how it will go with them. That is why we make mention of it here. We all know that experience is our best teacher, and we feel that we have had many lessons of this kind since we entered Camp Sept. 22, 1917. We believe that God has been with us and that he will deliver those that trust in him, as he has promised.[22]

Ministers, appointed by districts to visit Brethren men in the military camps, verified that conscientious objectors struggled against an unsympathetic system. Some of these visitors encountered many Brethren who had enlisted, while others discovered that all whom they met would "choose the church when the final test comes." But, the visiting ministers agreed that maltreatment was commonplace.

The only brethren we found at Camp Hancock were such as had enlisted, and were preparing for combative service in France. There are brethren of this class at all the camps we visited, but at this one we found such only. We conducted a short service for them, and gave such counsel as seemed expedient.[23]

Evidence showed that a few of the Brethren were in training for the trenches. A few others had yielded in part because of threats. Some had endured the sorest persecution, because they refused, to the last, to take up arms and be trained for the army. Almost every indignity conceivable was heaped upon them. They were cursed, called the vilest of names, threatened, and stood up as gazing stock of the soldiers, but they stood true as steel, and won a great victory. However, they were afterward placed in a servitude almost equal to imprisonment.[24]

It was my privilege to accompany our dear Bro. W. J. Swigart, chairman of the Central Service Committee, to visit Washington and several of the War Camps. We spent part of March 6 in

Washington, coming in touch with Congressmen and the War Department. We reached Petersburg, Va., which is about two miles from Camp Lee, sometime after dark. Some brethren from the Camp met us at the train, and received us very gladly.

A number of our boys are uniformed, and working at the remount station, doing the nearest noncombatant work available, tending horses and driving teams. They are becoming fearful that sooner or later they will be forced to drill and, of course, will have to decide which—war or church. We found some of our brethren in the guard-house for not uniforming and refusing to work. At this writing (March 14) we are glad to state that all of our brethren, whom we found in the guard-house, have been favorably located in the Detention Camp, with the other noncombatants. The guard-house is the fiery furnace way into the Detention Camp, where our brethren are well cared for and unmolested.

In this Detention Camp at Camp Lee we found seventy-six nonresistants or conscientious objectors, as they are called, absolutely under their own control. They do their own cooking and housekeeping and do nothing outside of this, except that they are required to take a hike of eight or ten miles daily, which, of course, is very beneficial to them. In the number we found fifty-five of our brethren (two of them ministers), eleven Mennonites, two members of the Church of God, two of the Apostolic faith (one a minister), one Primitive Baptist minister, two Progressive Brethren, one Old Order brother, and several others. Being mess time, we made our services rather short. I wish you could have heard them sing "Jesus, Lover of My Soul," and all unite with us in the Lord's Prayer.

At Camp Belvoir there had been seven brethren in the guard-house for seventeen days, because of their refusal to drill. Bro. Swigart had visited them two weeks before, and was then doing what he could for them. To our joy, they were released on Friday evening, and when we arrived on Saturday noon, March 9, they were all working in the kitchen, with the promise that they would not need to drill or learn the art of war. A second grilling [sic] may have to be gone through.

Those who stand firm from the start, fare the best. Our brethren will simply have to choose between war and the church. We have not found any of our drafted brethren who will not choose the church when the final test comes.[25]

M. C. Swigart, pastor of the Germantown congregation in Pennsylvania and a visitor to the camps, sought transfers for Brethren to noncombatant service and to prevent their assignment overseas. Although he obtained the aid of Governor Martin G. Brumbaugh, Swigart nevertheless often confronted a cumbersome system as authorities in Washington, D. C., and camp officers each waited on the other for recommendations on COs. Swigart was content to place Brethren as noncombatants ("that is all we ask"), and he suspected that some draftees asked "too much in the way of noncombatant service."

Having been elected by the Southeastern District of Pennsylvania, New Jersey, and Eastern New York, to look after the interests of our boys in the various Camps, I have thus far visited three Camps.

Nov. 12 I visited Camp Meade, spending two days there, visiting the boys in service and those of the Conscientious Objectors in the Detention Camp. I found a lot of the boys taking training whom I knew, and who were exceedingly glad to see me.

The first one I met is a cook in the Officers' Mess Barracks. He took me in, introduced me to the rest of the boys and served me with pie of their own making. I found a lot of the boys from our District in the 304th Company of Engineers. They surely seemed glad for my visit to them. I received the most courteous treatment from the officers in charge.

By permission of the Mess Sergeant, the boys invited me to mess with them, which I gladly accepted. The meal was very good, considering the conditions under which it was served.

The second day there I spent with the Conscientious Objectors. They were just moving that day and offered many apologies for the condition of their barracks. By permission of their superior officer, I preached for them at 4 o'clock. An officer was present at the service.

As many of our Brethren visit Camp Meade from the surrounding Districts, the boys there receive much encouragement, and my presence there was not so much needed, as the following will prove.

By far the most pressing need of help to our boys is at Camp Mills, Long Island, N. Y. Here the famous Rainbow Divisions are made up and many are sent from this Camp "somewhere." The soldiers here have canvas tents to stay in, while at Camp Meade they have wooden barracks. This proves that this Camp, so far as

I know, is but for a short stay. I am the only minister of our church that has been at Camps Mills and Merritt.

On information from California that two of our brethren were there and needed help, I immediately went over. I found eight Conscientious Objectors there but only two of our own church. Two were Mennonites, three Brethren in Christ and one is a Jew. Later I found a third one of our Brethren, also from California, but he is taking the service without objection.

Our boys asked for a transfer to another Camp or to non-combatant service. I took it up with the Chief of Staff and asked for the transfer. All the officers told me that Camp Mills was no place for a Conscientious Objector, that they were all fighting men there. I was told that they would gladly transfer them with the proper orders from Washington. I was promised that all the boys would be transferred to noncombatant service in the Camp.

More than a week passed by and no order for transfer came. One of the boys telegraphed me: "Come at once. Are going somewhere. No transfer yet." I immediately took it up with the Governor of our State, who gave me permission to send a telegram to the Camp Headquarters and sign his name as Governor.

This brought a response. Immediately the transfer was made for all the Conscientious Objectors. They were scattered throughout the Camp, and assigned to what the Camp officials regarded as non-combatant service—mostly in the Medical Companies of the different regiments. This, I think, is still questionable in the minds of many.

The boys all felt they ought not be sent over seas, and to this end we worked hard. I was treated with the kindest consideration and allowed the freedom of the Camp on days not visiting days.

I was compelled to make four visits to this Camp to help our boys, but still I fear that I did not get done what ought to have been done. The officials there told me they would gladly send the Conscientious Objectors to any other Camp on orders from Washington.

The private secretary of our Governor told me he heard Secretary of War Baker say to the Governor [Brumbaugh] that he—the Secretary of War—would gladly order a change on recommendation from the officers of the Camp where the Conscientious Objectors are. On account of this, we are handicapped and need to know where the real issue lies.

I lost valuable time in pressing this claim because of the shifting of this authority. I am convinced of a few things that we need to know definitely—a few things to advise our boys in such an hour as Camp Mills presents. The stand needs to be taken at the very beginning of Camp life. After the uniform has once been put on, and a gun taken, it is hard to retrace the steps.

Some of our boys may be asking too much in the way of non-combatant service. Can they compel our boys to go over to the other side? Lately we have learned that our boys will not be sent overseas, but some have already been sent—"through error"—Washington claims.

My visit to Camp Merritt was to head off these boys who were being sent against orders from Washington. But then I was too late. The boys were already on the waters, although on a venture we appealed again to Washington and had an order issued to the commander of this Camp to hold a certain brother. Washington says they don't understand why their orders are not obeyed and the young men held.

I do not know. Possibly it is like this: The officer in charge assumes that the Medical Company is noncombatant service and as that is all we ask for, we have a right to go where sent. . . .

I am thoroughly convinced we should have met the issue a little more bravely earlier in the strife. It would have helped a lot.

We need more uniformity of treatment for our boys in the various Camps. We need to know WHAT to ask for our boys and how MUCH we can ask.

Col. May, of the 162d United States Infantry at Camp Mills, in whose regiment are most of the Conscientious Objectors who came from Camp Lewis in the State of Washington, told me that he didn't want them in his regiment, and that it was a mistake to send them to this Camp. He didn't know what to do with them. He said that he never had them before. He acted the gentleman in every way, and told me I would have the thanks of every officer in the Camp if I could be the means of getting rid of them. It was he who secured me an interview with the highest officer of the Camp, but this highest officer of the Camp only shifted the responsibility on to Washington.

I trust we can find the key to unlock the difficulty.[26]

The Brethren, then, faced a trying moment. Hounded by public opinion and bullied by the nation-state, Brethren boys wound up in the guardhouse in limbo or, more often, in uniform. Many Brethren leaders suggested that clearer guidance from the fellowship would make a bad situation better.

CONFRONTATION

Amidst ambiguity and persecution, the Church of the Brethren called an unprecedented special conference to clarify its response to conscription. An extra annual meeting had no standing according to Brethren polity, and under the circumstances inviting all congregations to send delegates was unmanageable. Instead, approximately four hundred Brethren gathered on January 9, 1918, in Goshen, Indiana, with the Standing Committee, the Peace Committee, and the camp visitors comprising the approximately one hundred voting delegates.

Farm real estate made H. C. Early financially independent at age forty-six, after which he devoted his life to serving the denomination as an evangelist and eight-time Annual Conference moderator. He presided at the special gathering at Goshen. *Photo courtesy of BHLA.*

The emergency assembly approved an uncompromising statement that called for non-involvement with the military. The Goshen Brethren professed loyalty to the government, and their call for conservation of resources in a time of great need carried little controversy. But their statement drew strong limits on Brethren support for the war and urged believers to follow their faith when religion and government conflicted. Even more to the point, they advised Brethren to "refrain from wearing the military uniform" because the "tenets of the church" banned drilling and other military skills. The conference hoped that conscientious objectors would use its statement to verify status to camp authorities, but the language was so strong that a minority dissented because they considered it a treasonous violation of the Selective Draft Law.[27]

THE GOSHEN STATEMENT

The Church's Attitude
Toward the Government

I. We are loyal citizens of this great nation, which has been and is now a safeguard of our religious liberties and the protector of our homes and loved ones.

II. Our attitude towards Civil Governments and rulers should be carefully taken into account. We are taught that Governments are ordained of God, and that the administrators of Government are ministers of God. As such we are to be in subjection to them (Rom. 13:1-7). We are admonished to pray for the rulers and magistrates and for those in authority (1 Tim. 2:1-2).

The word and authority of God, however, must be final and supreme over all. And when the demands of men and of Governments conflict with the Word of God, we are then bound by the latter, regardless of consequences. "Whether it is right in the sight of God to hearken unto you [magistrates] rather than unto God, judge ye" (Acts 4:19). "But Peter and the apostles answered and said, We must obey God rather than men" (Acts 5:29). Therefore we urge—

First. That our various congregations pray without ceasing for the rulers of our nation that the nation may again enjoy peace, and that blood-shedding and destruction may cease.

Second. That they contribute liberally to the relief of human suffering, both in men and money.

Third. That they express their gratitude to God for our favored position and freedom from the devastation of war, by giving freely of our substance for constructive relief work, such as Red Cross, Y.M.C.A., Friends' Relief Work or through our own Service Committee.

Fourth. We urge our people to put forth their utmost effort in this world crisis, laboring with their hands, cultivating our fields and gardens and vacant lands, planting only such crops as will contribute to the real necessities of life; also that they practice the greatest economy in clothing, food, and all supplies which may, mechanically or otherwise, aid in the production and transportation of food, clothing and fuel, so that a suffering and hungering world may be clothed, warmed and fed.

Appeal for Greater Efforts in Church and Mission Work

The present crisis has aroused the self-sacrifice of all classes of people in the interests of suffering humanity. The spirit of sacrifice is with us. Our young people are restless to do something commensurate with the sacrifices of others, but they must have a cause.

We urge that the supreme cause of the Kingdom of God be held up before them so repeatedly and continuously that they will enlist in its service. Our young people should be made to see that there can be no permanent peace without Christianity, and Christianity can not become real in the world without the heroic, self-sacrificing work of missions. The world will not be safe for democracy until it is safe for truth. The greatest service we can render humanity is the promotion of the Kingdom of God. And all the pent-up energy of the church can here find an outlet in the work of religious education, which includes all Christian work.

We need more pastors, and churches should elect and encourage suitable brethren for this work. The Sunday-schools have a great task to inculcate the true Gospel into the hearts of men, in this age of materialism, skepticism, and carnage. We urge that special efforts be made to secure volunteers for our mission work. As others give their sons for the trenches, we should give ours for the salvation of the world. When the spirit of self-sacrifice is manifest on every hand, it is opportune to enlist the young people in the holy cause of missions, where they can give their lives in a living sacrifice for the "things that endure."

We urge upon the whole church greatly to increase her offerings for the cause of missions. The excess profits, due to the war, should all be given for the promotion of the Kingdom of God, of which the mission work is a most vital part. We believe, with Dr. [John R.] Mott* and Sherwood Eddy† that, during this world crisis, no one should "lay up treasure on earth," but give all that he can for the salvation of the world.

The Gospel of Jesus Christ is the source and foundation of all our blessings, and the only hope of an enduring peace. Therefore let us give our lives and our means to promote his Gospel, at home and abroad.

Other Provisions of the Goshen Statement

We are petitioning the Government to give our drafted brethren such industrial noncombatant service as will contribute constructively to the necessity, health and comfort of hungering, suffering humanity, either here or elsewhere.

We further urge our brethren not to enlist in any service which would, in any way, compromise our time-honored position in relation to war; also that they refrain from wearing the military uniform. The tenets of the church forbid military drilling, or learning the art or arts of war, or doing anything which contributes to the destruction of human life or property.

———————

We commend the loyalty of the brethren in the Camps for their firm stand in not participating in the arts of war. We do not wish to oppose the consciences of those brethren who, in some Camps, found work which they felt they could conscientiously do, but we urge them to do only such work as will not involve them in the arts of destruction.

———————

———————

*Mott aimed to create an international, ecumenical mission-oriented student movement. See Heather A. Warren, *Theologians of a New World Order: Reinhold Niebuhr and the Christian Realists, 1920-1948* (New York: Oxford University Press, 1997), 13-15.

†Prior to the war, Sherwood Eddy was an independently wealthy, unpaid evangelist for the YMCA in Asia. When the war broke out, he ministered to troops on the western front, and the life-changing experience turned him into a pacifist and social reformer. See Warren, *Theologians of a New World Order,* 28-29.

Provision for Special War Relief and Reconstruction Work. Committee appointed: J. E. Miller, Galen B. Royer, Clarence Layman.

Duties of Committee: It shall be the duty of this committee to devise ways and plans by which our people can do relief and reconstruction work, either independently or in cooperation with other organizations, and it shall be authorized to appeal for, and receive, funds, and carefully administer the disbursing of the same. . . .

The Publishing House shall be asked to print copies of this report, to which shall be appended a suitable church membership certificate blank [i.e., a form]. That the elders or clerks of each congregation be urged to procure from the House sufficient copies to supply one to each member now in the Camp, and to each one as he may be called in the future. That, if need be, these may be shown to the officers of Camps as the final and highest authority from the church to which they belong.[28]

For the moment the Goshen Statement clarified the denomination's approach to the draft, and when Moderator H. C. Early spoke to the Annual Conference in June 1918, at Hershey, Pennsylvania, he sounded confident. As he mounted the platform to preach, someone warned Early that government spies were in the hall, but the moderator's sermon apparently withheld little. Admittedly, his first words pledged loyalty to the government, perhaps to satisfy the snoops, but from their time in colonial America, Brethren had always considered themselves loyal, tax-paying citizens. Even the Goshen Statement began with a profession of allegiance. The majority of Early's talk was a firm, lengthy, and detailed defense of biblical nonviolence that denounced warfare as unchristian. He did not, however, specifically criticize the current conflict except to say that it should end quickly, and he did not repeat the Goshen Statement's recommendation that Brethren avoid military service. Instead, Early reiterated his belief that noncombatancy was consistent with nonresistance, and he urged his listeners to support the war as much as possible without violating their faith. Perhaps Early's frankness came from self-assurance of his own loyalty or from his preference for noncombatancy, a moderate position within the denomination that might persuade non-Brethren observers to view him thusly. Most notably, his mistaken assumption that the "government recognizes our scruples" must have reassured him.[29]

I. Introduction.

Before entering into the discussion, there are a few things that must be clearly understood.

. . . I shall make no effort to settle the question as to whether noncombatants should support the war, financially, or the difference, if any, between financial and personal support. There is confusion in the minds of some. However, it may be said that members of the Church of the Brethren have bought Liberty Bonds and War-Saving Stamps. But the question can not be regarded as a proper subject for discussion here, and so it must rest.

. . . Nor must any statement be interpreted as lacking love of country and true patriotism, loyalty to the Government and readiness to support the nation in all things not in violence of conscience. On the other hand, we openly avow and declare our love of country and government, and pledge afresh our fidelity to the nation in the name of our Master whom we serve and in the light of his teachings. We esteem our rulers, we love them, we sympathize with them in the cares of the State in this hour of trial, and pray that God will so direct them that they may lead us wisely, justly. Here the people stand for whom I have the responsibility to speak.

II. The Bible on Peace

And as we turn to the Great Book for light, my dearly beloved, you must not expect all its teachings on this subject to be given in this hour. Nor can we elaborate at any length the few passages we shall give. A few plain passages are sufficient. And if, in your judgment, there are passages on the subject of doubtful meaning, they must be interpreted in the light of the plain passages. The Bible is a unit, and upon the principle of its unity, what is taught by one of its writers is taught by them all. Any doctrine, plainly stated by one of the sacred writers, therefore, is virtually stated by them all.

First, take a glance at the Old Testament, but it can be but a word. Many of its examples teach victory by the sword. There were wars, many wars, in those days by the people of God, the victory falling to them as they obeyed the Lord, and escaping them as they failed to trust him, which shows that Jehovah led the battle. The most noted leaders as prophets and kings of Israel were great warriors. But the method of conquest under the New Testament is changed. And both Jesus and the nature of his Kingdom are set out in foreview in the Old Testament. Isaiah declared that he should be called "Wonderful, Counsellor, Mighty God, Everlasting Father, Prince of Peace. Of the increase of his government and of peace there shall be no end, upon the throne of David, and upon his kingdom, to establish it, and to uphold it with justice and with righteousness from henceforth even for ever" (Isa. 9:6, 7; see Ezek. 34:22-26; 37:20-28). Here are the King and his Kingdom. Jesus is a Prince, not the prince of carnal strife, but the Prince of Peace. And of his Kingdom, or his Government, which means Kingdom, there shall be no end. It shall increase, it shall subdue all other kingdoms, it shall fill the earth, it shall stand forever (Dan. 2:44). The Prince of Peace is to sit upon the throne of his Kingdom, to establish it and to uphold it in peace and right-eousness forever. And so, in the midst of the wars of the Old Testament, we must see the coming Kingdom of Peace and Righteousness. We must remember also that Christ is the end of the law and prophets, the fulfillment of them (Luke 16:16; Rom. 10:4), and that we are no longer under Moses, but under Christ, the Prince of Peace.

The teachings of Jesus and the apostles. When the New King came into the world, while the Judaean shepherds kept watch over their flocks by night, the angel of God brought them the mes-sage of good tidings of great joy which shall be to all people, and at once a multitude of the heavenly hosts joined in praising God, saying: "Glory to God in the highest, and on earth peace among men in whom he is well pleased." Jesus was introduced to the world in song. The basic principles and doctrines of the New King and New Kingdom were heralded by the angels. It was the com-ing of happy news and peace and good will to a world that had been plunged into strife and sorrow. It was the dawn of a new day, the beginning of great joy to all people, for it was to sweeten and sanctify with peace and good will all of life's relations. It was to bring back man and make him the friend of God again, and to establish peace and good will among men—a glorious day. Certainly, this was a fitting introduction to the world of the New King and his Kingdom.

The Sermon on the Mount, given by Matthew in the fifth, sixth and seventh chapters, sets forth the constitution of the New

Kingdom, it may be said. It holds much the same relation to the laws of the Kingdom as the Constitution of the United States holds to the laws of the nation. Jesus gave in the sermon the principles of his Kingdom, and they are the blood and bone of his teachings, relating to the Kingdom in the world. They are also a complete revelation, for the world had never had such teaching, and the people gazed in astonishment. And I am sorry that I have time to call your attention to only a few things in the sermon.

The teachings of the first chapter of the sermon concern us chiefly in the present discussion. The chapter divides itself into two general parts. The first sixteen verses, containing the Beatitudes, describes the citizens of the Kingdom of God in the world, with their blessings; while the second division, from the sixteenth verse to the end of the chapter, shows how Jesus fulfilled the Law, making it full and running over, and also how his teachings are above and beyond the requirements of the Law.

The subjects of the Kingdom are poor in spirit; mourn for sin; meek, yielding to the will of God; hunger and thirst after righteousness; merciful; pure in heart; peacemakers; persecuted and reviled for righteousness; salt of the earth and light of the world.

Isn't this a beautiful word picture of fine, high character? How does it fit the warrior and war? Do you see a way of making it fit him and his calling? If so, tell us how.

Jesus uses five illustrations in the second division of the chapter to show the superiority of his teachings over the Law and the olden time. "It was said by them of old time, Thou shalt not kill; and whosoever shall kill shall be in danger of the judgment; but I say unto you, that every one who is angry with his brother shall be in danger of the judgment; and whosoever shall say to his brother, Raca, shall be in danger of the council; and whosoever shall say, Thou fool, shall be in danger of the hell of fire." Hate is murder (1 John 3:15), and anger is the condition to hate, so that anger is the first step to murder. In the second illustration, forbidding adultery, the motive is put for the deed, for "every one that looketh on a woman to lust after her hath committed adultery with her already in his heart." So that the purpose to kill is equivalent to the act in the sight of God.

The third illustration forbids the civil oath. The fourth says, "It was said, An eye for an eye, and a tooth for a tooth; but I say unto you, Resist not him that is evil; but whosoever smiteth thee on thy right cheek, turn to him the other also. And if any man would go to law with thee, and take away thy coat, let him have thy cloak also. And whosoever shall compel thee to go one mile, go with him two." And the fifth, "It was said, Though shalt love thy neighbor and hate thine enemy; but I say unto you, Love your enemies, bless them that persecute you; that ye may be sons of your Father who is in heaven. . . . For if ye love them that love you, what reward have ye? Do not even the publicans the same?"

It would be difficult to state the doctrine of nonresistance in clearer, stronger language. It is the clearest and strongest statement of one of the fundamental doctrines of the New Testament, and there is no misunderstanding it. It is no longer the victory of physical force, the strong overpowering the weak, and the hate of an enemy. On the other hand, it is the victory of good over evil—resisting not him that is evil, turning the other cheek, giving the cloak, going the second mile, loving the enemy. It is purely the victory of goodness as coals of fire on the head of the enemy (Rom. 12:20, 21). The second mile victory only is victory. It is real victory, for real victory is the surrender of the WILL of the opponent and oppressor, and when men are thus overcome, they feel that they are the meanest of men, and would gladly kiss the feet of their victors.

Jesus taught these high, lofty principles that they might crystallize into human character, and such men, he says, are the salt of the earth and the light of the world. In other words, he delineates the character of the citizens of his Kingdom in the world, as already given, as concrete examples of these principles worked out in life. And the world has never ceased to marvel.

The nature of the Kingdom of Jesus. Hear Jesus' own words: "My kingdom is not of this world; if my kingdom were of this world, then would my servants fight, that I should not be delivered to the Jews: but my kingdom is not from hence" (John 18:36). That is to say, the Kingdom of Jesus is spiritual; it is divine. Its principles are above the world and beyond its comprehension. "The world by wisdom knows not God" (1 Cor. 1:21). If the Kingdom were of the world—worldly—then would its servants fight that its king should not be delivered into the hands of men; but since it is spiritual and divine, its defense is spiritual and divine, and not of physical force. Its subjects, therefore, can not fight with carnal weapons; and not any more now than when Jesus stated the nature of his Kingdom as forbidding carnal strife.

The weapons of the Kingdom of Jesus. Paul states: "For though we walk in the flesh, we do not war according to the flesh (for the weapons of our warfare are not of the flesh, but mighty before God to the casting down of strongholds); casting down imaginations, and every high thing that exalteth itself against the knowledge of God, and bringing every thought into obedience to the obedience of Christ" (2 Cor. 10:3-5). The Kingdom of Jesus is not armed with the weapons of the flesh, but it is equipped with weapons of victory, for the Kingdom is set for conquest, eternal conquest, complete, absolute. But it is not the conquest of the sword.

Jesus' instruction to Peter, when Peter used the sword and smote off an ear of the servant of the high priest at the time of Jesus' arrest, is clear and final on the point. Peter felt it was the time to strike. If any conditions justified the use of the sword, these did, in the judgment of Peter. But Jesus rebuked him and ordered that the sword be put up in its place, and then laid down the principle, that "all they that take the sword shall perish with the sword" (Matt. 26:52).

Now listen, friends. Jesus founded his Kingdom upon love. Its victories and triumphs are all the price of love. True, it is the only kingdom ever thus founded, and it is the only kingdom that shall stand. All other kingdoms are founded upon the sword and built upon its authority, and they must fail, because "all they that take the sword shall perish with the sword." And when the ideals of the Kingdom of Jesus shall have been realized, swords shall cease. They shall be beaten into ploughshares and implements of industry and progress, and the nations shall learn war no more. (See Isaiah 2:4.) And as a matter of fact, force settles nothing but physical ascendancy. It is the strong overpowering the weak. That's not victory. Love settles everything. It subdues and conquers everything. And it is the only all-conquering power in the world. Ultimately the whole world must lie in conquest at its feet. "The seed of the woman shall bruise the serpent's head." The ultimate triumph of truth and peace and love is pledged, eternally pledged.

He that is conquered by love surrenders at his own will. The conqueror rules over the conquered at his consent. This is victory, real victory—the only real victory in the world. The conquered yields in heart. It is also perfect government, complete, absolute, and the only perfect government in the world. And the subjects of such a government are volunteers to lay down their lives, if need be, for their King, for "the love of Christ constraineth them." Such is the Kingdom of Jesus.

Jesus is the Example of his teaching. He never used physical force upon man. He wins by love. Unlike the kings and monarchs of earth, he gave himself because he loved, and gained his eternal victory when the world thought it had defeated him. And so his subjects give themselves because they love, and gain their victory in apparent defeat. . . .

In the light of the foregoing teachings and examples the church declares herself in opposition to death and destruction, preparation therefore, and all that contributes to these ends. On the other hand, she stands for life, at its best and fullest, all interests and industries that make for real progress, and all that contributes to these ends. Upon this ground the church has planted herself, and here she has stood unflinchingly for two hundred years. And upon this principle we must determine our duty in the present war. Complications will arise that will puzzle us to the utmost to know, but the principle is true, and it will serve as a safe guide, if our perception is sharp enough. . . .

What the church should do in the present strife. Since Jesus came into the world to give life, and to give it abundantly (John 10:10)—for this was his mission—we share in the same mission. And since our mission is to promote the mission of our Lord, it is our duty to do all that's possible for the promotion of life against the works of death. Upon this ground the issue rests. Whatever, therefore, is essential to life we can and should do. The growing of grains to feed the hungry nations, providing clothing and shelter, caring for the sick and wounded and helping them back to life, all works of mercy and charity, moral and religious help, etc., etc., are essential to life. In fact, the field is very wide, and there is no excuse for doing nothing. In the Training Camps there is much to do that is essential to life, which, therefore, noncombatants can choose without sacrificing nonresistant principles, if wise discrimination is exercised.

A speedy and just peace. The biggest question before the world today and probably the biggest question in all the past history of the world, is the final settlement of the war. Practically the whole world has been drawn into the struggle, and it is to no purpose to discuss the conditions that have led into it. The question is to get out of the conflict of terms that will best serve the future interests of the nations of the world. It is a world question in which all the nations or the world are vitally interested. It must be clear also that our own nation will have great influence, if not the dominant influence, in the final settlement.

We should exercise our utmost influence in favor of a speedy peace, and peace upon terms that make the nations equal, granting to all the nations of the earth, small and great, equal rights and privileges for growth and progress, and upon conditions that will, in so far as possible, array the moral sentiment of the world against war. If future wars are made impossible, it will be done by educating the moral convictions of the people against it, placing war under the moral censure of the world. And peace can be maintained and the law of the brotherhood worked out in the life of nations only when nations are [sic] upon the basis of equality, with equal rights and privileges. These conditions are our only hope.

A League of Nations and Court of Arbitration. Certainly, at the close of the war there should be a League of Nations to enforce peace and an International Court of Arbitration for the settlement of disputes. This would be to set up the most formidable agencies for the promotion of peace, with universal sanction and the moral support of the world. The form or name under which these measures are provided is not vital, but such measures, in whatever form provided, would have the greatest moral weight. While they would not be an absolute guarantee of peace, I confess, they would be a strong guarantee.

Universal disarmament. A League of Nations and Court of Arbitration ought to open the way for universal disarmament. Any universal measure that bonds the nations together in a common agreement and covenant inspires confidence and friendship; it tends also to establish the doctrine of a community of interests. It is certain, it seems to me, that when the nations believe each other, and love each other, and realize that their interests are common, something will happen to the armament of the nations. . . .

In conclusion, I appeal to the people for whom I am speaking that you support with a liberal hand the Red Cross, the Y.M.C.A. in their splendid work in the war, and the Relief and Reconstruction work in war-devastated lands. We should keenly appreciate the consideration accorded us by the Government, because of our conscientious scruples. At the same time we must know that we must bear our part of the burden of the war in some form, and since the Government recognizes our scruples, we should support, with the greatest liberality, such measures as do not violate our conscience. . . . And as to money, we have never had so much to give.

It is the price of blood, it may be said, and no decent man can desire to enrich himself at the cost of another's blood. . . . This blood money should be used freely to relieve distress and suffering.[30]

Soon after the Hershey Annual Meeting, the denomination's differences with the government intensified. As intended, young men attempting to document their pacifism presented the Goshen Statement in pamphlet form to draft boards and military officials, but authorities concluded that because it discouraged participation in the military, it broke the law. Several complaints about the pamphlet arrived in Washington, including the following from Captain Spencer Roberts, acting intelligence officer at Camp Meade, Maryland:

Enclosed is a copy of the letter regarding the "conscientious objectors," and also publication "The Church of the Brethren." On page six of this leaflet there appears a statement in my opinion clearly advocating interference with the draft law and other peace propaganda.[31]

Within months of the publication of the Goshen Statement, the War Department summoned W. J. Swigart and J. M. Henry, members of the General Service Committee, to its offices. There an official accused the Church of the Brethren of sedition, which carried a severe prison sentence.[32] As Henry recalled,

Dr. Frederick P. Keppel, Third Assistant of War, who had been selected by President Woodrow Wilson to look after the questions arising concerning conscientious objectors, called one evening by telephone and asked that I come to his office at once. I had already had many conferences with Dr. Keppel on the problems arising in the camps, and had learned to admire his earnestness and fair-mindedness. He received me very courteously, took me to his private desk and picked up a document bearing the seal of the War Department from the office of the Advocate Generals.

    I listened to the reading of the document with its charges which still ring sometimes like a nightmare in my ears. After reciting the law, the document charged the officers of the Goshen Conference and authors of the Goshen Statement as guilty of treasonable intent of obstructing the cooperation of the Select Draft Law. Dr. Keppel turned to me and said, "What have you to say about this matter?" I studied a moment and quietly explained the facts about the Goshen

Conference, and then asked, "Will you have the case stayed forty-eight hours and give us time to prepare an answer?" The request was granted and the two other members of the Central Service Committee were called to Washington by telegram.

We met in the parlor at the parsonage on North Carolina Avenue. The Central Service Committee was facing a tragic situation. We stood between our dear brethren and the federal prisons. The honor and sacred name of our beloved fraternity were at stake. We needed wisdom and guidance, not born of flesh and blood, nor of the will of man, but from the Giver of all wisdom. To him we went on our knees in the parlor on that crucial morning. After a long season of prayer and meditation each member of the Committee was asked to write down his plea and answer.[33]

The government was not bluffing. Authorities had arrested a number of national figures, most notably socialist and labor leader Eugene V. Debs, for public criticism of the war. The Brethren leaders capitulated. Swigart had always favored noncombatant service ("that is all we ask"), and Henry claimed that at Goshen he "vigorously" contended that the majority's statement was treasonous. Now they returned to Keppel's office with a statement claiming that the recent Annual Meeting in Hershey had implicitly repudiated the Goshen doctrine with a less offensive resolution on the war, but for good measure the ad hoc Brethren delegation explicitly renounced the contentious Goshen pamphlet. Before government officials accepted the submission, they reviewed it line by line with the Brethren representatives.[34]

1. This "Statement of the Special Conference of the Church of the Brethren" was issued at a called meeting of the General National Conference, held Jan. 9, 1918.

2. This Conference was called to provide for conditions relative to the draft, prior to the President's pronouncements concerning noncombatant service.

3. At a meeting of Brethren and representatives of other non-resistant churches with the War Department in the latter part of 1917, officials asked for the creeds of the churches on the subject of war—the Mennonites leaving a copy of the creed with the officials.

4. It was deemed advisable by this called Conference, Jan. 9, 1918, that a clear statement of the church tenet on this subject be printed in convenient form.

5. This paper was intended for those who are members of this church, and for the information of officials who might desire to know the tenet of the Church of the Brethren, as it is related to the clause of the Selective Draft Law which provides exemption from combatant duty to "members of churches whose tenets forbid its members to participate in war." No other use of this paper was contemplated.

6. There has been no publication of this paper since its first issue in January, 1918.

7. Other parts of this paper specifically express love and loyalty to the Country and urge the members to contribute to the needs of the Government—indicating, according to our understanding, entire freedom of the whole paper from any willful intent to obstruct; the purpose being to restate to herself the position the Church has always held.

8. The Regular Annual Conference of June 5-12, 1918, passed resolutions of commendation for the liberal provision made by the Government for noncombatant service, and the spirit of the Conference was to leave the matter largely to the individual conscience.

9. The Church of the Brethren has ever sought to avoid any undue publicity, desiring only to be accorded the privilege of living quietly within the realm of conscience as the law and the Executives have so graciously provided.

10. The Central Service Committee was created and appointed after the passage of this paper, and is in no sense responsible therefore, yet we agree to use our influence for the discontinuance of the distribution of the Statement in its present form, and we humbly pray that any intended prosecution proposed may be withdrawn.[35]

The Church of the Brethren kept its pledge to withdraw the Goshen pamphlet. Swigart wrote an urgent appeal in the *The Gospel Messenger* instructing Brethren not to use it, conceding that the church had to curtail its witness, and warning of the high stakes involved.[36]

In accord with the recommendation of a joint meeting of various organizations, together with the Standing Committee, a "Bulletin of Information" for those affected by the draft will be issued within a few days. Our people must appreciate the fact that care is necessary in sending out printed matter, especially in the form of advice, and if this "Bulletin" is not specific, in some points, as you would like, you must read it with the full understanding of the position of our church, at all times, and in the light of the understanding. . . .

All persons in Camp and those going should have the regular church certificate, instead of this one. No use or display of the Goshen paper in its present form should be made, and the regular church certificate should be substituted therefore. If the paper should again be brought to the attention of the War Department, trouble again may arise.

Conditions are becoming more tense every day and conditions have changed much since the Goshen Conference. *We must all know that the world is at war and that the United States are a part of the world.* A man is entitled to his opinion and to the exercise of his own conscience, but *he is not always at liberty to give utterance to or exploiting his opinion, or to urge his conscience on the attention of others.* The Government is disposed especially to emphasize this fact, when that exploiting can, in any sense, be construed as affecting the raising or disciplining of armies, or the raising of means for the support of the Government. It is the word "urge" in the Goshen paper to which the authorities object—*the giving of advice to others that would interfere with their enlisting or taking the uniform.* It may be suggested also that advice or reference to Liberty Bonds that could, in any sense, prejudice their sale, may involve one in trouble. Our Brethren should take account of all these facts and govern themselves accordingly, in their utterances. *It will have to be understood by persons going to Camps that they should be settled and established in their own views, and in their personal consciences and choice, that it may not be necessary to convey advice to them.*[37]

Either many Brethren were unaware that the government had forced their leadership to recant under duress, or else they were remarkably forgiving, because the following year Annual Conference showered approval on Woodrow Wilson and Secretary of War Newton Baker for, among other things, their handling of draft issues. Meeting after the completion of the Treaty of Versailles but prior to its ratification battle in the U. S. Senate, the Conference thanked Wilson for his "generous and tolerant interpretation" of selective service legislation and praised his "advanced views" in the cause to prevent future wars, an implied endorsement of Versailles and the League of Nations. It should also be said that Conference added disapproval of proposals for compulsory military training, especially in schools. (Baker received a similar communication.)

> First: Three years ago, when the ominous and threatening clouds of war were gathering in our firmament, we made formal presentation to you, reciting our religious tenets forbidding our members to engage in war, and concerning our claims of conscience restraining us from militant service and learning the arts of war. With this we stressed our plea for provisions in the laws and the execution thereof that would release us from such service. We wish now, by formal vote and official sanction, to give expression to our deep sense of appreciation of the respectful attention which our appeals received. We also make recognition of the generous and tolerant interpretation you placed on the laws enacted by Congress concerning the claims of the conscientious objector.

> Second: We have followed with interest your course and policy in dealing with the tremendous issues that have rested so largely upon your judgment and conscience concerning the affairs of our own country and the wider and broader affairs of the earth. We hereby express our admiration of your advanced views, wise position and tolerant and Christian standards manifested in your attitude towards the subject of peace and the settlement and adjustment of the affairs of the world and its future protection from the menace and perils of war.

> Third: We take this occasion to renew to you the expression of our abhorrence of war and our testimony in favor of peace and the furtherance of those sentiments that make for peace.

> We desire and shall ever pray that our beloved country shall stand, in the interest of its own citizenry and in the presence of the wide world that look hitherward towards us, as a nation whose ideals and laws and standards and sense of citizenship all savor of peace and tolerance and righteousness towards all. And that we most respectfully but most earnestly and specifically protest against the enactment of laws that contemplate enforced military training—

especially against such training in the schools of our land—believing
that such action would be a step backward of several centuries in
the ideals of government and the civilization of the world.[38]

America was a tough place for nonconformists. The mature nation-state, with vast resources at its disposal, demanded that citizens answer the Hun in unison, and public opinion badgered those opposed to the war. Consequently, many Brethren entered the armed forces, often as noncombatants. Some, of course, became soldiers of their free will, some after the military's version of friendly persuasion had taken effect, and others fell victim to bullying and threats. Compounding frustrations for Brethren in this difficult time was a poorly articulated denominational position. Some thought that the doctrine of nonresistance ruled out military service in any form, while others considered noncombatancy consistent with traditional belief. When the Brethren recovered their voice with the firm Goshen Statement, the government considered them in the wrong key, and subcabinet level officials menaced Brethren leaders with possible imprisonment. Modern war surprised Brethren not only with its ferocity on the military front, but with its long reach on the home front.

"Wrecks of Time"

When in 1918 the Brethren gathered in Hershey, one of the first things they did was sing "In the Cross of Christ."

> In the cross of Christ I glory, Tow'ring o'er the wrecks of time.
> All the light of sacred story Gathers round its head sublime.

This old hymn must have evoked a variety of sentiments. Whether conferencegoers thought about death on the western front, lost civil liberties at home, questions about their loyalty, or brothers, sons, and husbands drafted, "wrecks of time" were apt words.

> When the woes of life o'er take me, Hopes deceive, and fears annoy,
> Never shall the cross forsake me: Lo! It glows with peace and joy.

With all the weight of the modern industrialized nation-state at war bearing down on the Brethren, they turned in song to the cross for comfort.

Bane and blessing, pain and pleasure, By the cross are sanctified;
Peace is there that knows no measure, Joys that thro' all time abide.[39]

NOTES

1. "Factory of death" and "industrial warfare" are the quotes of Omer Bartov, *Murder in Our Midst: The Holocaust, Industrial Killing, and Representation* (New York: Oxford University Press, 1996), 20-50; Michael Howard, *War in European History* (New York: Oxford University Press, 1976), 94-115; Paul A. C. Koistinen, "The Political Economy of Warfare in America, 1865-1914," *Anticipating Total War: The German and American Experiences, 1871-1914,* edited by Manfred F. Boemeke, Roger Chickering, and Stig Foster (Washington, D. C., and Cambridge, U. K.: German Historical Institute and Cambridge University Press, 1999), 57-76.

2. Woodrow Wilson quoted in Robert H. Zieger, *America's Great War: World War I and the American Experience* (Lanham, Md.: Rowman and Littlefield, 2000), 52. See also Zieger, 63, 78-80; John Higham, *Strangers in the Land: Patterns of American Nativism, 1860-1925* (New Brunswick, N. J.: Rutgers University Press, 1955, 1988), 204-12.

3. Zieger, *America's Greatest War*, 198.

4. Donald F. Durnbaugh, *Fruit of the Vine: A History of the Brethren, 1708-1995* (Elgin, Ill.: Brethren Press, 1997), 427-28.

5. Kermit Eby, "The Evolution of a Dunker: WWI," *Brethren Action* (July 1, 1937): 4.

6. Nora E. Berkebile, "Military Training in the Schools," *The Gospel Messenger* (January 26, 1918): 52.

7. Zieger, *America's Greatest War,* 60-61.

8. Albert M. Keim and Grant M. Stoltzfus, *The Politics of Conscience: The Historic Peace Churches and America at War, 1917-1955* (Scottdale, Pa.: Herald Press, 1988), 36-46.

9. Keim and Stoltzfus, *The Politics of Conscience*, 46; Frederick Palmer, *Newton D. Baker: America at War, 2* vols. (New York: Dodd, Mead, & Company, 1931), I:341.

10. Rufus D. Bowman, *The Church of the Brethren and War, 1708-1941* (Elgin, Ill.: Brethren Publishing House, 1944), 179; Durnbaugh, *Fruit of the Vine,* 423-24; Keim and Stoltzfus, *Politics of Conscience,* 46-47.

11. Zieger, *America's Greatest War*, 62-63.

12. Palmer and Baker, *America at War,* I:341-42.

13. Leo Blickenstaff, "A Plea to the Drafted," *The Gospel Messenger* (January 5, 1918): 4.

14. Rufus Bowman, *The Church of the Brethren and War,* 175.

15. Berkebile, "Military Training in the Schools," 52.

16. J. Maurice Henry, *History of the Church of the Brethren in Maryland* (Elgin, Ill.: Brethren Publishing House, 1936), 527.

17. "Daniel Long Miller," *The Brethren Encyclopedia, 3* vols., edited by Donald F. Durnbaugh (Philadelphia, Pa., and Oak Brook, Ill.: The Brethren Encyclopedia, Inc., 1983), II:835-36.

18. Daniel L. Miller, "The War Crisis and the Church," *The Gospel Messenger* (September 22, 1917): 594.

19. Elmer E. Frick, c/o Base Hospital Camp Sherman, Ohio, January 13, *The Gospel Messenger* (February 2, 1918): 75.

20. Kenneth G. Long's account in Rufus Bowman, *The Church of the Brethren and War,* 198-99.

21. Roy E. Peters' account in Bowman, *The Church of the Brethren and War,* 226-27.

22. Levi T. Angle, "Detachment C.O.2 Training Battalion, Camp Lee, Virginia," *The Gospel Messenger* (February 9, 1918): 92-93.

23. M. Clyde Horst, "A Visit to Four Training Camps," *The Gospel Messenger* (December 1, 1917): 764.

24. D. H. Zigler, "Our Visit to Camp Lee," *The Gospel Messenger* (December 3, 1917): 692.

25. Perry J. Blough, "A Trip to Washington, D. C., and Camps Lee and Belvoir," *The Gospel Messenger* (March 30, 1918): 199.

26. M. C. Swigart, "Our Visit to Camps Meade, Mills and Merritt," *The Gospel Messenger* (January 12, 1918): 21.

27. Durnbaugh, Fruit of the Vine, 424-25; Henry, *History of the Church,* 528; "Henry Clay Early," *The Brethren Encyclopedia,* I:413.

28. *Minutes of the Special General Conference of the Church of the Brethren, Held at Goshen, Indiana, January 9, 1918,* 5-6.

29. Durnbaugh, *Fruit of the Vine,* 426. The warning to Early that spies were in the congregation is oral history. According to Durnbaugh, Michael R. Zigler claimed that Early told him about the caution. Zigler told Durnbaugh, who passed along the source to me in an e-mail communication.

30. Henry Clay Early, "Peace Address Delivered at the Hershey Conference, In Two Parts—Part One," *The Gospel Messenger* (July 6, 1918): 415-16; "The Position of the Church of the Brethren," *The Gospel Messenger* (July 13, 1918): 434.

31. Spencer Roberts, Captain, Acting Intelligence Officer, 79th Division, Camp Meade, Md., to W. C. Smiley, Captain, Military Intelligence Branch, Washington, D. C. (May 9, 1918), National Archives, Military Intelligence Division, RG 165, 10902-14. The file also contains a copy of the pamphlet. For another complaint about the Goshen Statement, see 10015-62.

32. Durnbaugh, *Fruit of the Vine,* 425.

33. Henry, *History of the Church,* 530-31. See also W. J. Swigart's account of the meeting: "The Central Service Committee," *The Gospel Messenger* (July 27, 1918): 468-69. H. R. Gibble and I. W. Taylor joined Swigart and Henry in Washington; Durnbaugh, *Fruit of the Vine,* 425.

34. Henry, *History of the Church,* 528.   Swigart, "The Central Service Committee," 469.

35. Swigart, "The Central Service Committee," 469. For another version of the statement and an account of the browbeating of Swigart, Henry, and the others, see Henry, *History of the Church,* 31.
36. Durnbaugh, *Fruit of the Vine,* 425-26; Jeff Bach, " 'Our Conscience Is Bound': A Survey of the Brethren Peace Witness," *Brethren Life & Thought* (Fall 2000): 174-76.
37. Swigart, "The Central Service Committee," 468-69.
38. *Full Report of the Proceedings of Annual Conference of the Church of the Brethren, 1919* (Elgin, Ill.: Brethren Publishing House), 143. For the resolution addressed to Baker, see same, 143-44.
39. Sir John Bowring, "In the Cross of Christ, "No. 235 in *The Brethren Hymnal: A Collection of Psalms, Hymns and Spiritual Songs* (Elgin, Ill.: Brethren Publishing House, 1901).

PART II
The Interwar Period

III. THE TWENTIES
Change

At first glance, the 1920s were America's fun decade. The Jazz Age was awash with ticker tape, saxophones, automobiles, big-time sports, radios, movies, electric vacuum cleaners, fads, heroes, and prosperity. Babe Ruth, Dow-Jones, Rudolph Valentino, Henry Ford, Clara Bow, and Charles Lindbergh embodied this image of the twenties.

Yet momentous transformation surged underneath the carefree veneer. It is true that change is a constant as society undergoes unending evolution. But some forms of newness create more anxiety than others, and social change unnerves some eras more than others. In the twenties a lengthy list of changes particularly disturbed many Americans, especially traditionalists. After World War I, the flow of huddled masses across the Atlantic returned to normalcy with nearly one million immigrants arriving annually, many of them Catholic, Jewish, or Orthodox. Economic change, represented by chain stores and large corporations, threatened small, local enterprises. Labor unions challenged the balance of power in labor relations. In 1919 perhaps one million American workers participated in strikes, and socialists and other radicals, emboldened by the 1917 Bolshevik Revolution, offered an alternative to capitalism. In 1920 women cast their first presidential ballots, and throughout the decade young, trendsetting females rejected convention and declared independence. On large campuses, a youth cult emerged, grounded in a student subculture with distinctive clothing, vocabulary, music, and values. For the first time older adults imitated students. Dating replaced social calling. Diversity, economic change, labor strife, independent women, and unconstrained youth all marked the relative decline of traditional, small town, and rural white Anglo-Saxon dominance and the arrival of a more modern society.[1]

Likewise, though the Brethren exterior often appeared serene, inner Brethrenism underwent significant change. Revivalism and mission gave the denomination an outward appearance of stability, but professionalization and changing gender roles made modernization no less dynamic among the Brethren than the rest of society.

REVIVALISM AND MISSION

Despite the novelty of the period, familiar patterns of faith persisted. Revivals, added to Brethrenism after the Civil War, became ubiquitous and blazed the Brethren landscape with unadorned, mainstream Protestant orthodoxy. The denomination honored these services as the "first great work of the church" and offered no-nonsense advice on how to organize them.

> The first great work of the church is evangelistic. The last word of Jesus on earth emphasizes the work of making disciples. The secret of the rapid growth of the early church is recorded thus: "They therefore that were scattered abroad went about preaching the Word."
>
> It is not enough to believe in missions abroad. Missionary efforts are necessary at home also. If one is missionary at home, he will support foreign work also.
>
> Common terms for evangelistic meetings are "Series of Meetings," or "Revival Meetings." The former may comprehend more than the latter. A "series of meetings" may partake of both "revival" and "ingathering." The latter depends upon the former. The more thorough the "revival," the more sure the "ingathering." . . .
>
> Since song is such a universal gift and can be used to carry truth in such an appealing manner, it becomes a very vital agency in the evangelistic meeting. A spiritual and efficient song leader is essential. Congregational singing should be encouraged. Trained spiritual singers can render special messages in song to advantage and profit. . . .
>
> Good ushers are an important part of the organization. Men tactful in seating an audience; who can meet people both before and after service in a winning way; who can discover the unsaved and the interested, and seat them to advantage. Men whose every thought while handling the crowd is in the interest of the Kingdom.[2]

Revivals functioned as the chief mechanism for new members entering the fellowship, and congregations routinely tallied the number of souls harvested by these seasons of renewal. New converts were quickly baptized, usually outdoors, and although congregational reports ignored weather conditions, Brethren broke the ice, if necessary, prior to immersing the repentant sinner.[3]

It should be noted that we are having a most interesting revival in our congregation and school, held by our pastor, Bro. A. B. Miller. There have been 31 accessions. We praise our Father in heaven for this blessing.[4]

———————

Beginning on the evening of Jan. 2 and closing Jan. 30, our church conducted a most helpful meeting. Eld. J. H. Cassady, of Huntingdon, Pa., was the evangelist, and he was at his best. Bro. Cassady, having been our former pastor, the members and friends were especially glad to have him back, and entered into the meetings from the beginning, with a hearty cooperation and good will, which increased to the close of the campaign.

The church had been in prayer and preparation for several weeks, prior to the opening. Bro. George Berkley, leader of the music, had given several nights to the training of a chorus. He, with the assistance of Sister Mabel Lambert, conducted the music throughout the meetings. Bro. J. P. Coleman presided at the piano, and contributed much to the success of the song service.

Bro. Cassady is not afraid to expend money properly to advertise a meeting. By means of his special announcements of the meetings over Sundays, he was able to fill the house on Saturday nights, when other churches close down on occasions of that sort. No matter how cold or rainy the weather, the people came and filled the house—often to overflowing—and several times some were turned away. A very helpful and much appreciated feature of the meetings was the strong delegations, led by their pastors, from the other churches of the city. Many persons, affiliated with other denominations, also helped to swell the crowds. Of the more than one hundred and fifty persons, whose names we had on our prayer-lists, many were regular attendants. . . .

So far fifty-five persons have received baptism, two were received on former baptism, and one was reclaimed. There were several re-consecrations and a number more are expected to be baptized when they get well enough. Half of these are adults—sixteen being heads of families. Twelve new homes were reached. The membership has been greatly built up and a large increase in Sunday-school, church and prayer meeting attendance is noticeable. The last Sunday of the meeting it rained, and yet 355 were present in Sunday-school. Last Sunday our monthly Sunday-school missionary offering was $78.01.

While we greatly rejoice over the victories won, we are sad over the many who refused to yield. Many seemed near the Kingdom, and a week more of preaching might have reached them, but the fact remains that Satan has a wonderful power over people. Worldliness, indifference and hypocrisy abound, and this makes the success of the church difficult.[5]

We agree to differ,
We resolve to love,
We unite to serve.

Such was the motto adopted by the Goshen City church at the beginning of one of the greatest revivals ever held here, one which was conducted by Brother and Sister Oliver H. Austin, of McPherson, Kans.

The meetings proper began on Sunday morning, Nov. 8, and continued for two weeks, but the spirit of the revival began much earlier than Nov. 8. Twelve cottage prayer meetings were held during the month of October, with an average attendance of twenty-one, and the thought most expressed and prayed for was a revival in our individual lives, a revival for the entire congregation, and a revival in soul saving. The revival spirit among the membership was very pronounced when the evangelists opened their campaign, and from the start we had large crowds which continued to grow until scores were turned away.

Rally Day was also observed Nov. 1 at which time we had 345 in Sunday-school, and this was also a means of awakening the Sunday-school and church to the coming revival. We found the evangelist and his wife among the best we have ever had at Goshen. Bro. Austin gave us very strong sermons and proved himself to be an evangelist that any church might well be glad to claim. He is very ably supported by his good wife who had charge of the singing—and how the people must sing when she leads. Her pleasing personality and beautiful Christian character soon won for her a place in every heart. She found the large chorus of fifty voices well trained and ready and willing to be led in gospel singing. Many people were wonderfully blessed by the fine music and this, together with a strong gospel sermon each night, gave the people something well worth traveling miles to hear. We had members present from at least fourteen different congregations, some coming as far as South Bend and North Manchester. We especially appreciated the attendance of the members from the West Goshen congregation.

Brother and Sister Austin are also splendid personal workers. They visited in over one hundred homes. As a direct result of the meetings, there were sixty-five decisions for Christ—of these, fifty-two were baptized and six received on their former baptism, the balance are awaiting baptism. Of the fifty-two baptized, thirty-three are over twelve years of age; twenty are heads of families. Several who were baptized had been Christians but desired to serve him in our church. One lady, who has been an invalid for several years, requested baptism and was taken into the church.[6]

Mainstream Protestantism notably influenced Brethren revivalism. In 1921, a year of special emphasis on evangelism, the denominational press advertised several collections of sermons by Charles G. Finney, a well-known evangelist in the early nineteenth century, and a biography of Billy Sunday, the flamboyant contemporary evangelist. The Brethren Publishing House lavished praise on Sunday, in promoting the biography they wanted Brethren to buy:

Explains "Billy" Sunday; as readable as fiction. Tells the story of Mr. Sunday's eventful life, gives a keen analysis of his manner and methods, and also contains the heart of his message, which has changed the lives of over a quarter of a million. It reproduces his picturesque heart-stirring phrases and sayings, and retains all of the wonderful appeal of his platform utterances. It will give any minister, teacher or worker new ideas, new inspiration, new energy.[7]

More frequently the Brethren Publishing House advertised works by Reuben Torrey, another well-known revivalist. For a few years after the turn of the century, Torrey was America's favorite evangelist, organizing revivals in major cities in cooperation with leading laypersons, such as John Wanamaker and Asa Candler (of Coca-Cola). Torrey's critics charged that he was too literal and narrow-minded, that his revivals were too commercialized and showy, and that he ignored modern scholarship. But Torrey's simple, unadorned doctrine and his attacks on liberals, Darwinists, progressive politics, and modern immorality, such as dancing, theater-going, gambling, and card-playing, attracted many, including the Brethren Publishing House. A Brethren ad, for example, admired one of Torrey's volumes:

> A book by an evangelist of international reputation who has been greatly used of God to the saving of souls. Coupled with a large experience is an attractive manner of presenting the facts in the case. Sure to be helpful to the earnest seeker of the right methods in this great work.[8]

Support for evangelists like Torrey and Sunday placed the Brethren squarely within the mainstream of American evangelicalism, and their style of revivalism played a large role in congregational life. Many converts appeared to spontaneously accept a call from the evangelist, and others hit the sawdust trail because it was expected of people their age. For example, a member of the Elgin, Illinois, congregation remembered,

> My mother said to me one spring day, you're going to be baptized next Sunday. She said, you want to be a member of the church, don't you? It's time for these kids [a membership class] to be baptized, so we were.[9]

Although visiting evangelists, music leaders, rally days, and inspiration from Sunday and Torrey often made Brethren revivalism appear identical to the mainstream Protestant variety, some Brethren evangelists nevertheless sought to maintain their distance from this popular movement. They especially disliked the emotionalism and spontaneous conversion that was synonymous with the larger movement. According to traditional Brethren doctrine, conversion resulted not from impulse, but from sober contemplation and deliberate commitment to the faith community symbolized by baptism. Although converts might declare their intent to join the fellowship during a revival, doing so involved a longer process of growth and reflection rather than responding to an unpremeditated urge. Brethren conversion was not less heartfelt or regenerate than other forms of free-will conversion, but ideally Brethren hearts changed slowly, not suddenly.

I. J. Rosenberger, an admired and conservative evangelist from Ohio, mixed popular revivalism with traditional Brethren conversion in a sermon on the new birth. Most Protestant evangelicals assumed that the Holy Spirit sparked regeneration, but Rosenberger held that it entered the heart toward the end of the conversion process. He pointed out that a planted seed lives and grows even before it sprouts, making conversion a relatively long-term progression rather than a spur-of-the-moment event. He further Brethrenized the new birth by urging two traditional Brethren rites—baptism and the laying on of hands—which he believed preceded the infusion of the Spirit.

The sacred writers employ a number of symbols of conversion, seemingly with a view to having the interesting subject of conversion well understood. The potter's clay named by Jeremiah is an interesting symbol of conversion. Ezekiel's vision of the valley of dry bones is a figure of conversion of equal interest; but we now have conversion as symbolized by a birth. It should be noted with care that a birth is not a creation, but a change of state or relation; for that which is born existed before birth. Notice that this is true in grace. A birth in nature has a number of prerequisites or changes. These same changes are met within grace.

First, a birth in nature is preceded by conception; so in grace. The first thing that John did was to teach the people; that same first thing Christ did; that is the first thing that Christ bade His chosen to do, to teach the people. Place a something in their minds that would cause them to reflect and consider, grow and mature, a new sentiment; that they might conceive the truth. The prophet, alluding to the work of the gospel dispensation, said: "After those days, saith the Lord, I will put my law in their inward parts, and write it in their hearts." It was said of the Pentecostians: "Now when they heard this they were pricked in their hearts." Here conviction, spiritual conception was taking place, and their spiritual birth soon followed. In Acts 19 we have the interesting circumstance of Paul meeting twelve disciples, who reported that they were baptized unto John's baptism; but when they confessed that they did know that there was a Holy Ghost, the error in their teaching was made plain. Paul then opened up and taught them aright. It is said: "When they heard this they were baptized in the name of the Lord Jesus." Here spiritual conception, a change of heart, took place. And their spiritual birth followed. . . .

We read of those "to whom the word preached did not profit them, not being mixed with faith in them that heard it." Here was nothing received; so there could be no conception, and therefore no birth followed.

Second, a birth in nature is preceded by gestation, formation or development. So in grace. Paul says: "My little children, of whom I travail in birth again until Christ be formed in you." This text is a clear support of my proposition. The eunuch had been up to Jerusalem to worship and had doubtless heard of Christ, and this new doctrine. It made such an impression (conception) on his mind that gestation was now doing its work, for Philip found him reading, and he at once welcomed to a seat by his side Philip, who taught him and helped him fully to mature his mind as to this Christ. And his spiritual birth at once took place. Paul, preaching at Berea, produced spiritual conception, affected their minds and hearts. This led them to "search the scriptures daily to see if these things were so." Here was development (gestation) going on which matured and fitted them for their spiritual birth, or Christian baptism.

I once called upon a man and wife who had been coming to our service. From their attention I thought they were seekers. I gently rapped on the man's door and he was quickly there with an open Bible in his hand. He at once expressed his pleasure that I came at that time, as he and his wife had been talking the subject over. I was highly gratified, for I found that gestation (development) was maturing in their minds. After an hour's talk and a season of prayer we repaired to the afternoon service, after which their spiritual birth took place, to the joy of the saints. A sister whom I baptized said to me: "I could hardly wait to be baptized, ever since I attended your love feast. At that meeting I was fully convinced that this was right." Here conception and gestation had matured and she was ready for her spiritual birth. We have in nature what is called false conception, which no birth follows. We may have many of these. They are serious in nature and sad in grace. Simon the Sorcerer serves as a sample of these. He was put under the water, but was not spiritually born; hence, no baptism.

Christ in His further development of this new birth to Nicodemus, said: "Except a man be born of water, and of the Spirit, he can not enter the kingdom of God." This language implies two operations. . . .

[1.] The Order That Christ Gave Nicodemus Was, Water First and Spirit Second

This order was clearly manifested at the baptism of Jesus. As He came up out of the water the Holy Spirit descended upon Him. In the birth formula, given in our text, Christ gives water first and Spirit second. This same order was seen on Pentecost, at the conversion of the Samaritans and the rebaptism of those twelve in Acts nineteen. It would seem proper, that after the penitent is washed in holy baptism, cleansed and pardoned, the house being swept and garnished," then to welcome the new Occupant, to receive the Holy Spirit. This is good reasoning.

[2.] The Operation of the Birth of the Spirit Was Wrought by the Laying On of Hands in Prayer

Let it be understood and remembered that the laying on of hands was always an important sacred service, variously employed. Luke tells us of Philip successfully preaching at Samaria. Peter and John followed, and by prayer and the laying on of hands converts received the Holy Ghost. This is made more emphatic and clear when we read Luke, who says: "When Simon saw that through the laying on of hands the Holy Ghost was given," he sought to buy the power. This leaves no ground for controversy. Turn to Acts 19, where Paul retaught and rebaptized "certain disciples." He then "laid his hands on them and the Holy Ghost came on them." These citations clearly show that the birth of the Spirit, the second operation in the formula of the new birth, is wrought by the laying on of hands in prayer.

In the epistle to Hebrews we read thus: "Leaving the principles of the doctrine of Christ, . . . not laying again the foundation of repentance from dead works, or faith toward God, of the doctrine of baptisms, and the laying on of hands," etc. The fact that the laying on of hands in this text follows baptism, is evidence that it is the same laying on of hands that we have seen in former texts quoted. I raise the question: If the conversion of the Samaritans and the twelve disciples met by Paul was not complete without the laying on of hands in prayer, is your conversion with mine complete without the laying on of hands in prayer?[10]

Despite the efforts of Rosenberger and other traditionalists, Brethren revivalism absorbed much from the larger society, thereby bringing the fellowship a whiff of social change. Even so, revivalism often came across as little more than straightforward soul-saving, far removed from liberal higher criticism and the Social Gospel, and on balance reassured traditionalists.

Mission similarly reinforced stability during an age of change. In the twenties, domestic mission still won many hearts, most notably when Annual Conference backed the establishing of the Bethany Brethren Hospital in Chicago. This project owed its existence to the Bethany Seminary board, which had always envisioned a hospital adjacent to its school, and in 1921 it converted a residence into a thirteen-bed hospital.[11] The statement that authorized a Brethren hospital revealed a mixture of motives that included overseas mission and "practical" service.

[The] hospital is a desirable and needed thing in the church, **first**, to serve as an institution for the training of nurses and physicians (particularly missionary); **second**, to offer hospital and sanatorium facilities to our missionaries; **third**, to offer hospital facilities to members of the church; **fourth**, and above all, for the sake of furnishing an outlet for practical Christian service to mankind, of the sort that Christ himself taught and practiced.[12]

In the thirties Bethany Brethren Hospital operated a nursing school, but it ended in 1938. In 1968 Bethany merged with Garfield Park Hospital in West Garfield Park, Illinois, to create the Bethany Brethren-Garfield Park Hospital with two buildings.[13]

Foreign mission also provided a vehicle for continuity. Combining a popular program with an orthodox emphasis on winning souls, overseas evangelism appeared conservative in the context of twenties-era modernity. Major efforts in China and India continued, as did the smaller undertakings in Denmark and Sweden. In 1922 mission enthusiasts planted Brethrenism on another continent, Africa, with the arrival of H. Stover Kulp and Albert D. Helser in Nigeria. The following year their wives, Ruth Royer Kulp and Lola Bechtel Helser, joined them, although in 1924 Ruth Kulp and her infant son died of dysentery.[14] A fellow missionary lamented the high price of the Nigerian mission.

In the past month our knowledge of God's plan for the work here has been greatly altered through his calling to rest one of our number, Ruth Royer Kulp. Although we are sure his way is the best way, we can not but wonder why. If, for the foundation of the Church of the Brethren in Africa, God chooses to use such costly materials as human blood; before God, as a church, shall or dare anything less than our all adorn the remainder of the structure?[15]

Growth in Nigeria remained unexceptional except for a leprosarium founded in 1929, which won international recognition. After World War II, the Nigerian Brethren expanded dramatically; in 1981 membership was 40,000, and in 1995 it reached 120,000. At this writing the membership of the *Ekklesiyar 'Yanuwa a Nigeria (EYN;* Church of the Brethren in Nigeria) exceeds that of the Church of the Brethren.[16] It became autonomous in 1972.

An early baptism in Nigeria. Earl W. Flohr immerses the convert while locals observe and Clarence C. Heckman rolls the film. *Photo courtesy of BHLA.*

Missionaries freely borrowed from the Social Gospel, and in all major mission fields the Brethren opened schools and medical facilities. Lola Helser described the dedication of a hospital in Nigeria.

A good audience attended the dedication of the Mission Hospital May 11. As the basis of his sermon Bro. Kulp used the story of Peter and John and the lame man at the Beautiful Gate of the temple. Bro. Kulp made it plain to the people that we did not come with any money of our own to build houses or to work among them. The people understood that believers in Jesus in America had given the funds for this building because they loved God, and since they loved God, they naturally loved the Bura people who were his children, too. When Bro. Kulp asked the people, "Whose money built this house?" they said, "God's money." When he asked, "Whose house is this?" they replied, "God's house." It is our prayer that this expression of his love may always be used to his glory. The people were given to understand that the doctor could not help them in his own strength, any more than Peter and John could raise the lame man in their own strength. But that the doctor does his work in the name of the same Jesus that made the lame man leap for joy. And that God has helped the doctor learn many things about the bodies of men, and God would now use the doctor to help these people because he loved them.[17]

But evangelism, rather than the Social Gospel movement, predominated on the mission field. Lola Helser, for example, was effusive about an early preaching tour by her husband and Dr. Homer L. Burke. While the doctor vaccinated against smallpox and pulled teeth—an application of the Social Gospel—both of them preached the salvation gospel to eager listeners. In Helser's words, the Bura

learned of the love of Christ as they heard for the first time the story of God's love as the Father of us all, and that, being children of the same Father, we are brothers, regardless of the color of our skin. Once as they were preaching the Word, one old man said, "Bless God, bless Jesus the Son of God, bless Mohammed." When they were told the difference between Jesus and Mohammed, soon all were saying, "Bless Jesus." Old and young would clap their hands to the rhythm of the children's song "Jesus Loves Me." As they prayed the Lord's Prayer, a number of the village headmen would kneel by them and with their people repeat it after them line by line. At a number of the villages the people and the headmen begged the brethren to come and live among them and teach them and help them.[18]

Brief "notes" or news items in *The Missionary Visitor,* a periodical devoted to mission, described the risks and successes of spreading the gospel among the "heathen." In one of these accounts, Ellen H.

Wagoner, a missionary in India, told of disease, tigers, dazzling western technology, and a faithful remnant.

> Evangelistic work among the various villages continues with much interest. On account of sickness of some of the workers the effort has been hindered in the particular districts. Bro. [Jacob M.] Blough, because of fever, has not been able to get out the past few weeks in the Vyara District. His good wife [Anna Detweiler Blough], however, has done what she could by taking her tent and remaining with the native helpers.
>
> Miss [Kathryn] Ziegler has been out in the villages the whole month. Although the nights were cool for open-air meetings, large crowds of thinly-clad villagers attended the services. Her lantern, which showed pictures on "The Life of Christ," was an asset to her meetings. . . .
>
> Part of the month Brother and Sister [Benjamin Franklin and Nettie Pearl Brown] Summer were out in Raj Pipla District. They pitched their tents at two villages, working out from their head-quarters in the mornings and holding meetings at the tent at night. At one village they found a Christian community of twelve families, which appreciated very much the coming of these missionaries. At this place, two elderly women, a little girl and two boys were baptized. The Christians in these out-of-the-way places need our constant prayers, for they are surrounded by so much heathenism that has strong attractions for them. Brother and Sister Summer were made to realize very fully the protection of a kind heavenly Father when they were out in a tiger jungle. Two visits by night were made to their tent by tigers, but the beasts went on their way without any prey, because of the light which was kept burning on the outside.[19]

Anna Brumbaugh described to readers of *The Missionary Visitor* her visit to a Hindu religious fair in India. Brumbaugh, along with another missionary, Rosa Belle Wagoner Kaylor, and several "native Christians" traveled for two hours by oxcart to reach the gathering and preach about "salvation through Jesus."

> On arrival, we found carts and oxen under nearly all the trees, while the people were "bazaaring," going back and forth to see the idol, bathing, or sitting quietly, resting.

We stopped to spread our blankets under one of the nearest trees. There we rested, ate our lunch, and then began our work. First, we played the phonograph and sang, until folks gathered. Then the workers began preaching. "Jesus and the Samaritan Woman," as well as other Bible stories, was made the basis of teaching. Then, more songs were sung, and pictures and tracts were distributed to the hearers. After the audience had dwindled, we crossed the river and sat under a big tree on the opposite bank. There we sat for about three hours, singing, playing the phonograph, telling stories, and distributing pictures and tracts to an audience of from 80 to 100 people most of the time. Some listened for longer, some for shorter periods, but there was quite a change constantly going on.

. . . Our message, as they heard it, echoed the chord of salvation through Jesus, but because of the chains of custom and caste, we know it is hard for them to accept new doctrines. Some hearers seemed really interested, while others paid very little heed. We could but trust that the seed sown might some day bring forth fruit.

After thus giving the message, Sister Kaylor and I visited the native wares, brought there to be sold, and then went to the cart. About 4:30 we started on the homeward trip, reaching there about 6 P.M. We were very tired and thirsty, but glad for the day and the opportunity to witness in a small way for our Master.[20]

Also from India, Enoch Howe Eby assured American Brethren that Mohandas Gandhi's movement for independence indicated rising interest in Christ.

The power of vicarious suffering for a cause is well illustrated in India today. Mr. Gandhi is still in prison and his followers seem as devoted to him as ever, and are carrying on the propaganda for home rule though deprived of the inspiration of the presence of their leader. Mr. Gandhi is pointing his people to Christ as the great example of giving one's life for a cause. More people are studying the life of Christ today than ever before in India. While for the present the glory of Christ is obscured by the glory of India's hero, Christ will be able eventually to draw to himself the heart of India, IF WE ARE FAITHFUL TO HIM.[21]

Efforts to bring Christianity to China also received ample space in *The Missionary Visitor.* When missionary Anna V. Blough died of typhus, the periodical printed excerpts from her diary, recounting her success in teaching Chinese women to identify the "Babe Jesus as God's Son."

> Last spring when I left I felt I had made friends and hoped they would last. I hoped, too, that they would remember the teaching. Today I have been to see those on whom I had counted as friends. I find they have not forgotten me nor the teaching. They all recall the Babe Jesus as God's Son, and they all can say *"Kwan yiu I wei Chen Shen"* (a song that there is only one true God), that is, those most interested. I first went to Mr. Chi's home, and I felt that if everybody else turned me down it paid to come to his wife. Am going to teach her every day now. Last spring she took her first reading lesson. Today she had read three primers and was in Yu Chien Ju Shen, my second visit to her. And she understands well and has an open heart. God surely means great things for her. Now I am invited to her mother's home, nearly two miles away. God give me grace to give them something. Was in seven homes today. How I love these people and desire to be God's true servant! Mr. Chi presented me a duck, so my meat is provided.[22]

Revivalism and mission, then, underlined tradition. Whether revivals drew inspiration from I. J. Rosenberger or Reuben Torrey, they exuded conservative theology, and the ambitious enterprise in Nigeria gave new momentum to a foreign mission, an impulse underwritten by the same belief system as revivalism. Both movements enjoyed near-consensus. Both trod a familiar path for Brethren. Both coated twenties-era Brethrenism with constancy and stability.

Professional Ministry

Many of the same forces that transformed larger American society were at work at the Brethren core, underneath the traditionalism and orthodoxy. During the twenties modernization had an especially long reach, touching Brethren even on the local and individual levels.

Professionalization, for example, a common characteristic of modernization, steadily advanced within the ministry. During the first few decades of the twentieth century, patterns of local leadership changed noticeably as many congregations adopted professional ministers, that is, they paid a full-time, seminary-trained pastor. Of the 856 congregations, 203 employed professionals by 1925, and 297 part-timers filled pulpits; in all, 500 congregations (58 percent) had either a full-time or part-time clergy. Annual Conference added its weight to professionalization by urging congregations to hire ministers.

> It is advised that each congregation provide for pastoral care of its members. (a) The abler congregations will do well to provide full-time pastors. (b) Weaker congregations should provide at least part-time pastoral service. (c) Two or more weak congregations in close proximity with one another may unite in the support of a pastor who will divide his labors among them.[23]

Along with this change in the ministry, the informal educational requirements for Annual Conference moderators were revised. Between 1900 and 1920 most moderators were free ministers who earned their living by farming or teaching, but after 1920 moderators were typically college presidents and professors or professional pastors, reflecting the rising status of educated leadership. Transformation of the Brethren ministry appeared inevitable, although many congregations still relied on the free ministry and seminaries graduated more pastors than the congregations would hire.[24]

As professional leadership began to acquire wider acceptance, the free ministry suffered a corresponding long, slow decline. In the early twenties, however, the authority of elders over pastors remained clear. The *Pastor's Manual,* first published in 1923 and itself a sign of increased professionalization, advised pastors to exercise caution in asserting authority and to recognize free ministers in the congregation as partners. Eldership continued as the highest degree of Brethren ministry, and only ministers who had demonstrated their worthiness could attain it. Pastors who were not elders could not serve communion unless the elder was absent or requested it.[25] Moreover, the *Pastor's Manual* stipulated that elders retain overall responsibility for the spiritual health of the congregation and that important tasks, such as anointing the sick and training young ministers, belonged to them.

> The duties of the elder, in addition to the foregoing duties of the minister, are to feed the flock, to preside over council meetings, especially when official members are on trial; to anoint the sick, to have the oversight and general management of the church; training the young ministers in his charge and apportioning the work

among them according to their experience and ability—in brief, to be a faithful shepherd to the flock, guarding their souls as one who must give an account, and be willing to serve in any capacity authorized by the church.[26]

Pastors, however, gradually closed much of the gap between themselves and elders. In 1926 Annual Conference stripped elders of an important duty by empowering District Ministerial Boards to control ordination and placement and to settle disputes arising from the ministry. Previously these responsibilities belonged to the District Elders Body, all of whom were free ministers.

Each District Ministerial Board is definitely responsible:

1. To make a careful study of the congregations and the ministers of the District and make such reports to the General Ministerial Board as may be needed.
2. To distribute the ministers within the territory to the best advantage of the churches and the ministry. . . .
4. To examine and pass upon, by the approval of the congregation, candidates for licensing to preach as to educational qualifications, faith and doctrine and conduct the procedure of licensing in harmony with the Minutes of Annual Conference. . . .
6. To assist churches in the adjustment of difficulties arising from or affecting the ministry.[27]

On the congregational level, elders increasingly resembled figureheads, while pastors became active day-to-day chief executives of the congregation, anointed in the next decade, according to the *Pastor's Manual,* with the title of "spiritual shepherd."

The elder of the congregation should be considered its official head and should preside at all church councils, especially when the pastoral relationship is under consideration. He should be regarded as the chief counselor and adviser of the pastor in all of his work. The pastor should be considered the executive head of the church, the active leader in its program and activities, its spiritual counselor and "shepherd of the flock." [28]

Innovations in worship style, such as having choirs, a higher liturgy, marriage ceremonies with rings, organs, a baptistery, and the abandonment of kneeling during prayers, often happened with professionalization of leadership. Although professional ministers did not always initiate these steps toward mainline Protestantism, the arrival of a professional often coincided with the adoption of these innovations.

Church bulletins, another novelty, were also an example of the growing formality of Brethren worship.[29] The first example, from a revival in 1917, includes a choir and a "special offering" for the evangelist, but maintains the traditional opening of worship with several hymns. The second bulletin, from an urban congregation during the twenties, features an organ prelude and offertory, hymns throughout the service, the congregation rising to sing the Doxology, and an anthem by a "chorus" rather than a choir. The third, from the next decade, features even greater change with a processional, a choral anthem, a choral amen, and classical music, some of it secular. All three congregations had paid pastors.

Wiley, Colorado, Church of the Brethren
August 12, 1917[30]

Hymns Nos. 120, 136, 118	By Congregation
Prayer	
Scripture Reading, Mal. 3:7-12	
Announcements	
Special Offering for Evangelist [Oliver H.] Austin	
Special Music	By Chorus
Sermon Subject, "A Highway Robbery"	
Invitation	
Benediction	

First Church of the Brethren, Chicago, Illinois
December 16, 1928[31]

Prelude	Organ
Doxology	Congregation
Standing	
Invocation	
Hymn No. 1	Congregation
Offertory	Organ
Hymn No. 2	Congregation
Reading of God's Word	
Response	Congregation
Holy, Holy, Holy, Lord God Almighty	
Prayer	
Fair Eden Land	Wilson
First Church Chorus	
Sermon The Angel's Message	Pastor
Prayer and Benediction	

———————

Hagerstown, Maryland, Church of the Brethren
May 15, 1932[32]

Prelude: Cantabile	Franck
Processional: Holy, Holy, Holy	No. 17
Scripture Sentence:	Psalm 117
Invocation and the Lord's Prayer	
Hymn: How Firm a Foundation	No. 259
Scripture Lesson: Psalm 27	
Solo: Teach Me to Pray	Hewitt
Miss Catherine Miller	
Prayer and Choral Response:	
Hymn: Jesus, Savior, Pilot Me	No. 248
Announcements	
The Offertory: Rimembranza	Yon
Anthem: Gloria in Excelsis	Mozart
Sermon	
Hymn: Lead On, O King Eternal	No. 255
Benediction and Choral Amen	
Postlude: March in E Flat	Schumann

Offerings, another addition to worship, were often directly related to the arrival of a new pastor who needed to be paid. Rufus D. Bowman, twenty-nine years old and two years out of Yale Divinity School, argued for a fresh interpretation of loyalty to the denomination, a vision that included generous offerings to sustain full-time preachers.[33]

> The *new loyalty* demands that we teach stewardship of life and possessions. Since loyalty to church is not an end, but a means toward the most effective propagation of the Kingdom, we must exercise the methods which bring the best results. This idea necessitated the change from a free ministry to a paid ministry which could give more time to the work of the Kingdom. This fact, along with our expansion in missionary enterprises, created the demand for an active teaching of our stewardship obligations. The doctrine of stewardship is a great Biblical principle and we need to give no apologies when we teach it.
>
> There is nothing that brings greater spiritual enrichment than giving.[34]

With professionalization of the ministry came expectations of greater polish in the pulpit. One contributor to the *The Gospel Messenger* suggested more rational use of the minister's time to accomplish this.

> It is always desirable to maintain a proper balance between the elements of exhortation and instruction in the pulpit. One hardly goes to church to be instructed, but a sermon lacking wholly in instruction is not conducive to the wholesome development of the hearers. Any appeal of value must be based on accurate foundations, and any significant interpretation of events or experiences must issue from a critical knowledge of facts. At present there is too little rather than too much scholarship in the pulpit. The very nature and demands of a clergyman's activities make it difficult for him to be a consistent and constructive scholar. His work is subjected to all sorts of interruptions and a routine providing for stated periods of study is almost impossible. And scholarship requires a devotion and a jealous regard for time that will not admit of interruptions during the periods of careful and concentrated thinking.

But the scholarship in the pulpit is so important as to make necessary a schedule of hours that will include definite periods for study and research. Almost all of our social and business contacts are suggestive of the most discriminating observation and analysis. The mechanisms we use in the home and out, the methods of procedure in business, the entertainment and social affairs provided for us all give evidence of painstaking development, of critical thinking and investigation. We cannot follow the processes by which the inventors and organizers reached the satisfying results, but we are conscious of well-ordered and critically-developed schemes and devices which give us what we desire and need. Our young people in school and college are urged in many ways to think straight, to think things through, to think critically. Teachers do not announce it, but they use rather freely the text, "Prove all things, hold fast that which is good." Adults are faced every day with a considerable body of information and, whether they will or not, are required to discriminate and to evaluate what they read and hear and see.

All of this suggestion of careful thinking based on wide observation and critical selection argues most forcefully for the same regard for facts and tendencies in the pulpit.

And, still further, scholarship in the pulpit is not enough. But the man who is committed otherwise to his task of spiritual counselor and adviser will increase in power and effectiveness as he commits himself to the scholarly attitude in his periods of study. The pulpit of the future more than the pulpit of the past will demand the discriminating and critical thinker, the man of authority. He must be more than a thinker, but he can not be less. He must appeal to and interpret for the people, but the appeals and interpretations, he must know, can be effective only to the extent that their bases are sound.[35]

The rise of professional clergy even affected well-entrenched Brethren revivalism. The visit of a personable revivalist, frequently a widely-respected elder, potentially challenged the popularity of local ministers, whether free or paid. Perhaps the revivalist was a more gifted speaker than the congregational leaders. Perhaps those who responded to his invitation to convert considered him more effective than the local preachers. After all, it was the revivalist who led them to Christ. Consequently, free ministers and pastors alike suggested a revised role

Oliver and Hazel Austin, popular evangelists during the twenties and thirties. *Photo courtesy of BHLA.*

for evangelists. Professionals, who could be dismissed, thus enjoying far less security than free ministers, often became the spokespersons for this cause. Olin F. Shaw, a full-time pastor in the Midwest, made the case for combining soul-winning revivalism with local leadership but without claiming that guest evangelists undercut pastors.

> The ideal [revival] is the purely home evangelism with the pastor preaching a series of special evangelistic sermons and the whole church organized and cooperating with him. One week, or over two Sundays, may be long enough, if the campaign is well advertised and vigorously pushed. If two such campaigns are conducted they should come at the Easter and the Thanksgiving seasons. If there is only one, perhaps Easter would be preferable. These services should be the high points in every church calendar and should be closed with a love feast. When I say high point, I mean an effort to reach each time a new high standard to live up to and carry through the year. . . .
>
> The time was when as a church we disbelieved in revivals. Then we swung to the other extreme, where in practice at least, we believed in nothing but evangelism of the special revival type. We have become so saturated with the latter idea that neither the home ministry nor the laity has sufficient self-confidence when it

comes to evangelism. On one occasion it was being noised about that a special series of meetings was to begin in our church. The writer was met by a member who had been taken into the church at a revival, and who had seldom darkened the door of the church afterward. This brother inquired who was to conduct the revival meetings, and there was quite a noticeable falling of his countenance when I told him that I was going to do the preaching myself. This represents an all too frequent feeling about home evangelism. In the face of a consciousness of such a feeling it takes a rather unusual amount of courage for a pastor to urge his services for evangelism at home.

If any one who reads these lines is in doubt as to the comparative value of the two methods of evangelism you only need to look up the two methods and compare the results. Why not catch a vision of the real opportunity of every church being its own evangelist, take courage, have faith in yourself and your pastor, put on a program, and start a campaign? Let's go![36]

Leander Smith, a full-time pastor who served western congregations, frankly described the difficult situation that visiting revivalists created for local professionalized clergy, but he added that if revivals relied on congregational leadership, the bond between the professional shepherd and the flock would strengthen.

I hope that my position, with reference to evangelists and their work, will not be misunderstood. As to the office of the evangelist, it is as scriptural as that of pastor. There is no ground for controversy on this question, and we are glad that this is true, because of our appreciation of the work of the evangelist. We confess, however, that we are somewhat at variance with the views of some brethren as to his field of operation. We believe his efforts should be devoted, in the main, to weak churches and places of real destitution. Pastors and churches, holding their own meetings, enjoy special blessings which can not be received in any other way. . . .

The church and the pastor conducting their own revival meeting will greatly strengthen the tie between them. It will make the church believe in and love the pastor as nothing else will, and it will cause the pastor to love and appreciate his church more than anything else. A sure cure of the desire for a new pastor is for him to make preparation to hold a series of meetings with his church.

It will cure him of restlessness and make him feel that he has the best church in the Brotherhood. Many pastors have been forced to hunt a new field as a result of having some one else to do the preaching in a series of meetings. If a visiting minister does the preaching, the pastor will find it hard to maintain the interest created; and if he fails, both he and the church will feel that his work is done and that a change of field and pastor is a necessity.

The pastor and the church holding their own meeting will result in the best type of church members. There is less liability to get unconverted people into the church than is the case when questionable or high pressure methods are engaged in. It is perfectly natural for people to love their spiritual fathers as they love no one else. It is easy for a pastor and church to develop new converts of their own making, but if they are led to Christ by the visiting minister, he takes their hearts with him when he leaves, and they do not love the pastor as fondly as they would, had they been led to Christ by him. As a rule, when people are converted under the preaching of a visiting minister, they will feel, all through their Christian lives, that the only way to reach the unsaved is to have an evangelist or a neighboring pastor do the preaching in the meeting. They seldom have the same confidence in the soul-winning power of the church and the pastor as those who are saved during a meeting in which the pastor does his own preaching. . . .

In view of these considerations, it is best for the church and its pastor to hold their own meetings. . . . It is also our decided opinion that the office of evangelist is most effective in the interest of the kingdom when it is devoted to the weak churches and to places of real destitution. It will pay any church manifold to give unstinted moral and financial support to gifted evangelists to work in these virgin fields.[37]

Not surprisingly, the rift between revivalists and ministers came to the floor of Annual Conference. A query from a congregation in Indiana asserted that some revivalists did not preach the "established order of the church," i.e., sound Brethren doctrine. Of course, Brethren lacked consensus on the "established order," especially after the 1911 dress decision, but the Indiana query implied that revivalists undermined whatever version of Brethrenism the local ministers, both free and salaried, taught.

Inasmuch as the teaching of certain of the evangelists of the Church of the Brethren is such as to set aside New Testament teachings and the established order of the church, thus causing disorder and dissatisfaction in the churches, we, the Auburn church, petition Annual Meeting, through District Meeting of Northern Indiana, to devise some plan by which the church can control and direct the work of our evangelists.[38]

Conference suggested more emphasis on year-round, local evangelism, including pastoral efforts.[39]

In the first place we recommend that less exclusive reliance be placed upon the special revival for bringing people into the church, and that greater dependence be placed (1) Upon the religious training of our children in the home; (2) Upon the organization of Religious Education; (3) Upon the personal and pastoral evangelism, and (4) Upon the wise and fuller organization of the entire membership of the church for bringing men to Christ.[40]

H. M. Moore, a member of the committee that wrote the report on visiting preachers, bluntly concluded that de-emphasis on revivalists would benefit the spiritual health of the Brethren.

The committee felt that we were placing too much dependence upon the evangelist and, therefore that it was difficult for us to see the way clear to ask anything special of him. We felt that it was true in the local congregations that dependence was placed upon him absolutely to get people into the church in some cases. To lessen that and let people realize their own responsibility would be the first step towards solving the problem as we have outlined. The task placed upon this committee was to devise some plan by which the church can control and direct the work of our evangelists. It was presumed that in some instances there has been need of control and direction.[41]

Consequently, the Conference authorized District Ministerial Boards to create lists of appropriately qualified revivalists and to require congregations not using the list to secure approval for their evangelist. Delegates also reserved for local leadership the all-important task of preparing new members.

Each District Ministerial Board shall prepare a list of available men of such qualifications, and furnish information and advice to local churches, seeking the services of an evangelist.

Local churches should exercise proper care and wisdom in choosing and cooperating with evangelists.

Let the official board or special committee: Either (1) select from the list approved and furnished by the District Ministerial Board, or (2) submit their own choice to the Ministerial Board for approval. This choice should then be submitted to the voice of the church. . . .

The elder in charge, or the pastor, in consultation with the elder, shall have charge of instruction of applicants for church membership.[42]

Still, many Brethren esteemed revivalists, and Annual Conference rejected several proposals to put them on an even shorter leash. The delegates refused to hold local leadership accountable for the behavior of evangelists or to require local ministers to review the methods planned by the revivalists. But with this tinkering accomplished, the measure passed by consensus, and the balance of power shifted a bit more toward professional pastors.[43]

Although professionalization of the ministry was gradual, the results, including scholarly sermons, innovative worship, the diminished role of elders, and regulation of revivalists, were profound. As a result, congregational life changed—also slowly, but no less dramatically.

WOMEN

Modifications in the role of women, like those in the ministry, touched the congregational level, but gender issues struck the denomination more quickly and more passionately. Although Annual Conference often disapproved of the changes in gender roles in the larger society, many Brethren sisters adopted their own version of the modern woman.

Like their response to most aspects of modernization, the Brethren response to gender issues followed trends in the secular world. Throughout the Roaring Twenties many American women overturned tradition and became more self-reliant. In 1920 women secured the right to vote; then, the feminist political movement fragmented into disarray, but women asserted themselves in other ways. More women than ever worked for wages, though usually employed at the bottom of the scale, and young, middle-class women embraced the "flapper" image. With short, bobbed hair, high hemlines, heavy cosmetics, and discarded petticoats, these fashionable women were confident, brash, and athletic. They smoked in public, played golf, and used and misused the scandalous vocabulary of Sigmund Freud. Gender questions directly touch everyone in society, and the new women were daily reminders, especially to conservatives, that American society had changed.[44]

Many Brethren disapproved of this new woman, especially her fashions. In 1920 an Annual Meeting resolution condemned the emerging styles.

> We endorse anew our position on the simple life in every activity, and protest against the increasingly immodest, unhealthy and uncomfortable fashions in dress.[45]

Oliver Austin, a well-known Brethren evangelist, linked the rise in divorce to the new women's apparel.

> Daily we hear and read about divorce and immorality and we are made to ask, "Why?" It seems that many women and girls of today are making the wrong appeal to men, and a man who marries a maiden only because of the sex appeal, will soon tire of her and be looking for another. This appeal may be made innocently or deliberately, but it is being made to the sacrifice of the higher qualities of true womanhood. The dressing and the conduct of many of our women and girls today are such that a man cannot see the beautiful in womanhood for the simple reason that the other is made so prominent.
>
> One can scarcely pick up a newspaper without seeing the picture of some practically nude girl or girls in some beauty contest. No one is going to be so narrow as to object to the beautiful form of woman, but is beauty the thing that the world is seeking today? Why is it that society offers prizes for the girl who will appear almost undressed but we seldom if ever see prizes offered for the girl who will appear sanely dressed?
>
> Everything from bathing contests to auto shows must have partially undressed girls connected with it. Surely this will not help the married man to be a better husband and father and will not strengthen the morals of our young people, neither will it lessen divorce and immorality. Considering these conditions, is it not just about time for Christians to call a halt, at least among their own ranks?[46]

The General Welfare Committee, created by Annual Conference to promote peace, simplicity, and morals, had similarly harsh language for fashionable women.

> Public life, instead of home-making; love of wealth and pleasure, instead of home and children; the brazen vamp,* instead of the modest home-loving mothers of days gone by, the painted, half-dressed creature in the barber's chair—yes, these are **all** a part in the descending scale of morals in our "declining womanhood," but they are no joke; for just ahead is the nation's **imperiled Christian home.**[47]

Despite these spirited denunciations of modern women, Brethren gender conventions quietly shifted. This continued a long-standing pattern of non-mainstream gender roles inside the Brethren fellowship. The Brethren had always been patriarchal. During communion, preachers and deacons gave the elements individually to the sisters although male members circulated them among each other. An 1857 Annual Meeting decision that denied sisters the privilege of breaking their own bread at communion began matter-of-factly with the phrase: "Man being the head of women . . ." Yet Brethren women enjoyed a standing within the fellowship that was largely unparalleled outside it. Adult women, for example, who elected baptism made a choice about their spiritual lives independent of their fathers and husbands. Women had responsibility for preparing love feast, a central event, and they served actively as deaconesses. Sisters occasionally spoke in council meetings, exhorted, and testified, and they participated in the selection of ministers. Although the path to female ordination was slow, during the ordination of men, wives stood with their husbands and were installed with them. In 1910, after several decades of debate, Annual Meeting allowed women to distribute the bread and cup among themselves during communion. Historically different gender roles contributed to Brethren separation from the mainstream, and twenties-era sisters built on this.[48]

---

* Vamp is short for vampire, a predatory woman who sucked the blood out of men as she pursued sexual interests. By the twenties "vamp" had become the customary usage, and it still referred to a sexually-aggressive woman but one who no longer sucked blood. Robert Sklar, *Movie-Made America: A Social History of American Movies* (New York: Random House, 1975), 92.

During the twenties the pace of change in gender roles quickened. Particularly noticeable was a new, short hairstyle, the bob, popular in mainstream culture and adopted by many young Brethren women. Modern women liked bobbed hair for several reasons. It required much less care than long Victorian tresses and allowed for more spontaneity and participation in sports. Bobbed hair was also practical for women who were spending increasingly long days on campus or at work. But besides its practicality, the bob was explicitly sexual. The customary long-hair-in-a-bun created a sedate, controlled look, but the bob was free-flowing. It was the first time that grown women, not girls, had displayed their hair like this. Bobbed women believed that their hairstyle made them exciting, but opponents associated this "badge of flapperhood," as one contemporary put it, with promiscuity and a self-conscious rejection of decency. Almost everyone recognized that the bob represented a changed role for women, and conservatives complained loudly that the fashionable style was widespread among Brethren females.[49]

> . . . the sin of bobbing the hair is becoming almost universal in our southern District.[50]

Conservatives urged the denomination to make bobbed hair a test of membership.

> If you were back in Philadelphia, or Washington, D. C., and you were a bright young woman and applied for a position that is honorable, you would find in the recommendations you must have long hair, and can we as a Church of the Brethren accept in church fellowship any person whom the world will not accept to an honorable position? I hold that membership in the church of Jesus Christ is . . . the most honorable position the world can give, and the church of Jesus Christ is a kingdom separate from the world. I come here to say that we can come to an understanding that some of those things cannot be allowed, and [we should] say that by taking the substitute motion we cannot accept you as a member of the church because you have bobbed hair.[51]

Slick men and bobbed coeds among the sophomore class in Bridgewater College's 1927 yearbook. *Photo courtesy of Alexander Mack Library, Bridgewater College, Bridgewater, Virginia.*

In 1922 more formal change came to Brethren gender roles when the denomination began licensing female preachers. This allowed women to preach but not perform other duties associated with the ministry. Opponents, such as B. E. Kesler, leader of a conservative movement that would shortly bring schism (see chapter 5), cited scripture and New Testament practice.

> The Bible I read has been perverted. I would like to have the privilege of reading the Scriptures and reading from my Book. Romans 16:1: "I commend to you Phebe, our sister, who is a servant of the church that is at Cenchrea." That has been read *deaconesses.* It doesn't read that way in my Bible, and I must stand by my Bible, against all the opposition that may be brought. Philippians 4:3 was also read, and it doesn't read in my Bible like the reading that was given on the stand. I would like to look up your Bibles and see if yours read that way. . . .
>
>   Elder, apostle, minister, pastor, preacher are masculine terms used in the Bible, and used only in that sense, indicated by nouns and pronouns that refer to them. In First Corinthians we have those set in the church; in Ephesians 4:11, also Paul says they were set there for the work of the ministry. First Corinthians 12:28, "And

God hath set some in the church, first apostles, secondarily prophets, thirdly teachers, after that miracles," and so on. Then over in Ephesians 4:11, "He gave some to be apostles; and some, prophets; and some, evangelists; and some, pastors and teachers; for the perfecting of the saints, for the work of the ministry, for the edifying of the body of Christ." In the Bible, for persons who functioned in the ministry, are terms that indicate males. Where in all the New Testament was a woman licensed to serve in any of these relations: To license we are told does not exactly signify an official position. If it doesn't I don't see how one could be placed in a position; but anyhow, a licentiate may teach and not be a preacher. Licentiates must be males, because if a licentiate preaches, that licentiate is called a preacher, and preacher is a term that indicates males in the Bible, and in no way females.[52]

Supporters of women preachers countered that licensing them merely recognized current practice across the denomination.

As we now have it, we have sisters who are already preachers by permission, and they are not yet licensed. Now, if it is right for them to preach by permission, what is wrong with licensing them to preach, showing that the church is back of them? . . . We have sisters that I know of, and some of our good elders know of, that can preach better than lots of us ministers, and I think to take this away from them would be a step in the wrong direction.[53]

Wilbur B. Stover drew upon his experiences in India to add that women preachers were invaluable in the mission field.

I read over in Romans 16:1, "Let me introduce our sister Phebe, a deaconess of the church at Cenchrea," and down in the third verse, "Salute Priscilla and Aquila, my fellow-workers in Christ Jesus, who have risked their lives for me." As I think of these fellow-workers who had risked their lives for Paul and for Christ in the service of Christ, I think of our fellow-workers in India, women, our sisters, preachers, teachers, just as much as I am a preacher, just as much as I am a teacher, some of them better. It seems out of the question that any of us could raise a question as to their right to preach and teach and be sanctioned as preachers in our church.[54]

With some opposition but by more than a two-thirds majority (389-149), delegates approved women preachers. (Twelve of the thirteen speakers in the floor debate were male.) Female licentiates, unlike their male counterparts, could receive a permanent license, but they would never be ordained as full ministers. (For men, licenses were temporary until ordination.)

> We also decide that sisters, who are properly qualified, may be licensed by the church to preach. These licenses may be renewed from year to year. When, in the judgment of the church and the District Ministerial Board, their work and interest justify it, they may receive permanent licenses to preach.[55]

In addition to bobbed hair and licensed preaching, abandonment of prayer veils also contributed to the new Brethren woman. The sisters had always covered their heads during worship. In the nineteenth century they wore a simple black bonnet with a brim and drawstring tied under the chin. In the early twentieth century, the covering for women evolved into a brimless, circular, white mesh cap without drawstrings, known as a prayer covering or prayer veil because women wore them only for worship. Females with bonnets or hats exchanged them for prayer coverings in the vestibule before entering for worship.[56] Now, in the twenties, many Brethren women stopped wearing the prayer veil altogether, as noted by a query to the gathering.

> Whereas, the long-time-honored practice of sisters wearing the prayer veil is being greatly neglected over the general Brotherhood, and
> Whereas, many brethren and sisters no longer believe in Paul's teaching along this line [57]

Annual Conference created a study committee made up of two men and a woman, Bertha Neher, who was a licensed preacher.[58] The committee's report, which Conference passed, affirmed the traditional position on prayer veils and refused to give flexibility to local congregations to interpret the decision as they saw fit, but it stopped short of making the coverings a test of membership. The statement, nevertheless, left little doubt that patriarchy and prayer veils went together.

Paul [I Cor. 11:3-16] lays down a divine order of headship as a basis of his argument—God as the Head of Christ, Christ the Head of man, and man the head of woman (v. 3). Both men and women are instructed on this matter; therefore he says, "Every man praying or prophesying, having his head covered, dishonoreth his head [Christ]" (v. 4). And on the other hand, "Every woman praying or prophesying with her head uncovered dishonoreth her head—[man]" (v. 5a). . . .

He finally states that naturally a man's short hair and a woman's long hair suggest the appropriateness of man's praying with an uncovered head and a woman's worshiping with an artificial covering on her head (vs. 13-15). . . .

We therefore conclude that Paul's arguments on this subject, instead of being local in their application, are general and apply to the churches throughout all Christendom.[59]

Predictably, Conference's decision resulted in little change, and many continued to worship without a prayer veil. One sister, who still wore the covering, described the confusion and contradictions that she believed these circumstances generated.

"An honest confession is good for the soul," we have heard these many years; hence I think we as sisters of our beloved church would understand each other more fully, and feel better, if we make the confession that we do not understand as we should the interpretation of the prayer veil as taught in I Cor. 11:3-16. Now why do I say we do not understand? Because of our attitude toward the wearing of the prayer veil. Sometimes when the subject is approached, we are thought of as radical, as extremists, perhaps, and are afraid to voice our conviction. I wonder if that is Satan's means of approach?

. . . It has long been a question, dear sisters, why we should have Committees, and why have questions discussed at District and Annual Meetings if we are not going to be governed by the decisions of the same. There are parts of our Brotherhood where we observe this teaching of our church and Paul's teaching, while in other congregations and localities, we have very few who observe it. Isn't that the reason for the Committee's conclusion—or have I misinterpreted? Now I am not writing for an explanation of the teaching of our church. We know that, but I should like to know as a mother what we should try to teach at this point to our children, to the one who is seeking church relationship, to the one who is desirous of knowing our reasons for our church doctrine.

We, as sisters, obey the other decisions as to our belief; but when it comes to our head dress we are divided on the subject. "In union there is strength." Might that apply to our power as a body of intelligent women if we were a little more united at this point?

What shall the Sunday-school teacher stand before her class and teach on this subject if her hat takes the place of the prayer veil? Shall I, as a mother, teach my little daughters that their teacher is disobedient to her church? Is that the way to help create more interest in your child for its church?

. . . If I wear a bonnet am I helping or hindering the progress of the church? Is the belief in such too "old timey" for the modern age? If my husband is a minister, am I hurting the ministerial cause by still holding to our church teaching on this point? Sometimes, sisters, we joke about these differences of opinion when I believe we should be considering them seriously. It isn't a laughable matter if we are handicapping or retarding the work of the church. . . .

Can you explain to your daughter, mother, why you wear a prayer veil at the communion table and never again till the next communion you attend? The same reasoning holds true with some of our brethren. Can your daughter understand why she must wear a bonnet and veil against her will, perhaps, while you buy chewing tobacco by the box? Conference has given our brethren permission to wear ties, permission to look in appearance as any business man, and a number of privileges we have and take from a church standpoint that were not granted years ago. Can we wonder that our young sisters can not understand our point of view as a church, relative to their head dress?[60]

Thus, the character of Brethren sisterhood was altered. As progressive Brethren women cut their hair, preached, and discarded the prayer veil, they demonstrated that social change of the most basic kind had come to Brethrenism. These women were not short-skirted, cigarette-smoking, Freud-quoting flappers; instead, they remained evangelicals rather than fashionable rebels, and little historical record exists of the new Brethren womanhood except their actions. Just as in the larger society, conservatives only slowly accepted the modification of gender roles and often complained helplessly about a trend they could not halt.

"O HAPPY DAY"

During the twenties the Brethren were no less susceptible to change than other Americans. In progressive congregations particularly, the gradual but unrelenting transition from the free ministry to salaried professionals gathered force, and women demonstrated independence. Both trends illustrate the power of modernization to alter the Brethren.

Yet the appeal of traditional religion, including mission, endured perhaps because it represented stability and reassurance in an age of change. In 1928 the Brethren ended Annual Conference by singing "O Happy Day,"[61] a text dating from the early eighteenth century with a simple message of cleansed sin, set to the tune of "How Dry I Am."

> O happy day that fixed my choice
> On Thee, my Savior and my God!
> Well may this glowing heart rejoice,
> And tell its raptures all abroad.
>
> *(refrain)*
> Happy day, happy day,
> When Jesus washed my sins away!
> He taught me how to watch and pray,
> And live rejoicing ev'ry day;
> Happy day, happy day,
> When Jesus washed my sins away![62]

In the Age of Jazz, that old-time religion still felt good.

NOTES

1. Beth L. Bailey, *From Front Porch to Back Seat: Courtship in Twentieth-Century America* (Baltimore, Md.: The Johns Hopkins University Press, 1988), 19-24; Paula S. Fass, *The Damned and the Beautiful: American Youth in the 1920s* (New York: Oxford University Press, 1977), 5-8; John Higham, *Strangers in the Land: Patterns of American Nativism, 1860-1925,* 2nd ed. (New Brunswick, N. J.: Rutgers University Press, 1988; originally published 1955), 267, 308; Maury Klein, *Rainbow's End: The Crash of 1929* (New York: Oxford University Press, 2001), xvii-x, 1-18, 101-20; Nancy MacLean, *Behind the Mask of Chivalry: The Making of the Second Ku Klux Klan* (New York: Oxford University Press, 1994), 23-5; George Donelson Moss, *America in the Twentieth Century,* 4th ed. (Upper Saddle River, N. J.: Prentice-Hall, Inc., 2000), 117-53.

2. *Pastor's Manual: Suggestions, Outlines, Forms, Scripture Selections, Prayers, and Hymns for Conducting Religious Services of Various Kinds* (Elgin, Ill.: Brethren Publishing House, 1923), 235-37.

3. Donald Fitzkee interview with Luke Bachman (n.d.); Author interviews with Mary Greenawalt (November 2002), Earl Heckman (June 12, 2002), Monroe Good (May 20, 2004), Urban Long and Alma Moyers Long (June 17, 2002), Dorothy and Ray Summy (May 20, 2004), Stanley Wampler (May 2004), and Naomi West (July 2004).

4. Aubrey R. Coffman, "The Forward Movement at Bridgewater, Virginia," *The Gospel Messenger* (November 22, 1919): 743

5. Jerome E. Blough [Johnstown, Pa., Feb. 3, 1921], "The West Johnstown, Pa., Revival and Evangelistic Campaign," *The Gospel Messenger* (February 19, 1921): 124.

6. "The Goshen, Ind., Revival," *The Gospel Messenger* (December 12, 1925): 794.

7. *Yearbook of the Church of the Brethren, 1921* (Elgin, Ill.: Brethren Publishing House, 1921), 90.

8. *Yearbook, 1921,* 91. See also *The Gospel Messenger* (April 5, 1919): 223; (January 13, 1923): 31; (January 17, 1925): 47; William G. McLoughlin, Jr., *Modern Revivalism: Charles Grandison Finney to Billy Graham* (New York: The Ronald Press Company, 1959), 366-77.

9. Author interview with Mary Greenawalt.

10. Isaac J. Rosenberger, "Sermon XXV: The New Birth," *Practical Sermons for Bible Students and Social Reading* (Elgin, Ill.: Brethren Publishing House, 1922), 271-81.

11. "Bethany Brethren Hospital," *The Brethren Encyclopedia,* 3 vols., edited by Donald F. Durnbaugh (Philadelphia, Pa., and Oak Brook, Ill.: The Brethren Encyclopedia, Inc., 1983), I:123.

12. *Full Report of the Proceedings of the Annual Conference of the Church of the Brethren, 1922* (Elgin, Ill.: Brethren Publishing House, 1922), 108.

13. "Bethany Brethren Hospital," *The Brethren Encyclopedia,* I:123.
14. Donald F. Durnbaugh, *Fruit of the Vine: A History of the Brethren, 1708-1995* (Elgin, Ill.: Brethren Press, 1997), 363-64.
15. Mrs. H. L. [Marguerite Schrock] Burke, "Africa Notes for June," *The Missionary Visitor* (October, 1924): 370.
16. Durnbaugh, *Fruit of the Vine,* 364-65.
17. Lola Helser, "Africa Mission Notes for May," *The Missionary Visitor* (October, 1924): 369.
18. Helser, "Africa Mission Notes for May," 369-70.
19. Ellen H. Wagoner, "January Notes from India," *The Missionary Visitor* (May, 1923): 140-41.
20. Anna Brumbaugh, "An Interesting Day," *The Missionary Visitor* (August, 1922): 307.
21. Enoch Howe Eby, "Is Christ Able?" *The Missionary Visitor* (May, 1923): 139.
22. Anna V. Blough, "Sketches from Anna V. Blough's Diary," selected by Anna Crumpacker, *The Missionary Visitor* (September, 1922): 342. See also Minerva Metzger, "Anna V. Blough in Service," *The Missionary Visitor* (August, 1922): 311.
23. *Full Report, 1925,* 78.
24. Carl F. Bowman, *Brethren Society: The Cultural Transformation of a "Peculiar People"* (Baltimore, Md.: The Johns Hopkins University Press, 1995), 294-95, 308-10; Durnbaugh, *Fruit of the Vine,* 393-94.
25. Carl Bowman, *Brethren Society,* 304, 306.
26. *Pastor's Manual,* 65. Also quoted in Carl Bowman, *Brethren Society,* 304.
27. *Full Report, 1926,* 38.
28. *Pastor's Manual,* 122. Also quoted in Carl Bowman, *Brethren Society,* 304. See also 295-96.
29. Carl Bowman, *Brethren Society,* 310-11.
30. Worship bulletin (August 12, 1917), Wiley, Colorado, Church of the Brethren, Brethren Historical Library and Archives (BHLA), Elgin, Illinois. I am indebted to Ken Shaffer for locating this document.
31. Worship bulletin (December 16, 1928), First Church of the Brethren, Chicago, Illinois, BHLA. I am indebted to Ken Shaffer for locating this document.
32. Worship bulletin (May 15, 1932), Hagerstown, Maryland, Church of the Brethren, Brethren Heritage Center, Brookville, Ohio. I am indebted to Donald Bowman for locating this document.
33. Carl Bowman, *Brethren Society,* 295.
34. Rufus D. Bowman, "The New Loyalty" *The Gospel Messenger* (February 4, 1928): 66, 74.
35. C. B. Hershey, "The Herald of Gospel Liberty," *The Gospel Messenger* (May 1, 1926): 278.
36. Olin F. Shaw [Girard, Ill.], "The Pastor's Study: Home Evangelism," *The Gospel Messenger* (March 6, 1926): 150. See also "Olin F. Shaw," *The Brethren Encyclopedia,* III:1765.

37. Leander Smith [Muscatine, Iowa], "Advantages of Pastors and Churches Conducting Their Own Revival Meetings," *The Gospel Messenger* (January 22, 1916): 52. See also "Leander Smith," *The Brethren Encyclopedia*, II:1191.

38. *Full Report, 1919,* 118-19.

39. *Full Report, 1920,* 99-106.

40. *Full Report, 1921,* 45.

41. *Full Report, 1920,* 100.

42. *Full Report, 1921,* 45.

43. *Full Report, 1920,* 99-106; *Full Report, 1921,* 44-48.

44. Ellen Carol DuBois, *Harriet Stanton Blatch and the Winning of Woman Suffrage* (New Haven, Conn.: Yale University Press, 1997), 214-39; Lynn Dumenil, *The Modern Temper: American Culture and Society in the 1920s* (New York: Hill and Wang, 1995), 98-144; Fass, *The Damned and the Beautiful,* 22-25, 179-86, 292-300, 307-10, 332; MacLean, *Behind the Mask of Chivalry,* 31-32; Thomas C. Reeves, *Twentieth-Century America: A Brief History* (New York: Oxford University Press, 2000), 86.

45. "Resolutions," *Full Report,1920,* 238.

46. Oliver H. Austin, "Observations," *The Gospel Messenger* (August 25, 1928): 536.

47. "General Welfare Department," *Yearbook of the Church of the Brethren, 1926,* 39.

48. Pamela Brubaker, *She Hath Done What She Could: A History of Women's Participation in the Church of the Brethren* (Elgin, Ill.: Brethren Press, 1985), 45-60; Durnbaugh, *Fruit of the Vine,* 377-83; *Minutes of the Annual Meetings of the Church of the Brethren, 1778-1909* (Elgin, Ill.: Brethren Publishing House, 1909), 163; Stephen L. Longenecker, *Shenandoah Religion: Outsiders and the Mainstream, 1716-1865* (Waco, Tex.: Baylor University Press, 2002), 39; "Women," *The Brethren Encyclopedia*, II:1360-62.

49. Dumenil, *The Modern Temper,* 135; Fass, *The Damned and the Beautiful,* 20-21, 280-81.

50. *Full Report, 1926,* Phares Forney speaking, 122.

51. *Full Report, 1926,* Phares Forney speaking, 125-26.

52. *Full Report, 1922,* 106-7.

53. *Full Report, 1922,* William E. Baker speaking, 98.

54. *Full Report, 1922,* W. B. Stover speaking, 105-06.

55. *Full Report, 1922,* Report of the committee, 92. See also 91-107.

56. "Caps," *The Brethren Encyclopedia*, I:254; "Prayer Veil," II:1053; *Minutes of the Annual Meetings 1778 to 1909,* 98, 208, 339, 399-400, 582.

57. *Full Report, 1926,* 57-58.

58. "Bertha Miller Neher Stine," *The Brethren Encyclopedia*, II:1223.

59. *Full Report, 1926,* 57-58.

60. Margie John Garst [Salem, Va.], "What Should Be Our Attitude As Sisters of the Church of the Brethren?" *The Gospel Messenger* (May 15, 1926): 307.

61. *Full Report, 1928,* 138.

62. Philip Doddridge, "O Happy Day That Fixed My Choice," No. 454 in *Hymnal: Church of the Brethren* (Elgin, Ill.: Brethren Publishing House, 1925). Doddridge was a Baptist.

IV. THE TWENTIES
Conflict

During the twenties many Americans disapproved of the shifting social landscape, and conflict frequently occurred between those who contributed to modernization and those who disdained it. Indeed, opponents of social change enjoyed substantial popularity. The elections to the White House of three bland conservatives, Harding, Coolidge, and Hoover, stemmed from the public's desire for low-key politics in an era of uncertainty. Approximately four million white men joined the Ku Klux Klan, which gave life to the distress felt by small-town and rural white patriarchs about gender, diversity, ethnicity, and class as well as race. With quota legislation passed by Congress, nativists closed the door on immigrants. Temperance men and women defended Prohibition from widespread criticism and flagrant violations. Anti-union sentiment suppressed organized labor and crushed its radical wing. Even baseball hired a conservative judge to solve its labor problems after the Chicago White Sox, forever after nicknamed the Black Sox, conspired with gamblers to fix the 1919 World Series. Those who disliked the prevailing pitch of American society in the Jazz Age composed a very discordant countermelody. William Jennings Bryan, Warren Harding, Calvin Coolidge, Imperial Wizards, and Judge Kennesaw Mountain Landis personified this conservative era.[1]

Most Brethren hoped to tone down the Jazz Age, and some wanted to shut it down entirely. Like generations of Alexander Mack's followers before them, twenties-era Brethren bemoaned the sinfulness of worldly society and censured specific behaviors associated with popular culture.

But some Brethren added a new twist to separation from the world and joined fundamentalism in a more sweeping condemnation of modernity.

Popular Culture

Much about fashionable America during the twenties offended Brethren across the ideological spectrum. They particularly rejected the music that gave the era its moniker and the subculture most closely associated with it. Jazz and the youth cult did not play well with the Brethren, and in 1924 *The Gospel Messenger* gloated, prematurely to be sure, over the demise of jazz and the return to "good music" and "more sober values."

> The so-called "jazz age" is passing according to a referendum of 54,000 fans recently analyzed by the radio officials of the American Telephone and Telegraph Company. Two years ago letters from radio fans indicated an overwhelming desire for jazz music from broadcasting stations; but the January 1925 poll shows that only five percent prefer jazz while a greatly increased percentage desire good music. "Concert and standard numbers, philharmonic concerts and the like, are steadily growing in popularity." And thus history repeats herself. When the pendulum swings far in the direction of the light, inconsequential stuff, there is bound to follow a day of disillusionment when the pendulum swings back to more sober values.[2]

Jazz was perhaps the most conspicuous aspect of a larger culture of youth that during the twenties appeared suddenly and became a national obsession. America's first subculture of the young emerged from several consequences of modernization, especially growth in education and changes in the role of the family. Pre-industrial families had interceded between the individual and society by introducing children to the workplace, community, and church, but, with industrialization, family life withdrew from an increasingly rational, impersonal, competitive society and became an affectionate and nurturing refuge. Schools and peers replaced families as institutions that eased the entrance of children into the world of adults. Between 1900 and 1930 attendance at high schools increased by 650 percent and at colleges and universities by 300 percent with the largest expansion during the twenties. Middle-class young people delayed marriage and prolonged schooling to prepare for the modern economy and to protect their prosperity. Quite simply, because of schools young people spent more time together, thereby enhancing the peer group. Moreover, education was increasingly organized by age, which also stimulated peer development. By the twenties, then, modern trends in education and family life gave young people enough time by themselves to create their own subculture, complete with music, clothing, fads, values, and vocabulary.[3]

The new culture of youth exasperated many Brethren. Historians invented the term "youth cult"; consequently, it does not appear in contemporary Brethren sources. But when Brethren criticized jazz and popular amusements or worried about their own young people, they articulated their apprehension about this new phenomenon.

> In a world that is vocal with the strange music of jazz and fashion, we must maintain the integrity of the home.[4]

> Of course, we all know something is wrong, very much wrong. We are hearing that on every hand, and from leaders in every sphere of activity. Judges, law enforcement officers, reform associations and newspaper writers are pointing out that youth is on a rampage and crime on the increase. They tell us that parents have lost control of their children; that youth in revolting against parental rule, has set itself against all law; that crime is growing at an astonishing rate, especially among the young, not only in America but throughout the world; that 80 percent of all murders and burglaries of the last quarter of a century have been committed by boys and girls under 25 years of age; that 75 percent of the persons now in jail are under 25.[5]

Concern for youth contributed to the advancement of the Brethren camping movement during this period. Religious campsites had a long history that included Scots-Irish communion seasons, eighteenth-century awakenings, nineteenth-century camp meetings, and the Chautauqua movement, but in the late Victorian period, a back-to-nature impulse swept America. As society became increasingly urbanized, reformers rediscovered the virtues of the great outdoors, and religious educators promoted raw nature as the ideal place to learn about God. "In the rustling grass I hear Him pass," proclaimed Maltbie D. Babcock, the author of "This Is My Father's World."[6] Likewise, Henry Van Dyke's "Joyful, Joyful, We Adore Thee" found spiritual insights in the natural world.

Field and forest, vale and mountain,
Blooming meadow, flashing sea,
Chanting bird and flowing fountain,
Call us to rejoice in Thee.[7]

Reformers particularly thought that the outdoors held special benefits for children and youth, and summer camps quickly emerged in the
field and forest. By 1915 they were commonplace. Camps reconnected
children with America's outdoor heritage, which supposedly built character, but rather than woodcraft they increasingly emphasized athletic skills
and socialization that prepared young people for adulthood. Educators
liked the controlled atmosphere of summer camps and considered them
an ideal counterattack on the moral degeneration of summertime.[8]

The Brethren began their trek back to nature in the 1890s with meetings for youth in the Colorado mountains and in the late teens and early
twenties with organized youth conferences and summer assemblies. In the
twenties several districts purchased sites for these conferences. The earliest
were Camp Harmony in western Pennsylvania (1923), Camp La Verne in
southern California (1924), and Camp Alexander Mack in northern Indiana
(1925).[9] In the next decade Brethren camping became widespread.

Chauncey Shamberger (left) and friends traveled "field and forest, vale and
mountain" to promote Brethren camping. *Photo courtesy of BHLA.*

The dedication of one of the first Brethren camps, Camp Bethel
(1927), near Roanoke, Virginia, touched many themes that typically

inspired campers. More than one thousand listened to orations by Chauncey H. Shamberger, the first denominational youth director and the organizer of Brethren camping,[10] and Paul H. Bowman, president of Bridgewater College. Bowman's dedicatory address cited the singular spiritual benefits of unspoiled nature, and although the camp was not for youth exclusively, he predicted that "confused and tempted" young people would find "refuge" in the "mountain recesses of the Blue Ridge." Quite clearly, Camp Bethel's founders intended it as an antidote to the youth cult.

> A great many years ago a young man at the end of a perilous day's journey pillowed his head on a ledge of rock on the mountain side for a night of rest. He fixed his eyes on the distant stars and fell asleep. In that sleep he dreamed a marvelous dream. A ladder rested with its foot upon the earth and extended away into the heavens. On the ladder angel messengers ascended and descended bearing from God a message of assurance and hope. When the young man awaked from his slumber, he realized that his dream was a vision of unusual significance. He said: "Surely Jehovah is in this place and I knew it not. This is not other than the house of God and the gate of heaven." He built there an altar and named the place Bethel and entered into a solemn covenant with his Lord. Since the consecration of that rudely constructed altar on the mountain side, the name "Bethel" has symbolized in Christian thought one of our most vital and sacred religious experiences.
>
> In the summer of 1925 a still larger group of young people came and the spirit of devotion to God and consecration of life to his cause had seemingly multiplied many-fold in the hearts of those who came. In the summer of 1926 the group was enlarged to include ministers, teachers and officers of our churches and Sunday-schools. Like Jacob of old they all said: "God is in this place." In the light of those experiences the perpetuation of these conferences was as inevitable as were the recurring visits of Jacob and his descendants to the altar at Bethel. This young people's movement gained such momentum that a permanent place for these conferences was also inevitable. It is therefore fitting that this permanent camp site should be called "Bethel," and that we who have gathered here should devote ourselves to the task of making this a veritable meeting place between God and the souls of our young people and our church leaders. . . .

The changing conditions of life have required all religious bodies to develop new methods and new resources. Camp Bethel is not merely a name for a few rudely constructed cabins in the mountain recesses of the Blue Ridge, but is rather a symbol of a new vision and a new spirit in the hearts of our people. We now regard our youth as an undeveloped human resource which by nurture and guidance may be transformed into a great spiritual force for the moral enrichment of the world. The seclusion and informality of camp life we regard merely as a new method of accomplishing some of the things, which our fathers realized in other ways.

Therefore, in gratitude to Almighty God for his leadership in the development of the church and for his glorious handiwork which enriches this very spot, and in solemn acknowledgment of our obligation to our forefathers for the spiritual heritage which they have wrought out for us, we here and now dedicate this camp, which includes sixty acres of land, with beautiful hills and groves, gushing springs, and rippling streams; and its rustic cabins which have been and shall hereafter be erected, to the glory and honor of God, and to the enrichment of the life of his honor of God, and to the enrichment of the life of his children through a fuller knowledge of his will as revealed in nature and in his Holy Word.

Let this camp stand as a city of refuge to the youth of the church when confused and tempted; as a retreat for tired ministers, pastors, and professors, where they may find inspiration and an opportunity for communion with God; and as a beacon light to the religious teachers of our children where they may learn more of God, his holy will, and of the nature of his children.

Let this camp stand, not as a place for holiday trips and annual outings, but as holy ground where only such gatherings are held as are associated with the church and religion. Let this camp stand as a refuge where even wild life in all its forms may have every reasonable protection and may grow and develop unafraid in God's great out-of-doors. Let this camp stand for all that is good, true, and beautiful in human life and human relationships.[11]

Popular opposition to Prohibition, like jazz and the youth cult, disturbed progressive and conservative Brethren alike. The denomination had a long history of temperance advocacy. Throughout the nineteenth century, Brethren had remained aloof from the movement but consistently endorsed its principles. The denomination's refusal to approve participation in temperance organizations disheartened progressives, but conservatives objected to employing the power of the government—the sword—to legislate religion. But in 1908 progressives eased the Brethren into the dry campaign when Annual Conference created a Temperance Committee authorized to assist the "Brotherhood in defending their homes against the invasion of this evil."[12]

In 1919 Brethren and other temperance advocates hit a home run when the Eighteenth Amendment to the Constitution made the manufacture and sale of alcohol illegal. This monumental victory, however, settled little. Critics charged that Prohibition violated civil liberties, was unenforceable, and promoted crime, including gangsters. Popular circumvention of the law spawned a subculture of evasion with its own terminology: hip flasks, speakeasies, and bootleggers. The apparent breakdown in law and order impressed traditionalists as yet another example of the general decline of American society, making the temperance campaign part of the struggle over modernity and a conservative magnet. But as a basic stand against immorality and vice, anti-repeal also attracted moderates and progressives and, thus, appealed to almost all Protestants.[13]

Twenties-era Brethren, then, still harbored much passion for this century-old cause. A letter to *The Gospel Messenger*, for example, vigorously defended Prohibition from criticism that it created crime.

> No, indeed, prohibition has not increased crime—not even in New York and Chicago. . . .
>
> Cities, large and small, show encouraging decreases in the number of crimes committed. Clippings could be multiplied by the score to prove these assertions. From coast to coast cities and counties have closed their jails for lack of patronage—after the advent of prohibition.
>
> No, prohibition has not eliminated evil from the human make-up, but it has gone a long way toward curbing its worst expressions. And, better yet, prohibition has given many an unfortunate victim of the drink habit another chance—a chance to be the kind of man he aspired to be—the kind of man he never could be while surrounded by the temptations of the saloon.[14]

Anti-repeal expressions from Annual Meetings were commonplace. In 1924, for example, delegates resolved that

we assert our faith in the eighteenth amendment to the
Constitution of the United States as a providential blessing to our
country, and protest against all efforts to modify by revision or
interpretation either the Prohibition Amendment or the Volstead
Act* in any way to defeat the original purpose of the American
people; we commit ourselves in favor of law enforcement and
urge our Welfare Board so to organize the churches of the
Brotherhood as to conserve the traditional position of the
Brethren on the temperance question.[15]

In 1926 the General Welfare Committee proclaimed, "It is our duty
to do all we can to assist the forces of righteousness in upholding one of
the greatest reform movements ever enacted in the history of the world."[16]

Brethren temperance advocates distributed numerous pamphlets, including this one. *BHLA collection.*

Brethren on the congregational level similarly crusaded to keep
America dry. Many served as trustees for the Anti-Saloon League,[17] and
anti-repeal sentiments flowed freely from pulpits. A 1921 revival at West

---

*The United States Congress passed the Volstead Act to implement the Eighteenth
Amendment.

Johnstown, Pennsylvania, mingled affirmation of temperance and "denunciations of modern sins" with traditional components of the faith.

> Bro. [John Henry] Cassady preached thirty-six powerful Gospel sermons, giving us three meetings on Sundays. His messages for the first week or more, were to the membership, encouraging to fuller consecration, and a renunciation of worldly pleasure-seeking. His denunciations of modern sins were scathing. His afternoon meetings drew large crowds. His sermon on "Booze, Bootleggers and Boozers" was a powerful denunciation of law-breakers and a plea for all to support civic officials in carrying out the prohibition and anti-cigarette laws of the State. By a rising vote the entire audience pledged its support to this end. While denouncing the sins of the world and deploring the lukewarmness of many professors, he also dwelt strongly on the love of God, the steps into the Kingdom and the doctrines of the church. Faith, repentance, baptism, feet-washing, the Lord's supper, the communion, the anointing, heaven, hell, the second coming, the unpardonable sin, the judgment, the atonement, etc., all received due attention.[18]

Alcohol also contributed to the Brethren standoffishness toward Catholic Americans, especially during the 1928 presidential election when Democrats nominated Al Smith, a Catholic. Smith's candidacy opened another theater in the culture wars of the twenties, suggesting that many Protestants were uncomfortable with a more diverse America. Radicals flooded the nation with intolerant literature that accused Catholics of crude immorality and sinister disloyalty, but Protestant denominational spokespersons generally avoided Smith's religion and instead declared that the election was about drink. Smith, like most Catholics, was an avowed opponent of Prohibition, and this gave Protestants an opportunity to oppose his candidacy without overtly criticizing his faith.[19] One dry Brethren took this high road in an article titled "Shall We Vote as We Pray?"

> The presidential election emphatically presents a referendum, as it were, upon the attitude of the country upon the Eighteenth Amendment and enforcement of prohibition laws. . . .
>   I have no patience with religious intolerance, nor with Protestant preachers who would embarrass the situation by trying to inject religious strife into the campaign. Personal religious choice

is too sacred a privilege to discuss very loudly under present circumstances. That privilege is vouchsafed by the very constitution
whose eighteenth amendment we seek to defend. But prohibition
involves a government policy toward a gigantic economical, social
and moral problem, affecting our whole nation—and the world.
We shall not permit the evacuation of the ground we have won!
    Vote as you will. The Lord permitting, I'll vote as I pray.[20]

As November approached, Smith's Protestant opponents discussed
his religion more frequently.[21] Although at one point *The Gospel
Messenger* refused to print contributions that emphasized the
Democratic nominee's Catholicism, eventually the editor, Edward
Frantz, claimed that he received so many letters that he felt compelled to
confront the issue. He repudiated the crudest aspects of anti-Catholicism
but nevertheless objected to a Catholic president.

THE GOSPEL MESSENGER has not encouraged the discussion in its
columns of issues in the present Presidential campaign, other than
the one in which the church has taken a definite stand. Some of
our contributors who have not had quite as much liberty as they
desired could testify to this. And now the editor himself is breaking
over the line, which he has set for others. That doesn't look very
consistent but in the light of certain developments a few remarks
on one phase of the subject may not be out of place.
    . . . We are in no mood therefore to oppose a man's candi-
dacy for the high office of President merely because his religion is
different from ours. Neither have we been able to get much excited over the stories that the pope will move his residence from
Rome to Washington if Smith is elected and Catholics in general
have their cellars full of guns ready to rise up and slaughter the rest
of us as soon as they get into power. . . . Our decision to vote
against him is made quite independently of the religious question.
Nevertheless, there are a few facts bearing on that question which
do interest us, and if the Catholic candidate would give them due
consideration he need not affect surprise at the widespread intolerance and prejudice of which he complains. . . .
    The biggest factor of course is the Catholic theory of the rela-
tion between church and state as voiced from time to time by popes
and other dignitaries. The church is not only superior to the state in
its own proper realm of the things of the Spirit, but in temporal and

secular matters also. All civil rulers of whatsoever rank and type are by right subject to the church and to its head, the pope. . . .

Added to this are two other facts of considerable significance. One is the antagonism of the Catholic church to our public school system, involving not only the refusal to patronize it but also, in the case of many authorities, the desire to destroy it. Another is the exceedingly intolerant attitude of this church toward all other churches. It absolutely refuses to meet with them in conference and for the most part refuses also to associate with them in worship or in any definite program of social welfare. Complaints of Protestant intolerance come with poor grace from a candidate whose church is itself the incarnation of intolerance.[22]

Still, in its editorial endorsing Herbert Hoover, the Republican nominee, *The Gospel Messenger* avoided religion and urged Dunkers to vote dry.

THE MESSENGER does not advise mixing in politics in the common sense of that term, as there is often nothing really involved but a scramble for the spoils of office. It does, however, advise and strongly urge a lively interest in everything affecting the moral welfare of the public. The country has just entered on a presidential campaign in which there is a clean cut moral issue at stake, an issue in which our people have taken a great interest. They have spoken with no uncertain sound on the question and have no intention of relinquishing their interest or well-established position.

One of the leading candidates is an avowed wet. His whole record is plainly and consistently on that side of the question, and though he professes to stand for enforcement of the law, as long as it is the law he thinks the law should be changed and has indicated his purpose to use his influence to have it changed. That his influence, if elected President, would be very great goes without saying. It is absurd to claim that he could do little in that office to help the wet cause. He could do much and undoubtedly would.

We can hardly believe that our own people need instruction or exhortation on the choice of candidates. Our imagination is unequal to the task of picturing a member of the Church of the Brethren in the act of casting his ballot for a man with the record of [New York] Governor Smith on the prohibition question. But a failure to realize the importance of an active interest in the matter is our chief danger. The only chance of the Governor's election is in a large stay-at-home vote. The MESSENGER will expect every man and woman of the Brethren connection to do their part in seeing to it that the wet cause meets the overwhelming defeat which it needs and deserves.[23]

For most Brethren, movies were just as shocking as jazz, the youth culture, alcohol, or a wet Catholic president. The fast-growing film industry became a lightning rod for traditionalists, drawing condemnation by combining spectacular technology with several controversial trends of modernization, including secularism, diversity, and the youth cult. Commercial movies first appeared in the 1900s with nickelodeons, so-called for their admission charge, but these attracted mostly working-class audiences. World War I removed European competitors from the market, and during the twenties the American film industry exploded in growth. In 1921 film attendance averaged approximately forty million per week, and by the end of the decade it doubled. By 1927, 20,500 theaters had been constructed, many of them in small towns, and film was the nation's fourth largest industry even though still a relatively new phenomenon, especially as a middle-class amusement.[24]

From the beginning, dream-makers flirted with the bounds of propriety. Thomas Edison's *What Demoralized the Barbershop* (1901), created for vaudeville and peep shows, portrays a woman who raises her skirt to reveal her calves and adjust her stockings. In *A Daughter of the Gods* (1916), a champion swimmer appears in the nude; and in Cecil B. DeMille's *Male and Female* (1919), Gloria Swanson steps into a sunken bath, briefly displaying naked breasts. Plots often pushed the edges of middle-class morality, allowing viewers to participate in the fantasy. In *Male and Female,* for example, a romance between a high-born woman and a butler had shock value. Often film titillated but left convention intact. A married woman might be tempted by a suave male, often a foreigner, but in the end the seducer gets what he deserves while the marriage is stronger and its partners wiser.[25]

In the Jazz Age, movie-made sin grew too much for traditionalists to bear. Middle-class Americans had never warmed to the Jewish immigrant predominance in this industry, and they noticed that it produced for the mass culture rather than employing its new technology to forge American cultural unity. Additionally, movies had a symbiotic relationship with the youth cult. Many college students saw a film once a week, and movies spread the subculture of youth across the nation. In fact, the twenties saw the birth of a genre of films set on a college campus.

Finally, moviemaking technology captured the imagination; in 1927 the first "talkie," *The Jazz Singer,* amazed audiences. This was a breathtaking new technology, heavily influenced by the foreign-born, appealing to lower rather than higher impulses, and tempting youth; thus, movies exuded modernity—technology, cultural diversity, and secular values—and unsurprisingly became a battleground in the culture wars of the twenties.[26]

Brethren were soldiers in this war. An editorial in *The Brethren Evangelist,* the periodical of The Brethren Church,* reprinted in *The Gospel Messenger*, illustrates the linkage many made between two evils: movies and the youth cult.

Perhaps some do not realize we have a movie peril. Practically everybody knows that we have some sort of a peril, that something is radically wrong with the moral life of our day, that its tone and temper are at a decidedly low ebb. But many do not seem to have related this condition with the movie in any very definite way.

. . . But few, however, have had the vision or the courage to point out the large and definite way in which the movie is responsible for this lamentable condition, and so very little effective public sentiment has been focused against it. This has been due largely to two facts: first, that too many people have become enamored with the motion picture; and second, that many have been deceived by the maneuvering of the movie trust to give the people the impression of its high purpose and respectability. Will H. Hays†with all his talk about cleaning up the movie, is but a smoke screen behind which this powerful law-breaking corporation has gone on making merchandise of the baser passions of men, at the same time "throttling good pictures, terrorizing the better elements of the industry and corrupting politics," as is affirmed by Dr. Wm. Sheafe Chase, general secretary of the Federal Motion Picture Council, which is now in conference in Chicago. . . .

It is on our children that the movie is getting in its worst influence. It is the teenaged folks who are being transformed into criminals, or if not so bad, into frivolous, insincere, irreverent, godless throngs, who avoid the church, and find no enjoyment in the higher

---

*A product of the schism of 1882. See Introduction of this book.

†Hays ran the Motion Picture Producers and Distributors Association, a trade organization created in 1919 that assumed public relations responsibilities and facilitated labor agreements. Sklar, *Movie-Made America,* 82-85.

and finer things of life. In view of this fact it is evident that the situation cannot be ignored. If we care for our children, if we care for our national welfare, if we care for the church and for our duty, we must do something to stop this steady stream of corrupting influence.[27]

Critics charged that movies attracted young Brethren moths to the dangerous candle of sin.

Our young people are going [to the movies]. You are aware of the fact that our young people in the various churches of the Brotherhood are going to these motion pictures right along, and we hesitate to let them go if there is any possibility of preventing it. But if they are going, we ought to try to help clean the motion picture business so that we may be able to prevent the wrong influence being brought to bear upon our children from time to time.[28]

———————

Some of you people do not know what a motion picture is like, perhaps. Some of you have been so afraid that you would find out something about it that you have never seen one. Perhaps you had better go and see what the young people are seeing, and then perhaps you will be interested in getting the right kind of films shown to the public.[29]

J. W. Lear, a theology professor at Bethany Theological Seminary, recognized that motion pictures were big business, and he spoke harshly of what they put on the screen.

The [movie] business as it is run today is highly commercialized. The motive behind the scenes, very largely (I would not say wholly), is monetary. The folks who manage the affair have an eye for business. Therefore, they put on the screen or the stage what appeals to the largest percentage of theater and show goers. And since the larger percentage of constant theater goers are the non-Christian people, it is not to be wondered at that the managers, who for the most part are following pagan business methods rather than Christian, would run the business for personal financial profit rather than for moral educational reasons.

Just here is the most appalling situation. It cannot be denied that Christian principles are not only very largely omitted from the display but very often Christian ideals are held up to ridicule. It is safe to say, I think, that the devout Christian will find very little, if anything, in the average "show" or "theater" which will enlarge his conception of Christian living or inspire him to greater faithfulness in living or inspire him to greater faithfulness in living the "Jesus way of life."

If one can judge anything from advertisements on billboard and the daily paper, or the echoes from the conversations of theater goers, one must be convinced that the tone and content of most of these plays are not conducive to holy living, and in many instances are suggestive of evil if not wholly vulgar. With such a content it is not hard to imagine the type of crowd which attends; and hence, the kind of human atmosphere to which the Christian exposes himself in attending these places. There are exceptions, to be sure, but the exception establishes the rule.

Then, too, it is safe to say that no holy and helpful principle or standard of life can be obtained in the very best of these commercialized places that could not be gotten in places far removed from the deadening atmosphere of the playhouse. Moreover the lines of Pope are apropos here:

> "Vice is a monster of so frightful mien,
> As to be hated needs but to be seen;
> Yet seem too oft, familiar with her face,
> We first endure, then pity, then embrace."

May I say further, that since the causes of Christian education and evangelism are so needful for this generation, and since the promotion of these causes is constantly being held up on account of a lack of funds and of consecrated life, the Christian can ill afford to spend time and money helping on a godless institution and thus be guilty of robbing the treasury of the Lord. May I say to one and all, think it through on your knees before throwing your influence on the side of this sordid, mercenary, pagan business when your Lord's work is lagging for want of loyal support.[30]

Numerous Protestants, including many Brethren, supported censorship of the films. In 1926 the Church of the Brethren sent five participants to a national conference on the influence of films on American society. One of the returning delegates identified problems generated by motion pictures and endorsed legislation enabling the government to suppress objectionable content in movies.

The motion picture industry is only thirty years old but for twenty-five years it has been designated as "a school of crime."

The total daily admissions to movie theaters of the United States average more than twenty million, and seventy-five percent of these are under twenty-four years of age. The average daily attendance at public schools is only ten million.

The movies now represent the fourth largest investment of capital among the industries. One great combination of producers now controls ninety-five percent of all the films exhibited in this country.

The movies constitute the most subtle, the most dynamic of all the forces that touch child life. In one brief hour he may live through the events and experience the emotions that normally belong to many years of a life.

Any thoughtful observer must conclude that the movies have a greater potential power for influencing character, habits, dress, morals and ideals of our youth than do the schools.

While a few good pictures are being produced, by far the larger number of those being exhibited in the theaters are "unwholesome, indecent, immoral, make crime attractive and hold up to ridicule and treat lightly the most sacred and intimate relations of life."

Federal Regulation the Remedy

The industry has made repeated promises to "clean up the movies," but has failed to keep a single promise. Although they employ Mr. Will Hays at a salary of $100,000 annually (some say $300,000) to lead in this campaign, his chief boast is that he and his lobbyists have defeated censorship bills introduced in thirty-three State legislatures, thus leaving movie magnates free to exploit our childhood and youth at will.

Eight state and numerous local censor boards have done effective work by cutting out certain scenes in the films they view, but they often advertise the very worst pictures and increase their patronage during the months that intervene before the courts render a decision favorable to the censor.

"Better Films" committees have grown weary of trying to select a few decent pictures from the mass of those produced. The conference went on record as favoring federal regulation which concerns itself with production rather than exhibition, for once a bad picture has been filmed at an expense of thousands or even millions of dollars, it is not easily suppressed.

Bills Now in Congress

Two bills now in Congress propose to entrust a board of five, or seven, reviewers with this task. They are the Upshaw Bill (No. 6233) and the Swope Bill (No. 4094) and both have commendable features, such as removal from political influence and civil service examinations for reviewers.

Wholesale condemnation of the movies will not solve our problem. We must fearlessly analyze the facts concerning the effects of the pictures on our youth and then put on a nation-wide educational campaign that shall present these facts to the parents and teachers of our children.[31]

As therapy for undesirable social change, whether jazz or movies, many Brethren believed that the family was crucial, and family altars in the home became a favorite method to nurture religion in the household. In the safety of the home, parents could instruct children in the faith and gird them with the spiritual armor necessary to deflect temptation. The practice encouraged regular worship in a designated place in the home rather than literal construction of a domestic shrine. Of course, family worship was not distinctly Brethren and, in fact, was popular throughout evangelical Protestantism. Moody Bible Institute, for example, produced a popular radio program called the *Family Altar League*.[32] Echoing mainstream Protestantism, the Brethren *Pastor's Manual* decreed that "no home is complete without the family altar" and gave specific advice on how to achieve this.

A regular place is conducive to the truest and fullest worship. If breakfast is eaten in the kitchen, then around the dining-room table is the most homey place. It is not best to try to have worship around the breakfast table where sights and smells of food distract the attention of the children, suggesting insistently eating, not worship.

For the same reason, all work and toys and every distracting thing should be put away, so that all may concentrate on the worship.[33]

Franklin Crumpacker, a Brethren missionary to China, believed that if more homes had family altars, maintaining the Brethren order would be easier. "Irregularities," he suggested, would disappear from the fellowship.

> May we . . . go back to our homes and in our homes establish the family altar, and this family altar, friends, is the one method that will solve this whole question.
>
> If we had the family altar we would not have so many of these irregularities. I wish that that emphasis might be laid right there, that we get busy in all of our homes and have the family altar reestablished and do more praying and personal service; then we will get the results we are seeking.[34]

Wilbur B. Stover dedicated his book, *The Family Worship,* to the South Dakota legislature for its resolution urging family worship. Stover concluded that family altars offered protection from undesirable social trends, including worldliness, jazz, and movies, and that they enhanced worship with the full fellowship. He implored families to set aside an entire room for prayer.

> A prayer room in every home will be found materially helpful, a room in which the pictures suggest worship, the books on the center table are Bibles and song books, the best room in the house. What used to be called the parlor, or what is now called the sitting room or living room, can very easily become the prayer room. And in this room, at the appointed regular time, the *whole family* will assemble. . . .
>
> Would you have the Church free from the spirit of the worldliness? Your home must first be free, for what comes into the home must come into the Church, by the very nature of things. No home can foster jazz, and appreciate the grand old hymns of the Church. No home can patronize the movies every night in the week, and enjoy the Church services on Sunday, for the simple reason that Sunday and its services are a projection of the best religious experiences of the home. If the daily worship is maintained in the home, the worship of the Sunday will be the same in fuller measure. And they who find enjoyment in the one will find complete satisfaction in the other.[35]

In the cultural conflicts of the twenties, condemnation of jazz and the youth cult, defense of Prohibition, opposition to Catholicism, regulation of movies, and praise for family altars united most Brethren. This also gave them much in common with fellow Protestants.

BRETHREN FUNDAMENTALISM

Other consequences of modernity, especially the fundamentalist/modernist controversy, divided the Church of the Brethren. In fact, for Brethren and larger Protestantism, the battleground between fundamentalism and modernism contributed significantly to the discord of this period.

Fundamentalists were the most determined opponents of modernity. Their aggressive defense of the faith from so-called modernist or liberal trends and their vigorous defense of society from secular morality (movies, jazz, youth cult, etc.) distinguished them from the wider evangelical movement. (Evangelicals often agreed with fundamentalists about liberalism and secularism but were less militant about it.) Fundamentalists also self-consciously embraced what they considered the basics, or fundamentals, of the faith, usually listed as the virgin birth, biblical inerrancy, Christ's resurrection, the second coming, and the atonement. Finally, fundamentalists were adamantly premillennial, convinced that humans had no hope of realistic progress until after the second coming of Christ. A series of pamphlets, *The Fundamentals,* published between 1909 and 1914, attacked theological liberalism and higher criticism and gave the emerging movement its name.

The roots of fundamentalism extended into late nineteenth-century soul-winning revivalism, dispensational premillennialism, and the Keswick Victorious Life movement. Dispensational premillennialism divided time into distinct periods; the second coming would end the last one. The Keswick movement taught that after the new birth a second, intense spiritual experience could bring a spirit-filled life and triumph over sin. In the 1890s and 1900s, the movement gathered institutional momentum from the series of conferences on end-times prophecy, and World War I sharpened the divide between conservatives and modernists. Liberals charged that premillennialism undermined the idealistic war effort to recast the world. Conservatives, on the other hand, countered that the real danger was liberalism and higher criticism, developed by German seminaries and responsible for the brutal, degenerate German nation that now threatened international order.

In the twenties the split between fundamentalists, as they were now called, and modernists deepened. The postwar resurgence of immigration, often by non-Protestants, and trends in popular culture indicated to many conservatives that America was in danger of losing its Protestant

J. H. Moore, editor of *The Gospel Messenger* (1883-1884; 1891-1915), was a fundamentalist and determined anti-evolutionist. *Photo courtesy of BHLA.*

identity. Much of what troubled twenties-era fundamentalists flowed not just from the pens of liberal seminary professors, but from diversity, secularism, and higher education, all consequences of modernization.[36]

Brethren conservatives shared much with fundamentalism. When *The Fundamentals* pamphlets appeared, the editor of *The Gospel Messenger*, J. H. Moore, pronounced them indispensable in refuting "destructive criticism and the New Theology," and he urged every Brethren preacher to obtain a copy.[37] Likewise, Brethren fundamentalists occasionally expressed apprehension over an increasingly secular national morality. Although progressives and conservatives both denounced worldly sins, such as alcohol, jazz, and motion-pictures, linking these problems to the spiritual state of the nation was primarily fundamentalist.

> Brethren, there is something more than just mere moving pictures concerned here. It is the foundation of our nation. We read in God's Word that righteousness exalteth a nation, but sin is a reproach to any people and I believe it is our duty as members of a Christian organization that exalts the Lord Jesus Christ to do everything that we can to remove that reproach, that the reproach of sin be taken from our nation; and anything that we can do, and everything we can do in the name of our Christ to have that reproach removed, should be our earnest endeavor.[38]

The Brethren
During the Age of World War

by Stephen L. Longenecker

— Errata —

Chapter IV
Pp. 142 and 147: The photo on page 142 should
replace the one on page 147 and vice versa.

Brethren Press

I am living now in my mind in a city, or town, and the whole community is infested with dandelions, we will say, for instance, and
they are a menace. I can work and clean my little patch, but unless
I get the cooperation of all my neighbors, we will never get the
community clean from that menace. I think this cooperation [with
the Motion Picture Council] is what we need. Our Welfare Board
is doing very commendable work. It cannot go far enough within
itself to clean our country of this terrible menace [of movies].[39]

––––––––––

We are living in days of great danger to the Republic of the United
States of America. There is a well-directed, highly-financed program to break down the constitution and the laws and the moral
backbone of this country. The Anti-Saloon League was the instrument, forged by the united Christian forces of this nation, to do the
specific task of ridding this nation of the saloon, and of the organized liquor traffic. That task was accomplished and the entire liquor
traffic is outlawed, but there remains a great task yet before us, to
make that legal enactment actually operative in this country. Of
course, the liquor question is a political question and the Anti-
Saloon League is interested and engaged in political activity only
because it seeks to conserve the moral interests of this nation.
Surely our State Districts ought to have the privilege of cooperating in this great task, and of protecting the future not only of our
own boys and girls but of the nation and of the world.[40]

The Social Gospel movement provided direct confrontation
between Brethren progressives and fundamentalists. Many progressives
approved of the application of religion to social problems, typified by a
sermon on the dignity of labor tinged with class consciousness, preached
by Merlin C. Shull. Additionally, Shull's use of secular literature, emphasis on Jesus as a role model, and weight given to Jesus' humanity rather
than Christ's atonement were prototypically liberal.

Shull began his sermon by pointing out that between 1914 and 1920
dividends for U. S. Steel Corporation increased from $135,204,471.90 to
$523,454,890.89, yet the company reduced the wages of unskilled work-
ers to thirty cents an hour. Then, according to his sermon notes, he
argued that "we must think of work as being dignified," and he outlined
the biblical view of labor.

The Bible and work.

1st. Some Bible students say work is the penalty of the fall. "In the sweat of thy face thou shalt eat Bread."

Undoubtedly sin adds to the hardships of work, especially the sin of wrong attitudes. "Thorns and thistles prosper around the broken gate of the sluggard."

But this same passage says, "Adam was placed in the garden to dress it."

2nd. O[ld] T[estament]. Busy men called into special kingdom service.

Moses, tending flocks on hillside.

Saul, was seeking his Father's cattle when he found the Kingdom of which he was to be King.

David, busy in the sheepfold when the prophet called him to his work.

Ruth, gleaning in the field to earn a living for herself and mother-in-law.

Gideon was beating out wheat in the wine press when drafted for the Campaign to break the power of the Midianites.

Elisha was plowing the 12 yoke of Oxen when the mantle of Elijah fell on his shoulders.

Nehemiah was serving as cupbearer to the King.

Amos was among the herdsmen of Tekoa when the word of God took him captive and sent him on his prophetic career. God only calls busy men!

3rd. N[ew] T[estament]. Less specific but shows preference.

1. Matthew, at seat of custom.

2. James and John were engaged in their occupation as fishermen when they heard the voice on the shore and pulled their boats over the blue waves that they might become fishers of men.

3. The shepherds were in faithful watch over their flocks by night when they heard the evangel of song and were startled by the message of peace.

4. Someone has said, "the best reward for good work is more good work to do." The Bible shows a strong preference for the worker as against the shirker.

5. Christ, the best Example of a good workman. In his teachings He made the common work of earth the illustration of our responsibility in service to God.

The Kingdom of Heaven is like unto

A merchant and his pearls.
A sower and his field.
A woman and her leaven.
A fisherman and his nets.
A husbandman and his vineyard.
A merchant traveler and his trusted talents.

When he wanted to illustrate quickly, he gathered his material from the realm of toil.

1. The builder and his house.
2. The shepherd and the sheep.
3. The axman and the tree.
4. The tailor and the cloth.
5. The housewife and the coin.
6. The rich man and his steward.
7. The woman and her grinding.
8. The watchman and his vigil.
9. The man and his plowing.
10. The husbandman and the vine.

This is almost an Encyclopedia of labors. Jesus regarded the common work of life as representing the Kingdom of God.

Life would be a dreadful thing if we had to think of the work we do to earn a living for our loved ones as evil. . . .

1. As a carpenter he worked on material things.
2. As a healer on the bodies of men.
3. As a teacher on the minds of men.
4. As an Evangelist on the souls of men.

All the workers of the world can be brought under one of these divisions. We call Him Carpenter, the great Physician, the greatest teacher, the world Savior. The manual toilers claim him, the doctors claim him. He is at home in the shop, the hospital, in the school room and in the temple.

But Jesus made none of these distinctions. . . .

The shadow of the Cross may fall on all legitimate work. . . .

Shull ended his tribute to labor by drawing on hymnody: "Work, for the Night Is Coming," from the Brethren hymnal, and "Be Strong, for We Are Not Here to Play," which included a call to justice. The latter was not in the Brethren hymn book.

Work for the night is coming,
Work through the morning hours;
Work while the dew is sparkling,
Work 'mid spring flowers.

Work when the day grows brighter
Work in the glowing sun;
Work for the night is coming
When Man's work is done.

———————

Be Strong!
We are not here to play, to dream, to drift;
We have hard work to do and loads to lift;
Shun not the struggle,
     face it, 'tis God's gift.
Be strong, be strong, be strong!

Be Strong!
Say not the days are evil—who's to blame?
And fold the hands and acquiesce—O shame!
Stand up, speak out, and bravely in God's Name.
Be strong, be strong, be strong!

Be Strong!
It matters not how deep entrenched the wrong,
How hard the battle goes,
     the day, how long;
Faint not, fight on! Tomorrow comes the song.
Be strong, be strong, be strong![41]

C. C. Ellis, weekly contributor to *The Sunday School Times* and a Social Gospel foe. *Photo courtesy of BHLA.*

Brethren fundamentalists took exception to Social Gospel theology like Shull's; therefore, they protested when the General Education Board published a clarion call for liberal and Social Gospel thought, "The Social Message of Christianity." C. C. Ellis, a popular preacher, three-time Annual Conference moderator, and president of Juniata College (1930-43), particularly complained that the pamphlet spoke of the brotherhood of man—the only brotherhood, he said, was through Christ and the church—and that it incorrectly suggested that the kingdom could come through human improvement, a direct challenge to premillennialism.[42] Following is an excerpt from the pamphlet and then Ellis's rejoinder.

> In their confidence that the faithful application of the principles of Jesus Christ is the only adequate solution for the questions and problems of society, the Church of the Brethren stands for:
>
> The Fatherhood of God and the universal brotherhood of man.
>
> The sanctity of human life and the supreme worth of human personality, irrespective of social distinctions.
>
> The organized church as a practical means of fostering and propagating the ideals of Jesus.
>
> The observance of Sunday as a day of rest and worship.
>
> A single standard of purity for the sexes.

The home and marriage as divine institutions, which should be safeguarded by civil law and the regulations of religion.

Christian education as the buttress of morality, religion and democracy.

The promotion of friendship in the community, national and international relations, leading to the adoption of arbitration for the adjustment of differences.

The establishment of full and free democracy, founded upon knowledge and self-control, guaranteeing equal rights and complete justice to all men.

The simple life, as opposed to the life of selfish luxury, extravagant pleasures and sordid material interests.

The right, duty and opportunity to engage in useful work at a reasonable wage, and under conditions favorable to health and happiness.

The abolition of child labor and the protection of women in industry.

The cultivation of friendly relations between capital and labor, leading to the establishment of just wages and fair prices and ultimately to harmonious cooperation of capital, labor and the public, in the production and distribution of wealth.

The provision of wholesome recreation for the youth and those who labor.

The application of the principle of stewardship to the acquisition and expenditure of wealth.

The abatement and prevention of poverty and the effective relief of suffering and distress.

Prevention of crimes by civil restrictions, and humane provisions for the regeneration of criminals and the elimination of maladjustments and vicious institutions from the social order.

The life of love, sacrifice and service as the highest expression of the social ideal of Jesus.

The establishment of the Kingdom of God upon earth, through the Christianization of our social relations and the spread of the gospel of brotherhood throughout the world.

The establishment of the Kingdom—the Family of God—through the methods of Jesus' teaching, preaching, prayer, service, and vicarious sacrifice.[43]

Ellis's response:

> IT may seem a bit ungracious to criticize unfavorably a pamphlet put out by one of our authorized Boards, and one that contains so much that one could agree with. But the fact that it purports to speak, not for the authors alone, nor even for the Educational Board alone, but for the Church of the Brethren, makes it imperative to examine it not only in the light of our church position, but as well in the light of the Scripture upon which our church foundations rest. . . .

> On the fourth point a few things may be noted: The inconsistency appears in that, after twice stating that the term "Father" belongs properly to those who are "spiritually begotten," or "accept the truth of Christianity," the statement on page "12" commits the church to a belief in the Fatherhood of God and the Universal Brotherhood of Man, notwithstanding the fact that scriptures cited on page "7" lend but the very faintest support to such an idea, and ignore completely such scriptures as John 8:44 and John 3:3. With one possible exception all the scriptures quoted emphasize not universal Fatherhood, but the Fatherhood of God, in relation to Jesus himself or his followers. . . .

> The introduction states that the character of Christianity is determined by the personality and teaching of Jesus Christ. Is it not determined by what he did, especially on Calvary? . . .

> . . . However, there is another theological statement with which the church, as a whole, hardly has such unanimous agreement as to justify its being put out in this authoritative manner. Certainly the two statements about the Kingdom can not be sustained purely by reference to the Word. The writer happens to know that there are a great many in our fellowship who do not expect the establishment of the Kingdom by the method that is here set forth, but are "looking for the blessed hope and the appearing of the glory of the great God and our Savior Jesus Christ" (Titus 2:13) and they can not but wonder why, when we speak so much of the Kingdom, we should say no word about bringing back the King who alone can set up the Kingdom. The Scripture does not confuse the church and the kingdom, as the pamphlet seems to do, nor does there seem to be Scriptural warrant for calling the Kingdom the Family of God. The Gospel Message is a personal

message to men who need to be born again, and no abiding social uplift can come where this is ignored or where the social by-product is mistaken for the heart of the Gospel.[44]

Brethren also argued over other points in the fundamentalist/modernist controversy, including higher criticism and religion's ability to change with the times. Many of the first Brethren to pursue graduate studies attended liberal divinity schools, including Vanderbilt and Yale, and most of the faculty at the Bethany Theological Seminary earned degrees at the University of Chicago, well-known for modernist thought.[45] As might be expected, then, some Brethren preferred the new methods and agreed with liberalism that religion needed to accommodate itself to a new age. F. F. Holsopple, for example, chair of the English department at Juniata College (1901-1914) and president of Blue Ridge College (1917-1919), fully endorsed higher criticism.

> The rapid advance in the sciences, and man's conquest over the forces of nature along with changing philosophical conceptions, has made inevitable the challenge to traditional religion in its varied implications. That the Bible should be questioned in the light of modern research is inevitable. There could be no escape from such a result, nor should an escape be sought. The fundamentals of belief had of necessity to be probed to the very center. Truth has never suffered from the most rigid scrutiny, and never will suffer. Only superstition and error, however hoary with age, find themselves confounded when truth is insisted upon. With every new onslaught of criticism, the Cross grows more glorious, the Christ of God more majestic, and his claims are established as supreme.[46]

Brethren fundamentalists, however, feared the new methods of biblical study. Many felt skepticism and an alienation regarding higher education and higher criticism.

> Under this heading I beg leave to first give a brief survey of the conflict the Bible has ever been up against in educational circles. You will please note that when this Book invades the circle of intellectuals, it has certainly tackled a big proposition. It certainly will be tested by brains that have been sharpened with the wit of the ages. Paul stood in the midst of the Greek philosophers with this truth and in less than no time had them all sitting and taking notice, yet

they would not commit themselves to full acceptance till they could test it out by the truths already accepted as valid. This is the kind of thing that goes on in educational circles, and justly so, for no one would want to accept a bit of knowledge as truth if it will not stand the test of truth already verified. Our Bible has been through this kind of a sifting process ever since it has been a Bible.

During Old Testament times the contest was largely one of belief against unbelief within the Jewish circle. Moses and the prophets had a big job. True they always had a pagan environment against which they religiously contended with a true courage. When the Jews went into captivity, they struck paganism as never before. A remnant of them returned to Jerusalem to reestablish their faith. The masses never returned because the pagan intelligence was a little too much for them. When they came into contact with Greek culture, there seemed at first a generous exchange of truths and doctrines. But when the introductory period had passed by, the contest was long and bitter. The windup of all these siftings in the highest intellectual circles of the centuries gave to the New Testament times a body of Bible doctrines and literature head and shoulders above all contemporaries. This is as we would naturally expect, for God's truth will always make good when handled by godly men.[47]

Another Brethren conservative likened modern "intellectual education" to the ineffective pursuits of scholars in the Apostle Paul's time, and he accused intellectualism and modernism, which included higher criticism, of being "twin brothers." Both, he presumed, ignored God's plan.

"For after that in the wisdom of God the world by wisdom knew not God, it pleased God by the foolishness of preaching to save them that believe" (I Cor. 1:21). Intellectualism and modernism are twin brothers; they both in a large measure set God's plan of salvation aside, and build their structures on a human foundation. Their plans and doctrines are derived from human reasoning and much of God's Word and counsel is set aside and ignored. And much of the preaching and teaching of today is wholly based upon the counsel and reasoning of finite men.

Notwithstanding the definite, plain, simple teaching in God's word, intellectualism is being deified, and many are bowing to this man-made creed, and as a further result, men and women that

had espoused the cause of Christ are departing from the simplicity of the Gospel of Jesus Christ and are worshipping at the shrine
of purely human reason. It is a manifest fact "that the wisdom of
this world is foolishness with God." He looks upon intellectual
knowledge and earthly wisdom and ignorance (Acts 17:30).

The greatest intellectualists and most renowned educators in
the days of Paul got no nearer to God than to imagine there might
be such a Being, hence the altar erected to the unknown God. An
intellectual education today comes just as far from finding out God
as it did in the days of the ancient Greeks. If we would learn to
know God, we must study his Word. For therein and nowhere
else he is revealed in all his beauty and holiness. And if we would
know the mind of God and his will concerning us, and our salvation from sin, we must read and study the Bible, more especially
the New Testament.[48]

C. C. Ellis, one of the most influential Brethren fundamentalists,
represents their affinity for biblical study without higher criticism. For
many years Ellis published a weekly column, "This Week's Teaching
Principle," in *The Sunday School Times,* a prominent fundamentalist
journal. Ellis's piece was part of weekly "lesson helps" that supported
Sunday school teachers. In the twenties this service became a self-consciously conservative alternative to materials produced by suspiciously
liberal Protestant denominations, and although Ellis refrained from the
passion and anger of many fundamentalists, his theology was untouched
by higher criticism and straightforward rather than analytical or inter-
pretative.[49] In this representative passage, Ellis depicts the atonement
and second coming as literal, characteristically fundamentalist.

Important as is the teaching of Christ about himself in the Book of
Matthew, it seems hardly a competent discussion of the matter to
limit it to Matthew's report, especially when we recognize that the
different Gospels were written evidently with different purposes.
Nor can we be content in dealing with such a subject to limit ourselves even in Matthew to the designated portion of Scripture.
True, there are indications here of most important truths relative
to the person and work of our Lord. There are glimpses of deity
in what he says and does, and it will be well to let the class discover
them. However, that which is often inferential here is so plainly
declared in the Gospel of John that the teachings of Christ there

should be brought to bear upon the question of what he teaches concerning his own person.

Then, too, if we were attempting to tabulate the qualities of character which our Lord set forth concerning himself either directly or figuratively, it would surely be necessary to go to the other Gospels to be certain that none were overlooked. Again, if we would interrogate the Lord himself as to the purpose of his coming into the world, we find him making one statement, but not the only one, in Matthew 20:28. This statement indicates not only that his mission while in the world was one of service, but also sets forth the fact that he came to give up his life in sacrificial atonement. This is more fully set forth, however, by our Lord in the record of John, and this should be taken into account also.

One important teaching of the Lord not found in the selected Scripture, but elsewhere in Matthew, concerns his second coming. Our principle of correlation therefore seems necessary for an adequate treatment of the lesson theme.[50]

Similarly, J. H. Moore bristled at the thought that the virgin birth might include mythology. According to Moore, an admired preacher, former editor of *The Gospel Messenger*, and three-time Annual Conference clerk, the birth of Christ was a well-documented miracle, and attempts to strip religion of the miraculous threatened its core beliefs.[51]

Is it really a fact that Jesus was born of the Virgin Mary? All evidence, bearing directly on the question, says he was. Not only so, but Isaiah, who wrote 750 years before the beginning of the Christian era, said: "A virgin shall conceive and bear a son." By those who were best qualified to give reliable testimony, it is reported that this is what happened in the birth of Jesus. The story is told by two men who had years of training as writers—one a scholar, a physician, and the other a clerk in a Roman customhouse, where the utmost precision was required in recording statements.

Neither of the two wrote on the spur of the moment or while laboring under excitement. Both men gave themselves ample time to collect and sift their evidence. Then, too, they permitted all statements regarding this remarkable birth to go the rounds of public criticism—not for a time or two, but for years. After the public, both friends and foes, had discussed every phase of the subject, leaving only the bare facts standing out, then and not till then, did the two men proceed to record the facts that had defied all criticism.

One witness is Matthew and the other is Luke. Both of them lived at a time when the discussion was its keenest. They lived in the country where the thing happened—possibly knew those who were as familiar with the circumstances as it was possible for human beings to be, and it is not unreasonable to presume that both of them may have listened to the story that Mary herself related to her most intimate friends. After the ascension of her Son, Mary became the object of much love and great respect. She was the mother of the Lord, and while at Jerusalem, in the course of his travels, Luke, the earnest believer and skillful physician, would naturally seek an interview with her, while she was making her home with the Apostle John. The care, the grace and delicacy, that characterize Luke's narrative, would indicate that something of this kind may have happened. Matthew, while serving as an apostle, during the life-time of the Master, had scores of opportunities to meet the mother of our Lord, and it would seem strange indeed if she had not, on some of the many occasions, when she was in the presence of the apostles, said enough concerning the birth of her Son to enable Matthew to record the splendid story that completes the closing half of the first chapter of his interesting book.

The testimony of both Matthew and Luke would indicate, as clearly as it would be possible for words to state a fact, that Jesus was born of a virgin. Matthew says that before Joseph and Mary "came together, she was found with child of the Holy Ghost." Not only this, but Joseph believed this to be a fact, and with all becoming reverence treated Mary accordingly. There is no way of accounting for this, excepting on the ground that the conception was a miracle. The story has all the appearance of a miracle. There is no legend about it. It does not read like a legend or a myth. Matthew is not dealing with myths. He is recording well-authenticated fact—such as have stood the criticism of years.

Nor can this miracle be set aside or be ruled out. The story cannot be ruled out on the ground that it is unscientific. It was not intended to be scientific. No attempt was made to have it appear as being in keeping with nature. For this one instance science was set aside and the law of nature, regulating conception, dispensed with. This constitutes the real miracle—the very thing that God decreed to take place. The conception was by the Holy Ghost,

and the only way to get rid of the fact is to deny the miracle element altogether. And to get rid of this miracle means paving the
way to get rid of all the miracles of the Bible. Thus setting aside the
divinity of Christ and the inspiration of the entire Bible gives us
materialism, or nothing, in its place.[52]

Brethren conservatives also joined in the battle against evolution, the
great fundamentalist cause of the twenties. Opposition to evolution came
late to the antimodernist movement, but in the twenties this changed for
several reasons. William Jennings Bryan, who by the sheer force of personality elevated anti-evolution onto center stage, deserves some of the
credit for its emergence. Also, the continued growth of fundamentalism,
including premillennial dispensationalism and biblical inerrancy, encouraged a literalism that discouraged accommodation with Darwinism. The
rapid increase in secondary education meant that more families came into
contact with Darwin when their children studied science in high school,
and this raised difficult questions about academic freedom. Would parents and taxpayers control the high school curriculum or could liberal
teachers expose students to Darwin? Finally, anti-evolution represented
the last stand of the commoner against specialization and advanced education. Vocation after vocation had become professionalized, and now liberals wanted to make biblical interpretation a specialty, the domain of
archeologists, historians, and linguists. Would the Bible remain a divine-
ly inspired book of simple truths comprehensible to all, or did biblical
interpretation require a doctorate? Not surprisingly, then, evolution
attracted the attention of Brethren committed to the fundamentals.[53]

In 1923 Annual Conference first considered evolution when a congregation from Franklin County, Virginia, accused Brethren colleges of
teaching Darwin.

Whereas, a false theory of the origin of species, especially as it
relates to our primeval ancestors, to which reference is made in
the first chapter of Genesis, 26th and 27th verses, known by the
appellation of Evolution, or Darwinism, is being fostered in many
of the colleges and universities of the world, and, whereas, it has
been charged that the same false doctrine is held by some of our
educational leaders, and, whereas, the influence of these leaders is
detrimental to the spiritual development of our young people who
are passing through our colleges, and, whereas, our church,

through the ministry of our Annual Conferences, has appointed an Educational Board, whose office is to protect our schools from such influences which tend to lead the minds and hearts of our young people away from the simplicity and purity of life, as it is taught in the New Testament: therefore, we, the Bethlehem church, of the Church of the Brethren, do petition the Annual Conference to require the aforesaid Educational Board to make an exhaustive survey of all of our colleges and Bible schools in order to ascertain to the Annual Conference of 1924, with recommendations as to the proper course to pursue in order to conserve the best interests of the church.[54]

One outraged conservative pointedly referred to the appearance of Darwin in high school textbooks.

I have studied, and you have studied, the books of our high schools, and you know how far they are from the Word of God. You know that in some of our colleges these books are being used, and most of us, I suppose, are conscious of the fact that it is the best we can do. I have heard our teachers say, "We will use the book that teaches the untruth, and then brand it as an untruth." I believe we ought to be very serious about the use of such books.[55]

Debate focused on whether the accusations were accurate or hearsay, but nobody defended Darwin or academic freedom on the floor of Annual Conference.

I would like to ask the delegate [representing the district that brought the query] as to the correctness of his statement, when he says that this false teaching is being fostered by some of the schools in the Brotherhood. I would be very loath to think that any of our brethren, teaching in any of our schools, would for a moment consider teaching in favor of the evolutionary theory of the origin of man, and against the Divinity of Jesus Christ. If that condition exists in the schools of our Brotherhood, I am very much in favor of the thing which this inquiry asks for, but I think we should know whether this statement is correct.[56]

This paper says it has been charged that the same false doctrine is held by some of our education leaders. You notice the indefiniteness of that statement. In my pastoral experience I have discovered that hearsay is one of the biggest prevaricators I know of. Hearsay can not be run down, and I have come to the place where I do not believe more than one-quarter of the reports I hear, and not nearly all I see. I would very much regret to have this Conference refer a matter of this kind on a basis of nothing but hearsay.[57]

Unfortunately, the query suffered from a fatal stylistic flaw; the poorly worded answer from District Conference accompanying the query implied that the Divinity of Christ was a "false teaching."

This District Conference . . . respectfully requests that the Educational Board inquire as to the correct teaching concerning the Divinity of Christ and other false teachings.[58]

Conference returned the query to the district.[59]

Two years later the famous trial of biology teacher and alleged evolutionist John Scopes, in Dayton, Tennessee, caused ripples among the Brethren but not the tidal wave felt by the larger society. While journals of many Protestant denominations published major articles on the Scopes trial or sent correspondents to Tennessee, *The Gospel Messenger* ignored the trial of the century.[60] In fact, the Brethren's journal did not respond to this national controversy until December, months after the Scopes trial (July 10-21, 1925). But if the timing of the piece was unusual, its content was not. The author, J. H. Moore, a convinced anti-evolutionist, addressed several questions raised at Dayton when Scopes' attorney, Clarence Darrow, put William Jennings Bryan on the witness stand and interrogated him on biblical interpretation. By most accounts, Bryan had not answered convincingly, and perhaps Moore sought to finish the task.

IN literary circles the evolution theory regarding the origin of man is the burning question. Nine-tenths of the papers and especially the leading journals have something worth reading on the subject. The question has reached some of the popular pulpits, and some not so popular. In some parts of the Brotherhood we hear of well prepared addresses treating the subject at ministerial meetings. All of this means healthy thinking for the question is a vital one. . . . And then the way a leading attorney, who discards the Bible, grilled

Mr. Bryan and denounced religion at the Dayton trial, has put a lot of people to thinking and even to reading.

. . . In this communication . . . our only purpose is to take a common sense view of a few points relating to miracles. The points we are treating were brought out during the Tennessee trial. . . .

One point deals with the Book of Jonah, the whale swallowing Jonah, and retaining him for three days and three nights. This reminds us of a bit of experience. A five-minute walk brings us to a large lake where we do a little fishing now and then. The other morning we placed on the hook a minnow about three inches long. In due time we landed a fish twelve inches in length, that had swallowed the three-inch minnow. This put us to reasoning. If a fish twelve inches long could swallow a little fish one-fourth its length, what would be in the way of a Mediterranean fish twenty-four feet in length, swallowing a man less than six feet long? For a fish one-half larger, and there are plenty of them even larger than that, the feat would have been an easy matter, and that too without any miracle about it. It seems to us that a little common sense, without much faith, would enable the average man to accept this part of Jonah's story.

But we are further told that the fish took care of its man for three days and three nights, and then delivered him alive and unharmed, on dry land, ready for business. There is nothing about this hard to believe or difficult to understand. It is only necessary to remind the reader of the fact that the author of the Book of Jonah was a good writer, a man who measured his words, and with pen in hand understood his business. In the narrative he says, "Now the Lord had prepared a great fish to swallow up Jonah." From this we understand that the fish was made on purpose for the occasion, properly prepared to take care of the prophet any length of time desired. Certainly no one will question the ability of the Lord to make a fish. He made the whole earth, the sun, moon and all the stars. Why should he not make or prepare a fish for a special purpose? For the great Creator that would have been a very small matter.

During the late war the Germans made submarine boats capable of crossing the Atlantic and carrying a score or more of men. Why not the Lord make a fish equipped for taking care of one man? He could have made such a fish in less time than it took one of the submarine workmen to drive a nail.

. . . In short, with the application of a little common sense and a grain of reason it is a good deal easier and far more comforting to believe what is said about Jonah and the great fish, than it is to accept even half of the so-called scientific theories advanced in many of the schoolrooms regarding the origin of man, and a whole lot of other things calculated to undermine the inspiration of the Bible. Our Bible tells us that God made the heavens and the earth, that he prepared a fish capable of swallowing Jonah, and it also says that he made man and was not very long about it. One part of the Record must be regarded as truthful as the other.[61]

In the list of recorded incidents urged against the correctness of the Old Testament we refer to Joshua 10:12, 13, where we are told that both the sun and the moon stood still, at the request of Joshua, to enable his army to complete its victory over the enemy. It is urged that such a thing as the earth and moon coming to a standstill, in the course of their rapid movements, should be regarded as a scientific impossibility. Well, let us take a sensible view of the situation.

The incident itself, as narrated in the Sacred Record, reminds us of a bit of experience. For years we have been carrying a good Elgin watch that will now and then need a little touching up. Not so long ago we had our local silversmith look it over. Having opened up the watch so he could get at the works, we noticed that with a small pointer he touched the balance wheel and every wheel in the watch stood still. After examining the works a moment or two he lifted his pointer and the wheels resumed their motions and so continued as though nothing had happened. No one questions the correctness of the story which we are here telling, but had the watch been half as large as the earth some critic might call our statement in question.

Of course a watch is a small affair, but not one-tenth as small as the earth when compared with the rest of our solar system. Man made the watch but God made the universe, and the earth, when contrasted with the universe, is less than the size of a pea. For God to have held the earth and moon in check for a few hours would by comparison have been a far less task than for the silversmith to stop the wheels of our watch. And now, in the light of what we are here saying, pray tell us why it would be possible for the silversmith to make the movement of our watch stand still a few minutes and yet God not be able to stay the earth and moon a few hours? The critic who calls in question the truthfulness of what the Bible says about Joshua's experience with the earth and moon makes God by comparison far less powerful than man. As applied to the stopping of the sun and the moon you call our attention to the law of gravitation, saying that under such circumstances our solar system, including the sun and all the planets, might have gone to smash. By estimate, in comparison, God in staying the sun and the moon did not have half the force in gravitation to contend with as did the silversmith when he held our Elgin watch in hand. While what the silversmith did in overcoming gravitation is admitted to be practical, it is argued that what is ascribed to God in the incident concerning Joshua is unreasonable, unscientific. To us this is a funny way of reasoning. In fact there is no reason about it. It is not even good applied sense. This disposes of the objection urged against the Bible narrative about Joshua, the sun and the moon.

If what has been written about Jonah and the fish, as well as about Joshua's experience with the sun and the moon, comes within the range of reason why may we not accept what is said about the immediate and direct origin of man. The evolutionists, possibly the most of them, tell us that the story as set forth in the first chapters is not supported by modern science. Well, we are not seeking a quarrel with science, but it so happens that what is known as the scientific theory regarding the origin of man, is a hypothesis, "something assumed, . . . a theory to explain some fact which may or may not prove to be true; supposition; conjecture" (Universal Dictionary). . . . It is a theory at best and as such we regard it. . . . Every well read man knows what has been said about the "missing link," or rather links, for a new link is unearthed every few years, but the real link, the one that would, beyond doubt, tie up the human race with the animal creation, is yet to be discovered. So the evolution theory regarding man is still a hypothesis— a supposition, a conjecture. Suppose we leave the problem for science to work out and take a look into the Bible. In the early chapters of Genesis we have a splendidly written story about the creation of the heavens and the earth as well as the creation of man. The story is not a scientific hypothesis. Not even a conjecture. There is no guesswork about it. It is a straightforward historic narrative, so simple in form and language that a child may understand it. It has about it the ring of certainty. There is not an element of doubt in the whole story. The author writes as though he had first information, as though he understood, and knew that he understood, just what he was writing about. Everything about the story indicates that the writer was well educated, a fine, clear thinker, accustomed to writing, and knew how to say what he wanted to present. Furthermore, the Book of Genesis contains the first intelligent statement concerning the creation of the world and all living things ever given to man. . . .

Well, what did he [the writer] think of the beginning of things, of the origin of man? He says and says it in a way not to be misunderstood, that "in the beginning" God created the heavens, the earth and all things therein. And while at it [he] says that he made the man, and made the woman, and not only tells how it was done but names the material employed, and the process observed. No historian ever penned a plainer statement. All this he says was done in the beginning and names God, the great Creator, as the first great Cause. He puts God behind everything and when everything was completed and put in motion, the planets, the other heavenly bodies, the things of earth, the great historian closes his narrative so far as the creation was concerned, and left the future historian, the future scientist to discover and work out the rest.[62]

In 1929 Darwin appeared once more on the floor of Annual Meeting. Two congregations, one in South Dakota and the other in North Dakota, sent identical queries condemning evolution as unbiblical and detrimental to the morality of young people, and they requested federal legislation banning it from the nation's classroom.

There is being taught in our public schools, colleges and universities in this United States of America the theory of evolution. This teaching is diametrically opposed to the teaching of the Bible, and has the effect upon our youth of breaking down their faith in God and undermining their morals.

Therefore, we, the Minot church, in regular quarterly council, March 16, 1928, petition Annual Meeting, through the District Meeting of North Dakota and Eastern Montana, that Annual Conference authorize our General Education Board to use their influence with congress, that the teaching of evolution may be abolished from our public schools, colleges and universities.[63]

Before Conference could process the Minot query, another arrived from Virginia in 1930 arguing that education was a state and local matter and that Brethren should concentrate on teaching the biblical perspective in their own schools rather than passing national legislation.[64] Conference considered this persuasive and, as it emphatically endorsed creationism over Darwinism, rejected laws that would put the government behind its position.

Evolutionary theories propose to explain how higher forms of nature have developed from lower forms. They propose to show how man has evolved from a lower species. This is the part of evolutionary theory that has been disturbing religious thought and faith. But this form of evolution is only a theory. While many scientists strongly uphold it, many do not. Some scientists strongly deny the truth of the theory and especially many of the unwarranted deductions that have been made from it. Considering the lack of definite scientific proof of this theory and especially the disastrous influence of materialistic evolution upon the Christian faith, Christian teachers should emphasize the teaching of the Bible on man's origin, nature and destiny.

Genesis gives the most original and authentic information that we have on this subject. Other scriptures throw light on the subject. "The Lord God formed man out of the dust of the ground, and breathed into his nostrils the breath of life; and man became a living soul" (Gen. 2:7). "Then shall the dust return to the earth as it was; and the spirit shall return to God who gave it" (Eccl. 12:7). In these scriptures a few things are made clear: Man is a child of God who created him. Man has a physical nature, for his body was made out of the elements of the earth. Man has also a spiritual nature, for he was made in the image of God. Paul tells us that God hath made of one blood all nations of men (Acts 17:26). And again, "The spirit beareth witness with our spirits that we are the children of God."

With this knowledge and with the assurance of the truth of our Christian faith from the Bible and from history, reason, and experience, the church should not be disturbed over evolution or any other scientific theory. Neither should we ask for legislation against any of these theories, for it would have little effect on the teaching of them. Rather we would recommend that the church increase her efforts to teach, to preach and to demonstrate the truth of the gospel of Christ as the power of God unto salvation to all who believe.[65]

Brethren conservatives, then, agreed with fundamentalists about the Social Gospel, higher criticism, and evolution, but some of them conspicuously departed from the militancy of mainstream fundamentalism. As they stood at armageddon and battled modernity, they did it more gently and without the forcefulness the larger movement often displayed. Both C. C. Ellis and Otho Winger, president of Manchester College and six-time Annual Conference moderator, professed compatibility with fundamentalist doctrine but dissented from what Ellis called its "intolerant attitude." Following are criticisms of fundamentalist narrow-mindedness from Ellis first, then Winger.

I must confess that though my doctrinal attitudes are far more in line with the attitudes of the fundamentalists, so-called, than perhaps with any other group, I have been frequently disturbed in spirit at the intolerant attitude which certain ones of them seem to manifest; and I have taken occasion sometimes to suggest that important as it is to accept the doctrine of Christ, it is quite as important to manifest the spirit of Christ, for if one [does] not have this spirit, he is none of His. Whatever the outcome of our brethren controversies may be, I can but hope that this spirit will be manifest in them all and that ultimately we may all . . . deserve in the eyes of our Lord to be called evangelical Christians.[66]

———————

I want to say just a word about the so-called fundamentalism. First, I want it understood that so far as that name applies to doctrine I agree with them [the fundamentalists]. I doubt whether any of them have taught the fundamental teachings much longer and much more strongly than I have. I haven't done it from policy. I have done it from conviction. . . . I believe in the fundamental teachings of Jesus Christ, and doctrinally, I believe in all that fundamentalists teach so far as it relates to doctrine. But they have developed an attitude of mind which I believe is entirely wrong. Unless you believe in their interpretation in everything, you are entirely wrong.[67]

Conclusion

On one hand, the tents of all twenties-era Brethren appeared to be pitched uniformly in the conservative camp. Cultural pluralism and the growth of secular values dismayed all Brethren, and they united to resist the corrupting influence of the Jazz Age.

But modernity disturbed some Brethren more than others. The fellowship disagreed over the use of religion to promote social reform (except for Prohibition) and on the usefulness of higher education and intellectualism in religion. Brethren conservatives, then, joined the fundamentalist chorus in rejecting the Social Gospel, attacking higher criticism, distrusting intellectuals, and fretting over national morality. Evolution similarly troubled some more than others. Although Darwin was largely friendless in the fellowship, only militant fundamentalists sought to summon government assistance in subduing evolution. But, whether militant, moderate, or progressive, cultural change of one degree or another concerned all Brethren.

NOTES

1. Lynn Dumenil, *The Modern Temper: American Culture and Society in the 1920s* (New York: Hill and Wang, 1995), 8-13; John Higham, *Strangers in the Land: Patterns of American Nativism, 1860-1925,* 2nd ed. (New Brunswick, N. J.: Rutgers University Press, 1988, originally published 1955), 264-299; Nancy MacLean, *Behind the Mask of Chivalry: The Making of the Second Ku Klux Klan* (New York: Oxford University Press, 1994), 23-51, 79-91; George Donelson Moss, *America in the Twentieth Century,* 4th ed. (Upper Saddle River, N. J.: Prentice-Hall, Inc., 2000), 136-53.

2. "The Aftermath of Jazz," *The Gospel Messenger* (March 14, 1925): 169. A typographical error dates this issue as 1924.

3. Paula S. Fass, *The Damned and the Beautiful: American Youth in the 1920s* (New York: Oxford University Press, 1977), 5-6, 53-95, 119-27.

4. Rufus D. Bowman, "The New Loyalty," *The Gospel Messenger* (February 4, 1928): 66.

5. "Facing the Growing Movie Peril," *The Gospel Messenger* (March 20, 1926): 180. This is a reprint of an editorial (February 10, 1926) in *The Brethren Evangelist,* a periodical published by The Brethren Church.

6. Maltbie D. Babcock, "This Is My Father's World," No. 94 in *Hymnal: Church of the Brethren* (Elgin, Ill.: Brethren Publishing House, 1925. Babcock was a Presbyterian.

7. Henry Van Dyke, "Joyful, Joyful, We Adore Thee," No. 91 in *Hymnal: Church of the Brethren.* Van Dyke was a Presbyterian.

8. Peter J. Schmitt, *Back to Nature: The Arcadian Myth in Urban America* (New York: Oxford University Press, 1969), xvi-xxiii, 18-19, 96-105, 141-45.

9. "Camping Movement," *The Brethren Encyclopedia,* 3 vols., edited by Donald F. Durnbaugh (Philadelphia, Pa., and Oak Brook, Ill.: The Brethren Encyclopedia, Inc., 1983), I:248.

10. "Chauncey Howard Shamberger," *The Brethren Encyclopedia,* II:1171.

11. "Dedication Service of Camp Bethel," *The Gospel Messenger* (July 23, 1937): 478.

12. *Minutes of the Annual Meetings of the Church of the Brethren: Containing All Available Minutes from 1778 to 1909* (Elgin, Ill.: Brethren Publishing House, 1909), 871.

13. *Minutes of the Annual Meetings from 1778 to 1909,* 76, 262, 857-58; Carl F. Bowman, *Brethren Society: The Cultural Transformation of a "Peculiar People"* (Baltimore, Md.: The Johns Hopkins University Press, 1995), 176-181, 219-21; Martin E. Marty, *Modern American Religion: Volume 2, The Noise of Conflict, 1919-1941* (Chicago: University of Chicago Press, 1991), 233-241; Ferenc Morton Szasz, *The Divided Mind of Protestant America, 1880-1930* (Tuscaloosa: University of Alabama Press, 1982), 64-65.

14. Merlin G. Miller, "The 'Failure' of Prohibition," *The Gospel Messenger* (February 19, 1921): 114-15.

15. "Report of the Resolutions Committee," *Full Report of the Proceedings of the Annual Conference of the Church of the Brethren, 1924* (Elgin, Ill.: Brethren Publishing House, 1924), 190-91. See also *Full Report, 1921,* 137; *Full Report 1923,* 227.

16. "General Welfare Department," *Yearbook of the Church of the Brethren, 1926* (Elgin, Ill.: Brethren Publishing House, 1926), 38.

17. *Full Report, 1926,* 88-89.

18. Jerome E. Blough [February 3, 1921], "The West Johnstown, Pa., Revival and Evangelistic Campaign," *The Gospel Messenger* (February 19, 1921): 124.

19. Marty, *Modern American Religion,* 241-49; David M. Chalmers, *Hooded Americanism: The History of the Ku Klux Klan* (Durham, N. C.: Duke University Press, 1987; originally published, 1965), 300-03.

20. S. S. Sanger, "Shall We Vote as We Pray?" *The Gospel Messenger* (October 6, 1928): 630.

21. Marty, *Modern American Religion,* 245.

22. "The Religious Issue in the Campaign," *The Gospel Messenger* (October 20, 1928): 661.

23. "An Early Word on the Campaign," *The Gospel Messenger* (August 25, 1928): 533.

24. Maury Klein, *Rainbow's End: The Crash of 1929* (New York: Oxford University Press, 2001), 113-15; Thomas J. Schlereth, *Victorian America: Transformations in Everyday Life, 1876-1915* (New York: HarperCollins, 1991), 200-207; Robert Sklar, *Movie-Made America: A Social History of American Movies* (New York: Random House, 1975), 46-47.

25. Sklar, *Movie-Made America,* 23, 25, 91-103.

26. Fass, *The Damned and the Beautiful,* 126, 206-7; Sklar, *Movie-Made America,* 46, 89-91.

27. "Facing the Growing Movie Peril," *The Gospel Messenger* (March 20, 1926): 180.

28. *Full Report, 1926,* Michael W. Emmert speaking, 80-81.

29. *Full Report, 1926,* Forest S. Eisenbise speaking, 83.

30. John W. Lear, "A Query Worthy of Consideration," *The Gospel Messenger* (May 1, 1926): 277.

31. V. C. Finnell [North Manchester, Ind.], "Correspondence: National Motion Picture Conference," *The Gospel Messenger* (March 6, 1926): 149.

32. Joel Carpenter, *Revive Us Again: The Reawakening of American Fundamentalism* (New York: Oxford University Press, 1997), 130, 133; D. G. Hart, *That Old Time Religion in Modern America: Evangelical Protestantism in the Twentieth Century* (Chicago: Ivan R. Dee, 2002), 69-74.

33. *Pastor's Manual: Suggestions, Outlines, Forms, Scripture Selections, Prayers, and Hymns for Conducting Religious Services of Various Kinds* (Elgin, Ill.: Brethren Publishing House, 1923), 185-87.

34. *Full Report, 1926,* 124.

35. Wilbur Brenner Stover, *The Family Worship* (Mt. Morris, Ill.: The College Press, 1924), 42-43, 45-46. See also page 79. Stover, known primarily for his mission work in India, was pastor of the Cleveland, Ohio, Church of the Brethren when he wrote this book.

36. Virginia Lieson Brereton, *Training God's Army: The American Bible School, 1880-1940* (Bloomington, Ind.: Indiana University Press, 1990), 165-70; Paul K. Conkin, *When All the Gods Trembled: Darwinism, Scopes and American Intellectuals* (Lanham, Md.: Rowman and Littlefield Publishers, Inc., 1998), 49-77; Marty, *Modern American Religion*, 159-64; George M. Marsden, "Fundamentalism," *Encyclopedia of the American Religious Experience: Studies of Traditions and Movements,* eds. Charles H. Lippy and Peter W. Williams (New York: Charles Scribner's Sons, 1988), II:947-62; Szasz, *The Divided Mind of Protestant America,* 35-41, 68-91.

37. Donald F. Durnbaugh, "The Fundamentalist/Modernist Struggle Within the Church of the Brethren, 1910-1950," *Brethren Life and Thought* (Winter and Spring, 2002): 56.

38. *Full Report, 1926,* John R. Snyder speaking, 84.

39. *Full Report, 1926,* Homer F. Caskey speaking, 86.

40. *Full Report, 1926,* C. Ernest Davis speaking, 90.

41. Merlin C. Shull Sermon Book, manuscript, n. d.; "Work, for the Night Is Coming," No. 334 in *Hymnal: Church of the Brethren* (Elgin, Ill.: Brethren Publishing House, 1925); Maltbie D. Babcock, "Be Strong" (1901). Shull served a congregation in Detroit between 1928 and 1931. It is tempting to imagine him preaching this rousing sermon on labor to a working class fellowship. But Shull chose his words carefully, suggesting that his listeners were not members of organized labor. The sermon's first draft included the thought that laborers "have felt the Church to be unsympathetic to its struggles for justice. Protestantism always has a tendency to cater to the higher strata of life but in recent years has experienced a renewal of interest in labor." Shull, however, crossed out these words. Perhaps they were too hot for a congregation unsympathetic to organized labor, such as in his placements in Chicago and Johnson City, Tennessee. I am grateful to his son, Merlin G. Shull, for access to this source.

42. "Charles Calvert Ellis," *The Brethren Encyclopedia,* I:441-42.

43. "The Church of the Brethren and Social Problems," *The Gospel Messenger* (February 18, 1922): 99, 106.

44. Charles Calvert Ellis, "The Social Message of Christianity—A Critique," *The Gospel Messenger* (March 25, 1922): 180.

45. Durnbaugh, "The Fundamentalist/Modernist Struggle," 56-58.

46. Frank Ferry Holsopple, "The Revolt of Youth," *The Gospel Messenger* (May 30, 1925): 346.

47. "The Bible in the Public Schools," *The Gospel Messenger* (July 4, 1925): 419, 426.

48. Charles M. Yearout, "Intellectualism Versus the Counsel, Wisdom, and Will of God as Revealed in His Word," *The Gospel Messenger* (May 28, 1927): 340.

49. Hart, *That Old-Time Religion in Modern America,* 62-63.

50. Charles Calvert Ellis, "This Week's Teaching Principle" [lesson for March 2], *The Sunday School Times* (February 15, 1930).

51. "John H. Moore," *The Brethren Encyclopedia,* II:874.

52. John H. Moore, "The Virgin Birth of Christ," *The Gospel Messenger* (October 16, 1920): 618.

53. Edward J. Larson, *Summer for the Gods: The Scopes Trial and America's Continuing Debate over Science and Religion* (Cambridge, Mass.: Harvard University Press, 1997), 31-59; Szasz, *The Divided Mind of Protestant America,* 117-135.

54. *Full Report, 1923,* 92-93.

55. *Full Report, 1923,* Charley W. Guthrie speaking, 95.

56. *Full Report, 1923,* Silas S. Blough speaking, 93.

57. *Full Report, 1923,* John H. Moore speaking, 94.

58. *Full Report, 1923,* 93.

59. *Full Report, 1923,* 96. See also Herbert Hogan, "Fundamentalism in the Church of the Brethren, 1900-1931," *Brethren Life and Thought* (Winter, 1960): 34-35.

60. "The Issue at Dayton" (July 18, 1925): 8; "Not Tennessee Only" (July 25, 1925): 8; Forrest Davis, "Some Impressions from Dayton" (July 25, 1925): 12-13—all in *The Churchman.* "The Dayton Trial," (July 30, 1925): 8; R. M. Ramsey, "Tennessee and Evolution" (August 6, 1925): 14; "Learning to Think for Oneself" (August 13, 1925): 5—all in *The Presbyterian and the Herald and Presbyter.*

61. John H. Moore, "Scientific Theories and Common Sense," *The Gospel Messenger* (November 28, 1925): 754.

62. John H. Moore, "More About Science and Common Sense," *The Gospel Messenger* (December 5, 1925): 770, 771, 778.

63. H. L. Hartsough, J. E. Miller, and Ora W. Garber, eds., *Minutes of the Annual Conferences of the Church of the Brethren, 1923-1944* (Elgin, Ill.: Brethren Publishing House), 81.

64. Hartsough, Miller, and Garber, *Minutes of the Annual Conferences, 1923-1944,* 82.

65. Hartsough, Miller, and Garber, *Minutes of the Annual Conferences, 1923-1944,* 82-83.

66. Charles C. Ellis to Grant Mahan (February 4, 1943), Juniata College Archives, RG 4, President's Papers, Box 16. Also quoted in Durnbaugh, "The Fundamentalist/Modernist Struggle," 73.

67. V. F. Schwalm, *Otho Winger, 1877-1946* (Elgin, Ill.: Brethren Publishing House, 1952), 172.

V. THE TWENTIES
Division

With the changes that modernization bestowed upon American society and the Brethren community, conflict within the fellowship was nearly certain. Fondness for old time religion and a unified voice on several social issues suggest Brethren harmony, but twenties-era adjustments to modernity, layered atop old arguments about the Brethren order and separation from the mainstream, often generated friction. In 1926 the denomination suffered a small schism, but the departure of the disaffected failed to calm Brethren waters. The previous chapter described the different attitudes of Brethren toward modernization; this chapter explores the turbulence created within the fellowship by those disagreements.

CONSERVATIVE RESPONSE

Frustration haunted twenties-era Brethren conservatives just as it did those in the previous decade (see chapter 2). After World War I, traditionalists, still smarting over the 1911 dress decision, attempted once more to restore discipline and unity. In 1919 a conservative-inspired query called "Difference of Practice and Teaching" asked for a return to the Brethren's order on a list of causes. Citing Annual Meeting decisions, the measure notes:

> Accepting civil offices, in discharge of the duties of which the non-resistant principles of the Gospel are violated (Min[utes]. A[nnual]. M[eeting]., 1825 and 1918), affiliation with secret lodges (Min. A. M., 1859 and 1893), musical instruments in churches (Min. A. M.,

1890 and 1918), worldly games manifestly sinful (Min. A. M., 1892), sisters wearing hats (Min. A. M., 1867, 1898 and 1911), brethren or sisters wearing neckties (Min. A. M., 1898), or gold or pearls in the adornment of the body (Min. A. M., 1853 and 1911), is not in harmony with the established principles of our church and the Gospel. . . .[1]

The query proposed a committee of five elders, called the "Committee on Loyalty," with authority to deal with "disloyal churches in which these evils and irregularities are tolerated" and to "depose" elders, pastors, evangelists, teachers, and school officials who publicly or privately "encouraged" any of these alleged problems. A minority in a congregation could invoke the committee, but for complaints against individuals the proposal required only six members. In short, the proposition empowered a faithful conservative remnant with the ability to summon assistance from a denominational committee of weighty elders. Conservatives anticipated using this committee to purge the ministry and educational institutions, but congregations would still impose sanctions against individual members, in accordance with the traditional order.[2]

In 1920 Annual Conference brushed aside this call for a conservative super-committee and instead addressed one by one the specific issues in the measure: holding public office, membership in secret societies, musical instruments, "sinful games," and women's hats. Individualism and diversity versus community and unity dominated the discussion. Conservatives, for example, objected to a proposal that would allow members to accept civil offices if "by so doing no Gospel principle is compromised," because of the freedom this gave to individual conscience.

Who is the judge whether a Gospel principle is compromised? Suppose I decide that I would like to be treasurer of a county. I am the judge as to whether I sacrifice Gospel principles. Brethren, this is individualism. Every member of the church can decide for himself whether he sacrifices principle, and if he is anxious for the office, he will decide that he is not compromising principle and will push himself out for an official position. I oppose this, because it will take us in the direction into which our brethren have never launched.[3]

The measure tolerating Brethren office-holding passed by a large majority (379-142) but with significant opposition.[4]

Delegates found the ban on secret societies more difficult. Throughout the nineteenth century, Brethren had enforced, sometimes with difficulty, a ban on secret societies as a test of membership. Initially Brethren directed their proscription against the Masons, but as labor unions and the Sons of Temperance emerged, Annual Conference included them in its definition of associations unfit for Brethren. The Brethren had many reasons for avoiding secret societies. The secrecy itself was unbiblical, as were the oaths these societies required; their costumes disregarded plainness, their rituals were sacrilegious, and their behavior frivolous.[5] But by 1920 secret societies presented new dilemmas. Some Brethren worked in industries where union membership was beneficial, but because employers fired or blacklisted union workers, organizations often concealed their membership. Conference leadership assumed that the question on the floor referred to lodges and clubs because the annual gathering's minutes (1908) already held a hard line against unions. But delegates wanted to discuss labor organizations, indicating their relevance. M. R. Brumbaugh, elder of the Clover Creek Church of the Brethren in Fredericksburg, Pennsylvania, a coal mining region, pointed out that a ban on unions would create an unfortunate dilemma in his congregation.

> If this motion is passed, I will get into deep water. I am presiding elder in a church where the secretary is a member of a secret organization, as are two or three of my deacons. They belong to what is known as the union, the great menace of the day. I preach against it, as Bro. Funk has said, and I argue against it, but what shall I do with them if we pass this paper or this motion? . . . I want to know what I shall do with those brethren who support the church in every shape and form and who will be denied the privilege of taking up their pick and shovel to feed their hungry wives and children with daily bread, if we pass this decision and carry it in force?[6]

But anti-union sentiment was also strong.

> When our brother said something about those who would have no work if they quit the union, it set me to thinking. I used to belong to the carpenters' union. I was a member of it for about six years. The only thing that I can see in unionism today is that they want to be the big thing in everything. If there is any good in them—and

there is good in them—it is a selfish good, and it is not one that can be brought into church fellowship, as we see church fellowship. To find that out does not take long for a man who is trying to live a Christian life; neither does it take him long to find out that he can not be a member of a union and do efficient church work.[7]

Conference resolved the dilemma between its traditional ban on secret societies and the reality of industrial labor with a loophole that permitted membership in confidential associations that somehow did not violate scriptures. The blanket prohibition against membership in these organizations disappeared. Presumably Brethren could join a secret society, such as a union, if it did not require an oath, and Clover Creek could tolerate the union membership of its laboring brothers. Once more, congregations would determine what violated "Gospel principles." Once more, diversity expanded, and the order suffered.

> We decide that none of our members align themselves with, or in any way affiliate with oath-bound or secret lodges, or any other secret society that would require the individual to violate Gospel principles.[8]

Conservative hopes to reinvigorate the Brethren order suffered another setback when Annual Conference failed to restore the traditional ban on musical instruments, including organs, in worship. Delegates "advised that musical instruments not be used in the churches where they disturb the peace of the congregation."[9] This apparently permitted instruments when they did not disturb the congregation, which once more acknowledged a divided brotherhood. Conservatives complained that the wording on musical instruments was so vague that it made discipline difficult.

> I think the trouble with the Brotherhood is that we have compromised so long we are divided on many vital questions which are disturbing the spirit of the Brotherhood. We have got so far apart that we can not make a definite decision for or against the proposition, and I believe today is the vital day with the Brotherhood. We should decide this question so an elder or pastor can decide according to the decision of the Standing Committee. . . . We have to get to the things that are disturbing the peace of the Brotherhood so that we, as elders and pastors, will know where we stand. No elder in any

congregation can decide whether we are to have instruments in the church or not, according to this report.[10]

One prominent conservative condemned musical instruments as unbiblical and invoked the testimony of the fundamentalist Billy Sunday. (The best guess is that Sunday attended one of many Annual Conferences that the Brethren held in Lake Winona, Indiana, where he had a home and headquarters.)

David used instruments. David did lots of things that were worthy and some things very unworthy, and one of the unworthy things he did was to invent instruments of music. God said, "Woe unto them that invent musical instruments like David did." That is hanging over your heads. He elsewhere says, "I will not hear their viols." That is what the old law says. Now come to the new. Paul tells us how to sing, but he does not tell us how to play on the organ. I say we have not the law on this question. . . . Saul was led by the voice of the people and got into serious trouble. . . . We must not let the people decide this question; no, the law decides it. . . . We have had flattering results in our Annual Meetings. We have been praised for our fine music. Billy Sunday is a splendid singer. He said, "I never heard such fine music. I never led a congregation like you have got here." No. At Seattle the papers praised our fine music and we had no instrument. . . . I would not see any harm in the people learning music; no, but when you come to worship God, it is simply wrong to employ musical instruments.[11]

Yet another defender of the Old Order called for conformity to Annual Meeting and for unity on music.

It has been asked what we are to do with those churches that already have this instrument. I have no doubt the committee did the best they knew how, but that has been the mischief right along. I have been fifty years in the church, and the mischief was for churches to go ahead of Annual Conference, not heeding their decisions until it came to a point. Now, what shall we do? We simply have submitted to those who were not loyal to the decisions of the church. Jesus says, "You can not serve two masters." You can not serve those who have gone ahead of the decisions of the Annual Meeting and have organs in the churches.[12]

Casual remarks made by elders about musical instruments revealed their power in congregational affairs.

> So far as I am personally concerned, there has not been much pressure in our church at home. What little there has been I have been able to hold down.[13]

> I stand in bad light before the young people of my church because I blocked the way in my church for allowing the instrument to be used for public worship.[14]

D. W. Kurtz, a progressive, countered that musical instruments were already a fact of congregational life. He challenged the conservative interpretation of the scriptures, he compared the conservative passion for order and unity to the rule of Russian tsars, and he concluded that popular opinion among the Brethren heavily favored instruments.

> Now the facts of the matter are, there are scores, and I think I can say hundreds, of churches that have musical instruments. Some have had them for many years. This is a condition that exists. . . . We must have a decision that takes into consideration this senti-ment in the Brotherhood. If we want a decision to work together, we have to consider that sentiment. On the other hand, we are facing the future, and we have no right to make any decision that we can not defend by scriptural reason. I want a decision we can face with the one hundred thousand young people and tell them why we do it. They all ask, "Why do you have them in your homes, in your colleges, in your theological seminaries, teach it everywhere, and not allow it?"[15]

> We have to face the situation. The best way to make law breakers is to have a bad law. There would not be a bit of bolshevism in the world had there been no czar. You can not enforce in a democra-cy any law under the sun unless it is a just law. It is very easy for us to say we don't want it. It is another thing to say why we don't want it, and to say there are scriptural or reasonable grounds why.

One brother tried to do it, but he so completely misrepresented Amos in his clear teaching that it does not tell us anything. The whole ground of Amos is not against the instrument, but against the worship they have, with injustice back of it. Those people came and sang and had their music and worship and went home and robbed their neighbors and were unjust. It is the injustice he is condemning all the way through. Again, to say it is absolutely wrong—you can't show by the New Testament that it is wrong. Again, we are told about the harps in heaven. I would like to know how we can go before the world and before the church and before the young people and before the churches that have them and before the homes that have them and say it is wrong. In many of the homes the instrument is used in the religious services; how can we go before them and consistently say there is a scriptural and reasonable ground for saying it is wrong? That is the problem we are up against. It is no longer for us to say what we want. We have to make decisions that are in harmony with Christ—decisions that we can defend so clearly that our young people will love the church and abide by the decisions. That can not be done by looking backward. We have to give grounds, and I want to say again, . . . the committee was instructed to study the sentiment of the church. We have found that sentiment, and we believe that the sentiment in the church as a whole is just as strong, that under peaceful and proper conditions the thing should be allowed . . . our answer must be an answer that we can defend, and if you say "No," defend your answer, and I do not believe it has yet been done in any of the previous Conferences, or here.[16]

After a heated and lengthy discussion on musical instruments, delegates cried out for the "question," but the moderator still had trouble closing the debate. Finally, the gathering approved congregational autonomy on this issue by a majority (361-161) almost identical to that which allowed Brethren to hold public office.[17]

Exhausted delegates quickly passed two more recommendations: "We decide that all games manifestly sinful be forbidden" (cards, pool, gambling, etc.), and a requirement that sisters not wear hats. The injunction against sinful games was long-standing, and for women's hats Conference relied on the 1911 dress decision, which required

> that the sisters attire themselves in plainly-made garments, free
> from ornaments and unnecessary appendages. That plain bonnets
> and hoods be the headdress, and the hair be worn in a becoming
> Christian manner.[18]

Once more delegates discussed neckties but without changing policy. Conference still advised men not to wear them but declined to make men's neckwear a test of membership. Apparently the brothers who did most of the voting were willing to have the hatless sisters take the lead in upholding the order on dress while granting themselves elbow-room on neckties. Finally, Conference left in place the traditional ban against wearing gold and jewelry.

Conservatives attempted to add one last word as other delegates clamored to vote. The moderator, I. W. Taylor, a conservative elder from Lancaster County, Pennsylvania, perhaps sympathizing with the minority and perhaps hoping that they would not depart too dejected, resisted motions to close debate and allowed conservatives the floor.

> After we go home, we would like to have everybody feel he had
> a fair chance, even if we must take a little more time. It is the sense
> of the officers of this meeting that we should give Bro. Zigler an
> opportunity to speak.[19]

Conservatives left the 1920 Annual Conference with the lingering taste of defeat. After all the voting, they gained nothing, and the progressive erosion of the traditional order rolled on. Only approval of the already existing bans on sinful games, jewelry, and hat-wearing sisters affirmed the order, whereas the choice of diversity over unity, i.e., allowing congregations to set their own standards regarding neckties, union membership, musical instruments, and public office-holding, and the quick demise of the loyalty committee, were antithetical to the order and signaled the continuing decline of nonconformity. The future belonged to neckties and organs.

1926 ANNUAL CONFERENCE

Two years later beleaguered traditionalists founded a periodical, the *Bible Monitor*, to "oppose error, wrong and evil wherever found."[20] Reflecting on their setback in 1920, they concluded that the majority had treated their concerns unfairly by assigning their "Difference of Practice and Teaching" paper to a committee laden with progressives, whose unsympathetic report the delegates only narrowly approved. (In fact, even the controversial parts of the committee's report passed by margins of more than two to one.) According to vanquished conservatives, the committee "virtually sanctioned all the irregularities embraced in the paper and was adopted by a small margin in open Conference. And, as might be expected, conditions grew worse."[21]

In 1924 the evolving Old Order movement incorporated its journal and agreed on a Declaration of Principles, two big steps toward separation from the denomination.[22] They denied accusations of divisiveness and claimed only to "take God at his Word."

> Are we seeking to divide the church when we take God at his Word? If so, may he send us more who are trying to divide the church. The only division we seek is that of the church from the world, and we intend to continue seeking that. We are taking God at his Word, and we can only say as did the apostle long ago, "Whether it be right in the sight of God to hearken unto you more than unto God, judge ye." We do not want division; we want union, but the only union that is worth having is that which is based on the teaching of our Savior and his inspired apostles. What does any union amount to that does not have God behind it and all through it? We can do all things if we have God with us, but our condition is indeed pitiable if we obey man rather than God. . . .
>
> . . . We do not like to have anyone say that we are trying to divide the church, for that is not true. For some time we have known persons who wished to withdraw from the church and unite with some other body because of the departures of the church from the faith; but we have always urged them to stay with the body and do their best to help get the church back where it belongs. If there is any effort to divide the church, it is made by those who differ from us.[23]

As conservative aggravation grew, defenders of the Old Order yielded still more ground to progressives, this time over the ability of congregations to control membership standards. The rise of congregational independence, which allowed local societies rather than Annual Conference to interpret the Brethren order, led inevitably to confusing multiple standards for membership and, in practice, illogical situations. Liberal individuals, who lived closest to a conservative congregation in which they could not qualify for membership, could not join a more progressive group nearby because Brethren who were out of fellowship with their congregation could not join another. This prevented brothers and sisters from gravitating into meetings with whom they might be more compatible. Also, Brethren who had moved and needed to transfer membership encountered difficulties. Conservative fellowships could deny membership to newcomers even if they had full standing with their previous, presumably more liberal, congregation. Furthermore, conservative congregations could refuse certificates to members in full fellowship when they moved because questioning departing members was easier. In a *Gospel Messenger* article, H. C. Early gently rebuffed traditionalists by criticizing congregations for delaying transfer letters and by encouraging subordination of local interests to denominational unity, normally a conservative goal, but in this case a suggestion that conservative stubbornness created disharmony.[24]

> To be a member in regular standing and entitled to a certificate of transfer, if changing location, one should be sound in faith, believing in Jesus and his teachings whole-heartedly, unreservedly. For the New Testament is the ground of faith and the bond of Christian fellowship. It must mean upright walk also, and that the individual is at peace with the membership. Individual differences and offences must be cleared away. The church is justified, in fact it is her duty, to withhold certificates from those who are at fault in these respects, until adjustments are made and satisfaction given. For these conditions are purely fundamental and absolutely essential to the Christian life. They are plainly taught in the Word of God about which there can be no quibble.
>
>   . . . Practices belonging to localities are common to all bodies. It is true of the church [in] general; it is true of the Church of the Brethren. And it is true in more things than one. But local conditions must yield to general conditions in the adoption of measures for the general body, and which involve the interests of the whole body. This principle applies to church certificates as well as other matters, and it should unify and harmonize the body. The position of a body of people upon any question is to be understood in the light of their general practice. Therefore, the position of the Brotherhood in the matter of church certificates is the general practice of the church.
>
>   I need hardly say that when members move from one congregation to another, they should be given certificates promptly,

and then they should be presented promptly to the congregations into which they move. No opportunity should be lost. If, however, there are conditions in the way of giving certificates to outgoing members, they should be adjusted at once. In fact, congregations are not justified in carrying members, undisturbedly, who are not eligible to transfer. Undisturbed membership must mean not less than eligibility to transfer, for the requirements for the transfer of membership are the same as the requirements for membership.[25]

In 1925 Conference provided guidance on this thorny issue by deciding that transferring members deserved prompt certificates. Reluctant congregations could write the reason for the problem on the back of the document, but they should still issue it. The delegates included a statement of racial equality, noteworthy in a time when the Ku Klux Klan enjoyed widespread popularity. "The New Testament is the basis of membership. Neither race nor location is considered." Conservatives accepted this decision, not realizing until later that Conference had given those out of step with conservative congregations the right to transfer to liberal ones. Once more diversity trumped unity.

III. Basic Principles
    1. Since the local congregations are the units that constitute the general Brotherhood, to hold membership in a local congregation is to have membership in the general body. The New Testament is the basis of membership. Neither race nor location is considered. . . .
    2. The requirements for membership are the requirements for transfer of membership. Both are the same. **Therefore, the requirements for the transfer of membership must not be greater than the requirements for membership. . . .**

IV. Granting Certificates
    1. Certificates shall be granted promptly to those moving from one congregation to another, recommending them to the love and care of the congregation to which they go, that they may receive at once the care of the church and contribute to the work of the church. . . .
    3. Since the membership is practically one in faith in the principles of simplicity and modesty—the simple life in general—but not all are in complete harmony with all the methods employed to teach

and enforce these principles, a congregation, when it cannot see its way to grant a certificate in full fellowship because of a lack of harmony with the order of the church in dress, or any other subject, may state the exception on the back of the certificate, after all reasonable effort has been made for reconciliation.[26]

Although the membership decision elicited momentary consensus, the next Annual Conference, 1926, felt a sense of urgency. Papers submitted by the populous eastern and southern districts in Pennsylvania carried the conservative flag and catalyzed the crisis. The statements, virtually identical and obviously collaborative, rebuked several trends in popular culture, including fashionably dressed and bobbed women, which suggested a fundamentalist influence, as does the title of the papers: "Reaffirmation of Fundamentals." But the conservative complaints concentrated on the passing on of the Brethren order, including unacceptably progressive missionaries, membership in secret societies, the decline of kneeling during worship, the prayer veil, and the holy kiss.

Whereas, the Church of the Brethren has been, and now is, passing through a remarkable period of transition;

And whereas, a part of this change is regarded by many as being a departure from the faith (Jude 3), a violation of Scripture and Annual Meeting decisions, as will be seen from the following, to wit:

(1) Missionaries having been sent to foreign fields, holding views on the simple life in dress who would be deprived from holding fellowship in the congregations which are paying for their support.

(2) Elders and pastors receiving into fellowship those who are members of secret societies and oathbound organizations.

(3) Teachings of Scripture and rulings of Conference on the dress question ignored. Sisters bobbing their hair, wearing jewelry for adornment by members and wearing of apparel in quality and style that border on indecency and shamelessness.

(4) A general neglect and discarding of daily prayer and wearing of the prayer veil.

(5) Kneeling in prayer in public worship largely abandoned.

(6) Salutation of the holy kiss as taught by the Gospels and adopted by Annual Conference is gradually being dispensed with.

Because of the foregoing facts and conditions and the craze for worldly amusement, many times irreligious and Christless, serious apprehensions have [been] obtained, causing many honest souls to place a question mark in all seriousness on the propriety of supporting church work and missionary activities.[27]

J. H. Longenecker, an elder from Lebanon County, Pennsylvania, explained the intent of the papers. Twice he remarked that "we are not for a fight," but he left little doubt that if Conference did not reinstate lost portions of the order, schism was possible.

I desire to explain just why this paper is here. In the first few lines there is mention made of a period of transition, and it takes no sage to see that this has been and is true, that our beloved church has been and is passing through a period of transition. Where I come from we do not think that all this has been wrong, but a part of this has caused uneasiness and doubt, and departure from what we regard as Scripture teaching and the former rules of the Conference.

The origin of this paper, as the delegates would get it now, would seem to come from two State Districts of the east, and it is true the paper came through these two State Districts comprising a membership of about 14,000, but the uneasiness and the doubt that have come through some of the departures do not all rest in Eastern Pennsylvania or in Southern Pennsylvania. The reason perhaps, largely, that this came is because throughout the Brotherhood letters have come to us, asking whether something could not be done and we could come back again to some things that we have departed from. . . .

As to the design of the paper, we are not for a fight. I think we should be here because we love and want to be loved. I might say that the design of the paper . . . is to regain unanimity of faith and practice in the church, that confidence and quiet may be restored, and in framing this paper there was a thought that this paper does not do any good, for it is not radical enough. We ought to ask for much more than this paper asks for. There are those who think perhaps the paper that is here should not have come (I mean in our own State Districts), and who think that it will perhaps avail nothing, that we should be satisfied with present conditions and so the paper was brought in a kind of compromising nature, a kind of middle ground, with the hope that we may be unified. . . .

I say again we are not here for a fight; we are here because we want to have peace and quiet restored. You may not in some of the sections of the Brotherhood have just the information as we have it of this unrest and doubt that is at present staring us in the face, and unless something can be done by which we can again get us a little nearer together, there may be results that we would very much feel sorry for and would not want to come.[28]

Otho Winger also feared that conservatives would leave the denomination if it casually dismissed their manifesto. Winger labored late into the night to formulate a compromise that would placate traditionalists, yet win approval from the progressive majority of delegates at the 1926 gathering.

Otho Winger, president of Manchester College (1911-1941), six-time Annual Conference moderator, architect of the 1926 compromise, and moderate fundamentalist. *Photo courtesy of BHLA.*

On Monday night before the Conference was to begin on Tuesday, I began to think seriously. To have those papers come before Annual Conference and be turned down would have been an insult to eastern and southern Pennsylvania. I was afraid some harsh things would be said. To have that happen with this other organization at hand [the *Bible Monitor* movement] might have resulted seriously. I spent most of Monday night in my hotel trying to write out a substitute answer to that paper. I wrote it again and

again. The papers were long. I tried to cover the points in the
paper, restating the principles of the church in them, but leaving
out the teeth and the reactionary part of it.[29]

Winger explained his proposal, which included a substitute resolution, in a conciliatory speech to Conference. He agreed with conservatives that many Brethren "must apologize for some things that do exist,"
i.e., widespread departure from the Old Order, but in a mild rebuke of
discipline, he also counseled that "too rigid, drastic decisions" were
counterproductive.

In the first place, I think we ought to receive this paper with all sincerity. It comes from two Districts, well-known Districts, in our
Brotherhood. We have been told that they represent 14,000
members. These two Districts accept these queries here. That of
itself is evidence that there is a large number of our people who
are thinking seriously and earnestly desiring something, and I
would like to remind you, too, that these queries come from
Districts that are doing things. The District from which this first
paper comes stands at the head of all our Districts, I understand
this year both in the amount of mission giving and also in per capita of mission giving. Many of us know by working with these
brethren who represent these Districts on the Standing
Committee that their heart's desire is for the good of Zion, for the
work of the church and for the forward movement, in which they
have been interested.

I want to say, first of all, this paper ought to have the greatest
respect. More than usual, I think, consideration because of the large
number of good people who are back of it. That is my feeling.

This paper represents, as has been said, that on the part of a
large, conservative membership there are many things in the
Church of the Brethren in the way of practice of some of her
members that do grieve them, and rightfully so. The fact of the
matter is, there are some of us who do not live in such conservative sections, not quite as old as some others, that can scarcely be
satisfied with some of the things that do exist, and a great many
people from all parts of our Brotherhood, at least, must apologize
for some things that do exist.

Taking all that into consideration, I say again we ought seriously to consider this matter. There are a lot of people today,
good, honest people in the Church of the Brethren, who are won-

dering what we are going to do with this paper. I say again, if I know the situation, I doubt whether a large part of you would feel like passing these two papers, putting them on our minutes with the answer which in some respects perhaps is more drastic, or, should I say, more positive, in its statement, maybe so much so that after all, it would not have the desired effect.

I know there are some people who say, "What is the use to pass anything at all?" The minutes have already been referred to. That would indicate on every one of these questions we have minutes referring to these things. Yet I would like to remind you, like the subject of peace, we do not hesitate to put on our minutes some things that will refresh our minds. Sometimes folks ask the question, "Does the church still stand for some of these things?" Every now and then some one will say, "I don't think the Church of the Brethren does stand for some of these things."

For my part I still believe (at least I hope) that I am a member of a church that does emphasize some of these things mentioned that do violate the principles of the simple life, and if we can get something that will be an urge to some of our folks, I favor it, but I am frank to say I do not believe that too rigid, drastic decisions have done us much good. When they are too drastic, they become a sort of suggestion to some folks to violate, and where they are enforced too drastically, in most sections at least, they do not do the greatest amount of good.

If I were to express my own heart's desire on this, I would wish that we might send out again to our beloved Brotherhood, as that first Jerusalem council sent out some things that did pertain to moral questions, that somehow or other we could send out and renew an expression of our faith and belief in some of these things. For that reason, as a substitute motion, I have a resolution that I would like to offer as a substitute answer to this query, with the understanding that this might be our answer without placing on our minutes these four pages. I should like to offer this as a substitute motion, and I shall read it since I have written it in my own hand:

Realizing that in many ways the members of our beloved church are prone to drift into worldly thought and conduct, and sincerely desiring to do all possible to keep our church true to the teachings of our Lord and his Word, therefore, the Annual Meeting of 1926 reaffirms some of her fundamental teachings and urges renewed faithfulness to them.

1. That all our ministers be true to the declaration of principles and purpose as required of all delegates to Annual Meeting.

2. That we continue our opposition to our members belonging to secret societies and oath-bound organizations and insist that pastors and elders do not receive into, or hold in church membership, those who are members of such organizations.

3. That elders and pastors be faithful in teaching the simple life; that our members refrain from wearing immodest dress and jewelry and from worldly amusements. We decide that the world[ly] custom of women bobbing their hair is contrary to Scripture and Christian modesty, and urge all sisters to adorn themselves as women professing godliness.

4. That all members make a united effort to have the family altar erected in every home; that worship in our churches be made as spiritual as possible; and that the Lord's Prayer and the kneeling posture in prayer be not neglected.

5. That we renew our vows of love for the Church of the Brethren and for one another and urge that the Christian salutation of the holy kiss, that great symbol of Christian love, be properly observed.[30]

Although Winger acknowledged conservative grievances, he subtly reworked their document to remove suggestions of discipline. Conservatives sought enforcement of the order, even though they never used that term. Instead, the key word in Winger's version was "urge," found three times in his statement. According to Winger's vision, Conference would urge faithfulness, observation of the holy kiss, etc., but the Brethren would not restore a system that expelled nonconforming members. Winger employed stronger language only twice. He recommended that Conference "decide" that bobbed hair was unbiblical and immodest, but he dropped the conservative description of Brethren women with dress bordering on "indecency and shamelessness." Secondly, Conference would "insist" that elders and pastors not receive into membership those who joined secret societies. Otherwise, Winger gave the conservatives an emasculated version of their objectives.[31]

Winger's substitute attracted support. Several progressives rallied to the compromise because they opposed "legislating" church discipline.

> I believe we have just scores and scores of young men and women, middle aged young men and women, whom the proper kind of life will bring around right.
>
> If we go to legislating, off they will go. Legislation cannot reach them as love can.[32]

Protectors of a traditional role for women complained that Winger's substitute removed their ability to discipline for bobbed hair. By the mid-twenties the bob had arrived in American society and was no longer a novelty; glamour queens of the silver screen, such as Gloria Swanson, sported the sleek look, which was standard on campuses and in fashion advertisements.[33] Brethren traditionalists were upset, and just before the vote on Winger's compromise motion, a delegate bluntly asked, "If that substitute motion is granted, does it mean that we must receive our members who have bobbed hair?" The moderator asked Winger to reread the relevant portion of his motion. ("We decide that the worldly custom of women bobbing their hair is contrary to Scripture and Christian modesty, and urge all sisters to adorn themselves as women professing godliness.") This was the only answer the delegate received.[34]

Winger's substitute passed by a wide margin. According to the minutes, "most all stood" in support of the measure and "not many" opposed it. Winger believed that the eastern conservatives backed his efforts and that only the *Bible Monitor* followers dissented.[35]

DUNKARD BRETHREN SCHISM

Winger forestalled a major conservative defection, but he could not keep the "Bible Monitor family," as they called themselves, within the fold. One week after Annual Conference this group of alienated conservatives and fundamentalists met in Plevna, Indiana, and founded the Dunkard Brethren Church. The newest denomination to trace its origins to Alexander Mack proclaimed,

> We have taken this step deliberately. We do not expect large numbers to follow. Indeed we suspect the number to be small. God's minorities were never large. Majorities are often wrong. Minorities are sometimes right, especially when changes from former restrictive customs to modern liberalism are made. We commend our course to all lovers of truth and fidelity to Christ, conscious of the fact that God knows our hearts and the motives from which we act.[36]

As the Dunkard Brethren resisted change in the Old Order, they condemned the new one, including female preachers, professional pastors, the youth cult, higher education, and popular culture. Most assuredly, Dunkard Brethren belonged to the Old Order movement, but fundamentalists also objected to many of these trends, giving Dunkard Brethren commonality with America's great conservative counter-revolution.

> Standing in prayer?
> Omitting the Lord's prayer?
> Praying over the collection plates?
> Ministers dressing like Catholic priests?
> Sisters wearing hats?
> Sisters wearing bloomers?
> Sisters bobbing hair?
> Sisters waxing, painting and powdering?
> Ministers reading Mutt and Jeff?
> Members going to dances, shows, picknicks [sic], etc., etc.?
> Churches holding chicken and waffle suppers to pay their drone pastors that put the name Rev. to their name which belongs to God alone?
> Setting the deacon office aside?
> And the pastor selecting a bunch of men that are as worldly as he is, calling them his cabinet, and taking members into the church of other denominations contrary to the teaching of the gospel?
> Brethren taking the name of God in vain?
> In short doing and acting like the world? Are they not the world? They conform to the world in dress and conduct. The scriptures teach plainly that we are not to conform to the world. Rom. 12:1, 2; 1 Tim. 2:9; 1 Pet. 3:3, 4.
> It is impossible to know the church members by dress or actions.
> Will we stay with them and go where the world goes? Or will we obey Christ's teaching and separate ourselves from them? It takes courage but the Holy Spirit will strengthen us for all trials if we ask him.[37]

> Christian women may function, and should be encouraged to be helpful in many ways, but a female ministry in the sense of preaching, or a female official in the church, is without Scriptural authority.[38]

The duty of the church to properly support the ministry is recognized but a salaried ministry is without warrant from the Scripture and contrary to the custom of the church for over 200 years.[39]

The youth, reared in such an atmosphere, comes to regard chastity as a cheap and worthless virtue, and gives unbridled rein to his passions. A scandal thus becomes a matter that relieves the tedium of a dull and prosaic existence, and lends freshened interest to the news items of the day.[40]

If education, however great a blessing it may be, educates away from the Bible, that education is wrong even tho it may fill our schools and colleges with students. If the opinions and theories of the pupil are wrong, the means by which they were inculcated can never be right—the teaching that produced them must forever be wrong—the school which furnished an opportunity may be good but his teaching was wrong, hence wrong results, a mind filled with wrong ideas.[41]

Just think of the modern D. D.'s, Ph. D.'s, L. L. D.'s and so on, subscribing to the system of ethics or the code of laws and doctrine and the childlike faith of those men. How humiliating to our long-handled-named men to allow such men as James Quinter, John Umstead, R. H. Miller, Sr., D. Hays* or even A. Mack himself, to formulate a system of faith and practice for them!

Just imagine, if possible, yourself back in the days of those men, in a modern $30,000 or $40,000 Brethren church with a fashionable young lady with no marks of a Sister pounding away at

----

*James Quinter, John Umstead (Umstad), Robert H. Miller, and Daniel Hays were nineteenth- and turn-of-the-century denominational leaders.

a lifeless instrument in a hopeless effort to pump out praise to God in the assembly of the saints! This will show the contrast between then and now, between the idea of worship in their day and ours.[42]

Seeking defectors, Dunkard Brethren sent representatives into the conservative Brethren heartland of eastern Pennsylvania,[43] but they won few converts. Three Brethren elders—I. W. Taylor, J. H. Longenecker, and Samuel H. Hertzler—who comprised the District Ministerial Board, sent a mimeographed letter to district leaders persuasively arguing against division, and most conservatives remained with the Church of the Brethren.[44]

According to what we regard as reliable information, the thing that some of us have for some time been fearing, and which it seems to us none would really want, has happened, or is at the point of happening.

We are told that a group of our dear brethren and sisters have about decided to withdraw their fellowship from the Church of the Brethren with a view of forming another and separate organization. We would indeed deeply deplore a step of this kind. It would bring back again as from the grave all the dark record, the painful experiences, and horrors of things that happened some forty years ago, which in large measure are forgotten by the present generation.*

Experience has taught us that division was no cure then. We have no reason to believe it will mean a cure now. Above all, there is no assurance that it would meet the approval of the Father of mercies. Isa. 54:7-10; Jer. 31:35-37; 1 Cor. 12:25. Scripture has no plain case where God countenances division.

The story of Elijah and the record of the seven churches of Asia, Rev. 2 and 3, cannot be reconciled with the idea of forsaking the church, or of bringing about a rupture in the church. Some of us who felt there was just cause for complaint were greatly encouraged at our last Annual Conference by the attitude of our church leaders. We therefore think it would indeed be very unfortunate to agitate or disturb the church with a spirit of division at a time when there is hope of a check to the worldly trend in the main body of the church.

---

*This refers to the schism of 1881/82.

While we are not unmindful of the many problems with which the faithful are confronted in these last days, and the trials and tests it brings to them, we, however, do not think that our people in eastern Pennsylvania would be ready for another break in the Brotherhood.

We take this opportunity, which may seem to be a late date to earnestly plead with our dear brethren and sisters, to be cautious and move slow in an issue fraught with such grave and tremendous responsibilities.[45]

CONCLUSION

On occasion the worldview of twenties-era Brethren appeared black and white. The debate over the role of visiting evangelists notwithstanding, almost all Brethren believed that revivalism was the right way to admit new members into the fellowship (described in chapter 3). Likewise, almost all Brethren, even progressives, agreed that some elements of popular culture were wrong. In the culture wars against jazz, movies, the youth cult, and the violation of Prohibition, most Brethren fought on the same side (described in chapter 4).

Beyond these few areas of accord, blends and shadings highlighted the Brethren ideological spectrum, suggesting that culture wars also divided the denomination. Conservatives and progressives disagreed over the Brethren trend toward diversity and individualism, and they skirmished repeatedly over markers of the Old Order, such as prayer veils, the free ministry, plain dress, secret societies, and musical instruments. But fundamentalism also tinted Brethren conservatism, as indicated by quarrels over the Social Gospel, higher criticism, and national morality. Conservatives, including the Dunkard Brethren, with their focus on maintenance of plainness and nonconformity to the mainstream, appear primarily Old Order, but their antagonism toward modern women and "wrong ideas" in higher education suggest at least a small debt to fundamentalism. Yet another hue to the Brethren spectrum came from moderate fundamentalism, which embraced old-time religion except for its militancy. Moreover, most Brethren opposed evolution, but only militant fundamentalists called on Uncle Sam to suppress it. Thus, evangelicals, progressives, Old Orders—some in the denomination and some departing—and fundamentalists—some moderate and some militant—colored the Brethren rainbow.

Just before Moderator James M. Moore closed the 1930 Annual Conference, he told a story about a factory and its machinery to illustrate his anxiety that the church's institutional growth had outgrown the ability of the faithful to support it. Then, he looked forward to greater harmony among Christians and remarked that he would like to see the "little broken parts" of the Brethren restored to unity. He could have been referring to the splintering of Alexander Mack's movement in 1881/82, to the Dunkard Brethren schism, or to continuing division within the denomination.

> I heard a story not long ago, relating to a great factory. That factory was operated by a great engine, and they kept adding one piece of machinery after the other to the machinery of the factory until one morning the engineer went down into the boiler room, fired up the engine, got the requisite quantity of steam, pulled open the throttle, and not a single wheel moved. The fact was that the engine no longer had power to move the machinery of the institution. I think there is such a thing as that true in the life of the church, and I am glad today for the merging of organization. I am hopeful that the day will come when there will be a general merging of Christian interest and Christian effort. I am very anxious to see that day come, and I would be glad for the day when the little broken parts of the Church of the Brethren might be brought back into one groove and one communion, one fellowship. I hope that day will come.[46]

Moore's "machinery" metaphor, a commonly used term among the Brethren during this period, and his reference to the "groove," slang borrowed from phonographs and jazz, both show the contribution of modernity to the language of the Brethren. To be sure, modernization did not consistently divide the Brethren; on the secularization of popular culture they stood shoulder to shoulder. But bringing the Brethren "back into one groove" would be difficult, as long as modernization and some of its offspring—professionalization, urbanization, industrialization, individualism, higher education, and changing gender roles—cut cleavages in the fellowship.

NOTES

1. *Full Report of the Proceedings of the Annual Conference of the Church of the Brethren, 1919* (Elgin, Ill.: Brethren Publishing House, 1919), 123.
2. *Full Report, 1920,* 106.
3. *Full Report, 1920,* Reuben Shroyer speaking, 108-9.
4. *Full Report, 1920,* 109-10.
5. "Secret Societies," *The Brethren Encyclopedia,* 3 vols., edited by Donald F. Durnbaugh (Philadelphia, Pa., and Oak Brook, Ill.: The Brethren Encyclopedia, Inc., 1983), II:1163-64.
6. *Full Report, 1920,* M. R. Brumbaugh speaking, 112-113.
7. *Full Report, 1920,* Edward A. Markey speaking, 113.
8. *Full Report, 1920,* Daniel W. Kurtz speaking, 114.
9. *Full Report, 1920,* J. W. Lear speaking, 114.
10. *Full Report, 1920,* Verley K. Meek speaking, 115-16.
11. *Full Report, 1920,* Isaac J. Rosenberger speaking, 117-18.
12. *Full Report, 1920,* John Herr speaking, 118-19.
13. *Full Report, 1920,* Peter S. Miller speaking, 116.
14. *Full Report, 1920,* H. H. Helman speaking, 118.
15. *Full Report, 1920,* D. W. Kurtz speaking, 115.
16. *Full Report, 1920,* D. W. Kurtz speaking, 119.
17. *Full Report, 1920,* 110-123.
18. *Full Report, 1920,* reading clerk speaking, 123-24.
19. *Full Report, 1920,* 125-28.
20. "Origin and Purpose of the Bible Monitor," *Bible Monitor* (July 15, 1924): 2.
21. "Origin and Purpose," *Bible Monitor,* 1.
22. "Origin and Purpose," *Bible Monitor,* 2; "Minutes of the Meeting of the Bible Monitor Family," *Bible Monitor* (July 1, 1924): 1-3.
23. "Trying to Divide the Church," *Bible Monitor* (July 1, 1924): 6-7.
24. Carl F. Bowman, *Brethren Society: The Cultural Transformation of a "Peculiar People"* (Baltimore, Md.: The Johns Hopkins University Press, 1995), 263-65.
25. Henry C. Early, "Granting and Receiving Membership Certificates," *The Gospel Messenger* (May 8, 1926): 290-91.
26. *Full Report, 1926,* 56. See also Carl Bowman, *Brethren Society,* 264-65.
27. H. L. Hartsough, J. E. Miller, and Ora W. Garber, eds., *Minutes of the Annual Conferences of the Church of the Brethren, 1923-1944* (Elgin, Ill.: Brethren Publishing House, 1946), 36. *Full Report, 1926* titles the papers, "Restatement of Some Fundamental Teachings," see 147.
28. *Full Report, 1926,* 117-18.
29. Winger to H. C. Early (1933) in V. F. Schwalm, *Otho Winger, 1877-1946* (Elgin, Ill.: Brethren Publishing House, 1952), 133.
30. *Full Report, 1926,* 120-22.
31. Carl Bowman, *Brethren Society,* 281.

32. *Full Report, 1926,* Franklin H. Crumpacker speaking, 124.

33. Paula S. Fass, *The Damned and the Beautiful: American Youth in the 1920s* (New York: Oxford University Press, 1977), 456-57n35-36.

34. *Full Report, 1926,* Michael Kurtz speaking, 129. See also Carl Bowman, *Brethren Society,* 279-82; Donald F. Durnbaugh, *Fruit of the Vine: A History of the Brethren, 1708-1995* (Elgin, Ill.: Brethren Press, 1997), 444-46.

35. *Full Report, 1926,* 130; Schwalm, *Otho Winger,* 134.

36. "Minutes of the Open Meeting of the 'Bible Monitor' Family, Greentown, Ind.," *Bible Monitor* (August 1, 1926): 8-12.

37. J. G. Mock, "What Would Jesus Say of His Church?" *Bible Monitor* (February 15, 1927): 12-13.

38. "Declaration of Principles," *Bible Monitor* (July 15, 1924): 7.

39. "Declaration of Principles," 7.

40. "Bishop Freeman on the Church and Social Conditions," *Bible Monitor* (August 1, 1926): 5.

41. "Conviction or Policy," *Bible Monitor* (August 1, 1926): 2.

42. "Honor to Whom Honor Is Due," *Bible Monitor* (November 1, 1923): 3-4.

43. Loring I. Moss, "A Recent Trip to Maryland," *Bible Monitor* (February 15, 1927): 11.

44. Carl Bowman, *Brethren Society,* 406-7, 469–34; Durnbaugh, *Fruit of the Vine,* 444-46.

45. Schwalm, *Otho Winger,* 135-36.

46. *Full Report, 1930,* 145.

VI. The Thirties
Economic and International Crises

If the conflict and anxiety of the Roaring Twenties was concealed behind a carefree image, the social anxiety of the thirties was unmistakable. In the first decade of the interwar period, conflict seethed just beneath the surface, but during the thirties the modern economy's collapse and the inability of modern nation-states to coexist were agonizingly obvious.

Both the Depression and international tension engulfed the Church of the Brethren. Like most Americans, however, the Brethren met the economic crisis with perseverance, enduring what they could not change and waiting for prosperity to return. Brethren, similarly, could do little to prevent the resumption of global war, but they nonetheless witnessed for peace and increased relief efforts. Above all, both crises illustrate the power of distant forces to impact individuals and shape institutions, a classic trait of modernity.

DEPRESSION

The Great Depression callously displayed a modern economy's mysterious ability to influence local and personal welfare. Individuals paid a heavy price for the economy's collapse. Between 1929 and 1932, stocks lost three-fourths of their value, and local banks, college endowments, the wealthy, and those people approaching retirement watched assets disappear from their accounts. Between the Wall Street crash (October 1929) and Franklin D. Roosevelt's inauguration (March 1933), five thousand banks failed and $7 billion in deposits evaporated. In 1930 some 150,000 homeowners defaulted; in 1931 that figure increased to

200,000; and 250,000 lost their savings and shelter in 1932. State and local governments cut services and failed to pay creditors. During the winter of 1932-33, Chicago compensated its teachers with tax warrants, then paid them nothing. Macrostatistics were just as gloomy. By 1933 the gross national product fell to half of its 1929 level. In 1933 automakers produced only one-third as many vehicles as they had in 1929. Agricultural income dropped from $6 billion in 1929 (which was, in reality, a poor year on the farm) to $2 billion in 1932. In 1933 unemployment stood at 25 percent. Economic numbers, however, tell only part of the story. The marriage rate fell by 22 percent, the birth rate dropped by 15 percent, and the divorce rate declined by 25 percent as the hard times locked couples into failing relationships. Unemployed husbands and fathers lost self-respect, and in some families the balance of power shifted as nontraditional providers contributed a larger percentage of the household income. Undoubtedly, the Great Depression changed lives and altered society.[1]

Yet much about the Brethren reflected continuity. Even the Depression could not alter practices that Brethren had enjoyed for generations. Congregations continued to report revivals,[2] and church camps were popular. Love feast, as fondly remembered by one sister, remained a high point of the church year.

> Love feast was a big thing. We'd always have revival before love feast. We didn't have love feast at each little preaching point. We had it at the biggest church in the congregation and people would never miss it.* That was a big thing. They had seats made so that every other one, you could lift them up and put a little peg in [so] that they made a table and two people sat facing each other.
>
> We always had mutton, and then the ladies would bake homemade bread with the broth. My folks always helped with the food. My daddy helped butcher the sheep and mother would bake homemade bread, and we had bread and homemade butter on the table with that. They had extra bread and butter besides meat and the sop. [Deacons] would always go out and visit with all the members before love feast.[3]

Mission continued as another popular feature of church life, and furloughed missionaries returned home to warm welcomes.

---

*Congregations with scattered membership sometimes used several meetinghouses.

Congregations who supported missionaries over the years liked to see these saints in the flesh and blood, and a well-spoken testimony from a returning hero from the mission field could stimulate fresh donations. One Brethren woman recalled the thrill that a visiting missionary added to love feast.

> We had a lady in the church who went to Japan as a missionary and I remember as a little girl sitting at the same table with her and thinking that was so special because I always thought that I wanted to be a missionary. That was so special.[4]

The Mission Board, therefore, counted on furloughed missionaries to itinerate. Ella Ebbert, who served in India from 1917 until 1954, was typical. When she returned to her native Kansas for a furlough in 1933, H. Spenser Minnich, educational secretary for the General Mission Board, shared his expectations with her.[5]

> Now that you are getting acquainted with America, I wonder what plans you may have in mind for the visiting of Sunday-schools in Northeastern Kansas. They have been very faithful in providing your missionary support and, we feel, quite anxious to see and hear you. We are writing especially because Ernest E. Watkins, superintendent of the Sunday-school at Ottawa, writes asking when it will be possible for you to visit their school. He says, "Our birthday offerings are given for her support and we would like her present at the annual event." . . .
> Likely some definite tour in the District should be arranged so that you can economize in travel. If you feel that way about it, we should arrange to have some person, perhaps the Conference Budget field man, there to plan your itinerary.[6]

Communications from local organizers in Kansas further indicated the importance of Ebbert's appearance.

> [The district board] is wondering just what the wish of your office is, or whether you have a definite program in mind. Do you wish her to visit each church in the district, or would you rather have her meet groups? Would you expect offerings to be taken in each church, or would there be a stated sum which she would be expected to be paid?[7]

Unfortunately, some missionaries were not powerful speakers. Local organizers wondered whether a speaking tour by one missionary would be a wise use of scarce resources, especially in economic hard times.

> This next is confidential but I think you should know. It seems that [Alexander/Anna] has been in a number of the churches of this district in years past and seemingly did not "go over" very big. Please understand there is no objection to [him/her]. Everyone thinks [he/she] is a FINE [person], but it seems [he/she] just did not get away very well with a pulpit program. I think the churches of the district are willing to use [him/her] in most any way that the Board suggests but we are just questioning a little what is best. It has been a number of years since [Alexander/Anna] has been in the District and perhaps [his/her] work is different, or possibly the people different.
>
> The attitude of the Board was that if we put on a Missionary program in the District we want it strong enough to really do some good or it might be better left alone. In these times of serious depression it is very difficult to accomplish all we should like to accomplish and it is very important that our money and energy be expended to the very best advantage.[8]

Brethren esteemed missionaries like Lloyd Studebaker, who poses here with a poisoned leopard. A string tied from Studebaker's wrist to the big cat's neck allowed him to lift its head. *Photo courtesy of BHLA.*

Westernized teachers at the Ping Ting Girls' School, a Brethren mission in China. *Photo courtesy of BHLA.*

Temperance persisted as another Brethren priority. Even during the 1932 presidential election, when banks crashed, unemployment lines lengthened, and Hoovervilles (shanty communities for the homeless, so-named for President Hoover) expanded, Rufus D. Bowman, secretary of the Board of Christian Education, complained that Brethren voters faced a hard choice because neither candidate vigorously defended Prohibition. Franklin D. Roosevelt, the Democrat, openly supported its repeal, and the incumbent, Herbert Hoover, favored a substitute amendment to the Constitution giving states authority over alcohol. Bowman reluctantly encouraged Brethren to vote for Hoover. He allowed that other issues also deserved consideration, but he mentioned only world peace and said nothing about the economic misery that in a few weeks would trigger a Democratic landslide.

In regard to the two major parties, may I say that I do not endorse either party platform on prohibition. Neither do I endorse the stand of either candidate on prohibition. But when we consider the past records of the two men, their qualifications, their grasp of the present world situation, their world peace attitudes, and even their prohibition stand, my personal opinion is that there is weight in favor of President Hoover. And I think it will be unfortunate if good people stay away from the polls.[9]

As love feasts, missionaries, and temperance brightened Brethren hearts, debates about the Old Order and modernism/liberalism (another sign of continuity) and the Depression cast shadows across the denomination. Despite the departure of the Dunkard Brethren in 1926, most conservatives remained within the fold, loyal to the denomination but upset over its direction. In the 1930s they published a booklet, *The Gist of the Church of the Brethren,* authored by Grant Mahan, which enumerated their complaints. Mahan, a former associate editor of the *Bible Monitor,* argued for restoration of traditional Brethren practices, such as kneeling during prayer and plain dress, while other grievances, including opposition to the doctrine of human brotherhood, explaining away miracles, teaching civic righteousness and social reform, and updating the Bible to meet the twentieth century, were antimodern attacks on higher criticism and the Social Gospel.

> We believe that the present tendencies to worldlyism in the church are due to the unfaithfulness and laxity of the church in carrying out these Annual Meeting Minutes as listed below:
>
> 1. That the brethren wear plain clothing. That the coat with the standing collar be worn, especially by the ministers and deacons.
>
> 2. That the brethren wear their hair and beard in a plain and sanitary manner. That the mustache alone be forbidden.
>
> 3. That the sisters attire themselves in plainly-made garments, free from ornaments and unnecessary appendages. That plain bonnets and hoods be the headdress, and that the hair be worn in a becoming Christian manner.
>
> 4. That the veil be worn in time of praying and prophesying (1 Cor. 11:1-16, R.V.). The plain cap is regarded as meeting the requirements of scriptural teaching on the subject. (It is wise to stand directly on verse 5, also 1 Thess. 5:17.)
>
> 5. That gold for ornament and jewelry of all kinds shall not be worn (1 Tim. 1:9; 1 Peter 3:3).
>
> 6. That no brother be installed into the office of minister or deacon who will not pledge himself to observe and teach the order of dress.

7. That no brother or sister serve as delegate to District or Annual Meeting, nor be appointed on committees to enforce discipline, who does not observe the order of dress.

8. That it is the duty of the official body of the church to teach faithfully and intelligently the simple, Christian life in dress; and bishops, who are the shepherds of the churches, are required to teach and to see to it that the simple life in general is taught and observed in their respective charges.

In view of paragraphs 2 and 7, our hearts are burdened to behold what was once a plain sister, now with her hair cut and fashioned, short-sleeved, jewel-bedecked, a fashionable woman. Brethren, in a number of cases, have the "put on" and "put off" feeling to suit the hour. The fashionable necktie is common. Let us prayerfully consider. Because we have come short in prayerful consideration, we have the "falling away."

PRESENT-DAY INHIBITIONS AND TEACHINGS

We believe that there are many present-day inhibitions and teachings that are undermining our very faith, and that these teachings are not in accord with the New Testament teachings of Jesus and his apostles. We list some of these below:

1. We oppose the general omission of the Lord's Prayer. Luke 11:1, 2 says "When ye pray, say." This is a specific command.

2. We oppose the general standing posture during prayer. The preponderance of Bible testimony is in favor of the kneeling posture. Jesus in the garden. Matt. 20:39; Isa. 45:23; Rom. 12:11; Philipp. 2:10; Acts 21:5; Ezra 9:5; Dan. 6:10; Luke 22:41. Two exceptions are Mark 11:25; Luke 18:11.

3. We oppose the use of the word Reverend as a title for ministers. The word occurs but once in the Bible (Psa. 111:9) and then it refers to God. It is contrary to the decision of our general Conference. Further, it smacks of "Romanism" and smells of professionalism for the ministry. Even the titles "Mr.", "Mrs.", and "Dr." are without precedent in the Bible, and should be omitted in Brethren literature and religious services.

4. We are opposed to the growing disuse of the Christian salutation of love, as taught five times in the New Testament (Rom. 16:16; 1 Peter 5:14; 1 Cor. 16:20; 2 Cor. 13:12; 1 Thess. 5:26) and practiced by our church for more than two hundred years.

5. We oppose the increasing disuse of the sisters' prayer covering. See Paul in First Corinthians, eleventh chapter.

6. We denounce church suppers, festivals, fellowship suppers, lawn parties, measuring parties, dramas, theatricals and plays in churches. We do favor liberal, cheerful systematic, sacrificial giving as taught in the Scriptures.

7. We oppose the open communion and the use of the individual communion cup.

8. We oppose the preaching of world and human brotherhood other than by evangelism through Christ and the Holy Spirit in Christian Brotherhood.

9. We oppose the use of musical instruments in worship.

10. We denounce and teach against such statements that there is no merit in any precise form of baptism; that some Scripture may not be true, as, for instance, the Jonah story (yet Jesus makes reference to this incident, Matt. 12:40); that the miracles of Jesus may not be genuine; that feet washing, being merely symbolical of service, might be omitted; that the revelations of God in the Old Testament were merely emotional experiences; that we should teach civic righteousness and social reform rather than salvation through Christ; that the Bible does not meet the needs of the twentieth century.

11. We oppose associate membership.

12. We urge prayerful consideration on the subject of "Fraternal Relations," since there is great danger of compromising and sacrificing our gospel principles.

THE CONCLUDING PRAYER

1. We earnestly and sincerely pray in these last times for the conservation of the Church of the Brethren as she existed for two hundred years.

2. We fervently pray for each congregation and all to return to the plain and simple life, non-conformed to the world and that we may all take our stand for Christ and the Church.

3. We pray that every lawful opportunity in harmony with the Word of God may be extended to our young people for personal work in soul-winning, the preparation necessary for Christian service.

4. We pray for the official brethren of the ministry and the deaconship to be the guiding wisdom of the local church, the coun-

selors of the Truth in love and harmony with the Word of God; that this simple, co-operative effort for the preservation of our true Brethren Heritage and the teachings of our Blessed Lord Jesus and His chosen Apostles may bring honor and glory to His Name.

5. We deplore the worldward trend in our church, and pray that it may cease ere it pass the "danger point" on the stream of time or it will be doomed for a fall. We pray that at least a remnant may be preserved, that they often confer with each other, and will think much upon His Holy Name as they contend for the faith (Jude 3) and preach the Word in season and out of season. We pray that they may remain steadfast, immovable, always abounding in the work of the Lord, that they may be willing to deny themselves of ungodly and worldly lusts and live soberly, righteously and godly in this present world, looking for the realization of their blessed hope, the glorious appearing of our Lord Jesus Christ and thus be ready for the crown that is for all those who love his appearing.

6. We pray in the Name of our Blessed Lord Jesus that all presiding Elders with their officials may prayerfully and thoughtfully consider the contents of this booklet and we urge the approval and adoption and teaching of these Holy and Necessary things which are so highly essential in leading the souls of men into a higher spiritual relationship with Jesus Christ, their Savior.

And now unto him that is able to keep us from falling, and to present us faultless before the presence of his glory with exceeding joy, to the only wise God our Savior, be glory and majesty, dominion and power, both now and ever. Amen.[10]

Aroused conservatives once again threatened schism. At decade's end they assembled for an annual Bible conference in the Mummert meetinghouse in southern Pennsylvania, expecting I. N. H. Beahm, a well-known conservative, to lead them to independence. This time Otho Winger, architect of the 1926 compromise, sat as a powerless spectator in the back row without an invitation to join the preachers. But when Beahm's turn came to speak, he urged the packed gathering to stay with the denomination and to work for change within it. Hence, the Brethren dodged a major division, again assisted by conservative leadership loyal to the fellowship, but the gap between Old Order/fundamentalists and progressive/modernists remained wide.[11]

Despite the constancy of religion during the thirties, embodied by revivals, love feasts, missionaries, and familiar disputes, the

Depression's impact was profound. Throughout the Depression years, denominational spending diminished, making budget cutbacks unavoidable. Meeting in 1929 before the Wall Street crash, Annual Conference budgeted $275,500 for the General Mission Board. A year later it cut the Mission Board to $269,900, and by 1935 Mission Board spending had declined to $211,500, where it lingered until the beginning of World War II. (When the war broke out, mission fields closed and spending declined even further.) In 1930 Annual Conference awarded Bethany Biblical Seminary $35,000, $30,000 in 1931, and $25,000 in 1932, where it stayed for the rest of the decade. Total budgeted spending for all Annual Conference boards dropped from $346,000 in 1929 to $275,000 in 1932, remaining at that level until the war began. Twice (1930 and 1932) economic conditions forced Annual Conference to make mid-year corrections and adjust its budget lower. Institutionally, the Depression years were difficult.[12]

Not surprisingly, the hard times inflicted a high human cost. One woman, whose father worked in the denominational publishing house, harbored painful memories of the impact of cutbacks on her family.

> Our livelihood depended on the fortunes of the publishing house. R. E. Arnold was president of the publishing house. He was saying that this institution made money every year of the Depression. We turned money over to the Mission Board to carry on the work of the church in the three or four corners of the earth and it's true, they did; it's just a few thousand dollars but they never went in the red. But it was on the backs of people who worked at the publishing house. And so we have rather painful memories of the Depression. My dad's job went down to a day and a half a week.

Financial problems forced one member of this same family to withdraw from Manchester College. The student's father appealed to Manchester for a financial break, like those given to pastors' children, because he worked for the denomination, but the college declined. The student never returned to campus.[13]

Missionaries also had to stretch their resources. Charles D. Bonsack, for example, secretary of the Mission Board, informed H. Stover Kulp in Nigeria that salaries would be cut ten percent and support fifteen percent.

> We pay little attention to budgets as we are guided more by what the church gives. We shall have to stay within this in these times of

uncertainty as nearly as we can. There is very little change in the economic situation in America. Quite as uncertain as in the past. The stock market the last few days has gone down quite a great deal, and I think no one knows the future.[14]

In early January 1933, among the bleakest moments of the Depression, Bonsack had similarly discouraging words for Raymond Cottrell in India.

The financial situation still remains very distressing indeed. Our receipts in December fell off fifty percent compared with a year ago and we may be facing the worst situation yet, if this should happen again in the Achievement Offering at the close of our fiscal year, but we shall wait and see. Meanwhile, I am sure it behooves all of us to use the greatest economy possible to avoid anything more drastic than we have been resorting to.[15]

Missionaries on furlough or in retirement also suffered cuts. Adam and Alice Ebey, longtime workers in India, were in retirement in North Manchester, Indiana, when they received this letter from the General Mission Board.

In the face of the present situation the Executive Committee feels that we must make some reductions in the support of missionaries at home and those under missionary relief, if possible. They have asked the staff here to make some adjustments. We have therefore decided that your next check, due April 1st, instead of being for $250.00 will be for $200.00. This of course will be subject to the consideration and approval of the [Mission] Board at their meeting April 4-5. We are sorry indeed that this becomes necessary but know that we will have your sacrificial cooperation so far as possible. Of course, if any great emergency occurs, the Board will no doubt give consideration and if any undue hardship is incurred I am sure they would be glad to hear from you.[16]

Response to victims of the Depression encouraged Brethren to think of service without conversion. In this excerpt, Brethren in rural Illinois describe their donations of food to urban poor.

Indications are clear that there will be as much need of doing relief work this coming winter among the poor of Chicago as there was last year. Perhaps the opportunities of service will be greater. As a church we will have more experience to our credit. We will know better to whom it is wise or expedient to give assistance. We should be able to do some follow up work from our efforts of last year. We are beginning operations earlier and as a church are better organized to do more effective work. Our own Ladies' Aid has canned hundreds of quarts of fruit and vegetables.

Last winter we were highly gratified over the response from our brethren and friends in the country and near-by towns. Hundreds of people, upon learning of the need, went into their cellars and pantries and brought forth provisions to load on to trucks, and several kind-hearted farmers drove these trucks into the city that our people might not go hungry.

Why another winter of need is facing us I do not know, nor do I try to answer. Whether it is because God is disciplining the people of the nations for their ungodliness and materialism, or whether he is testing the patience, charity, and love of the saints, you may guess as well as I. But I believe you will agree with me that God does have his hand on the wheel and is trying to lead his people. Let us seek to learn the lessons he has to teach us through these trying times.

. . . The relief station is to be opened for the beginning of distribution, November 15.[17]

As the "trying times" squeezed missionary budgets and inflicted hunger upon city-dwellers, they created a new context for mission evangelism and the gospel of service. In 1938 Vernon F. Schwalm took the podium at Annual Conference to reflect on the contrast between these two interpretations. Schwalm's sermon was a thoughtful outline of the big picture, and he considered a variety of subtopics, including recent industrial violence and the state's assumption of the church's role in education and charity. After describing the confusion over the needs of those who suffered from the Depression and those who suffered from sin, Schwalm urged the Brethren to adapt to modernity by preaching both salvation and social justice.

There are at least four very clear reasons for the relatively small place of religion in our life today. First, for reasons which I can not detail here, there has been an enormous growth in the power of the state. Many of the activities once assumed by religion have now been taken over by the state. This is especially true in education and the administration of charity. . . . Increasingly, the church tends to become like the Russian church where worship of God is permitted, but where the privilege of making any comments on, or criticisms of, the social order is denied.

Second, the great developments in the field of the sciences have affected the role of religion. . . .

Since then science has gone on to push back the horizons of knowledge. It has put into man's hand the power to master his environment in a much more effective way than before. The great progress in the cure of disease, the vast increase in the comforts of life, the rapidity with which we have conquered space and time, and the enormous facilities for doing the work of the world have come about through science. . . .

Modern man is extremely this-worldly. He is occupied with his material environment. Secular education, the modern press, motion pictures, and the everywhere present radio serve to keep his material environment daily before him. He has little time to think of God, of spiritual realities, or the life beyond.

A third reason why the church has been playing a diminishing role seems to lie in the church itself. Institutionalized religion often is occupied with its own institutional or creedal problems. . . .

. . . At such times it often forgets the interests of the masses of men whom it is designed to serve. So the masses, struggling with the day-to-day problem of earning their daily bread, and finding the abundant life for themselves and their families, pass the church by. . . . In Russia, in France, in Mexico and in other lands, the church has been repudiated; even in America, the great sweating, struggling masses of men in the breadlines or in the picket lines of labor have but little time for religion.

Fourth, the badly divided condition of American Protestantism has so weakened our forces that it becomes impossible to speak with any voice of authority in our day. It was not until our Roman Catholic brethren with their millions of constituents dared to speak that the motion picture world took much note of the protests of the church against indecent pictures.* Our little denominational chirps must sound weak in the councils of the nation. What a

---

*Catholic complaints were largely responsible for the self-censorship of the motion picture industry.

tragedy that we are so divided that we can not now protest against the evils of intemperance, the vast and unnecessary armament of the nation, and other major evils in our nation.

What should be the role of religion today? What place should the church have amid the organizations competing for attention in modern society? . . .

There is a large group of Christians who conceive the function of the church to be that of a life-saving station, or to be that of snatching the souls of men like brands from the burning in order to bring them salvation—salvation now and in preparation for the life to come. The interest of this group is prevailingly spiritual and in a sense other-worldly. They hold to the view that if you save the individual, you will save society, and that the church should not concern herself so much about social questions as about the souls of men. . . .

At the opposite pole is another wing of Christendom, interested primarily in making this world a fit place in which to live. This group is not so much interested in saving men from the flames of eternal fire as in redeeming society from crime and vice and poverty, inequality and injustice. Their point of view is primarily this-worldly. They are interested almost exclusively in bringing the abundant life to men here and now. They talk very little about individuals or personal salvation, but a great deal about saving society, or social salvation.

Between these opposite poles all shades of emphasis prevail so that today the modern minister is in utmost confusion as to what should be his emphasis. Should he be primarily an evangelist seeking to lead individual souls into a saving, religious experience? Should he be primarily a teacher giving the most of his time to the religious educational program of the church? Should he be primarily a playfellow with the young people of his church in conferences and camps? Should he be primarily a shepherd helping his flock over the rough places of life? Or should he be a reformer using all his effort to bring about a more equitable distribution of wealth, better working conditions for labor, less unemployment and a war-less world? . . .

May I then without assuming to be dogmatic, or entirely exhaustive, venture to suggest some things that I think religion should accomplish in modern life? Any single address on so vast a subject must needs be incomplete. You will fill in the omissions according to your own point of view.

I. The church must continue to bring to individual men and women a gospel of personal salvation. . . .

This doctrine has often been made odious because of an insistence upon a particular method of entering into the experience. Whether the method be cataclysmic, or whether it be quiet and without great visible demonstration is not so important as that there be reality at the heart of it. And the fact that some have been crude in method, and irreverent in the manner of presenting it, does not warrant a neglect of the doctrine. . . .

If we are to grow great Christian souls for the trying times which are undoubtedly ahead of us, we shall need to see to it that there is in the inner recesses of men's souls a sense of security against the outward storms of life, and an inner island of peace and quiet to which they can retreat and take their stand securely when the outward props and stays of life crumble. . . .

II. Religion should teach and exemplify a personal and social ethic, that makes for a righteous nation. . . .

Our God is an ethical God. We are taught that he can not look upon sin with any degree of allowance. It is impossible to have fellowship with an ethical God if our lives are unethical. Sin makes men hide from God, as did Adam. Just why this is true, I know not, but I know that we are so made that when our own lives are consciously unethical, we lose fellowship with him. When we are knowingly living unethical lives, we are inclined either to forget God and religion, or else we try to rationalize our wrongdoing, in which case our religion becomes an unreal and meaningless thing. It seems to me that the greatest danger to us now is the danger that grows out of the fact that men and women live comfortably within the church; men and women who through lack of teaching or the nature of their surrounding, through spiritual callousness that results from long practice or from a species of self-deception, are unethical in their relation to their fellowmen and apparently know it not. . . .

There is nothing equal to genuine religion for motivating the good life. America needs desperately a great influx of integrity of character, of social justice, of purity of character, of common honesty. If it is to come to us, it will be preceded or accompanied by a revival of genuine ethical religion. . . .

III. The church should create the spirit of kindliness and a sense of brotherhood between men so as to heal the flaming antagonisms between classes, between races, and between nations.

Between these divisions of our humanity, there grow up tensions that now and then break out into open conflict. In the great cities of America, during the last year, there has been going on the bitterest kind of industrial warfare—a conflict which involved hundreds of thousands of homes and millions of men, women, and children.* Hatreds that have been smoldering for a long time, and that have no doubt been cultivated, have broken out into open flames of passion. It baffles the imagination to comprehend the suffering and loss of it all. . . .

. . . If you read the speeches you will be impressed with the depths of race feeling existent even in our country. Meanwhile the suffering from war in other lands is sufficient to break the heart of any lover of humanity. . . .

What is the church doing to release these tensions? What is she doing to release the causes of the tensions? Is the voice of Jesus or the voice of Karl Marx heard in the turmoil and confusion? . . .

These are grave problems that face us. On many of these problems one can scarcely speak in many American congregations for fear of dividing his own flock. . . .

But individual Christians must serve as leaven in the midst of the strife and conflict. For I fear that if the church does not Christianize our social order, then an unchristian, atheistic and materialistic social order will arise and do to the American church what is being done to the church in Russia and other lands. . . .

Let us therefore, as a church, preach the gospel of grace to the personal salvation of men, exemplify and teach the high ethical ideals of Jesus, and bring to an angry and divided world something of the kindliness, the love and goodwill of our Lord—keeping the church free, but serving the children of men for whom Christ died.[18]

As the Depression wore on with no visible light at the end of the tunnel, Americans learned to cope with hard times, even if they could not end them. By 1938 the Depression continued in its ninth year and unemployment lingered at over ten million, yet Americans felt more secure and the sense of crisis had passed. Capitalism was safe, banking reformed, and the Constitution secure from dictatorships, which was not

---

*In winter 1937, a massive sit-down strike hit the auto industry, and during the summer eighteen workers died as "Little Steel," i.e., companies other than United States Steel, resisted unionization.

the case in Europe. Franklin Roosevelt's New Deal had kept America's head above the water until the storm subsided. Between 1938 and 1941, Annual Conference did not mention the Depression, though recovery remained elusive.[19]

Peace

While Main Street and Wall Street pondered who could spare them a dime, international relations grew increasingly bankrupt. World War I, for all its cost in lives and wealth, had settled very little. The Treaty of Versailles could not reconcile the competing national interests of Europe and Asia, and it lacked the necessary framework to enforce the patchwork system it created, especially in eastern Europe. Particularly upset with Versailles were the upstart fascists, who combined intense nationalism with aggressive foreign policy. To be sure, all modern nation-states competed with religion through their vast resources, unquestioned potential to influence personal lives, and insatiable demands for allegiance. But facism took this a step further by proclaiming that only service beneficial to the nation held value. Moreover, the dominance enjoyed by the western democracies, confirmed by Versailles, especially angered these expansionist nations, and they made the world increasingly unsafe for Americans.[20]

On the Asian front, U. S. relations with Japan gradually deteriorated. During the twenties Japan had hitched its economy to the dollar, but when Wall Street collapsed, the Japanese looked elsewhere for economic security. In 1931 they seized the northern Chinese province of Manchuria, a move that abruptly aggravated U. S.-Japanese relations. For American policymakers, Japan's aggression and threat to block access to Asian markets set dangerous, unacceptable precedents. With each year it became more likely that Woodrow Wilson's war would not be the last, as he had promised.[21]

Many Brethren applied their denomination's traditional peace position to the precarious international scene. They eagerly supported Wilsonian idealism in foreign policy, hoping that greater international cooperation would encourage peace; through the twenties Brethren leadership had endorsed the League of Nations, the World Court, and the Washington Naval Conference, and an arms limitation agreement. This *Gospel Messenger* editorial opposing naval expansion is typical.

> In its issue for Jan. 18 the "Chicago Daily Tribune" printed in the same column, and under a common head, naval news from

Washington, D. C., and London, England. The column started out bravely with the statement of Admiral Hughes before the house naval committee to the effect that Secretary Wilbur's $740,000,000 program would give the country only a "reasonable degree of security." What is needed, according to this big navy man, is overwhelming superiority over any other sea power—"a fleet second to none." Admiral Hughes is credited with saying that we need a billion for new naval construction and not a paltry $740,000,000. All of which leads the writer to ask: if we are doomed under a $740,000,000 naval program, what assurance is there that $1,000,000,000 will be enough? Is there really any limit to what might be urged for naval defense so long as we depend on might rather than goodwill? In the opinion of this paragrapher the figures used by the naval man prove nothing so clearly as the futility of the big navy idea. Suppose we pass England in naval power, and England should turn again to Japan? Would it not then be urged that we would have to outbuild these two nations? This would force England and Japan—if they were so foolish as to trust in might alone—to gather other nations into a defensive alliance, with the result that the United States might conceivably soon be pitting her resources against the world. Thus the big navy idea, when pushed to its logical conclusion, is disclosed as an utterly futile policy. Indeed a tithe of the sum asked for the big navy, if spent in the interests of goodwill, would promote a type of security which a naval force equal to that of all the other nations of the world could not bring. . . . In view of all this, how big a navy do we need? Certainly not the biggest in the world, for such a navy promises nothing but such ill will and fear on the part of other nations that the biggest navy we could build would rather aggravate than solve the situation. How big a navy do we need? Certainly not as large as England's, since she seems to be trying to get out from under the untenable situation which her historic big navy problem has brought upon her. The big navy idea has not brought England security, but a giant competitor in the United States. Do we want to find ourselves in a similar position in the course of a generation or two? How big a navy do we need? Certainly not more than our share toward the needed naval police force of the world. And we could get it down to this if we would quit taking on billion dollar naval construction plans and cultivate the new and promising defenses based upon understanding and goodwill.[22]

In 1928 the Kellogg-Briand Peace Pact attracted Brethren support. This treaty emerged from a request from Aristide Briand, the French minister of foreign affairs, for a bilateral Franco-American ban on war against one another. American religious organizations quickly backed the idea, but the American secretary of state, Frank B. Kellogg, suspecting a French attempt to lure Uncle Sam into an alliance, counter-proposed a multilateral pact in which signatories renounced war as an instrument of foreign policy. After heavy lobbying by women's peace organizations, the U. S. Senate ratified the treaty 85-1, and in total sixty-two nations signed the document.[23] D. C. Reber, who taught education and classical and modern languages at Manchester College, strongly approved of this application of idealism to foreign policy.

> The Treaty of Versailles grew out of a desire to liquidate war. America refused to ratify or be a party to it. This is considered to be the greatest organized instrument or assurance to achieve world peace. Now comes the Pact of Paris born out of the collective will for peace to reinsure or reinforce the aim of the Treaty of Versailles. America too has had a leading part in its consummation and undoubtedly will ratify it through the United States Senate. By it, now universal peace and goodwill to all peoples are proclaimed without military threatenings. But this is only a noble beginning, a first step toward a worthy goal proclaimed by the Prince of Peace under whose leadership the cause of peace will triumph.
>
> Since war has been discarded on civilization's junk heap, a substitute must be instituted so that peace may be maintained, and not merely proclaimed. France's famous foreign minister, M. Briand, proposed that this latter treaty be dedicated to the memory of the dead who fell in the World War. So let it be.[24]

In the thirties many Brethren sustained their concern for peace. A poll of American clergy found that 96 percent of Church of the Brethren ministers believed that churches should place opposition to war on record. In contrast, approximately 60 percent of Reformed, Congregational, and Baptist preachers and 38 percent of Lutheran clergy agreed with the statement.[25] Emma Horning, a China missionary, personified this urge for peace with a *Gospel Messenger* article that emphasized the influence of parents and the home in a campaign for nonviolence.

> "On earth peace, goodwill towards men." This song of the angels has re-echoed in the hearts of men all down the ages. All the

world has prayed for peace, but war always seemed a necessary evil. Only since the world war has light broken on this dark spot in civilization. Now we are planning for world peace, for world reconstruction, forever advancing civilization. . . .

Yes, it is wonderful how the peace spirit is beginning to permeate all lands and races and organizations, but it has great odds to work against. It is only a drop in the ocean of turmoil—militarism, capitalism, greed and jealousy.

. . . Consequently we must look to the home for the permanent development of the peace principle. . . .

What is the psychological basis of war? Where does it begin? I would say that the basis is an antagonistic mentality, and it begins in the home because of the parents' attitude in child training. What misery and suffering are caused in the world through mental antagonism between parents, between church factions, between labor organizations, between nations! And why this antagonism? Again I would say, because of the parents' attitude in child training. Why all the mental conflicts in the home—the quarrels, the nagging, the scolding, the angry words, the tears? Is it not because the parents do not know how to train their children?

. . . This war spirit may begin to develop in a babe a few weeks old, and unless the parents understand child psychology, and devise proper means of training it, the antagonism will continue to grow until he is a little warrior. . . .

We need to teach parents how to cooperate with their children in work, in play, in their school work, in forming good habits, in developing a Christian character. We need to teach them how to develop initiative in their children, how to be creative, love industry, peace and progress. . . . Never give toys that will develop the war spirit, or produce antagonism.[26]

Brethren peace activists still praised the League of Nations. Andrew W. Cordier, a history and political science professor at Manchester College, applauded it as a means to create understanding in a "complex world."*

---

*In 1944 Cordier left Manchester College for an extraordinary diplomatic career. He served in the U. S. delegation at the conferences in San Francisco and London that organized the United Nations. From 1946-1962 he was executive assistant to the U. N. secretary-general and under-secretary to the General Assembly. In 1962 he became dean of the Graduate School of International Affairs at Columbia University, and in 1968-1970, a critical time, he served as president of the University. In 1973 Cordier received nomination for the Nobel Peace Prize. See "Andrew Wellington Cordier," *The Brethren Encyclopedia,* 1:344.

Andrew Cordier (1901-1975), educator and diplomat. *Photo courtesy of BHLA.*

During the last ten years a new element—the League—every native Genevese will admit, has been introduced into the Geneva atmosphere. Indeed the influence of the League has developed so rapidly that the Geneva spirit in the press and into her countries now generally signifies that sense of internationalism that grows here in the fertile soil of the League environment. More than fifty world-wide societies have their international headquarters here. …Nations like individuals can not live in isolation in a complex world. The leaders who come here year by year are learning each other's vocabulary, strength, and weaknesses, and find a much larger degree of solidarity than existed eight years ago. They establish fast friendships. They frequently find out that they can work with the representatives of fifty other nations as easily as they can with their own fellow-countrymen.[27]

At the center of the Brethren peace movement was Dan West, a young and creative member of the Church of the Brethren denominational staff. Originally a school teacher, West devoted his summers to itinerant leadership at Brethren church camps between 1927 and 1930, and in 1930 (at age 37) he accepted an appointment as the denominational director of youth work. His responsibilities included peace work, and in 1931 he published an article in *The Gospel Messenger* challenging the denominational leadership to encourage, not discourage, young people to work for peace.[28]

Parent eagles, we are told, push their eaglets out of the nest. There is some risk in that; the young birds have never flown; their wings may not be strong enough; and if they can't fly, they will fall. Might it not be better to avoid those risks and try to keep them safe in the nest?

Every active church has young people. They hold the promise of the future. But what shall we try to do with them—keep them safe in the nest? Make them think and believe exactly as we do? Urge them to do something never done before in spiritual adventure? Would we be wise to push them out of the nest?

Perhaps this reckless suggestion should be explained. The energy of youth is abundant, and it shows in a dozen ways. It may go in a dozen directions, too, or it may be guided, but it must have action. However, we can not give them our tasks. In a large measure their activity must be their own. They want to be persons, not things. We do well to learn to respect those whom we would guide to more abundant life.

Suppose you do want to urge them out in a good adventure of their own; in what direction shall it be? I suggest some fields for small beginnings. . . .

Peace on Earth. This ancient dream has not yet come true. The recent air maneuvers may still be fresh in your memory.* Put those hundreds of planes in charge of one man with a sick mind— sick with the pride of power and the fear of other peoples, and they can bring quick destruction. The maneuvers were evidently intended to make our minds sick, too, with the same pride and the same fear, after our government has solemnly "renounced war as an instrument of national policy" [i.e., the Kellogg-Briand Pact].

When I see so much that the warmakers are doing and so little that the peacemakers are doing, I wonder why the difference. But I find a chance for adventure here. Find me one hundred Dunkers between the ages twenty-one and thirty who will give as much for peace as a soldier gives for war, and we will change the thinking of Congress in three years' time. Would you like to push your young people in that direction?

Maybe you don't like these suggestions. All right. Make up some that you do like, or ask your young people to help do it.

---

*In a stunning demonstration of the potential of airpower, American airplanes under the direction of General James H. "Jimmy" Doolittle sank an obsolete battleship in minutes.

Then "push them out of the nest." Nothing binds people closer than fellowship in a great adventure. And nothing without adventure will keep our youth in the church.

The Church of the Brethren ought to be not a circumference, but a center for her youth.[29]

Soon West organized "One Hundred Dunkers for Peace," a call for Brethren to sacrifice as much for peace as soldiers did for war, and in 1932 he participated in a meeting of young people that founded "Twenty Thousand Dunkers for Peace," which sought pledges from individuals not to participate in war.[30] Ben Stoner, another peace activist, explained the group's goals.

Einstein on his recent visit to America said that if 2% of the world's population would refuse to bear arms or support war, international conflict would be rendered impossible. His statement was immediately picked up by the press and intelligent public opinion all over the world. An Einstein 2% organization was immediately set up in the U. S. as well as in many other countries for the purpose of enlisting this needed 2%.

The young people of the Church of the Brethren meeting at Anderson, Ind., in June, 1932, in our Annual Conference, felt that they would like to enlist the efforts of our young people to mobilize the forces of our church for peace. One part of this constructive program, they felt, should be in cooperation with the Einstein 2% group. With this latter purpose, the 20,000 Dunkers for peace organization were set up. . . .

Second, a query to Conference by the young people was accepted in the delegate body on June 14 without a dissenting voice or vote. The resolution was a petition to the church—

1. To build up a church program of international goodwill.

2. To investigate and provide a program of service in cooperation with the Society of Friends or otherwise in establishing special arrangements for neutral relief work in time of war or periods of national crisis.

3. To authorize the Board of Christian Education to make the necessary investigation and build up the program needed for the above action.

Third, on the basis of these two, the young people took the next step, inaugurating the "20,000 Dunkers for Peace" organization to start the work for peace at once.[31]

Twenty Thousand Dunkers for Peace

"Love your enemies, do good to them that curse you, pray for them that despitefully use you."—Luke 6:27-28.

"The Son of man has not come to destroy men's lives but to save them."
—*Luke 9:56*

"Let us therefore follow after things which make for peace."—Romans 14:19.

"The High Contracting Parties agree that the settlement or solution of all disputes or conflicts, of whatever nature or of whatever origin they may be, which may arise among them, shall never be sought except by pacific means."—Kellogg Pact. (Signed by 62 nations. Ratified by the U. S. Senate January 15, 1929, by a vote of 86 to 1).

I, ..., as a Christian citizen, hereby declare my love for my country, my purpose at all times to be a good citizen, and my willingness to lay down my life in the service of humanity.

I further declare that, because of conscientious religious convictions, I cannot engage in war, and do protest the appropriation of my taxes for military purposes.

Name...

Address ....

Date...   ....

Use Opposite Side for Remarks

As the world situation deteriorated, Brethren signed this "Twenty Thousand Dunkers for Peace" pledge card. *BHLA collection.*

In 1937 West's One Hundred Dunkers for Peace added a newsletter, *Brethren Action,* to their movement. They expected their periodical to provide a forum of exchange, but One Hundred Dunkers also anticipated challenging assumptions about Brethrenism and its relationship to American society. In the first issue, they criticized the Brethren for hiding in "rural oases" and avoiding engagement with society, and they exhorted the fellowship to greater involvement in world affairs.

> The 100 Dunkers and other like-minded Dunkers need a news letter to keep them informed about the activities of the group and of the members. There has been need of a publication which would serve as a medium for the exchange of their thinking. Many young members of the Church of the Brethren are today groping to find answers to questions such as: What things in our Dunker heritage are worth conserving in an age of high-powered automobiles, scientific advance, and the urbanization of rural life?
>
> Should the Church continue its former isolation from the "world" and attempt to build up rural oases in which the customs, patterns of living, and *weltanschauung* shall be relatively little influenced by those of the world outside? Would it be possible for it to do so if it wanted to? Can the principles and practices of the Church of the Brethren be made universal? How can we help to make this a better world in which to live?

What should we do toward the elimination of war, racial discrimination, and economic justice? What should young married people strive for—an income that will enable them to live in comparative luxury and to go in for elite society? What advantages should they be able to give their children? This paper should help to find the answers to these questions.[32]

As West and the other Dunkers for Peace chided the denomination to "make a better world," the international situation only worsened. In March 1935, Adolf Hitler disavowed the disarmament portions of the Treaty of Versailles and announced a program of national rearmament that included a 500,000-man conscript army and an already existing, covertly built air force. Meanwhile, Italian dictator Benito Mussolini invaded Ethiopia, and the Japanese digested Manchuria. Otho Winger expressed the frustration felt by many pacifists.

All news reports indicate that the nations of the world are spending unprecedented amounts for armaments and for preparations for war. We seem to stand in helpless amazement at the madness of nations which threatens to engulf what we call our present civilization. Is there anything we can do about it? Many indeed are trying to help conditions in one way or another. What will the church do?[33]

Rufus Bowman, thirty-six-year-old pastor of the Washington, D. C., congregation, challenged "young people" to reply to the growing crisis posed by "communism, materialism, and nationalism" with the kingdom of Christ. Bowman offered Christianity as a liberal social justice alternative to Marxism and identified communism and fascism as dangerous competitors to Christianity.*

Picture in your minds a celebration of Peace Day in Moscow. Thousands of boys and girls of the Communist Youth Movement are addressed by Chinese, Japanese and American communists. At the sound of the bugle these young people chant, "We are changing the world." These Russian youth are thrilled with the conviction that their cause will triumph. They are shown the map of the world, areas in which fifty million Chinese are under red rule. Their minds are filled with stories of the missionary successes of

*In 1937 Bowman became president of Bethany Biblical Seminary.

communism. The real competitors with Christianity for the allegiance of youth are not the old faiths of Hinduism and Buddhism. They are communism and nationalism. Communism which offers youth a saved world here with the beyond eliminated. Communism which holds before youth the ideal of a planned, cooperative, classless world society of workers; but without God and without Christ. Communism is godless and fatally materialistic. When it has achieved economic material comfort in a classless society, it has reached its goal.

The battle ground of the world is in the realm of philosophies. What can meet the growing faith of communism? Jesus Christ! His revelation of the fatherhood of God and the brotherhood of Man. His vision of a new world order in the family of God. His command for social and economic justice based upon his conception of human worth. His doctrine of the immortal worth of the soul which is eternally calling us to fresh horizons and higher planes of living. What has communism with its godless materialism to offer in comparison with Christianity's doctrine of the kingdom of God? The question is, do we have faith enough, consecration enough, and courage enough to give the message of Christ to the world?

Another rival of Christianity is the rising tide of nationalism. The world is witnessing the development of nationalism different from any nationalism that has existed hitherto. The totalitarian nation-state has arisen which "asserts itself as the final object of loyalty for its citizens." The nation-state repudiates belief in the family of God. It threatens freedom of conscience. Germany is trying to displace Christianity with paganism. It is going to cost something to follow Jesus Christ in Germany. Maybe out of the fires of persecution a more powerful Christianity will be born. Christianity has the only program that transcends in attractiveness the program of the dictator. In the early centuries, the candidates for baptism made covenant with Christ through these words: "I enlist with thee, O Christ." With that pledge in their hearts they went out to propagate Christ's gospel and to die for their cause. No lesser loyalty will win the victory. Christianity is facing a deliberate test of its strength. It is in a life and death struggle. Christ asks us for our lives. He must have our lives. Personality consecrated to the cause of Christ will save the world.

. . . We can not allow any feeling to develop that peace and missions are separate. These programs are one. Many of our young people are stirred with an undying enthusiasm to work for world peace. I share their enthusiasm. The nations of the earth are preparing for war. Young men are being drilled for the slaughter. May our young people go on with their peace work feeling in their own hearts that they are missionaries. May we consecrate ourselves toward the bringing of a new internationalism realizing that sturdy bands of Christians in other lands are the best prophecy of its coming.

Missions tomorrow must present a more adventurous challenge to youth. Youth everywhere are on the march. They are marching at the call of hard tasks. They are shouting the name of Hitler in Germany, the name of Mussolini in Italy. On a Hitler banner were these words: "The highest duty of German youth is to die for the Fatherland." These dictators are not promising rewards. They are offering death. Youth will respond to a marching leadership.

Have we got a Captain who can offer youth a more adventurous challenge than a dictator? Yes! Jesus Christ! He is the only one sufficient to call youth from the camp of the dictator. He captures youth because he is always going somewhere and because his tasks are hard. Jesus does not offer ease. The reward for following him is a cross crimson with pain. Civilization's ultimatum is Christ or chaos.

Young people respond to the call of personalities. They are being touched constantly by world leaders. The farthest man by means of the radio is but one-tenth of a second away. Nothing is so needed now as a new Christian world leadership. Leaders whom young people will follow. Leaders who have consecrated themselves to follow Christ no matter what the cost. Leaders who are able to face triumphantly the philosophies of communism, nationalism and materialism, and in their stead place the ideal of the kingdom of God. Young people, this is your marching call.[34]

Like Bowman, Sara Fogelsanger Murphy appealed for renewed emphasis on nonviolence. Murphy, national president of the Women's Work in the Church of the Brethren, charged that the Brethren had "stalled long enough" on peace.*

---

*Murphy was the wife of the pastor of the Philadelphia First Church of the Brethren, and in 1935 the congregation installed her in the ministry. Also, she was the first Church of the Brethren woman to earn a doctorate, awarded by the University of Pennsylvania. See "Sara Florence Fogelsanger Murphy," *The Brethren Encyclopedia,* II:897.

Another opportunity is the desire of the world to have Christ's attitude toward peace and war interpreted in a way that is sufficiently practical to meet the needs of today. Certainly Dunker women ought to find a large place in their program through which they may make a peculiar and distinctive contribution toward the solution of this problem. In this phase of our program we shall need to do some things and do them strenuously and with conviction. Not the least of which will be to strengthen and support the morale of our young people as they are launching out in a program of peace, which is bound to call for important and definite decisions on their part, decisions which may not always be easy to make. It is no longer necessary to establish our convictions. We, as Dunkers, have stalled long enough. We have, to use the words of the author of Deuteronomy in the Old Testament, "Encompassed the mountain long enough, it is now time to move northward."[35]

Annual Conference, too, responded to the increased likelihood that the Versailles system would collapse. In 1935 it updated the denominational peace position with a bold statement that addressed the current international situation. The paper included a mildly sarcastic reference to Woodrow Wilson's "war to end war," a simple declaration that "we hate war," and unambiguous condemnations of warfare as undemocratic, futile, and sinful.

Conscious of the growing danger of war in the world today and feeling the need of a reaffirmation of our stand on peace and war, we, the Peace Commission of the Church of the Brethren, through the Board of Christian Education, recommend to the Annual Conference of 1935 the adoption of the following statement, which statement shall be submitted to the proper officials of our federal government and to the leaders of other churches in America:

As a people we have opposed wars at all times throughout our entire history of over two hundred twenty-five years and we have stood with equal consistency for constructive peace principles in all relationships of life. We hate war because we love peace, our way of life at all times. It has been the practice of the church through the years to require of applicants for membership a pledge not to engage in war nor learn the art of war. In our constant attempt to be truly devoted to the highest interests of our country, we have recognized that our supreme allegiance is to God, and we believe that recognition commits us to the highest standard of Christian citizenship by which we can serve our country and our God. We believe a Christian regard for other peoples increases rather than decreases our respect for and our attachment to our own nation.

We believe that all war is sin; that it is wrong for Christians to support or to engage in it; and that war is incompatible with the spirit, example and teachings of Jesus. We believe that war is not inevitable. Those beliefs are not based upon a peculiar peace doctrine of our own; they arise from our application of Christian standards to all human relations, whether individual, group, class, or national. To settle conflicts in any of these relationships by war is not efficient, not constructive, not permanent, and certainly not Christian. We believe that nonviolence, motivated by goodwill, is more powerful than the sword, making possible the survival of both parties, while warfare insures the ultimate destruction of both. War is a far greater calamity, to victor and vanquished alike, than would be the hazards incidental to a renunciation of war by a nation and the settlement of all their disputes by peaceful means. We believe that armaments for nations, like weapons for private defense, do not bring security, but rather intensify the dangers of conflict, as present world conditions tragically testify. We do not believe in the expenditure of our substance for those instruments which endanger our peace and safety. We believe in the only real preparedness for our nation—goodwill, and the agencies through which it may be expressed and maintained.

We believe the whole war system is futile, always leaving more problems than it settles, if it settles any. Today, only a few years after winning the "war to end war," the United States is in the midst of the greatest of war preparation, and our country shares with other nations the general feeling of insecurity throughout the world. We believe that true democracy, "government of the people, by the people and for the people," is consistent with the spirit and principles of Christianity. But the fruit of war is not democracy; war destroys democracy as the prevalence of dictatorships of the communist, fascist, or other varieties, testifies. We cannot "make the world safe for democracy" by war.

Consequently, we are committed to such interests as a program of peace education for all people; the development and support of the necessary international institutions to settle the disputes between nations by means other than war; the promotion of better relations between conflicting social or economic groups within our country; and honesty and a spirit of public service in our government.

Likewise we are committed in our active opposition to all such interests as appropriations for military purposes; the manufacture of munitions of war either for private profit or by the government; the teaching of the doctrines of military preparedness which are so unsound and so unchristian; voluntary or compulsory military training in our secondary schools and colleges; the challenge of our so-called "war games" to other nations; the enactment of laws conscripting men or property for military purposes; neutrality laws that permit our citizens to profit from the trade of belligerents and draw us into wars; and the secret influence of munitions makers and military officials in conferences called to reduce or abolish armaments.

Therefore, as Christian citizens, we are devoted in principle and in action to the furtherance of every effort by our own nation to promote peace in the world, and we are equally devoted in our opposition to those forces within or without our country which make for war, for class struggle, for civil disorder, or for personal conflict.[36]

Anticipating the reinstitution of national conscription, the 1935 annual gathering also established a Committee on Legal Counsel for Conscientious Objectors.[37] In 1938 this committee recommended that conscientious objectors perform alternative service supervised by civilians, and it ruled out work controlled by the armed services, including military chaplaincy, medical attendants, the YMCA, and the Red Cross if supervised by the military.

The Committee on Counsel for Conscientious Objectors desires to make the following recommendations to the Conference of 1938 on the positions that our people should take in the event of war:

I. Types of service considered consistent with the historic position of the church:

1. Constructive service under church or civilian direction, such as housing, road making, farming, forestry, hospitalization, and recreational work.

2. Relief work under the church or civilian direction in and outside of the war zone, or in neutral zones, either as a denomination or in cooperation with the Friends and Mennonites.

II. Types of services not considered consistent with the historic position of the church:

1. Chaplaincy in the army or navy.

2. Red Cross service if this organization is definitely committed to render active service under military command in the event of war.

3. Hospital service if under military command.

4. Y.M.C.A. work if under military command.

5. Services of any kind within the ranks of the army, all which are without question under direct military command.

III. Types of peace testimony to register our convictions and to avoid our participation in war-related activities:

1. The refraining from the purchase of such as Liberty Bonds to finance war.

2. The renunciation of, or the sacrificial use of, profits derived from industry, farming, or invested securities as a result of war; sacrificing always during war periods to build a fund for the furtherance of goodwill and for the support of families who suffer because of their conscientious objections to war.

3. The protesting against federal taxes if used for military purposes.[38]

Some Brethren, however, did not share the zeal for biblical nonviolence advocated by the One Hundred Dunkers for Peace or Annual Conference. Dan West faced this situation as he attempted to rally support for his cause.

The Brethren Peace Action Program was launched more than six months ago. In some places it is going well. In others a few persons are just becoming awake. In many the leaders and led are still sleeping. How is it in your church?

Maybe you are not labelled a leader. Do you care enough for the peace cause right now, and for the coming kingdom, to rouse those who are labeled leaders if they are not already up and doing? "Who knoweth but that thou art come to the kingdom for such a time as this?"

And who knows but that the Church of the Brethren is come to the kingdom for such a time as this?[39]

Similarly, Chalmer Faw, a member of a peace caravan in the summer of 1936, met a membership that lagged behind the denomination's official position. (Peace caravans were teams of youth who visited camps and congregations to urgently advocate peace.) Although Faw did not use the word *fundamentalism*, the obstacles to biblical nonviolence that he found in congregations—literalism, pessimism about human progress, and emphasis on individual salvation—all belonged to that movement.

> The summer's work gave us an opportunity to look at the church, not through its own eyes, but through the eyes of the larger task of the church, the establishment of the kingdom of God on earth. We could view the church, as God must often do, from the standpoint of the great cause of peace.
>
> Some of the fruits of this new perspective were encouraging. For example, some of our most faithful and effective supporters came from the ranks of the church. The young people and, for the most part, the pastors were very responsive to the challenges we tried to bring.
>
> Other aspects of the situation, however, were discouraging. Some of our most severe opposition came from the church members. The school and school men, as well as various civic organizations, responded well, but many church members, they who should have the clearest message of all on the question of peace, opposed us, either actively or by their apathy and indifference.
>
> Perhaps the foremost cause for opposition lay in the narrow interpretation of the task of the church entertained by some. Those who would limit the church to the simple task of saving individual souls, and who carry that philosophy to its logical conclusion, are sure to resist any effective effort to bring peace and economic justice. In their zeal for a narrow type of evangelism they forget that "saved souls" in great numbers made possible the World War of bloody and unhallowed memory, and that the kingdom of God will not come on earth until society itself has been set running along the lines of the spirit of Jesus.
>
> Another so-called "Christian" tenet which has bemuddled the issue is the tendency to take Old Testament standards as on a par with New Testament principles of right. To do this is to forget that the peak of revelation came in Christ. People who find sanction for war by recourse to the Old Testament should be consistent and advocate slavery, polygamy and concubinage, for they too are endorsed there.

Overliteralism in biblical interpretation is a third factor contributing to false views on the gospel of peace. Sincere Christians sometimes find excuse for war in the letter of the New Testament, but they do so only as they ignore the great loving and sacrificial spirit of Jesus. "The letter killeth but the spirit giveth life," said one who was dealing with this kind of folk.

Close on the heels of this literalism follows a deadly form of fatalism which says that what is predicted has to be and there is nothing which can or should be done. To this type of biblical fatalists any attempt to eradicate the basic evils of society is to fly in the face of God.

Illustrations of all these types might be multiplied. The reader can supply his own well-known examples. The tragic fact is that in each case the reader need not go outside our own church to make this research.

Is it possible that heirs of the Dunker peace tradition are resisting the very purpose of the kingdom of God on earth by their opposition to efforts for peace?[40]

Faw's observations were accurate, and a growing number of Brethren enlisted in the military service. In 1939 Annual Conference recognized this by urging "brotherly love and forbearance" toward uniformed brothers, but the delegates also said they were not in "full accord" with the church. As with other issues, such as dress, military service was not an explicit test of membership, and Conference left room for congregational interpretation. Some congregations could declare enlisted members as not in full membership, but others could reinstate them if the soldier or sailor still desired fellowship.

It is evident according to Annual Meeting Minutes, Art. 9, 1840, and Art. 7, 1886, Sec. (1) that one who enlists in military service is not in full accord with the faith and practice of the general brotherhood. The attitude of the church toward such should be one of brotherly love and forbearance, endeavoring by faithful teaching to restore him to full accord as long as he expresses desire to continue membership in the Church of the Brethren.[41]

Thus, Brethren adjusted as international relations slid from arms limitations, peace pacts, and international cooperation in the twenties to fascist ambition and rearmament in the thirties. They supported attempts at international cooperation, but when the renewal of global war appeared likely, Brethren revised their peace statement and planned for conscription. Much of this, however, was top-down, and many in the pews rejected the view of biblical nonviolence. Peace activists worried that the denomination faltered in its witness and was unprepared for what looked increasingly inevitable.

RELIEF

In 1936 world peace received a body blow when civil war erupted in Spain and the following year Asia went to war when Japan attacked China. Both were preludes to broader strife just over the horizon. As in World War I, civilians suffered heavily, and the extensive misery caused by these conflicts stimulated new Brethren interest in international relief. The 1938 Annual Conference authorized an unbudgeted $30,000 for relief in these devastated areas.

> That our testimony of love and peace may be made more positive and helpful in the war-torn lands of China and Spain; The Council of Boards in session at Lawrence, Kansas, recommends to the Conference that we urge our church to give this year in love and sacrifice that we may help relieve the suffering and reduce the extent of starvation that must result.
>
> We believe a fund of $3,000 for China and $1,000 for Spain per month, or a total fund for the remaining fiscal year of $30,000 or more could be provided, if we really try and make a sacrifice worthy of the need and our Lord. This would certainly be true if the suffering were in our own land and among our own kindred.
>
> We feel this fund should be prayerfully considered and provided without reducing our gifts to the spiritual witness of the church at home or abroad. For the love and message of the church with its fellowship and institutions was never more needed than now and these must be stimulated and increased rather than weakened.[42]

The fighting in Spain erupted when General Francisco Franco, a fascist, attempted to overturn an elected, leftist, republican party. The conflict quickly became a proxy war for several of Europe's major powers. Although Britain and France avoided involvement, Germany and Italy aided Franco, and Stalinist Russia assisted the republicans. The civil war lasted for three years and inflicted much horror on civilians, but many Americans, including their government, cared little about Spain.[43]

Dan West, however, thought the Spanish Civil War deeply disturbing, and in 1937 he arrived in Spain to assist the American Friends Service Committee relief work. Other Brethren workers in Spain were David E. Blickenstaff, Martha Rupel, and Paul Hoover Bowman.[44] At a meeting of the One Hundred Dunkers for Peace, West listed the motivations behind his Spanish project.

> There are several reasons for my wanting to go to Spain: 1) If Europe breaks into war, cooperation in Spain will be the spring board for neutral work for any later war. 2) My work there will help save lives—especially mothers' and children's. 3) There is no direct way to stop the Spanish war; this is the best indirect way to help out. 4) It may help to let everybody know that we are working on both sides.
>
> I will go to Spain with the consent and cooperation of the Quakers, Brethren, and Mennonites. They are sending about $4,000 in money with me. . . . However, money, food, and clothing will be distributed to children and mothers on both sides, although I do not favor both sides equally.[45]

Once in Spain West vividly described to readers of *The Gospel Messenger* the conditions he found there.

> Civil War has been destroying the country that was Spain. Two years ago twenty-four million persons lived there, but more than a million have been killed. More than a million soldiers—perhaps 600,000 on each side—are now attempting to destroy each other. There are said to be three million refugees, and more than a million of them are children.
>
> This bitter struggle grew out of a deep-seated conflict between classes; it is part of an old story, too. This is the third civil war in slightly over a century. Whatever the merits of either party, now it is an endurance test with suffering increasing on both sides. Several times there has been talk of some kind of an armistice, but it has not happened yet. Meanwhile the killing goes on and hunger takes a growing toll on the lives of innocents. . . .
>
> Many outside agencies are helping there, and both governments have extensive plans to save the suffering civilians. But it is wartime and all that every agency can do will not keep them all

alive. How many must die this winter no one knows—but thousands certainly, likely tens of thousands. Since they can not all be saved, we have developed the policy: "Save the children first"—the neediest children in the neediest places in the neediest regions. This means refugee children on each side first, who are far from home and most helpless. Dependent mothers and old people are cared for too, but not first. On the Loyalist side the need is far greater; and so we are doing more there. Because of the different conditions, we are maintaining some hospitals, colonies, workshops and schools, but they are not first; and we are not expanding these. We must save the children first, and that means feeding them first. As winter comes on, we will give out clothing—to the neediest children first.

On the Franco side we worked most in the mountains of the north last winter. (It was colder weather than Chicago had.) In the spring we worked along the Ebro near Belchite Lerida and Teruel—the neediest places. On the Loyalist side we are working in and around Barcelona and Murcia. The former territory is filled with refugees from northern Spain who came over through France more than a year ago. The English workers are still doing most of it there. Our work is done mostly in the region around Murcia where refugees have come there from central and southern Spain. Perhaps that is the neediest region of the whole country as most of the other agencies from outside Spain are not working there.

In a letter from Murcia, Sept. 27, Florence Conard writes: "Some time ago I was at the hospital for supper with the English nurses. After the meal, they slipped into the babies' room to see a little tyke that they didn't think would last the night. The child was supposed to be suffering from kidney trouble, but was actually an excellent example of a typical 'war baby.' It was about six months old, its head one third of all its tiny body. Its arms, I'm not exaggerating, were no bigger around than my forefinger and its loosely-covered fingers just hung from the wrists. Its eyes and cheeks were sunken and its jaw and cheek bones were so prominent as to seem completely naked of skin. Already it had begun to gasp a bit for breath, moving its head back and forth on the pillow as though the very motion would give it more air. Calcium was lacking in its body among other things. No bomb holes, or refugees, or women's tears and sob stories can move me so much as that struggling little life, so helpless against external diabolical forces. Just a P. S., the baby died."

Never before have I known what food really meant. Not roast pork and mashed potatoes, not good American ice cream, not even spinach and lettuce and cabbage—just food, with no particular taste or form—fuel and nourishment for the weakening flesh.

Bread! Only now am I beginning to understand the meaning of "Give us this day our daily bread." (Perhaps our "daily bread" today is but 100 grams—3 1/2 ounces, but father and mother will pool their grams, forget their hunger and give the extra pieces to the young ones. Tomorrow, God willing, "our daily bread" may be 150 grams. We can not bear to think that perhaps tomorrow there will be no bread. It may be wiser not to think of the morrow. "Give us this day our daily bread."

Not long ago ten long-looked-for tons of wheat arrived. The men staggered in under the weight of the big sacks and dumped them in limp piles in our warehouse. The little puffs of dust that squirted out from between the sacks as they fell seemed to hang still and golden on the air. Yesterday the bread from the wheat came in—good bread, brown bread, wheat bread, symbol of health and strength and work, of plenty and friendship and peace.[46]

Brethren relief workers also grieved for the plight of Chinese civilians. In July 1937, Japan resumed its war against China, intending to create a buffer for recently acquired Manchuria and to reach its long-term goal of economic self-sufficiency. Japan's actions outraged many Americans, yet isolationism heavily influenced American public opinion and war was unthinkable, despite an apparently deliberate Japanese attack on a U. S. gunboat, the *Panay,* in the Yangtze River.[47]

The depredations of the Japanese army bore heavily on Chinese civilians, and Brethren missionaries cared for them as best they could. In Shau Yang three Brethren missionaries—Minneva J. Neher and Alva C. and Mary Hykes Harsh—opened their compound to a wide variety of refugees, including Chinese Christians and local magistrates. A note posted by a Japanese officer on the compound door kept soldiers away, but on a rare foray outside the compound to haul coal, Alva Harsh saw numerous bodies and witnessed "one man tied to a tree, being tortured."[48] In December 1937, Minneva Neher described the situation to her parents as "forlorn and desperate," but a unique opportunity to share the gospel.

I have another opportunity to send a note through to you; so will send you word again. . . . So far, we have no other way than through Japanese officials. I sent a letter to you on November 11, which was supposed to have gone to Japan through military and be mailed from there to you.

Today marks a month since the Japanese entered our town. Our mission compound has continued as a haven under the protection of God. The last couple of weeks we have been made to rejoice as we have been able to get in touch with our Christians and get many of the women and girls back into our fold here. It has been marvelous and faith-strengthening to hear the various experiences of them all and how the Lord has kept and protected. So far as we have been able to learn, none of the Christians have been killed or injured although many of them have suffered the loss of their homes and personal belongings. We have now within our court over one hundred of our church people or their relatives. Besides this, we have about as many of the leading gentry, merchants, and officials living here at present. They are here at our invitation and have succeeded in effecting an organization which takes the place of the county government. They work, of course, in connection with the Japanese authorities. Their being here is giving us the most unique opportunity to preach the gospel that I have seen since I have been in China as many of these folks never had anything to do with the mission before. Now they are most grateful for the protection that our court affords and thus are able to help get things organized so that the needs of the Japanese army can be supplied. And also help to get folks back into the city again. This has been a most forlorn and desolate place, but it is beginning to be better just a bit now. We have had troop movements to and fro, which greatly aggravated the problem of getting folks back.

The Lord has been graciously supplying all our needs. We have been able to get a good supply of millet and more coal and we trust that when this supply is used, He will have another way to meet our need. We have been living comfortably within our little haven. How thankful we are that we did not go away and that we are here to take advantage of the great opportunity which is here. Each evening we are having evangelistic services and they are well attended and we believe the Lord is at work. . . . You can rest your heart that I am well and safe and have everything I need. Oh, yes, even my cook got back several days ago, for which I was most thankful as I have done my own work for almost a month.[49]

The same day that Neher wrote this letter, she and the Harshes answered a call for assistance outside the compound after dark and never returned. Their colleagues assumed that someone lured them into a trap, but the motives behind their deaths remain obscure. A Chinese claimed to have witnessed their death at the hands of the Japanese, but other reports blamed Communists in a distant part of the province.[50]

Chinese converts working for the Brethren also paid with their lives. In 1940 the Japanese arrested eight Chinese—six women and two men—from the mission compound at Liao, more or less randomly except, according to Brethren missionary Ernest Wampler, "the women taken were of the better dressed and more attractive ones." Shortly after this, occupation authorities detained another eight Chinese workers, including the mission's doctor, its head nurse, the principal of the girls' school, and two teachers.[51] In Wampler's words,

> We did all we could to get the release of these workers, but were always put off by good promises that they would soon have their freedom. . . . The Chinese county official, whom the Japanese had brought in from another province, told us several times that six of the eight had no serious accusation against them. It was the beginning of October and the nights were becoming cold. We tried to get blankets to the prisoners but the Japanese refused, saying they would likely be out soon. But when on October 7 eight more were arrested we began to despair about the release of the ones who had been detained so long. The history of the Japanese army, as we had known it these years at Ping Ting and Liao, was always to retaliate on some innocent victim in their hands whenever they suffered reverses—and they were suffering plenty those days in the Liao section.
>
> On October 13 three of the last eight who were arrested were taken out and bayoneted to death by the Japanese soldiers. It was in an open lot just back of the home of some of our neighbors. They saw the ghastly act and reported to us in the east compound. I was returning from prayers the next morning when I heard it. It was told me by the husband of one of the women who had been killed. I was speechless as I looked into his sad face. . . . The morning following this execution, the three remaining women arrested in the last group were released, having been raped at the will of their captors during the entire time of their detention. I presume death was almost welcome instead of a life like that. The

three released told these stories of how they were treated. Two of these girls were about sixteen years old.[52]

On October 19 the Japanese shot the eight who were first arrested.[53] Wampler reflected on the Japanese tactics.

One method the invading army used in forcing the Chinese people to submit to Japanese rule was to threaten to punish some innocent person of the family if they did not obey orders. This punishment would fall upon the aged parents or women and children of the individual the Japanese were trying to force to do their bidding. So they used that method on us. Outwardly they were friendly, but when we did something they did not like or failed to follow their wishes they would punish some of the Chinese who were the most faithful to us and the church work. That method brought us more pain than if they had punished us. It was very subtle and often we did not know for sure just why the punishment was inflicted.[54]

At this point, with rumors circulating that all Chinese who still worked with Americans would be executed and with visits between Chinese and Americans impossible, little could be accomplished. In December 1940, therefore, most Brethren missionaries left China, except for three who stayed behind in Beijing to assist Brethren students.[55]

As mission work in China became more difficult, the Brethren turned to relief. To supervise the distribution of aid to civilians, they selected Howard Sollenberger, a twenty-one-year-old son of missionaries. Born and raised in China, Sollenberger was fluent in Chinese and could banter in the vernacular with common folk. He also spoke with an urban or aristocratic accent, the result of a Chinese education, which made peasants deferential toward him. When the Japanese invaded the Brethren Chinese mission fields, Sollenberger, a student at Manchester College, persuaded the Brethren Mission Board to send him back to China. He arrived late in 1938.[56]

Conditions determined Sollenberger's methods. He frequently organized a home industry project that provided women with cotton for spinning. The women kept two-thirds of the cloth, and Sollenberger sold his third for more cotton.[57] Sometimes he and a colleague, Louis Whitaker, and several Chinese workers distributed grain.

We have found it advisable to work in cooperation with the local authorities. They often understand their own situation better than we who are just passing through. We first pay a call on the county magistrate. He is asked for suggestions and introductions to the city and village elders. The elders are requested to call together some of the leading citizens of the community for a short meeting to make a list of the most needy. . . .

Thus far most of our relief has been in the form of millet, the staple food of Shanxi. The distribution of this grain has amounted to about 500 tons. During the fall and winter we also provided considerable cloth and cotton for winter clothing.[58]

When circumstances did not permit the distribution of grain, Sollenberger dispersed cash.

During the two weeks that we were working in that area we distributed twenty-five hundred dollars in grain and cash. I wish that most of it could have been given out in grain, but the situation makes it impossible. It is impossible to get the grain carried from place to place. And even if we could get it to the place of distribution, there would be danger of losing it before it could be distributed. The [Chinese] government had all manner of trouble when it tried to distribute a little grain. The Japanese tried several times to get their supplies. Our relief is not for the Japanese army, so we had to do the next best thing and give out cash. This can be done much more rapidly and with a greater degree of safety. Being able to carry cash with us we were quite mobile. We never stayed in one place more than a day, nor slept in the same village more than two nights. We were also very careful not to let anyone know where we were going.[59]

Sollenberger witnessed firsthand the wrath of war. Departing Japanese troops left behind animal manure, destroyed homes, raped women, and dead men. Sollenberger described two villages recently occupied by the invaders.

The Japanese spent a night and two days in this village [Nan Yu] less than a week ago. You don't have to ask questions to know where they have been. The mess that they leave behind gives them away. The doors and windows of the peasants' homes have mostly gone into fire wood. Benches, tables, cabinets, beds, water and grain crocks, and cooking kettles have mostly been smashed up. The rooms are full of straw and debris. Some of the homes where they have stabled horses look like manure yards.[60]

Just before dark I went down past the Chinese lines to a village in no-man's-land. There are still a few peasants there, mostly women. The men were either killed or kidnapped by the Japanese. Could hear the women wailing long before we got to the village. The whole section stinks from dead cows, horses and people.[61]

Sollenberger required residents of recently occupied villages to clean their community before receiving aid.

. . . We are insisting on a thorough cleaning before we help any one. Our reasons are two: one, that the peasants will return to their normal routine sooner if their surroundings look normal (psychological reason). And second, a good cleaning may help prevent the spread of typhus fever.
It's fun to see the whole village out sweeping their homes, airing their bedding, and straightening up places that have been disturbed by the Japanese.[62]

Dangers abounded for Sollenberger, Whitaker, and their Chinese colleagues. Front lines were more or less nonexistent, which allowed them to move about the landscape, dodging the Japanese and distributing relief. Sollenberger described his methods as "guerrilla relief."

I call it guerrilla relief because we have to use guerrilla tactics to distribute. It's give and run before the Japanese and their helpers know where you are and what you are doing.[63]

Disease added to the risk. Sollenberger and Whitaker almost died from typhus, and later Whitaker perished of typhoid.[64] Even when healthy, the physical demands were severe; Sollenberger complained that

I can't keep going at this pace for very long—particularly on the refugee diet which consists mostly of millet and parched corn flour. My digestive system doesn't work well on such fuel.[65]

The Japanese disapproved of Sollenberger's activities because they wanted Chinese civilians in cities, and Brethren aid allowed them to remain in the countryside. Spies followed his activities, and soldiers attempted intimidation, once searching his premises. On another occasion, a Japanese officer pulled a book off a shelf and, while Sollenberger listened, recited most of his activities for the past six months.[66] Several times Sollenberger came under fire.

> It's been a hectic day. We were planning to distribute relief after breakfast. But while we were eating an aeroplane came over and circled once. Nieh* got scared and left his breakfast. Louis [Whitaker] and I finished eating in spite of the aeroplane's return. But when the alarm sounded again we went to the south edge of the village and luckily too. The plane circled twice and then dove from the south releasing two bombs. I watched the bombs all the way down. At first it looked like they were headed directly for us, but they went over our heads and exploded in the village about 40 yards back of us. Again it went up, circled, dove, machine gunned, and released two more bombs. These hit the fields 50 yards in front. The little ditch we were in was right in line of the plane as it dove each time. After the second I decided to move towards the S. E. corner of the village to get out of the direct line. But alas, I went the wrong direction. Two more bombs, one fifty feet above and one fifty feet below, machine gunning too, just a few feet to the right. A piece of shrapnel went through the corner of my coat. And a fourth time the plane dove releasing two more bombs a bit to the west. They were all around us. Pretty lucky I guess. Got a bit excited, but not scared. Was too busy taking pictures. Got six or seven good ones I think. Twelve people were wounded and two killed. Several had terribly messy wounds. Found a little boy of twelve who had a double compound fracture in the leg. Carried him in to the military hospital and fixed him up as much as possible.[67]

In addition to assisting victims of war, Sollenberger occasionally practiced amateur medicine. Chinese medicine was poor, and often missionaries filled the void. Sollenberger learned basic medical procedures from a missionary friend who was a doctor and allowed him to observe operations.

---

*Nieh Chih Hau, an "old friend and colleague" doing government relief work. See Sollenberger, "Two Years in Guerilla Relief," 205.

One morning while I was down in Chen Chow a man brought his twelve-year-old boy around to see if I couldn't do something for him. The poor little boy had a tremendous abscess on his back. I had an idea that the thing should be opened, and in the near future. But I told him that I could not do it for him. He took the boy home but the next morning was around again. He had just come from a Chinese medicine man who said that it should be opened immediately. I didn't know what to say, but advised against letting the Chinese quack operate. They have absolutely no knowledge of sanitation or disinfection. Again I had to refuse to perform the operation myself. But on the third morning he brought the little boy around and delivered his ultimatum. If I wouldn't do it, he would take the boy straight down to the medicine man. The boy had spent a terrible night having considerable pain. There was also a breaking out all over his body. My Chinese relief helpers urged me to do it, saying that no matter what happened it would be better for me to do the job than the medicine man. Their logic and the pleading of the father finally prevailed in part. I told the gathering that I would prepare all the equipment and direct the operation, but that he should do the actual work. He agreed, to my regret.

The operating table was fixed in front of the window. It was nothing more than a board on some high benches. For a knife I clamped one of my injector razor blades in a pair of forceps and sterilized it in the fire. After it was almost white hot, I cooled it in alcohol, and then burned the alcohol off again. Our hands we soaked in near boiling water and continued by scrubbing them with soap. I then prepared the sterile gauze and bandages, and a drain pan to catch the pus.

The brave little fellow was stretched out on the board. Three men were commissioned to hold him. I then painted the entire vicinity of the abscess with iodine. The father's hands underwent the same process.

Every thing was ready for the operation, so I put the knife into the father's hand. After explaining that the opening must be deep enough and long enough for adequate drainage, I indicated the place and direction in which the gash should be made. For a moment I thought everything was going to move along fine. Then just as I was ready to give the command to cut, the father turned around and I saw that my plan had failed. He was pale and trembling. "Please do it for me. Please," he begged.

If it had to be done, I might as well proceed. So I painted my hands and resterilized the knife. But just as I was about to make the initial cut, I lost my nerve. After two or three turns about the room, I got enough cowardly courage to proceed. The first cut was about an inch and a half long and half an inch deep, but nothing happened. It took more cuts to get to where I wanted to go. I had no idea that the thing could be so deep and yet appear so near the surface. I'll not describe what happened other than to say that we got at least a pint of pus out.

I never heard so much yelling except at a football game as that little fellow let out in those few minutes. I did pity him, but could pay no attention once I got started. The assistants told me later that the little boy cursed and damned me as well as all my ancestors from the beginning, and my descendants to come for ten thousand years. But the next day he thanked me profoundly for relieving him of so much pain.

We kept the drainage open for five days and then closed it. The last time I saw the boy he was well and happy. My reputation in Chen Chow was established. From then on I was known as Dr. Sollenberger.[68]

Like Dan West in Spain, Sollenberger emphasized service rather than mission. Absent from his letters and reports are words like "soul-winning" and "converts." When the opportunity arose, he explained his motives to recipients, but he hoped for nothing in return except gratitude.

On the day of the distribution the recipients all gather in some central locality. They are told why they have been chosen to receive relief, and the spirit that is behind it. We also try to give them what encouragement we can. Our reward is the appreciation that they express. God, through their American friends, is kind to them.[69]

Once a village anticipated Sollenberger's arrival and prepared a huge welcome with slogans, singing children, banner, and posters. Sollenberger noted that his unassuming appearance disappointed them, but he used the encounter to explain his purpose.

It was quite obvious that they were surprised and not a little disappointed to see me come in without pretense. They had expected me to come on horseback and with an armed escort like a general of the Nationalist Army.* And here I was trudging along beside my donkey without even a personal pistol at my side for protection. I made use of this situation to explain what I was trying to do. The peasants and guerrillas understood rather easily, but the soldiers of the Second Route Army† couldn't quite get the point.[70]

As Dan West, Howard Sollenberger, and Brethren missionaries learned in these regional conflicts, modern war quickly and brutally turned civilians into victims. The efforts of the Brethren to assist these unfortunates without asking for their conversion indicated another stage in the shift from mission to service.

INVASION OF POLAND

In the late thirties, the atmosphere of a building crisis deepened, and war edged closer to the western democracies. Anxious Brethren contemplated what might be next and prepared for the draft, which had already arrived.

Central and eastern Europe became the latest hot spot. In April 1938, Germany annexed Austria; then in the fall Hitler gave Czechoslovakia an ultimatum demanding cession of the Sudetenland, a territory that contained German-speaking Czechs. Britain and France, both Czech allies, called an emergency conference at Munich, which narrowly avoided war by agreeing to Hitler's demand for the Sudetenland in exchange for a pledge of future German cooperation. H. A. Brandt, assistant editor of *The Gospel Messenger,* applauded this compromise in the name of world peace.

Recent events in Europe suggest some real gains are being made in the technique of international procedure. No, we do not announce perfection. But there has been significant hesitation. Premiers have not plunged nations into war like they once did. With all their bluster, there has been a stopping short of the actual deed, a respect for public sentiment, that comes very near being a new thing under the sun. But most significant of all, people now know that wars can be averted through conference. All this is why we say that a new statesmanship emerges and, because of its

---

*the army of Chiang Kai-shek's Nationalist movement

†Sollenberger was in a Communist-controlled area.

emergence, is certain to force higher standards of international dealings in the future.[71]

Brandt's anticipated higher standards never materialized. Instead, in spring 1939, German troops occupied the rest of Czechoslovakia, and through the summer Hitler prepared for war against Poland. Britain, and France, also Polish allies, promised that this time they would not bail out on their partner, as they had done to the hapless Czechs. In September 1939, Germany invaded Poland and, after a twenty-one-year hiatus, world war restarted.

Many Brethren leaders lamented the renewal of warfare, and they desperately hoped that this time the United States would avoid the conflict. Dan West compared the German invasion of Poland to the beginning of the previous war in 1914. He urged Brethren to keep their nation out of the fighting but to prepare a relief program for its expected victims.

> The long rumbling in Europe has broken into violent eruption again. Twenty-five years ago it was Serbia and other problems; this time it is Poland and other problems. The "other problems" are not all clear; but millions of young men are at the business of killing one another. The horrible stupidity of it all cannot be put into words.

A Half Dozen Suggestions

1. Hold steady. "The alarmist has already ceased to be a Christian." And the people who are inflamed emotionally are not following their Master. He was calm.

2. Guard against propaganda. Truth is the first casualty in war. It is impossible to get a fair picture of daily events with censored presses and radios. Watch the British particularly. Nye's report* on their advance plans to get the United States into their war opens the eyes. Write me at Elgin for free copy.

3. Determine to help keep America out of this war. President Roosevelt has declared that our country is to be neutral. Write him commending that action. Many people will want that policy changed so that they might make money off the killing of their brothers across the ocean.

---

*In 1935 Senator Gerald P. Nye had investigated the causes of U. S. entry into World War I and concluded that bankers and arms manufacturers were responsible.

4. Refuse blood money. Prices are rising already. It is a terrible temptation. We might put the whole eleven millions of unemployed to work and have "prosperity" again for a while—and then a real depression. If you cannot avoid war profits, turn the extra toward relieving suffering.

5. Get ready for an expanding relief program. Women and children will be suffering more this winter than last; and the longer the war, the more they suffer. We dare not let them die while we have means for help. "Inasmuch as ye did it—."

6. Go right on building according to the Lord's Prayer. This war will stop some day. Then some weary spirits will turn again to the building of the world they helped to destroy. Since our Christian faith keeps us from being destroyers, we have an extra duty to work harder to build for the kingdom of God. "Thy will be done on earth" must express our determination.[72]

Edward Frantz, editor of *The Gospel Messenger,* called for Brethren to retain their sanity as the world leaped into insanity.

We stood once on the old suspension bridge below Niagara Falls, and looked intently into the depths below. Strange fascination! What makes one almost want to see how it would feel to jump in? Perhaps they are wise who refuse to visit an insane asylum, lest they also go crazy. . . .

It is for us to keep the charge committed to us, not asking too insistently when the kingdom will be restored to God's true Israel, but faithfully go on witnessing for Christ. In a world gone mad it is the part of the church to stay sane, that is, to love and work and pray and trust and wait.[73]

Kermit Eby encouraged Brethren to avoid any participation in the conflict. "It must be stated now, while we yet have freedom of press here, that war is incompatible with Christianity. That ends do not justify the means. Either we have nothing to do with war, or we accept all its brutal implications."[74]

In April 1940, as German troops unleashed *blitzkrieg* on western Europe, Bonnie Keller reminded Brethren of war's cost.

War or Peace?

War is a cruel, gruesome thing
That takes the lives of youth today.
But have the war lords stopped to think
What the mothers of these boys would say?

How can they cause the suffering,
The moans, the cries of pain, the dread?
Have not their hearts been touched by all
The wounded and the rows of dead?

Must we have hatred, greed and fear
That rule our war-torn world today?
Let's challenge those who say we must.
Lead on to peace, oh, U. S. A.![75]

Some Americans, however, believed that the international situation was so grave that the U. S. should prepare for military action. Consequently, in summer 1940, the nation debated the reinstitution of conscription, and as the draft legislation (the Burke-Wadsworth Bill) worked through Congress, the peace churches lobbied hard for their interests; M. R. Zigler alone visited twenty-four members of Congress. The final version of the bill, which produced the first peace-time conscription in U. S. history, authorized alternative service for those whose "training and religious belief" did not permit participation in the military. It did not require membership in a peace church. But the law gave no recognition to those whose conscience prevented cooperation with the conscription apparatus. As in the previous war, local draft boards would bestow upon the process an image of community democracy, absorb any controversy that might arise, and determine the sincerity of objectors, subject to appeal. Conscientious objectors would be assigned to noncombatant military service or work of "national importance under civilian direction." Because the government preferred to relate to only one organization, peace groups formed the National Council for Religious Objectors* to serve as liaison with the authorities. Friends,

---

*Soon this organization changed its name to the National Service Board for Religious Objectors; later it became the National Interreligious Service Board for Conscientious Objectors; currently it is the Center on Conscience and War.

Mennonites, and Brethren shouldered most of the burden for this agency and Zigler chaired its board, but other denominations also participated.[76]

With the right to alternative service secured, the peace churches then turned toward exercising it. They proposed Civilian Public Service, modeled along the lines of the Civilian Conservation Corps with church work camps as additional inspiration. The religious bodies wanted the government to share the costs of the program, but President Roosevelt insisted that if the churches ran the camps, they had to pay for them. Otherwise, the government would fund the program but also administer the camps; it was all or nothing for the churches.[77] Unwilling to allow the government to supervise its conscientious objectors, a special meeting of the Church of the Brethren Standing Committee, held in December 1940 in Chicago, agreed to fund alternative service even if it cost "large amounts." In its statement Standing Committee

> 1. Reaffirmed that we continue to advise our young men that noncombatant service within the army is inconsistent with the teachings of the Bible and the Church of the Brethren. Further, that it cannot be reconciled with our historic peace positions.
>
> 2. Voted to assume financial responsibility for training our young men, with or without government aid (it not yet being clear what position the government will take as to financial aid) in projects of national importance under civilian control which are in harmony with our convictions regarding military training and service. This may run into large amounts.[78]

The government viewed denominational bodies as its agents, managing alternative service units on its behalf, but the peace churches saw themselves as engaging in church-state cooperation and "then going beyond that," in the words of Paul Comly French, director of the National Service Board for Religious Objectors, by paying for it. Critics charged that the peace churches had sold out to the government by funding one of its basic functions.[79]

By November 1941, Brethren-sponsored CPS camps were open, and America was only days away from declaring war. Through Lend-Lease and other arrangements, the United States had already aided Britain in every way possible short of committing troops, and in the North Atlantic, American sailors shot at German submarines on sight as part of an undeclared naval war. Meanwhile, negotiations with Japan had broken off over U. S. demands that Japan withdraw from China, something to which no Japanese government could agree, and the only question was where the first shots would be fired. One week before Pearl Harbor Dan West wondered how Brethren would respond to the "whirling chaos" around them.

> We are deeper in war now than any other time in the last twenty-three years. The approval of arming merchant ships and sending them anywhere in the world virtually nullifies the whole neutrality act. Unless something unforeseen—a genuine miracle—prevents, we shall turn our minds as a nation to the brilliant and exhilarating activities of hating and killing. I have no doubt of the sincerity of many people who wish this were not necessary, but who believe it has to be done before we can rebuild the world on a better basis. Some of our own people feel that way, too; and there is a danger that more will move in that direction. Can Brethren, with a history of peacemindedness across centuries and through wars in Germany and America, hold steady under this increasing strain? If that is possible, how can we keep perspective in the whirling chaos around us?[80]

Conclusion

During the thirties modernity impressed Brethren with its ability to influence society from afar as large, unseen, powerful economic forces bore down on Brethren institutions and personal lives. Brethren up and down the denominational ladder coped with the diminished resources of the Great Depression and assisted those who suffered even more than they.

Modern nation-states were just as distant, mysterious, and dangerous, particularly in their fascist form, as economic forces. Another total war between industrialized powers became increasingly likely, and where conflict had already broken out, warring nations left in their belligerent wakes conditions that fostered relief rather than evangelism. Abroad as well as at home Brethren continued their trek from mission to service. In a world of Depression and war, in a "world gone mad," to borrow Edward Frantz's phrase, modernity had a heavy hand in the global insanity.

NOTES

1. David M. Kennedy, *Freedom from Fear: The American People in Depression and War,* 1929-1945 (New York: Oxford University Press, 1999), 162-67.

2. For examples see; "News from Churches," *The Gospel Messenger* (September 19, 1931): 24-25, 28-29; "News from Churches" (June 10, 1933): 20, 24; "Kingdom Gleanings" (March 23, 1935): 16; "News from Churches" (March 23, 1935): 29, 30.

3. Author interview with Alma Moyers Long (June 17, 2002).

4. Alma Moyers Long interview.

5. "Ella Ebbert," *The Brethren Encyclopedia,* 3 vols., edited by Donald F. Durnbaugh (Philadelphia, Pa., and Oak Brook, Ill.: The Brethren Encyclopedia, Inc., 1983), I:417; "Herbert Spenser Minnich," *The Brethren Encyclopedia,* II: 848.

6. Spenser Minnich to Ella Ebbert, (May 19, 1933), Brethren Historical Library and Archives (BHLA), Elgin, Ill., Missionary Personnel/ Correspondence file, Box 49, "Ella Ebbert." file.

7. Earl M. Frantz to H. Spenser Minnich (July 6, 1933), BHLA, Box 49, "Ella Ebert" file.

8. "Alexander/Anna" is a *nom de plume.* In exchange for access to missionary files, the General Board required that none of the missionaries, dead or alive, suffer public disclosure of personal foibles.

9. Rufus D. Bowman, "For Whom Shall We Vote?" *The Gospel Messenger* (October 15, 1932): 5-6. See also in *The Gospel Messenger* F. A. Vaniman, "Morals vs. Politics," 6-7; Thomas Nixon Carver, "Common Sense and the Liquor Issue," 7-8.

10. Grant Mahan, *The Gist of the Church of the Brethren* (a Dunkard Brethren booklet), February 22, 1936: 7-11.

11. Carl F. Bowman, *Brethren Society: The Cultural Transformation of a "Peculiar People"* (Baltimore, Md.: The Johns Hopkins University Press, 1995), 407; Donald F. Durnbaugh, *Fruit of the Vine: A History of the Brethren, 1708-1995* (Elgin, Ill.: The Brethren Press, 1997), 446-47. Bowman and Durnbaugh are unsure whether this meeting took place in 1939 or 1940.

12. H. L. Hartsough, J. E. Miller, Ora W. Garber, eds., *Minutes of the Annual Conferences of the Church of the Brethren, 1923-1944* (Elgin, Ill.: Brethren Publishing House, 1946), 64, 67, 84, 90, 100, 106, 113, 120, 128, 141, 145, 151, 161. Conference did not include Bethany in its budget until the 1931 budget year. I added Bethany's 35k to the Annual Conference board budget to make it consistent with other budgets in the thirties.

13. Author interview with Mary Greenawalt (November 2002).

14. Charles D. Bonsack to H. Stover Kulp, October 6, 1932. BHLA, Missionary Personnel/Correspondence, Box 23, "1926-1934" file.

15. Bonsack to A. Raymond Cottrell (January 3, 1933), BHLA, Missionary Personnel/Correspondence, Box 48, "Drs. A. R. and Laura Cottrell, 1910-1938" file.
16. General Mission Board to Adam Ebey (March 23, 1933), BHLA, Missionary Personnel/Correspondence, Box 49, File "Adam/Alice Ebey."
17. "Facing Another Winter of Relief Work, *The Gospel Messenger* (October 15, 1932): 26.
18. Vernon F. Schwalm, "The Role of Religion in Modern Life," *The Gospel Messenger* (June 11, 1938), 5-10.
19. Kennedy, *Freedom from Fear,* 362, 365-80; Hartsough, Miller, Garber, eds., *Minutes, 1923-1944,* 139-67.
20. Kennedy, *Freedom from Fear,* 381-83.
21. Walter LaFeber, *The American Age: United States Foreign Policy at Home and Abroad Since 1750* (New York: W. W. Norton and Company, 1989), 336-39, 369-70.
22. Edward Frantz, "How Big a Navy Do We Need?" *The Gospel Messenger* (January 28, 1928): 57; see also LaFeber, *The American Age,* 329.
23. LaFeber, *The American Age,* 329.
24. Daniel C. Reber, "The Paris Peace Pact," *The Gospel Messenger* (October 6, 1928): 631.
25. Gerald L. Sittser, *A Cautious Patriotism: The American Churches and the Second World War* (Chapel Hill: University of North Carolina Press, 1997), 25.
26. Emma Horning, "The Psychological Basis of World Peace," *The Gospel Messenger* (September 10, 1932): 20, 24.
27. Andrew W. Cordier, "The League of Nations as Seen from Geneva," *The Gospel Messenger* (March 14, 1931): 5.
28. "Daniel West," *The Brethren Encyclopedia,* II:1330-31; Durnbaugh, *Fruit of the Vine,* 459-60. For a biography of West see Glee Yoder, *Passing on the Gift: The Story of Dan West* (Elgin, Ill.: The Brethren Press, 1978).
29. Dan West, "Youth and the Church," *The Gospel Messenger* (June 13, 1931): 7-8.
30. "Daniel West," *The Brethren Encyclopedia,* II:1331; Durnbaugh, *Fruit of the Vine,* 459-61; Yoder, *Passing on the Gift,* 53-55.
31. Ben Stoner, "Twenty Thousand Dunkers for Peace," *The Gospel Messenger* (October 22, 1932): 5.
32. *Brethren Action* (June 1, 1937): 1.
33. Otho Winger, "What Will the Church of the Brethren Do This Year for the Kingdom of God?" *The Gospel Messenger* (June 1, 1935): 12.
34. Rufus D. Bowman, "Missions: Tomorrow," *The Gospel Messenger* (June 22, 1935): 10-12.
35. Mrs. Ross D. [Sara Florence Fogelsanger] Murphy, "Women's Work, the Five Year Period," *The Gospel Messenger* (June 29, 1935): 8-9.
36. "A Restatement Concerning War and Peace," *Minutes of the Annual Conference of the Church of the Brethren, 1935,* 40-41.

37. "Legal Counsel for Conscientious Objectors," *Minutes, 1935,* 34.
38. *Minutes, 1938,* 39-40.
39. Dan West, "Peace Action?" *The Gospel Messenger* (November 7, 1936): 10.
40. Chalmer Faw, "Peace and the Church," *The Gospel Messenger* (November 7, 1936): 13.
41. *Minutes, 1939,* 6.
42. In 1938 Conference again allocated funds for relief in China and Spain. *Minutes, 1938,* 42.
43. Kennedy, *Freedom from Fear,* 398-400; LaFeber, *The American Age,* 365-66.
44. "Spanish Civil War," *The Brethren Encyclopedia,* II:1208.
45. *Brethren Action* (June 1, 1937): 2.
46. Dan West, "Saving Lives in Spain and China," *The Gospel Messenger* (December 17, 1938): 12, 15. See also Yoder, *Passing on the Gift,* 89-99.
47. LaFeber, *The American Age,* 336-39, 369-70.
48. Anetta C. Mow, *In Memoriam: Minneva J. Neher, Alva C. Harsh, and Mary Hykes Harsh* (Elgin, Ill.: Brethren Publishing House, 1947), 83-86.
49. Letter from Minneva Neher (December 2, 1937), in Mow, *In Memoriam,* 51-53.
50. Mow, *In Memoriam,* 23-27.
51. Ernest M. Wampler, *China Suffers, or My Six Years of Work During the Incident* (Elgin, Ill.: Brethren Publishing House, 1945), 161-63.
52. Wampler, *China Suffers,* 163-64.
53. Wampler, *China Suffers,* 167.
54. Wampler, *China Suffers,* 171.
55. Wampler, *China Suffers,* 171-78.
56. Howard Sollenberger manuscript, "Two Years in Guerrilla Relief: Howard Sollenberger's Diary, Journals, Letters and Recollections, 1938-1940," edited by John Wampler, v-vii. I am deeply indebted to John Wampler for providing access to this manuscript.
57. Sollenberger, "Two Years," 16-17.
58. Sollenberger, "Two Years," 14-16.
59. Sollenberger, "Two Years," 39-40.
60. Sollenberger, "Two Years," 233.
61. Sollenberger, "Two Years," 235.
62. Sollenberger, "Two Years," 235.
63. Sollenberger, "Two Years," 37.
64. Sollenberger, "Two Years," 171-98, 342.
65. Sollenberger, "Two Years," 76.
66. Sollenberger, "Two Years," 80, 82.
67. Sollenberger, "Two Years," 226.
68. Sollenberger, "Two Years," 13.
69. Sollenberger, "Two Years," 14-16.
70. Sollenberger, "Two Years," 56-57.

71. H. A. Brandt, "A New Statesmanship Emerges," *The Gospel Messenger* (November 5, 1938): 4.

72. Dan West, "The Brethren in Wartime," *The Gospel Messenger* (September, 16, 1939): 12-13.

73. Edward Frantz, "When the World Is Mad," *The Gospel Messenger* (September 23, 1939): 3.

74. Kermit Eby, "The War Is On," *The Gospel Messenger* (September 23, 1939): 5.

75. Bonnie Keller, "War or Peace?" *The Gospel Messenger* (April 13, 1940): 8.

76. Donald F. Durnbaugh, *Pragmatic Prophet: The Life of Michael Robert Zigler* (Elgin, Ill.: The Brethren Press, 1989), 126-27; Cynthia Eller, *Conscientious Objectors and the Second World War: Moral and Religious Arguments in Support of Pacifism* (New York: Praeger, 1991), 24-27; George Q. Flynn, *The Draft, 1940-1973* (Lawrence: University of Kansas Press, 1993), 10-20; Kennedy, *Freedom from Fear,* 632-33; Albert N. Keim and Grant M. Stoltzfus, *The Politics of Conscience: The Historic Peace Churches and America at War, 1917-1955* (Scottdale, Pa.: Herald Press, 1988), 78-105.

77. Durnbaugh, *Pragmatic Prophet,* 129-30; Keim and Stoltzfus, *The Politics of Conscience,* 108-14. For a history of Civilian Public Service, see Leslie Eisan, *Pathways of Peace: A History of the Civilian Public Service Program Administered by the Brethren Service Committee* (Elgin, Ill.: Brethren Publishing House, 1948).

78. Hartsough, Miller, Garber, *Minutes of the Annual Conferences, 1923-1944,* 166.

79. Durnbaugh, *Pragmatic Prophet,* 131-32. French was a friend.

80. Dan West, "Perspective Now," *The Gospel Messenger* (November 29, 1941): 8.

PART III
World War II

VII. WORLD WAR AGAIN
Brethren Seek an Alternative

As historian David Kennedy has noted, the 1939 German invasion of Poland made World War I merely the "opening chapter in the twentieth century's own Thirty-Year War."[1] In this second phase of the century's world conflict, industrialization loomed larger than ever. Motorized vehicles, including tanks, trucks, and mechanized artillery, dominated the battlefield, and lengthy, bureaucratized, and complicated logistical lines supported this gas-driven warhead. Technology was critical, especially in air and sea warfare, but also for land armies, dependent upon transport and radio communications. Those with skills useful to industrialized warfare, such as scientists, dock workers, and accountants, were just as valuable to the war effort as soldiers, and many of the estimated fifty million who died in the war did not wear a uniform. Among major belligerents, only the U. S. suffered no direct civilian casualties, though 292,000 soldiers died in combat. The British suffered the death of 60,000 civilians (and 244,000 combatants); 200,000 Dutch perished in the war, only 10,000 of them soldiers; and half of the Soviet Union's 14,000,000 deaths were nonmilitary.[2]

For the Church of the Brethren, this mechanized tempest also became another chapter in a terrible age of war, and the struggle profoundly influenced it. Overseas mission efforts, especially in China, suffered a setback from which they never recovered. Mission further declined as World War II's impact on civilians made many Brethren increasingly service-minded, a change of heart that hastened Brethren ecumenism. Nonresistance again conflicted with the nation-state's demand for the loyalty of Brethren men. Most answered Uncle Sam's call, but a significant minority of draftable Brethren clung to the traditional peace position. For the second time in twenty-three years, the Brethren lived in a nation at war.

WARTIME MISSION

One of the most apparent Brethren casualties of the war was mission. The mission field in China closed prior to Pearl Harbor (see previous chapter), but as the war wore on, all mission fields suffered.

Of course, preaching the gospel in many foreign lands continued despite the conflict, and every week *The Gospel Messenger* urged prayer for several of its missionaries and remembrance of them on their birthdays.

> **What to Pray For**
> Week of April 3-10
> **Pray for the missionaries whose names are listed in the Prayer Calendar this week.**
> B. Mary Royer
> Goldie E. Swartz
>
> **Remember the missionaries on their birthdays.**
> **Africa**
>   Gladys Hawbaker Royer, April 1, 1902.
> **China**
>   Susie M. Thomas, April 15, 1910.
> **India**
>   Dr. Barbara M. Nickey, April 5, 1886.
>   William G. Kinzie, April 19, 1906.
>   Everett Fasnacht, April 19, 1912.
>   Joy Cullen Fasnacht, April 11, 1915.[3]

But World War II touched mission fields far removed from the battlefield. Leland S. Brubaker, general secretary of the General Mission Board, reported the "stress and strain" that the war caused among the Brethren in Nigeria, although he ended on a positive note, as missionaries so often did.

> The Africa mission staff has been cut off from the home church as far as transportation is concerned as it never has been before. Many letters do not reach their destination. Provisions and supplies are ordered and reordered, but even then fail to arrive.

Almost all the present staff are either due or past due for furlough. They are trying desperately hard to arrange furlough schedules in such a way as to care best for their work, their health, and their future plans. This is a most difficult problem, but the staff is meeting it with excellent spirit and fortitude.

Three missionaries have returned to the field in the last few months: Brother H. Stover Kulp, and Brother and Sister Herman B. [Hazel Minnich] Landis. They went by way of South America to South Africa, a route which is long and expensive, but it enabled them finally to find their place with their comrades on the field. Plans are already made for Dr. Howard Bosler and wife to return next spring. Others, we hope, will be able to go just as soon as travel restrictions are less stringent.

Nigeria, British West Africa, is feeling the stress and strain of war. New problems have arisen in new areas without removing many of the ever-present ones. In spite of this, almost every letter from our folks there points to encouraging facts: renewed strength in local indigenous church groups; revamping of the education work in order to serve the church more truly; new communities and areas asking for teachers and for those who can dispense simple medicines; a deeper consecration of individual lives, and always faithfulness and loyalty of the mission group to their many tasks made so difficult because of present conditions.[4]

As Brubaker noted, travel to the wartime field was difficult. Particularly perilous was the experience of Ruth Utz, Mary Alice Engel, and Sylvia M. Oiness, Brethren missionaries to Nigeria, who in early 1941 sailed on an Egyptian passenger ship, the *Zamzam*. On board were refugees from England plus 120 missionaries representing twenty-one faiths, all heading for South Africa. As German submarines roamed the Atlantic, the *Zamzam* departed from New York, stopping in Baltimore for hundreds of sacks of ammonium nitrate, an ingredient in ammunition. The ship also carried aviation gasoline. Its captain took orders from the British Admiralty, and it maintained radio silence, sailed in blackout without navigation lights, and flew no flag. The *Zamzam's* contraband cargo and the manner in which it traveled marked it as a target. Oiness related her story.[5]

At 5:45 a.m., Thursday, April 17, just five days and 1,500 miles from Capetown, we were shelled without warning by a German raider. We were awakened by what at first seemed to be thunder; then we heard the boom of heavy guns. The air trembled with a terrible vibration. The ship shook and quivered as salvo after salvo came. The noise was tearing and rending. Shrapnel burst over and around the vessel. One shell destroyed the wireless apparatus; one shell blew a life boat in two; another hit the forward lounge; still another blew a tremendous hole in the funnel, destroying all wire connections between the bridge and the various departments of the ship. Three shells punched great holes in the engine room below the water-line. The captain's quarters were smashed. A shell tore through the hull aft the midship watertight door and crashed into the main passageway, injuring passengers. Shells burst into cabins on the port side. The wounded were screaming and crying in pain for help; children were crying from fright; Arabic oaths from the Egyptian crew were heard here and there.

All in all, the shelling lasted about ten minutes, and at least ten shells hit their mark, causing destruction and tragedy. Stories vary as to the number of shots fired, but the German gunnery lieutenant later told us he had fired 55. The Zamzam began to list to portside immediately. . . .

When the shelling started, one of my cabinmates, Ruth Utz, rushed in from the outer deck, where she had been sleeping, and called out, "Get your lifebelts on." Then Mary Alice Engel and I knew what we had feared—a German attack! I jumped quickly out of the upper bunk, praying, "O Lord, help us." I tried to grab a few clothes, keeping as close to the floor as possible, should a shell come through our cabin. Between shells I threw on a housecoat, put on my winter coat and a pair of sport shoes, snatched my lifebelt and purse and hastened on deck. By that time the firing had ceased, so I went back into the cabin to retrieve a washcloth, a toothbrush, ankle socks, and a kerchief as protection from the burning sun. Yes, a toothbrush and washcloth would aid me in keeping clean during anticipated days in a lifeboat. Carrying my Bible and purse I struggled down the rope ladder, swinging against the side of the sinking ship, and into a lifeboat.

Passengers maintained complete calm but the crew members lost their heads. Pushing women and children aside, they rushed madly down the ladders into lifeboats. Fear gripped their unchristian hearts as they saw the ship listing to its side. Screaming and bellowing at the top of their lungs, they fought to pull away when boats were only half-filled, and they refused to go back for passengers clinging to the bottom rungs of ladders. Because of this, some had no alternative but to throw themselves into the sea and swim to rafts which had been cut loose; others were compelled to remain on the sinking ship until rescued by German motorboats.[6]

If a shell had struck oil drums, gas tanks, or the aviation gas, a violent explosion would have quickly sunk the craft, but only three persons were injured seriously and no lives were lost. The Germans rescued everybody in the water, pulling children up to their ship in blankets and allowing adults to climb rope ladders, and they promptly operated on the gravely wounded. The captors finished off the *Zamzam* with explosives in its hold, and most of the baggage went down with the doomed ship. The *Zamzam's* passengers, including the three Brethren missionaries, spent their first night in captivity locked in a hot, unventilated hold three decks down as children whimpered and cried all night. The next day the Germans transferred everybody to a prison ship.

Motorboats were busy all forenoon the following day, Friday, April 18, now taking supplies from the raider to the auxiliary ship. By mid-afternoon we all went aboard the Dresden, the German prison ship which was to be our jail for almost five weeks. Mothers and children were given the few cabins; these cabins, ordinarily accommodating two persons, now accommodated eight. Single women occupied the lounge and smoking room, where dirty mattresses were lined up on the floor. Eighteen slept and lived in a room the size of an ordinary living room. One blanket apiece served as bedding; lifebelts became pillows. Water was rationed—2 quarts per person per day. True, we had ample sea water, but salt water does not remove dirt. Plumbing again was atrocious; toilets would not flush. One public bathroom and lavatory served over seventy people.

The men fared even worse. They were ordered into the front hatch, given sacks and raw cotton, and told to make their own pallets. Of course, they had no washing facilities or lavatories in the hold, except as they themselves built them. The Germans furnished lumber, and told them to go to work. Each man was given one spoon, one tin cup, and one enamel bowl. This bowl, the one receptacle, was used for many purposes: for bathing, for shaving, and for eating! 108 white men occupied a space 50 x 50;

one small ladder was the only exit to the deck above. The Egyptian crew had similar accommodations in the next hold.

From sunset to sunrise we were all locked inside. Windows were closed, wooden Venetian blinds were closed, heavy cardboard was placed in front of the windows, and then blankets were nailed on top. We were indeed sailing under strict blackout; no ray of light must escape to the outside. With no fresh air, the atmosphere stifling, we almost suffocated.[7]

Food was bad and clothing scarce. As the ship sailed north into colder weather, colds, flu, bronchitis, and dysentery beset the prisoners. After running the British blockade, the ship docked at St. Jean de Luz in occupied France, and the Germans placed the *Zamzam's* crew and British, Canadian, and French citizens, including women and children, in prison camps. This separated several multi-national married couples and sent to internment a young English woman who had planned a marriage shortly after arrival in Capetown. Americans, however, were still neutrals, so the Germans dispatched the Yanks, including Utz, Engel, and Oiness, to Biarritz, France. Oiness complained about the overbearing German presence there.

In the mornings I was awakened by "glee clubs." These were groups of German soldiers marching through the streets singing lustily the war song, "Germany Over All." I can still hear the sound of hobnailed boots marching up and down, up and down the streets of Biarritz. May those hobnailed boots never march up and down the streets of America![8]

After ten days authorities transferred the Americans to Spain and then to Portugal for repatriation. In Spain Oiness found conditions were even worse than in Biarritz.

As we stopped at stations, starving Spanish children rapped at our train windows, with outstretched arms begging and pleading for food. It was a pitiful sight![9]

Entry into Portugal was joyous. At the first stop, local citizens, who had been helped by the Red Cross and American Express, prepared a huge feast for the hungry Americans. The train waited an hour while they ate. Oiness returned to the United States on a Portuguese liner, accompanied by Jewish refugees, many of whom were children of parents the Nazis had either killed or jailed. Although Utz, Engel, and Oiness were the only Brethren missionaries captured while in transit, their sojourn illustrates the difficulties of travel to wartime mission outposts.[10]

In China the obstacles were much more grave than difficult transportation or wartime shortages. As described in the previous chapter, the Japanese occupation became so oppressive that most Brethren missionaries finally left. Only three stayed behind—V. Grace Clapper, Minor M. Myers, and Hazel Rothrock—and the Japanese detained them for approximately six months until they were exchanged for Japanese civilians. Hazel Rothrock reflected on her time as a prisoner.

> It is worthwhile to think of the end results of our months spent in internment, and I give here a few thoughts that have come to me. We were not mistreated. Annoyances, inconveniences, limitations were our lot, and no doubt to be expected. Uncertainty and isolation were probably the hardest to bear, but these very facts made prayer more vital and faith more essential. A very real benefit was to be found in our simple living with much of the day spent outdoors, not far from God's best plan for humans perhaps. . . . Housekeeping was simple and entirely lacking in modern conveniences. We lived in crowded rooms, carried all our water, did laundry in wash basins in many cases, used Chinese style latrines, retired at 10 o'clock, or soon after, when lights were turned out . . . and ate stew served from large dingy metal pails out of unbreakable soup bowls on tables "untouched by linen cloths."[11]

Several other missionaries spent almost the entire war in detention in the Philippine Islands. When the Brethren evacuated China, eight missionaries, instead of returning home, went to the Philippines, where their language school had relocated. But shortly after Pearl Harbor, the Japanese invaded this American possession and captured them.[12] Rolland C. Flory, one of the imprisoned Brethren, described the beginning of the war and the arrival of the Japanese.

> One beautiful morning in December 1941, the students from the College of Chinese Studies in Baguio were standing in little groups discussing the attack on Pearl Harbor. It was time for school but there was not much incentive to start classes that morning. Soon after classes began, we heard the roar of planes and the thud of

exploding bombs. Were the planes just Americans practicing or were they Japanese? It was impossible to carry on school work and so several fellows went to find out the truth of the situation. Upon their return we knew war had actually started in the Philippines. . . .

As the Japanese advanced, the American army in Baguio left, leaving the city undefended. Most of the American civilians assembled together in Brent School, an American boarding school. We felt there would be safety in numbers. The mayor and a couple of other Americans and the leading Japanese civilian of the city went down the road to contact the Japanese army and to inform them that Baguio was undefended. In this way we were saved from being shelled. At midnight, December 27, the Japanese army arrived at the school. We were all searched by the soldiers and then crowded into a small building. The next day, loaded with a very few personal belongings, we were marched several miles to Camp John Hay, the American military camp, our home for the next four months.[13]

Approximately one-third of the detainees in the camps were missionaries, and the others were involved with mining or business. In April 1942, the Japanese moved them to another location, a former Filipino police camp where conditions were much better, and for the next thirty-two months they lived here. According to Flory, relations with the Japanese guards varied.

When we were first interned, the civilian Japanese who had been in Baguio were in charge of us but soon the army gave closer supervision. The civilian Japanese were then employed by the army as an office staff to manage us through our committee. An army guard was maintained to guard us at all times. The guard was frequently changed. When a new guard came in, the soldiers would control with fixed bayonets and were very careful to see that we behaved as we should. Sometimes a guard would slap an American who did something contrary to the Japanese standards. A day or two later, however, they would dispense with the bayonet and as they saw more of us, they would walk among us unarmed. Frequently they spoke to the children and even to an adult now and then. That was a sign that we had tamed a new group of guards. They found that we were not so terrible as they had been led to believe.[14]

Rules changed constantly, and clothing was limited. Detainees spent most of the time outdoors, which relieved overcrowding except during the rainy season, but generally cramped quarters added to the stress, as reported by another of the captives.

> The typical remark that would fit the picture from beginning to end would be, "If you want privacy, shut your eyes." There are always means to be found to ease physical discomfort. But what can relieve the strain when so many personalities are thrown closely together? And this was not merely the question of overcrowding like peas in a pod, but there was the added stress of hunger, anxiety and physical exhaustion and sickness.[15]

Conditions were unhealthy but rarely life-threatening. The camp suffered a dysentery epidemic and a typhoon, but in late 1943 medical supplies from the American Red Cross arrived, probably saving lives. Also, each person received a Red Cross kit of approximately fifty pounds of food, which many used over the year to vary their diet of rice and corn.[16] Food was adequate, if simple.

> Many times we wondered if our rice would arrive in time for our next meal. Every time but one it did come, although sometimes meals were late because of its delayed arrival. On the one day it failed to come, the Japanese guards loaned us a sack from their stores so that no day passed foodless.[17]

The Brethren detainees had almost no contact with the outside world, leaving friends, family, and the church in doubt about their safety. A news item in the April 17, 1943, issue of *The Gospel Messenger,* more than fifteen months after detainment, reported only that several names had appeared on Red Cross lists and that a "British woman," interned with the missionaries but repatriated, knew little except that they were healthy and that two of them had given birth inside the camp.

> The only communication that we have had from our missionaries in the language school at Baguio since December 7, 1941, was a cablegram received from them on December 11, 1941, stating that all were well. We have tried every known method of getting in touch with them or receiving information from them.

We are sure that our readers will be happy to know of the following news. A British woman was interned in Baguio with our people. . . .

"Concerning the names you [Leland S. Brubaker] listed in your letter, I remember all of them with the exception of Miss Susie Thomas.

"Doctor [Ernest L.] Cunningham was very fit and doing a great deal of medical work in the camp—his specialty was dietetics—trying to see that we had enough calories with the limited supply of food at our disposal and also trying to look after the needs of the people who had diabetes. His wife and son were also well when I left. Miss Bessie Crim was very fit and extremely active in camp work in her capacity as a trained nurse. As far as I can remember, both Mrs. [Josephine Keever] Flory and Mrs. [Helen Francis Buehl] Angeny had sons. Mrs. Angeny had hers in January, I think, and Mrs. Flory had hers, I think sometime in February or March.

"I cannot give you very much news about the men as they were in the next building to ours and were not allowed to associate with us in the women's dormitory, and as the camp consisted of over 500 people and it is a year since I was in Baguio my memory for names or faces is not so good."[18]

When in early 1945 American troops landed in the Philippines, the Japanese transferred the American civilians to a prison in Manila. Food, disease, and sanitary conditions were much worse there, and several likely would have died had not American forces captured the city within a month. Shortly thereafter, the liberated Brethren missionaries returned to the U. S.[19]

Most missionaries had much less harrowing lives than those who were interned by the Japanese or aboard the ill-fated *Zamzam*. Many fearless Christians, strengthened by the prayers of those at home, continued the challenging work of overseas evangelism, but all mission fields felt the strain of war, regardless of their distance from the front lines. Undoubtedly, global conflict made the goal of winning the world for Christ much more distant.

Wartime Service

As mission lost steam, service shifted into high gear. The global conflict bore responsibility for both aspects of this trend; it kept missionaries at home and made civilians in its path harder to ignore. For many Brethren, then, overseas service became more important.

Theologically this trend owed a debt to a growing international variant of the Social Gospel, usually called "realism" in non-Brethren traditions. Protestant realists hoped to make the world better, and they focused on the immediate, the "here and now," rather than crusading for perfection or America's destiny or waiting upon Christ's second coming. International in perspective, in the crucial pre-war period the realists encouraged greater American involvement in world affairs at a time when that was controversial. They were also ecumenical, believing that unified Christianity represented the one ideology with enough power to counter fascism. Protestant realists were not necessarily pacifist, but the nonresistant Brethren version of this movement consistently urged a greater international role for the church through relief and service.[20]

A sign of the rising stature of relief work was the redesignation of the Brethren Service Committee as a major board, equal in status and independent of the denomination's other main agencies, including the General Mission Board. A report on the "Reorganization and Function of Brethren Service Committee" delivered a ringing call to service.

> The Brethren Service Committee finds its charter in the words of the Master: "I was hungry and ye gave me to eat; . . . I was a stranger and ye took me in; I was naked and ye clothed me; I was sick and ye visited me; I was in prison and ye came unto me . . . inasmuch as ye did it unto one of these my brethren, even these least, ye did it unto me." [ellipses in the original]
>
> This committee represents the Church of the Brethren in the area of social action. Its primary function is that of personal rehabilitation and social reconstruction in the name and spirit of Christ. Its fields of service are as follows:
>
> 1. To arrest and eliminate, insofar as possible, those forces in human society which contribute to the disintegration of personality and character, and to social instability.
>
> 2. To relieve human distress and suffering around the world without regard to barriers of race, creed or nationality.
>
> 3. To represent the church in the area of creative citizenship and Christian testimony on issues of national and international significance. This includes the program of Civilian Public Service and the relation of the church and its members to the government in regard to peace and war and situations where the principle of religious freedom is involved (1 Peter 2:12).

4. To develop, organize and apply the spiritual and financial resources of the church to the above areas of service as a concrete and practical expression of the spirit and teaching of Christ as the Brethren understand and interpret them. This shall include the expressional side of our peace program in an effort of world reconciliation and the preservation of goodwill and human understanding among all peoples and races.[21]

The highly recognizable Brethren Service cup was made of Oregon myrtlewood and bore a decal illustrating a cup of cold water given to a neighbor in Christ's name. *Photo courtesy of BHLA.*

Service loomed large in congregational life. Many congregations dedicated Brethren Service cups, which were wooden communion chalices into which they placed weekly donations for relief. Women sewed and canned for CPS camps, and youth raised money for Brethren Service. Although some local societies did not participate in these activities, reports filed in *The Gospel Messenger* demonstrate just how deeply into some pews the call to service had penetrated. In 1943 one issue of the denominational periodical included the following:

Cherry Grove, [Illinois].—The Red Cross received some money from the church and the ladies' aid.

Battle Creek, [Michigan].—Our ladies' aid sent five bags of clothing for relief this winter. On the evening of March 21 Brethren Perry Hoover of Beaverton, Mich., and A. E. Taylor of Flint, Mich., were with us and showed interesting pictures of the C. P. S. camps.

Swan Creek, [Ohio.]—Our ladies' aid canned fruit and vegetables and sent several kits and comforters to the C. P. S. camps.

Zion Hill, [Ohio].—The [Easter] forenoon service was for parents and their children; the members brought eggs to send to the C. P. S. camps. The ladies have been taking home relief sewing to work on. They are planning to do more canning for the camps this summer.

Maiden Creek, [Pennsylvania].—The Easter morning service was in the charge of our young people; they rendered an impressive peace play entitled "Early American." The offering lifted at this service amounts to $328 and will be used for Brethren Service.

Midway, [Pennsylvania].—On April 11 Bro. Galen Kilhefner presented his illustrated lecture on Brethren Service. Our young people and young adults are sponsoring refreshment stands at public sales and are giving the proceeds to Brethren Service.

Valley River, [West Virginia].—[The ladies' aid has] sent two more packets and eight comforters to C. P. S. camp. They also canned 150 quarts of vegetables and fruit for the camps.[22]

While the war persisted, most relief efforts went to the home front. The Brethren Service Commission's major task during the war was running Civilian Public Service, but it also developed several relief centers that collected and processed material aid, such as food, medicine, soap, and clothing. The largest and most significant of these was at New Windsor, Maryland, on the campus of Blue Ridge College, a former Brethren institution secured for the denomination by M. R. Zigler.* (The Brethren still own and operate New Windsor, but Church World Service and other organizations use it extensively.) Much of the material remained stateside.[23]

---

*Blue Ridge College had a long and troubled existence. Founded in 1899 by the Eastern Maryland district conference, Blue Ridge became a nonaccredited junior college in 1927, and three years later it affiliated with Bridgewater-Daleville College. In 1937 Bridgewater-Daleville sold Blue Ridge to a private foundation, which failed, and the following year the school returned to Brethren control. In 1944 Blue Ridge declared bankruptcy, and the Brethren Service Commission bought it at public auction. See "Blue Ridge College," *The Brethren Encyclopedia,* I:152-53.

Among the earliest beneficiaries of the growing service impulse were displaced Japanese Americans on the Pacific Coast. Ralph E. and Mary Blocher Smeltzer, teachers and members of the La Verne, California, congregation near Los Angeles, spearheaded this effort. In February 1942, Ralph Smeltzer aided the first evacuees, a fishing community in the Los Angeles harbor that had forty-eight hours to dispose of its property. Mary Smeltzer recalled the early weeks of Japanese American resettlement.

> Ralph took a day off from school to help. He had already been demoted from a regular to a substitute teacher in the Los Angeles schools because he expressed his conscientious objection to selling defense stamps. He was shocked at seeing army jeeps with machine guns patrolling the streets while looters were raiding houses from the alleys. The Quakers rented an abandoned school near our home to use as a temporary hostel for many Terminal Island refugees and their belongings. Within a few weeks all Japanese Americans in the Los Angeles area were evacuated, usually early in the mornings. We helped serve them breakfast at the train and bus stations, getting up at five o'clock, helping at the stations, then hurrying off to school.[24]

During the summer of 1942, the government targeted Japanese Americans in the California interior for removal, and, coincidentally, the Smeltzers directed a summer work camp in the San Joaquin Valley. They organized an interdenominational group of sixty-five people, including Methodists, Friends, Nazarenes, Baptists, Presbyterians, thirteen Brethren work campers, and local Brethren, to assist the evacuees.[25] Some local residents, however, bitterly objected to their efforts. In his monthly report to M. R. Zigler, Smeltzer told the head of the Brethren Service Commission that he had encountered opposition, centered in the American Legion and "Mr. Bandy."

> Bandy threatened [the pastors] with "the consequences" if they went through with the plans. He said, "We won't bother you at the station today, but you will be sorry for what you are doing. You prefer to have the friendship of 500 Japs and incur the animosity of 4000 Lindsay [California] folks. And if you don't believe it, just ask any man on the street." At that he called a man in off the street, the Legion's adjutant general incidentally, and asked him fairly and impartially what he thought of the churches feeding the Japs that

afternoon. The answer was obvious. Parrot-like he repeated Bandy's point of view.[26]

Sobered but undeterred, the interdenominational Samaritans assisted evacuees with transportation to the train station and served lunch to all, including soldiers, bystanders, and Legionnaires.

> So on Thursday, July 16, the allotted day, we went into action. Six of our cars transported approximately 35 evacuees and most of their baggage to the depot through the direction of Mr. Imote. Our activities were well organized and went smoothly. Our closest estimate is that 65 workers helped prepare and serve 45 gallons of punch, 1800 sandwiches, and 12 lugs of peaches and other fruit to 576 evacuees. The greater portion was served at the depot, but the sandwiches and fruit which were not used at the depot were put into boxes and distributed to the different coaches of the train. . . .
>
> We all made a special point of serving all persons impartially—Japanese, soldier boys, spectators, and sour-looking Legionnaires alike. As you can image, our responses were indeed interesting. Our actions seemed to activate Christ's words, "But if thine enemy hunger, feed him; if thirst, give him drink; for in so doing thou shalt heap coals of fire upon his head. Be not overcome of evil, but overcome evil with good."[27]

After the United States government had placed all West Coast Japanese Americans in detention camps, the Smeltzers secured teaching positions at one of the them, Manzanar Center in southeastern California, an isolated location just below the Sierra Nevada mountains. They also served as house parents for a group of twenty Kibei boys (American born, educated in Japan, and less Americanized than most their age), although most non-Japanese at Manzanar stayed in separate housing. Circumstances were difficult. Approximately ten thousand Japanese Americans lived within one square mile surrounded by barbed wire, guard towers, sentries, and searchlights. The Smeltzers' students sat on newspapers on the floor and leaned against the wall.[28]

In one instance, Ralph Smeltzer undertook personal risk to assist one of the Japanese American leaders inside the camp. When detainees staged a mass rally near the gate and administration buildings to protest their treatment, soldiers attempted to disperse demonstrators with tear gas but also fired several shots into the crowd, killing two, including a high school boy shot in the back. According to Mary Smeltzer,

[T]hat evening the camp became very tense. The anti-American faction vowed to kill pro-American leaders. A friend two doors from us came over frantically asking Ralph to find her husband, who was hiding at this brother's apartment and to take him to the guard house for safety. Ralph took our Model A Ford, found him, had him crouch down on the car floor, drove without lights around the edge of the camp, and made a beeline across a field to the outside-gate guard house. Although they arrived safely, the guards said that if they had been on their toes they would have shot at the car. About sixty were rescued from the camp during the night and housed in the military compound. The army and AFSC [American Friends Service Committee] arranged housing for them in Death Valley.[29]

In 1943 the Smeltzers became instrumental in a Brethren program to relocate Japanese Americans away from the west coast. Resettlement was one of the few passageways out of camp, but the government required freed detainees to have employment secured prior to release, an almost impossible condition. So the Brethren Service Committee started a relocation hostel, directed by Ralph and Mary Smeltzer, in Chicago, first at Bethany Biblical Seminary and then in an old mansion near Lake Michigan. The hostel staff assisted with housing and employment, easing the transition from camp to life in a strange city. By April 1944, the

Ralph and Mary Smeltzer provide support for Japanese internees in Brooklyn, New York. *Photo courtesy of BHLA.*

home had resettled over one thousand Japanese Americans in the Chicago area, and the Brethren decided to move operations to Brooklyn, New York, where Mary Smeltzer reported hostile public opinion.

> The house was located in an area of doctors' and dentists' offices. Because of fear and prejudice none of them wanted us nearby. New York's Mayor [Fiorella] LaGuardia and New Jersey's Governor [Walter E.] Edge also publicly opposed any such resettlement project, even though we had received the encouragement and cooperation of the WRA [War Relocation Authority]. Local newspapers carried frequent articles for a month regarding the hostel and related problems. The New York WRA administrator finally called us into his office to review the situation, pointing out the threats that had been made to our lives and property. He offered to allow us to back out of the resettlement project, but we declined.[30]

In May 1944, the Smeltzers moved to Elgin so that Ralph could become M. R. Zigler's assistant. The hostel remained open for another two years. Never before had the Brethren undertaken relief work on this scale for people so distant from their fellowship community.[31]

Brethren also sought to aid foreign victims of the war, and a program to restock wartorn regions with farm animals caught on quickly. This initiative emerged from Dan West's experience in the Spanish Civil War, where starving children haunted him. West concluded that milk cows were permanent sources of nutrition and a simple, efficient way to reduce hunger in war zones. He, therefore, proposed shipping heifers, already bred, to them. (A heifer is a cow that has not yet given birth.) Each new owner would donate the first female offspring to another needy family, then that household would do the same, and so on, quickly turning recipients into donors. In 1939 West's neighbors in northern Indiana formed a "Heifers for Relief" committee, and in 1942 the Brethren Service Commission accepted oversight of what became known as Heifer Project. *The Gospel Messenger* appealed for donations for this novel initiative.

> In Belgium, because of war conditions, dairy cattle have been lost, either by capture and removal or by being killed and eaten for food until at the present time scarcely more than seven cows of ten are left to produce milk. The situation is becoming worse instead of

better. Under these conditions innocent people—women, children, babies—suffer. Starvation faces many. It has already caused the death of unknown thousands.

The Brethren Service Committee of the Church of the Brethren is sponsoring a project to send dairy cattle to the stricken areas of Europe or elsewhere. Because of the cooperation of her government-in-exile, Belgium has been chosen as the first country with which to work. The Belgian Commission for the Study of Postwar Problems has agreed to undertake the shipment of these cattle from an eastern seaport to Belgium whenever world conditions are such that safe transport and placement of these cattle is assured, subject to incompleted plans of the Allied Shipping Pool. A qualified representative from our group will accompany each shipload to follow the cattle to their destination and report back to the donors. . . .

How Can You Help in This Cause?

It is planned to secure and care for these heifers in various ways. Individuals with clean herds may wish to donate a heifer of the proper age at the time of shipment. Some heifers may be collected at C.P.S. camps, to be cared for by the men there. Some farmers may wish to care for a number of these animals with the feed furnished by other individuals. Any 4-H Club member may help to raise these calves—calves for relief—with his own calves. Donations of feed or cash may be made to help in the purchase of calves or their care.

Good animals, purebred or grade, of any recognized dairy breed will be acceptable. Milking Shorthorns, Holsteins, Jerseys or Guernseys are preferred. Heifers should be bred for good quality offspring, preferably with sires of the same breed. . . .[32]

Within one year, one thousand heifers were ready for delivery, but due to wartime travel limitations, shipments went to Puerto Rico and sharecropping families in the American South. The first heifer, "Faith" (the second and third animals were "Hope" and "Charity"), found a home in Puerto Rico with a family of ten children. Faith had nine calves, unfortunately all male, and Faith's owner sold her at old age for meat, but several of her granddaughters became a small dairy herd. [33]

The Brethren also managed to send several workers overseas. Two Brethren established a boys club in Quito, Ecuador, that served two thousand underprivileged boys; and in Madrid, Spain, David Blickenstaff aided refugees from occupied France. John W. Barwick, supported by the Brethren, became the director of the entire YMCA effort for German and Italian prisoners of war held in English camps. Under his guidance, the YMCA's program provided recreational facilities, musical instruments, libraries, educational programs, and secretaries who made regular camp visits.[34] Luther H. Harshbarger, who arrived in Britain in January 1945 to assist with this program, recalled the difficulties of the assignment.

> Certainly we can all agree that the caging of human beings in barbed wire enclosures is an unmitigated evil. Yet we were not to ask why they were there or when they would be freed. Our task was to serve them while they were there. This kind of constraint calls for a high degree of discipline and not all people, unfortunately, could meet the test. The temptation, obviously, was either to become calloused or overly sentimental. . . .
>
> Basically, the task during this period was one of amelioration of the prisoners' lot in every way under our command. They especially welcomed a face from outside the enclosure. It was a time of waiting—waiting for escape, for the end of the war, for going home. It was also a time of great educational opportunities for those who could meet the test.[35]

The Brethren Service Commission also sent two relief workers to China. In the fall of 1941, Ernest Wampler and O. C. Sollenberger, veterans of the China mission field, returned to the portion of China controlled by Chiang Kai-shek's Nationalist forces. They hoped to travel overland to their former mission area, but when that became impossible, Wampler accepted a position as field supervisor for the American Advisory Committee for China Relief, a combined church relief agency, and Sollenberger became an assistant. Assigned to a district suffering famine, they supervised local committees that organized food distribution, soup kitchens, orphanages, camps and nurseries for children, medical aid, and work relief projects.[36] Sollenberger and Wampler labored in China until 1943, and as they traveled across the countryside, they often met desperate refugees fleeing war and famine. Wampler described one of those encounters.

> As we stopped along the road to drink water or to eat, children begged for food. One day, having bought peanuts, I was shelling them and letting the hulls fall on the ground. The children were soon

scrambling for and eating the hulls. I gave them the peanuts and went without any. One morning, after Osee [O. C. Sollenberger] and I had been riding on the train all night, we were tired, hungry and thirsty. Near the station were food stands. We went to one that looked rather clean and purchased a bowl of steaming noodles. Since there was no place to sit down, we stood and started to eat. We had taken only a mouthful or two when several old women and children began to beg for a few mouthfuls. I stepped back, trying to get a little farther away from their dirty bowls and chopsticks, but they kept following, getting closer, even trying to get their bowls between my bowl and my mouth. I finally put some from my bowl into the bowl of an old woman, hoping that would stop the begging but, alas, that only increased it! A dozen others saw what I had done and then they came insisting on a few mouthfuls. In desperation, not able to eat, I divided the entire bowlful among those empty bowls. Others were still crying for food.[37]

Without a doubt, during World War II service and relief work inspired more Brethren than ever. True, Brethren realism surfaced prior to the war and probably would have grown without the global conflict. Nevertheless, for Brethren of the previous generation, gifts of service and requests for conversion usually came hand-in-hand, but now service often walked independent of soul-saving and threatened to overshadow it. Service, rather than mission, caught a wave.

ECUMENCITY

Parallel with the surge in service came a rising tide of ecumenicity. For much of their history, Brethren had resisted collaboration with other denominations, and cooperation was a comparatively recent development. Their first tentative ecumenical steps, other than hymn-borrowing, came with involvement in the temperance movement. About the same time, Brethren missionaries discovered that cooperation with other Protestants was more helpful than emphasizing differences. In 1919 denominational staff had committed the Brethren to the Interchurch World Movement, an ecumenical scheme to use business methods and social science to win converts and assist the needy, but Annual Conference vetoed it. It was during the thirties that interdenominational cooperation became more acceptable. The denomination joined forces with other historic peace churches to assist conscientious objectors (see previous chapter), and M. R. Zigler, always a vigorous ecumenist, attended meetings of the Federal Council of Churches (FCC) as an observer. In 1938 the Brethren Council of Boards approved cooperation with the Federal Council, particularly in peace, temperance, relief, missions, and evangelism, and contributed with a small grant to support these endeavors.[38]

In 1940 the denomination was prepared to join the Federal Council. Paul H. Bowman, president of Bridgewater College and recent Annual Conference moderator (1937), defended the impending Brethren membership. Bowman maintained that membership in the Federal Council would not compromise Brethren independence and that interdenominational tolerance was consistent with Brethren heritage. His was a creative reinterpretation of a past dominated by separatism. Finally, he appealed to Christian cooperation "in this hour in the history of the world," a reference to the troubling international situation.

As the Church of the Brethren becomes a member of the Federal Council, we advance one step further in kingdom promotion. This conviction arises out of the following considerations:

1. The unity of Christians is in harmony with the will of our Lord and Master. His most earnest prayer was "that they might be one." The followers of Christ should be united in *love* and *loyalty* to him. This action of our Conference is a testimony to the spirit of our own church and to that extent adds to the spiritual dynamic of the Church of Christ at large. The Federal Council has been one of the greatest influences in the world for unity and mutual understanding among Christian peoples.

2. The spirit of co-operation and tolerance is in harmony with Brethren philosophy. Our church was born in an atmosphere of Christian fellowship, honesty, sincerity, and comradeship in search for truth and right. The Church of Brethren has throughout its history been a protesting church. It voices its convictions without fear or hesitation on all questions of moral and spiritual significance. We have usually been prompt to join other Christian bodies in interpreting and advancing the way of life revealed by our Savior. The way of brotherhood is one of cooperation, mutual trust, and common sharing of each other's burdens.

3. Membership in the Federal Council in no way limits or restricts the Church of the Brethren. We make no compromise of any doctrinal position, we modify in no way our faith or policy, and

we maintain all freedom we have ever had to declare our position and chart our own course of action. The Conference reserved this right and the council guarantees it.

4. Finally, this hour in the history of the world, so tragic and so pregnant with evil, demands new attitudes, new spiritual resources, and new approaches to moral problems. It is necessary that there be a complete mobilization of the forces of Christianity against the onslaught of paganism which now strikes at Christian ideals and Christian institutions around the world. A new heathen world is arising before our eyes. The spirits of men are being impoverished by hate and bitterness on a scale never before experienced by the human race. It may be that Christianity in Europe is being set back one hundred, or, who knows, maybe even five hundred years. The Church of the Brethren cannot in this hour withhold any of her resources from the struggle in which all Christendom is involved.[39]

In 1941 Annual Conference approved membership in the Federal Council, but with an unconventional decision-making process. At the initiative of M. R. Zigler and J. Quinter Miller (a Brethren pastor and an associate secretary of the FCC), the Brethren Joint Council of Boards sent a resolution to Standing Committee requesting membership in the ecumenical agency. This procedure was consistent with Brethren polity- the Board had entree to Standing Committee—but the normal route to Standing Committee and the floor of Annual Conference went through congregational councils and district conferences. After a lengthy debate, Standing Committee placed the resolution on the agenda, and Conference approved it by a large majority that overwhelmed fundamentalist opposition.[40] The statement stressed the Federal Council's interest in the peace movement and maintained that global ecumenism strengthened the Protestant voice "in the many strategic situations which now exist throughout the world."

Since the Church of the Brethren has for a number of years shared partially in the program of the Federal Council of Churches of Christ in America by unofficial representation in certain sections of the Council; and since the Conference was officially represented at the World Ecumenical Conference of Oxford and Edinburgh in 1937 [by M. R. Zigler]; and since much progress has been made toward a World Council of Churches in order to give Protestantism a strong voice in the many strategic situations which now exist throughout the world; and since the World Council as well as the Federal Council is now actively engaged in peace movements of major proportions and is concerned especially with the problem of the conscientious objector, which has been an important concern of the Brethren for more than two hundred years;

Therefore, the Council of Boards recommends that Annual Conference of 1941 authorize constituent membership both in the World Council of Churches and in the Federal Council of Churches in America. . . .[41]

Although conservatives lost this battle, their fight against the FCC had just begun. Tracts circulated throughout the denomination, describing the Council as breeding ground of modernism and lamenting that the unusual parliamentary path of the resolution had unfairly surprised Annual Conference with a quick vote.[42] Harold Snider, pastor of the Lewistown, Pennsylvania, Church of the Brethren authored a bitter denunciation of Brethren membership in *The Christian Beacon,* published by Carl McIntyre, an outspoken fundamentalist with a national following. Snider attacked the procedural grounds on which Conference approved the resolution to join the Federal Council.

Who carried the petition to the La Verne [Annual] conference that the Church of the Brethren be affiliated with the Federal Council of the Churches of Christ in America? And when was the matter put before the churches before action at the Annual Conference? How many pastors knew that such a matter was coming up at the said conference (1941)? . . . Does it always obtain because the majority manages to thrust a matter into the docket of the church and passes it that ALL must abide by it? Do minorities always have to abide by the majority?[43]

Snider continued that the "crux of the matter" was the attempt of Bowman ("you and your pro-Federal Council friends in the Church of the Brethren") to purge the fellowship of fundamentalism. He condemned the *The Gospel Messenger* for advertising a book critical of premillennialism (Adventism by William Peter King) and accused Federal Council supporters of hostility to literalism, a fundamentalist cornerstone.

The truth is, virtually all of the Federal Council men (and if I knew the real theology of all I might be able to truthfully say ALL of the Federal Council men) hate the literal interpretation of the Bible—that which is normally dubbed "Fundamentalism," and it is to this end you men have lent your energies to drive it out of the church.

I am making the statement, and can support it with plenty of evidence in the literature of the church, that this type of Bible interpretation is no longer welcome. It is not considered scholarly by some—but I think there are some scholars in this good old land who could put your Federal Council men to shame, and who believe the Bible literally, and who interpret it after the fashion of Fundamentalism, if you please.[44]

As specific evidence of liberal error, Snider pointed to the progressive distaste for editor Cyrus I. Scofield, a premillennialist darling of the fundamentalists.

For exhibit A, I offer the antagonism of the church and many of its ministers to the Scofield Bible. . . . we send our young people to the church camps and they come back and say some of the leaders advise the youngsters not to use the Scofield Bibles. Why? Because Dr. Scofield believed in the Bible, and your Federal Council men do not. That is simple. Dr. Scofield has done more to aid the beginner in his search for real Bible truth than any other human being in the last 100 years, but the modernistic-intelligentsia hate him with unbounded hatred. God pity them.[45]

The protests of Snider and other fundamentalists notwithstanding, Brethren ecumenists carried the day. Henceforth, the Church of the Brethren would cooperate with other Christians that they might better fulfill their calling "to serve the present age," as Charles Wesley's great hymn put it.[46] The quarrel over the Federal Council, however, remained unresolved, and only worsened after the war.

CONSCRIPTION AND ALTERNATIVE SERVICE

For many young men, the most pressing issue of the war was not Heifer Project or the Federal Council of Churches, but conscription. Within many Brethren meetinghouses, individual conscience had vanquished discipline, even more than during World War I, leaving young men free to make their decisions about the draft with little pressure from congregational councils and elders. Consequently, there was diminished unity on this question.

Olin Mason, for example, from Bridgewater, Virginia, was a pacifist, but one of his brothers entered the Air Force. Mason cited the crucial role of individual conscience as he and his brothers pondered how to respond to the draft.

> Another item in our training was that you respect each individual's right to reason out their plan and their way of action. And respect each other and their right to make their decisions. Therefore, there were three boys in our family. Two of us were in CPS, and the third one was in the Air Force. . . . No strain in the family at all; a disappointment to parents but other than that. . . .[47]

Thus, although the Church of the Brethren was still a peace church, many of its members entered military service. In fact, most Brethren men of draft age cast aside their fellowship's traditional teaching about nonviolence and chose the uniform over conscientious objection. Statistics show that 21,481 Brethren became combatants, 1,484 were noncombatants, and 1,386 entered alternative civilian service. Yet commitment to the peace position remained noteworthy, especially compared with other denominations. Mennonites had a higher percentage of members who became conscientious objectors than any other fellowship (42 percent), Friends were second (10 percent), and the Brethren ranked third (8 percent). The denominations with the next highest percentage of COs were the Congregational Christians (0.2 percent) and the Methodists (0.1 percent), both significant drop-offs from the levels of the three historic peace churches.[48]

Congregations demonstrated a wide range of opinion on the peace position. Some candidly discussed it with little rancor. One local society divided over military service until a deacon remarked, "Are you gonna stand here in the church and say it's ok to kill people?"[49] Another fellowship said little about the question prior to the German invasion of Poland, but afterwards many members hoped that the United States would avoid involvement. In the words of one sister,

> When they were first starting to talk about the draft, I remember a high school meeting about this, and we wrote letters to our congressman saying we didn't like that. But I think the attitude of the

older people in the church at that time was very much "America first."* Let's stay out of this. It was not our quarrel.[50]

On the other hand, the peace position disappeared in some congregations, with so many men entering the military that occasionally conscientious objectors in these local societies became marginalized. In the Midway, Pennsylvania, congregation, ten to twelve men entered the service, some as noncombatants, but only two chose alternative service. One of them, Luke Bachman, felt isolated.

> I felt I was alone with a partner: Christ. . . . It was like being a loner. . . . [I] felt a total support from my parents and my grandparents [but] of the church I felt a partial [support], depending who they were. The officials of the church, yes. With the membership, there seemed to be some differences of feeling, and it's hard for me to understand that because I felt that we all went to the same church. We had the same type of Sunday school, Bible school lessons, and everything else, and how one could interpret so differently from the others?[51]

In the Stonerstown Church of the Brethren (Saxton, Pennsylvania), none chose alternative service. George Daniel Baughman, a young member at that time, was aware of the Brethren peace position "only up to a point." When Baughman's oldest brother was drafted, the preacher visited their home to discuss nonviolence, but he could not persuade Baughman's father, a nonpracticing Lutheran with a family tradition of military service. All of Baughman's four older brothers accepted conscription; Baughman wanted to enlist but his mother, who was Brethren, made him wait until Uncle Sam wanted him.

> It was my heart's desire at that time to go into the service. I felt that my duty lay with going to the service because of several things. Number one, I had four brothers in the service, and I wanted them back home. I had five sisters and a father and mother and did not want it—if I could help it in any way, shape, or form—want them under the influence of Hitler and Germany.[52]

---

*"America First" was an isolationist movement that opposed President Franklin D. Roosevelt's proposals for a military build-up and a draft.

Stanley Wampler also held membership in a Virginia congregation that virtually ignored the peace position. Although three men in his fellowship became conscientious objectors, the congregation never discussed nonviolence or nonresistance, and Wampler received "no encouragement" for it. Wampler worked in a defense plant until he was drafted.

> I never really gave [alternative service] any thought nor was anything said about . . . CPS. . . . I didn't have any hesitation about the draft. I had a sense or feeling that I owed some loyalty to the country. We had a lot of freedoms and that kind of thing for Americans as a result of persons entering the military, and I felt like I owed some service to the country as well. That's where I had run-ins with my alternative service people, who had no sense of responsibility at all except to be in alternative service.[53]

Wampler served in a machine-gun squad in General George C. Patton's division. His unit eliminated pockets of resistance left behind by fast-moving armor, and he witnessed American soldiers taking no prisoners. Later he worked in the mailroom and composed letters explaining to parents how their sons had died in combat.[54]

Of course, young men from congregations with a strong peace emphasis also entered the service. Ray Summy, from Chiques, Pennsylvania, had a Sunday school teacher who made a "pretty strong argument" for nonviolence, and his uncle offered financial support if he entered Civilian Public Service. But Summy thought only briefly about conscientious objection—"yes and no," in his words. He explained his motivations to another member of his congregation, "a righteous fellow [with a] big beard, and everything."

> What would you do if a guy came into your house and started raping your wife? [The other member replied,] "Well, I tell you right now, I'd kill him." That's what we're going over for.[55]

One option for conscientious objectors was noncombatancy. Noncombatants received no weapons training and were unarmed, but otherwise belonged to the military. They wore the uniform, followed orders, received pay and dependency allowances, won medals, and got shot. During the first year of the war, noncombatants filled an assortment of roles, including the signal corps, engineering, and the quartermaster corps, but in 1943 Secretary of War Henry L. Stimson placed them in the medical units. He hoped that concentrating their numbers would give their status more respect and that if medical service were guaranteed, more COs would volunteer for it.[56]

In fact, some Brethren did regard noncombatancy as compatible with their faith. Monroe C. Good, a conscientious objector from the Springville (Pennsylvania) congregation, elected noncombatancy after assessing its contribution toward his long-term goal of becoming a missionary. Good faced an educational hurdle before he could fulfill his call to the mission field; he needed a college degree but lacked even a high school diploma. Elizabethtown College agreed to design an individualized program that would yield both a high school certificate and a college degree, but only if Good obtained draft deferment, which was possible only if his home congregation designated him as a ministerial student. Springville was inclined toward nonviolence, with several in CPS and others with agricultural deferments, but its board accused the would-be missionary of draft-dodging, despite his agricultural deferment for the duration of the war, and refused his request. Good then devised another plan and volunteered as a medic, anticipating that this training would someday contribute to his college entrance and prove useful on the mission field.

> It turned out that I got one-third of the credits for the training I had in the service. My going into the service was a big credit toward my getting a high school certificate, and I actually got into college a year earlier than we had thought might happen than with me working on the farm and working on my high school studies, unless the church had sent me as a special ministerial student. So we believe that it was God's doing that I went into the service. . . .
>
> If God calls you, . . . that he has a plan for your life, there are ways to accomplish that. If one way doesn't turn out to be possible, if you're really supposed to do it, why there'll be another way.[57]

After the war, Good graduated from Elizabethtown College and Bethany Theological Seminary; then he and his wife, Ada, served in Nigeria for fifteen years. Another Pennsylvania Brethren, Roy E. Longenecker, from Lititz, chose noncombatancy for reasons more typical than Good's.

I went into the [army as a] noncombatant. . . . The noncombatant was set up for people who had a religious opposition to war. CPS was put up where you wouldn't even wear a uniform. Noncombatants was for ones that didn't believe in going to war, but they weren't dead set against wearing a uniform or anything like that, or being in the service. When it was my time and my number came up and I knew I was going to be drafted, I was 4F the first time they called me up. I didn't pass the physical. The second time I knew I would pass, because they were taking almost anybody breathing. So I went to see what CPS was like. Kane, Pennsylvania, was the CPS camp, the closest one around. I went out there, and I knew some of the guys that were there. They were spending all their time planting trees; that was their program. I felt that if I'm going to have to give up a year of my life, I wanted to do a little more than plant trees. I thought that was not enough. Later on, the church came up with the idea of guinea pigs, and a lot of service work in hospitals and everything, but they weren't there yet. So I went in noncombatant, and was called in and went to Lancaster, and then went to Harrisburg, and when the guy went over my record to assign me to a place, he looked at it and said, "You've got a mistake here. It says noncombatant. You don't want to go noncombatant."

And I said, "Yes, I do."

He said, "Now why would you want to do that?" He was really very nice to me. He said, "You know, if you go noncombatant, you're going to be in the forefront of the medics, in the first line of defense for helping the wounded."

And I said, "Well, I don't have much choice." He let it go at that when I explained that I just wouldn't change it. So I went in as a noncombatant and was assigned to the medics.[58]

Longenecker was near the front lines in Europe during the Battle of the Bulge.

For conscientious objectors who rejected any role in the military, even as a noncombatant, the decision to enter Civilian Public Service often came effortlessly, with little conflict. The denomination had always taught peace, and when the draft arrived, CPSers accepted the traditional position, uncomplicated, unquestioned, and unambiguous. A conscientious objector from Rocky Ford, Colorado, reflected that he was "always taught that killing was wrong."[59] Others similarly became pacifists with little hesitation.

I have no idea why some would take the other position. I just automatically took it. This was the position of the church. I was born into the church. Baptized into the church at a young age. I always felt that was the position you should take. No question about it.[60]

_____

We knew something was going to happen. We were the ripe age, the age that was perfect to go, to be involved. I knew quite a ways ahead that I would be involved. And so I made up my mind pretty early that I was not gonna go out with a rifle. I was gonna go some other way. I didn't know what it would be. Whatever the church came up with, I was going to participate in.

I never considered the military. I never felt that it was quite the thing to go to prison. I suppose that if there had not been any CPS, I would have considered that option but I was enthusiastic all through the formulation of the concept that's the thing I wanted to participate in.[61]

_____

The main thing I knew was that I could not participate in the killing machine. I could not see myself leveling a rifle at any of God's children under any circumstances and pulling the trigger.[62]

_____

A pretty formative experience that I had—George Phillips was my pastor. He was very much on the side of this issue. I remember that I was just a kid and I played the cops and robbers business, and I came home and decided one day that a little Brethren boy should not play with war toys. So I threw them in the wastebasket, and my mother told George Phillips about that and he preached a sermon about me. I don't know how old I was—just a really little kid, but it really impressed me that I was the subject of a sermon.[63]

Conscientious objectors faced occasional harassment. Verna (Schlosser) Sollenberger, whose boyfriend and future husband was in CPS, taught elementary music and struggled to make her colleagues understand his situation.

I had to explain to a lot of my teacher friends where my boyfriend was. And what kind of a camp it was. Why wasn't he drafted? Why wasn't he in the military? They had no idea what Civilian Public Service was. I didn't defend him, but I had to do a lot of explaining, because it wasn't a popular stance at that time.[64]

In 1943 Olin Mason, a senior in high school in Bridgewater, Virginia, was put on the spot in math class as graduation approached. Mason explained his beliefs to his classmates.

When they were discussing plans for what they would do after they finished high school, most of them had grad plans for the Air Force, Marines, Navy, Merchant Marine—some phase of the national warmaking machine. One of the young men realized that Olin wasn't saying anything and one of them said, "Olin, what are you gonna do when you graduate from high school." I said, "Well, guess I'll stay on the farm for awhile." They said, you mean you're not going into the military, you're not going to be patriotic, and I said, "Yeah, I think I'm gonna be patriotic. I'm gonna produce food, but I can't participate in the military because I said I can't take another person's life." Of course, you got the regular guff for it, calling me various names and stuff, and I took a little of that. We were in the algebra classroom when this was going on and the teacher hadn't come into the room yet. I remember very vividly that I finally rose to my feet in the classroom by my desk, and they got quiet and listened. "I cannot see myself leveling a gun at another person who is a child of God. Therefore, I would be of no value in the military machine. But it also takes more strength to stand against the majority of the crowd." I sat down. They thought about that a little bit, and about that time I noticed the teacher standing in the door—he didn't reprimand me for causing a commotion in the classroom, and he went on with the class as if nothing had happened. But I never had any problems with my friends after that. They realized that I had it thought out and had made a decision as to what was right for me and that was okay. Part of my philosophy was that if David and Goliath had done what God would have wanted them to do, they would have set down on a rock by the brook and talked it over. You don't have to kill the Philistine giant to solve your problems. There are other ways to do it that are closer to the heart of God.[65]

Although their conscience kept CPSers apart from military service and distant from public opinion, they nonetheless cooperated closely with the government. CPSers served for the duration of the war, and the government considered them in the same legal category as draftees with few rights. But unlike servicemen and women, they received no pay, and to avoid signs of favoritism, the government delayed their release after the war. A federal agency, such as the Forest Service, trained the CPS volunteers and supervised their labor, while individual denominations fed, clothed, and managed the campers in off-hours at specific projects. CPS specifically resembled the New Deal's Civilian Conservation Corps (CCC), extending big government's alphabet soup to conscientious objection. In fact, the first camps used old CCC barracks and tools to perform forestry management, soil conservation, or some other form of manual labor, tasks similar to those of the now defunct New Deal program and described by one scholar as a "Rube Goldberg approach to alternative service." The collaboration between church and state led critics to charge that CPS was too obliging to the government.[66]

Later in the war, the CPS emphasis shifted from denomination-run camps to special or detached projects that private agencies supervised and funded. Most volunteers in these projects served in mental hospitals, schools for the mentally impaired, or public health projects, but a few became forest fire fighters or control patients in medical experiments. Meanwhile, the lack of meaningful work, the government's unwillingness to pay wages, and the church's collaboration with the military significantly damaged morale in the camps. By January 1944, more CPSers served in detached projects than in camps.[67]

The varied response of Brethren men to the draft makes several points. First, it demonstrates shrinking harmony within the fellowship. Once unity formed a beloved cornerstone of Brethrenism, but during World War II few pretended that the Brethren had consensus on military service. Instead, the heterogeneous approach to conscription reveals the supremacy of individualism within the fellowship. Although some conscientious objectors felt marginalized by their local societies, generally members decided on military service, as they did on dress, with little intrusion from the congregation. Secondly, the disagreement over military service was much more congenial than the fight over the Federal Council of Churches because nonviolence now belonged to individual conscience. The Federal Council question, however, required a corporate decision and could not devolve to the individual realm. Therefore, it sharply divided the fellowship. Thirdly, the Brethren response to the draft illustrates diminished nonconformity with the larger society. As

Brethren men entered military service, they joined mainstream America. During World War II nonviolence, once a conspicuous contributor to Brethren outsiderness, almost disappeared as a practice that separated Brethren from the larger society. Almost, but not quite. The conscientious objectors who opted for noncombatancy or alternative service and the denomination's strong support of Civilian Public Service testify to the persistence of traditional Brethren values. Despite the thousands of uniformed members, nonviolence remained strikingly Brethren.

"WHERE CROSS THE CROWDED WAYS OF LIFE"

As Brethren struggled on the war-time mission field, provided for victims of modern warfare, joined councils to enhance the Protestant response to the times, entered the armed forces, and volunteered for alternative service, they experienced the impact of renewed world war on their gathered community. None of the significant Brethren motifs during the war—service, ecumenism, fundamentalism, individualism, declining unity, and diminished nonconformity—were new, but all became more noticeable in wartime Brethrenism.

In 1925 Brethren added F. Mason North's powerful hymn "Where Cross the Crowded Ways of Life" to their hymnal. Written in 1905, North's hymn applied faith to urban problems, a classic Social Gospel approach to what religious progressives considered one of the most perplexing problems of their era.

> Where cross the crowded ways of life,
> Where sound the cries of race and clan,
> Above the noise of selfish strife,
> We hear Thy voice, O Son of man!

The fourth verse, with its reference to the "cup of water," became especially appropriate for the World War II era because the Brethren Service logo featured a cup offered in assistance.

> The cup of water given for Thee
> Still holds the freshness of Thy grace;
> Yet long these multitudes to see
> The sweet compassion of Thy face.

And the final verse called for faithfulness.

> Till sons of men shall learn Thy love,
> And follow where Thy feet have trod;
> Till glorious from Thy heav'n above,
> Shall come the City of our God.[68]

How appropriate that the Brethren adopted this great Social Gospel hymn when modern war made a cup of cold water and God's "sweet compassion" more needed than ever.

NOTES

1. David M. Kennedy, *Freedom from Fear: The American People in Depression and War, 1929-1945* (New York: Oxford University Press, 1999), 381; Paul Preston, "The Great Civil War: European Politics, 1914-1945," *The Oxford Illustrated History of Modern Europe,* edited by T. C. W. Blanning (New York: Oxford University Press, 1996), 148-49.

2. Michael Howard, *War in European History* (New York: Oxford University Press, 1976), 133-35; John Keegan, The Second World War (New York: Viking Press, 1989), 590-93; Richard Overy, "Warfare in Europe Since 1918," *The Oxford Illustrated History of Modern Europe,* 222-23.

3. "What to Pray For," *The Gospel Messenger* (April 8, 1943): 22.

4. Leland S. Brubaker, "Just a Word," *The Gospel Messenger* (December 4, 1943): 4.

5. Sylvia M. Oiness, "The Sinking of the Zamzam," *The Gospel Messenger* (September 20, 1941): 10-12.

6. Oiness, "The Sinking of the Zamzam," 24-26.

7. Sylvia M. Oiness, "The Sinking of the Zamzam (cont'd)," *The Gospel Messenger* (September 27, 1941):11-13.

8. Sylvia M. Oiness, "Concluding 'The Sinking of the Zamzam,' " *The Gospel Messenger* (October 4, 1942): 9-11.

9. Oiness, "Concluding," 10.

10. Oiness, "Concluding," 10.

11. Hazel Rothrock, "Internment," *Missionaries Speak: From Internment Camps in China* (Elgin, Ill.: General Mission Board, Church of the Brethren, n.d.), 11.

12. *Flashlights from Our Missionaries: Interned in the Philippines* (Elgin, Ill.: Brethren Publishing House, n.d.), 2; "You Will Remember," Missionaries Speak, 28.

13. Rolland C. Flory, "General Survey of Events," *Flashlights from Our Missionaries,* 3.

14. Flory, "General Survey of Events," 4.

15. E. T. Angeny, "Housing in Prison Camp," *Flashlights from Our Missionaries,* 9-10.

16. Bessie Crim, "Experiences as a Nurse in an Internment Camp," *Flashlights from Our Missionaries,* 8.

17. Ellen E. Cunningham, "Food Under Difficult Conditions," *Flashlights from Our Missionaries,* 15.

18. Leland S. Brubaker, "News from the Philippines," *The Gospel Messenger* (April 17, 1943): 17.

19. Flory, "General Survey of Events," 5.

20. Heather A. Warren, *Theologians of a New World Order: Reinhold Niebuhr and the Christian Realists, 1920-1948* (New York: Oxford University Press, 1997).

21. H. L. Hartsough, J. E. Miller, Ora Garber, eds., "Report on Reorganization and Function of Brethren Service Committee, 1941," *Minutes of the Annual Conferences of the Church of the Brethren, 1923-1944* (Elgin, Ill.: Brethren Publishing House, 1946), 180-81.

22. "Church News," *The Gospel Messenger* (May 22, 1943): 14-16.

23. Donald F. Durnbaugh, *Fruit of the Vine: A History of the Brethren, 1708-1995* (Elgin, Ill.: Brethren Press, 1997), 479.

24. Mary Blocher Smeltzer, "Japanese American Resettlement Work," in *To Serve the Present Age: The Brethren Service Story,* edited by Donald F. Durnbaugh (Elgin, Ill.: The Brethren Press, 1975), 124.

25. Ralph E. Smeltzer, "Report on the Japanese-American Relocation from Lindsay, California, 1942," edited and introduced by Craig Enberg, *Brethren Life and Thought* (Spring, 1977): 73.

26. Ralph Smeltzer, "Report," 76. See also Mary Blocher Smeltzer's description of this event in "Japanese American Resettlement Work," 124.

27. Ralph Smeltzer, "Report," 73, 77.

28. Mary Blocher Smeltzer, "Japanese American Resettlement Work," 124-26.

29. Mary Blocher Smeltzer, "Japanese American Resettlement Work," 126-27.

30. Mary Blocher Smeltzer, "Japanese American Resettlement Work," 129.

31. Mary Blocher Smeltzer, "Japanese American Resettlement Work," 129-30.

32. "Heifers for Relief: A Rehabilitation Program Sponsored by the Church of the Brethren," *The Gospel Messenger* (June 5, 1943): 12.

33. Durnbaugh, *Fruit of the Vine,* 463-64; J. Kenneth Kreider, *A Cup of Cold Water: The Story of Brethren Service* (Elgin, Ill.: Brethren Press, 2001), 131-33; Thurl Metzler, "The Heifer Project," *To Serve the Present Age,* 144-45; Glee Yoder, *Passing on the Gift: The Story of Dan West* (Elgin, Ill.: The Brethren Press, 1978), 100-08; "Down-to-Earth Project," *Time* (July, 24, 1944): 44-46.

34. "David Emerson Blickenstaff," *The Brethren Encyclopedia,* 3 vols., edited by Donald F. Durnbaugh (Philadelphia, Pa., and Oak Brook, Ill.: The Brethren Encyclopedia, Inc., 1983), I:146; "World War II," *The Brethren Encyclopedia,* II:1373; Durnbaugh, *Fruit of the Vine,* 479; Luther H. Harshbarger, "Work with Prisoners of War," *To Serve the Present Age,* 132-36; Kreider, *A Cup of Cold Water,* 62-65.

35. Luther H. Harshbarger, "The Brethren and YMCA Services to Prisoners of War During World War II," *Brethren Life and Thought* (Spring, 1981): 77, 78.

36. Wendell Flory, "A History of the Brethren Involvement in China," *Brethren Life and Thought* (Autumn, 1966): 42.

37. Ernest M. Wampler, *China Suffers, or My Six Years of Work During the Incident* (Elgin, Ill.: Brethren Publishing House, 1945), 236-67.

38. Durnbaugh, *Fruit of the Vine,* 447-49.

39. Paul H. Bowman, "The Church of the Brethren and the Federal Council," *The Gospel Messenger* (November 15, 1941): 5-6.

40. Durnbaugh, *Fruit of the Vine,* 449-50; Hartsough, Miller, Garber, *Minutes of the Annual Conferences, 1923-1944,* 174.

41. Hartsough, Miller, Garber, *Minutes, 1923-1944,* 162.

42. Durnbaugh, *Fruit of the Vine,* 450-53. Durnbaugh has also published his thoughts on the conflict over the Federal Council of Churches in "The Fundamentalist/Modernist Struggle Within the Church of the Brethren, 1910-1950," *Brethren Life and Thought* (Winter and Spring, 2002): 62-69.

43. Harold Snider, "Church of the Brethren Meets Issue of Federal Council As Pastor Files Protest," *Christian Beacon* (December 30, 1943): 2. The article consists of Paul Bowman's defense of the decision to join the FCC and Snider's rebuttal.

44. Snider, "Church of the Brethren Meets Issue," 2.

45. Snider, "Church of the Brethren Meets Issue," 2.

46. "To serve the present age" begins the second verse of Charles Wesley's "A Charge to Keep I Have," No. 328 in *Hymnal: Church of the Brethren* (Elgin, Ill.: Brethren Publishing House, 1925).

47. Donald Fitzkee interview with Olin Mason (July 6, 1990).

48. Cynthia Eller, *Conscientious Objectors and the Second World War: Moral and Religious Arguments in Support of Pacifism* (New York: Praeger, 1991), 50; "World War II," *The Brethren Encyclopedia,* II:1372.

49. Author interview with Alma Moyers Long (June 17, 2002).

50. Author interview with Mary Greenawalt (November 2002).

51. Donald Fitzkee interview with Luke Bachman (n.d.).

52. Author interview with George Daniel Baughman (April 1, 2004).

53. Author interview with Stanley Wampler (May 2004).

54. Author interview with Stanley Wampler (May 2004).

55. Author interview with Ray Summy (May 20, 2004).

56. Eller, *Conscientious Objectors and the Second World War,* 28-29.

57. Author interview with Monroe Good (May 20, 2004).

58. Author interview with Roy Longenecker (February 4, 1999). The interviewee is the author's uncle.

59. Author interview with Earl Heckman (June 12, 2002).

60. Donald Fitzkee and Ruth Carey interview with William Cable (July 6, 1990).

61. Donald Fitzkee and Ruth Carey interview with Bob and Verna Sollenberger (June 21, 1990).

62. Donald Fitzkee interview with Olin Mason (July 6, 1990).

63. Donald Fitzkee interview with Jim Garber (July 6, 1990).

64. Fitzkee and Carey interview with Bob and Verna Sollenberger.

65. Fitzkee interview with Olin Mason.

66. "Rube Goldberg . . ." in George Q. Flynn, *The Draft, 1940-1973* (Lawrence: University of Kansas Press, 1993), 10-20. See also Eller, *Conscientious Objectors and the Second World War,* 30-32; Albert N. Keim, T*he CPS Story: An Illustrated History of Civilian Public Service* (Intercourse, Pa.: Good Books, 1990), 27-101; Albert N. Keim and Grant M. Stoltzfus, *The Politics of Conscience: The Historic Peace Churches and America at War, 1917-1955* (Scottdale, Pa.: Herald Press, 1988), 114-20.

67. Eller, *Conscientious Objectors and the Second World War,* 31; Kreider, *A Cup of Cold Water,* 17-26; "World War II," *The Brethren Encyclopedia,* II:1372; Keim and Stoltzfus, *The Politics of Conscience,* 120-26.

68. Frank Mason North, "Where Cross the Crowed Ways of Life," No. 339 in *Hymnal: Church of the Brethren* (Elgin, Ill.: Brethren Publishing House, 1925).

VIII. POSTWAR RECOVERY
The Greatest Generation?

"The world was never the same again." In the popular mind, World War II was a defining moment, a social continental divide that forever changed life. The war gave America prosperity, expanded the middle class, lifted the South and West into the national economic mainstream, and bestowed upon the United States global economic dominance. Wartime technology invented radar, nuclear weapons, penicillin, insecticides, and plastics. Wartime politics introduced Keynesian economics and the military-industrial complex, and wartime experiences created new opportunities for women, African Americans, Native Americans, and Mexican Americans.

Popular thought, however, overlooks the strength of continuity during this period. Many of the changes, such as large suburbs, independent women, civil rights, a less marginalized South, and a more powerful federal government, appeared before the war and continued afterwards. Perhaps the war complemented or hastened these tendencies, but it did not create them. Moreover, there was much about American society that did not change. When peace returned, traditional thought still governed in race, gender, and family, and the feminist and civil rights revolutions took decades to find success. Politics and the distribution of wealth and power shifted little. Postwar Americans wanted a return to normalcy, except for more prosperity. For an alleged age of great change, conservatism was remarkably persistent.[1]

Thus, for the Church of the Brethren, the years immediately after the war represent a rich mixture of continuity and change, including its interaction with modernity. Ecumenicity and bureaucratization reached new levels, but these trends had begun before the war. The desire to assist victims of modern war soaked deeply into the Brethren grassroots and the magnitude of the Brethren service effort was unprecedented, yet expanding interest in service had appeared prior to the invasion of Poland. Cultural conflict ebbed, but clashes between progressives and conservatives still erupted, now more closely associated with the security of the nation-state. The pressures of modernization remained, but its influence stemmed more from wars, nations, and politics and less from cultural disagreements.

Postwar Relief

The most apparent change in postwar Brethrenism was a spectacular expansion in service. Brethren relief efforts, of course, had precedent. As described previously, relief without soul-saving became much more noticeable during the Depression, in the international conflicts prior to World War II, and during the war. When the fighting finally ended and transportation restrictions gradually disappeared, Brethren overseas relief soared.

Despite the growth of service, planting the gospel in distant lands still motivated many Brethren, and numerous missionaries driven from their field by the war resumed their labors. A small notice in the *The Gospel Messenger* praised the renewed vigor of these Christian ambassadors.

> By train, ship, and plane our missionaries are returning to their fields. Not since the peak year of 1920-21 have there been so many active missionaries serving the church as at the present time. There are now two in Scandinavia; in India, 41; in China, 6; in Africa, 39; in South America, 2, making a total of 90 on the fields, counting those on furlough.[2]

Ernest Wampler and Wendell Flory were the first missionaries to return to China after the war. In April 1946, they arrived in Ping Ting, a center of Brethren activity prior to the Japanese occupation. Already the conflict between Chiang Kai-shek's Nationalist government and Communist revolutionaries overshadowed the landscape, as Flory described his first days back in China.

> The situation was tense. Nationalist army officers had arrived to accept the surrender of the Japanese troops, but the men were

not disarmed. Instead, they were used to hold the main lines of communications against the Communist Eighth-Route Army, who still dominated the rural areas.

We first visited Ping Ting, Shou Yang, and Tai Yuan, all in nationalist control along the main railway, reopened a real relationship with Christian colleagues, established contact with all governmental authorities, established three area relief committees, and filed requests for return of all mission property. All seemed most cooperative. However, it must have seemed a most amusing sight to see these two pacifist missionaries asserting their will and rights among thousands of armed Japanese soldiers, many of whom were living in our property and all of whom meticulously saluted us whenever we met, in whatever capacity.[3]

Wampler and Flory returned to Beijing and acquired military passes that facilitated further travel.

Returning to Shansi, we completed plans for a trip through the rural areas. We crossed no-man's land on May 9, 1946, going south from Ping Ting. Word of our coming had indeed preceded us. We were welcomed, feasted, and deluged with information concerning their political views by the communist political commissars, much of which had real justification. We spent three weeks in this trip, traveling on foot and donkey back. . . . We . . . met with numerous Christians all along the road, counseled with them, and heard their stories of the war years. Christian activity was obviously at a minimum, with limited freedom for expression of views. This trip was the only postwar contact with this part of our former mission area.[4]

Several other missionaries arrived, and Flory was optimistic.

The churches were booming. A great number of very heart-touching stories were heard on the profound contribution of their Christian faith to their lives during the difficult days of the war. The door definitely seemed open to welcome a great movement to the Christian faith, if political conditions permitted. The writer baptized seventy-five in one day at Ping Ting, and the next day, April 9, 1947, conducted a love feast in the Ping Ting church with about six hundred present.[5]

The revival of Brethren mission in China was short-lived. The victory of the Communist Revolution made the Brethren presence there impossible, and in 1951 the last remaining missionaries left. But, the determined postwar effort to resuscitate the mission in China and the more stable programs that continued in India and Nigeria indicate that postwar Brethrenism remained committed to mission.

On the other hand, the immediate human needs, not the souls, of the millions who suffered from the effects of World War II became the denominational priority. Consequently, most western and central European nations received Brethren Service volunteers and material. The first projects were in Belgium, the Netherlands, and France. Four Brethren served on the Dutch island of Walchern, a major German base in the Scheldt River devastated during the war. In Dunkirk (Dunkerque), France, where fighting destroyed sixty-eight percent of the homes and many residents lived in barracks, Brethren helped furnish and staff a community center that provided washing machines, irons, sewing machines, public showers, a library, woodworking machinery, and play equipment for children.[6]

In Belgium Helena Kruger, a volunteer from Hershey, Pennsylvania, met an elderly Polish woman who had labored as a slave in a Belgian mine for much of the war. Upon her return Kruger frequently told the story of this sad figure.

> She was a tiny bent old lady, sitting in the sun near the gate of a camp in Belgium. She seemed to be holding something in her hands and talking to it. . . . [S]he crouched there, swaying a bit, mumbling, leaning protectively over her folded hands. I spoke to her as I passed, and I wondered. The camp was for Polish slave laborers who had been brought to Belgium [by the Germans] to work in the mines during the war. Now they were being sent home; well, at least back to their native land. Their homes had all been bombed before they left Warsaw.
>
> The next morning when I went in the camp gate, there she was—crouching, swaying, mumbling or was it praying? There she sat all day. I nodded, smiled, and again I wondered.
>
> The third morning I could no longer wait. I must know. Going over to her I said, "Mother, what are you doing here?" She looked up sadly.
>
> "Waiting," she said. "Waiting to go home. My daughter and her husband were brought to Belgium from Poland as slave

laborers. They brought me, too. We had to work in the mines. My daughter is dead. The war is over. Now we go back. I am old and feeble and should die here but I must go back. Back to my home."

"Mother," I said gently, "what have you in your hands?" She looked up quickly, her face breaking into a beautiful smile, her eyes taking on a gleam of light as she proudly opened her hands to show me—a little salt cellar.

"Madame," she said as she lifted her hands still nearer, "my salt cellar. It is my salt cellar. My home in Warsaw is bombed . . . I live in fields . . . I go back to my home . . . all is gone . . . I hunt through the brick and stone . . . I hunt long hours . . . Nothing do I find of all my things . . . My hands bleed . . . I must go . . . I turn one more brick. And there, Madame, I find my salt cellar!" She straightened a bit, her face shining. "Madame, I'm waiting to take my salt cellar back home." [ellipses in the original][7]

Efforts in the Low Countries continued until 1947, and in the following year Brethren work in France ceased.[8]

Brethren relief workers also quickly became involved in Poland. In December 1945, Brethren first visited the wartorn eastern European nation with a shipment of heifers, and the next year the first on-site workers arrived. Between 1945 and 1949 the Brethren distributed a variety of relief goods, including not only food and clothing, but also horse harnesses and two incubators. Russell Eisenbise, from McPherson, Kansas, described a poignant story about his ability to help a destitute Polish shoemaker.[9]

I had an experience today that I must pass on. Jon Szezsbaki, an old shoemaker, lives in a near-by village and supports eleven people, including himself. I found a note in our files stating he had asked for some old or odd shoes that he could repair or rebuild and sell. To make a long story short, I loaded three big boxes of odd shoes, together with quite a bit of shoe thread, nails, new leather half soles, rubber heels, and several large sheets of composition for half soles, and a few new tools, such as rasp, shoemaker's hone, etc., into the jeep and trailer and with Jennie for an interpreter took off to pay old Jon a visit.

We knocked at the door and were invited in. He was working in a corner of the kitchen, repairing an old shoe. I introduced myself and asked how things were with him. He said, "Very bad. I have nothing to work with any more. Last month I earn 100 zotych." This is equivalent to twenty-five cents legal money and about ten cents black market. It does not go very far with bread at eighty zotych per loaf. We carried in one big box of odd shoes and Jon began to express his appreciation. When we came in with a smaller box of shoes, he was swallowing rather hard. Then when we came in with a smaller box of shoes and the new materials his old eyes could no longer hold the tears and they overflowed down his cheeks. I opened the boxes and had the names translated. He held the new tools as gently as a scientist with a five-hundred-dollar piece of equipment. Here in Poland for a man to kiss a woman's hand is the accepted thing to do. As we prepared to leave, old Jon, with tears still on his cheeks, took Jennie's hand and kissed it very tenderly. I went to shake hands with him in parting and he kissed my hand, patted me on the shoulder and said, "Surely God has remembered me today."

An incident like this lingers in my mind a long time and, of course, stirs the desire to do more for these people. But really to help them after our goods are gone requires more than we are able to give.[10]

In 1949 relief to Poland ended when Polish Communist authorities expelled Brethren workers along with other Western agencies. But an agricultural exchange program managed to survive the Cold War. In 1947 the project began with ten graduate students in agriculture, who lived on Brethren farms and enrolled in American universities. The Polish government cancelled the endeavor after only ten months, but in 1956 it resumed, lasting until 1990. Over the life of the program, 1,023 Poles studied in the United States, usually on the graduate level, while 129 Americans went to Poland, mostly to teach English in agricultural universities.[11]

In China, a traditional mission field, Brethren Service also found a role. Its major Chinese project was a cooperative effort with the United Nations Relief and Rehabilitation Administration (UNRRA), which sought to reclaim land flooded by a mile-long break in Yellow River dikes. Tractors with ploughs were critical to this project, but the Chinese had little experience with mechanized agriculture and required outside expertise to train drivers and assist with maintenance. Brethren Service recruited fifty volunteers, not all Brethren, while UNRRA provided two thousand tractors and paid expenses. Howard Sollenberger, the daredevil hero of the Brethren relief efforts in 1938-39 (see chapter 6), headed this "tractor unit." Determined to exhibit political impartiality, the "tractor boys" worked in both Nationalist and Communist areas, while both sides fired at them on occasion and confiscated vehicles at gunpoint.[12]

Sollenberger's description of an assignment in Communist territory illustrates typical high and low points of the tractor unit.

> While operations in the contested areas of Honan were short-lived, it was felt that efforts should be made to set up a project in an area where Communist control was not contested, to demonstrate the neutrality of BSU [Brethren Service Unit] operations. Shantung was selected as a possible area. However, it was not until April, 1947, that forty tractors with farming equipment were released for the Communist area. Three BSU men accompanied the shipment, which was unloaded at Chefoo for transshipment to an operational site. Unexplained delays held the equipment in Chefoo for six weeks during which time a training school was held for thirty students. During June the forty tractors were transshipped to Yang Chiao Kou and convoyed by the BSU men three hundred miles overland to a project site near Lin Ching, traveling at easy stages, mostly in the early mornings and evenings, to avoid bombing and strafing by Nationalist planes.
>
> The land reclamation area selected by the Communist authorities consisted of approximately 100,000 acres of good flat sandy soil. Differences of opinion over whether the equipment should be kept together and operated as a single unit or disbursed to a number of smaller projects again held up operations. The BSU men objected to dispersal of the equipment during the initial training period on the grounds of lack of experienced operators and maintenance men. Even though verbal agreement was reached on this issue, local CLARA (Communist counterpart of CNRRA [Chinese National Reconstruction and Rehabilitation Administration]) officials refused to release the equipment. Mr. Thomfordo of UNRRA and William Hinton, a BSU volunteer, were sent up from Shanghai to replace the original BSU team and to negotiate arrangements for putting the equipment into operation. They were later joined by Raymond Hoff, also of BSU. Forty additional students were finally trained and 1,665 acres plowed before the gas supply ran out.[13]

The civil war, Chinese inexperience with mechanization, and the unfamiliarity of volunteers with Chinese society limited the tractor project, and authorities spread the tractor boys over thirteen provinces— another disappointment. Nevertheless, by the middle of 1947 the unit had trained 660 Chinese and reclaimed 49,000 acres, including one site where they plowed under a former Japanese air base. The tractor unit ended on December 31, 1947, a casualty of the growing political violence in China.[14]

Most of the Brethren relief effort went to defeated European nations. Although Japan received Heifer Project shipments, and several volunteers served in Italy, it was Germany and Austria that gained special attention. Initial reports from the war zone indicated that modern war's inability to distinguish soldier from civilian had taken a heavy toll. At first, the Trading with the Enemy Act banned American civilians from the former Third Reich and frustrated Brethren relief efforts, but in the fall of 1945, M. R. Zigler gained entry. One of the first American religious leaders permitted inside the defeated nation, Zigler interviewed military authorities in Berlin, including General Lucius D. Clay, who wondered, "Where in the hell is the church?" Clay confided that he had instructions to limit the diet of German civilians to 1300 calories per day until French civilians were better fed.[15] The *Chicago Daily Tribune* reported Zigler's conclusions, which combined a bleak image of conditions with a call for donations by the "carload."

By the Rev. John Evans
Dr. M. R. Zigler of Elgin, head of the Church of the Brethren's service committee, has returned from an inspection of conditions in Belgium, the Netherlands, and Germany. He reports that in some localities, only one child of families of three or four will survive the winter. The church, with headquarters in Elgin, has been sending heifers and blooded bulls to European lands.

Which to Save?

"Which one of three or four children to save is the heart-rending decision many European mothers face today," Dr. Zigler said, as he told the story of exposure, starvation, and disease, "which hardly can be imagined here by us." He said that in one city, out of 108 babies born in July, 98 were dead in August. Dr. Zigler himself lost 14 pounds in weight during his few weeks in the Low Countries.

"The 12 millions likely to perish abroad from cold and hunger this winter lend urgency to our appeal to congress for the granting of deficiency appropriations and additional funds for UNRA activities," Dr. Zigler said. "The need is so tremendous that no one agency can possibly meet it alone."

Asks Carload Lots

"Persons of all faiths owe it to themselves to provide more than token help by sending material aid abroad. It is time for American churches to think in terms of carload lots of goods for relief," said Dr. Zigler, adding that cases of canned soybeans, corn, dehydrated soups, dry peas, and soap may be sent prepaid to the United Church Relief centers at New Windsor, Md., or Modesto, Cal. From these points the relief items will be allocated by material aid committees organized in the various countries cooperatively by the Jewish, Catholic, and Protestant faiths, and the International Red Cross.[16]

Zigler also published stunning reports of German conditions in the *The Gospel Messenger*. In the periodical's 1945 Christmas issue, printed in seasonal green ink, he described a dire situation of homelessness and hunger.

A journey from Aachen, Hannover, Schwarzenau, Berleburg, Marburg, Heidelburg, Karlsruhe, Stuttgart and Berlin reveals that Germany has been largely destroyed. Millions have died. Thousands are in prison and work camps. More are being put into prison. Others are being executed as criminals. The war is not over. Millions are hunting for homes.

The Bishop of Berlin told me that five times as many people will die this winter in Germany as died through the entire war period. Starvation has set in. There is not enough food. Since last April people in general have lost fifteen to twenty pounds and the winter is just beginning.

By February, women will have lost interest in life. They will no longer have mental or physical power to care for themselves or their children. They will not be able to provide food for newborn babies. They will hunt grass and leaves but will have no strength. Already (November 1) mothers must face their children daily with not enough to feed them. The amount of calories is now lower than the subsistence level. A mother starves for her children; therefore, death takes her first; then her children must go down the lonesome road to death by starvation. We must answer the question, Why must this be? . . .

I have talked with many soldiers and they have all agreed that the churches ought to be very busy sending materials to the suffering of Europe. Every soldier knows that many innocent people are going to suffer and die this winter.

. . . Let us flood New Windsor, Modesto, and other warehouses with materials and pray that the Congress of the United States and the businessmen of the United States will make shipping available so that some will be saved this winter. Let us give in the name of Christ all we can spare. I sincerely feel that unless the Christians who have materials to spare really sacrifice and help now the Christian church will not recover for many years the place she deserves in the life of the world.[17]

In the winter of 1946-47, Zigler made another trip to Europe. He learned that the second winter was worse than the first because the weather was colder and reserves were gone. Zigler's first cable from Berlin, reproduced in *The Gospel Messenger*, read:

Urgent need German civilian population. Reserve resources exhausted; conditions growing steadily worse. Harvest and imports fail to provide subsistence. Clothing need extreme and absence [of] raw materials makes textile production impossible. Widespread sickness. Suffering inevitable owing to lack of fuel, housing, clothing, food. Desperate need for shoes and clothing aggravated by refugee population.[18]

On Christmas Day 1946, Zigler and two other Brethren workers visited Schwarzenau, the denominational birthplace. The small village sheltered two hundred and fifty of its own, made homeless by aerial bombing, and three hundred refugees expelled from Eastern Europe. After Zigler returned to Elgin, he received a letter from Schwarzenau's pastor pleading for help in longhand English, and *The Gospel Messenger* printed a photograph of it under the headline "The Pastor of the Schwarzenau Church Writes."

I am glad that you had visited us just at Christmas day and we had heard together the gospel: "Glory to God in the highest, and on earth peace, goodwill toward men." We know that we are brethren for the sake of our Saviour Jesus Christ. Therefore I dare to beg that you, Mister R. Zigler, would take care of the distress of the community Schwarzenau. Our poor community had to receive 300 refugees. We have no clothes and shoes to give them. Please, say to the brethren in U. S. A. how great the distress is here. Now we ask you for the sake of our Saviour Jesus Christ to help us.[19]

Brethren Service immediately sent fifty bales of clothing to Schwarzenau and established a special fund for its benefit.[20]

Before long, Brethren Service contributions to German reconstruction became wide-ranging. In Bremen Eldon Burke, a Brethren working with the YMCA, secured a complex of former military buildings for relief efforts sponsored by German churches. Among the projects here was the Christopher Sauer Workshop, a vocational training center for veterans handicapped by the war and named after a father-son team of German American printers in colonial Pennsylvania. (Christopher Sauer I was denominationally unaffiliated; Christopher Sauer II was a Brethren minister.) In Kaltenstein, Brethren Service again cooperated with the YMCA to establish a shelter for homeless and jobless youth. The YMCA rented an old castle, and the Brethren supplied seventeen tons of food and clothing plus the services of Byron and Ruth Royer who, along with three Germans, served as house parents. An article in *The Gospel Messenger* described the project.

About 100 boys have been brought to the Castle of Kaltenstein, or will join the youth village soon. They will live here and get a chance to learn and work in agriculture and trades. Above all, they will work on the farm land belonging to the castle and in apprentice workshops which will be established there. A Christian community life where they themselves have responsibility will give them the opportunity to develop a fine Christian character. . . .

The majority of the youth who are becoming established at Kaltenstein have no parents or homes. Some are refugees. Practically all are either juvenile delinquents or in danger of becoming such. Some even have prison records of a less serious nature. The object of the entire project is to help these youth to turn from a world which has very few standards of conduct and responsibilities to a new life in which the standards become a basic and

natural part of their lives. The program will have vocational, educational, recreational and religious emphases. . . . The government
of the village will be almost entirely handled by the boys themselves, and as they gain the ability to assume responsibility, they will
take over the operation of Kaltenstein. This, of course, will be with
the help of adult leaders. . . .

These German boys roaming since the war through the
streets of Germany with nothing to do, improper food and clothing, and no homes or care need, along with these necessities, the
knowledge that Christians throughout the world are concerned
with their welfare and interested in their future. It is not enough
that Brethren send them food and clothing. Of greater importance
is the knowledge that Christians remember that they have need
and that in the spirit of love, they are willing to share with a nation
who was once counted their enemy.[21]

Kassel became the hub of Brethren Service in Germany. Close to
Schwarzenau, but also near the Russian or eastern zone of occupation,
thousands of refugees poured through the bombed-out city. Yet Kassel
retained favorable rail and autobahn connections, and the local occupation authorities were cooperative. The first Brethren building in Kassel
was a Gauleiter's house, i.e., the home of a Nazi official, assigned to
them by the army. The spacious structure came fully furnished with a
maid and gardener, whom the Brethren retained to provide employment
for the two individuals. In 1951 Brethren Service began construction of
a new facility, which it completed in 1953. With rooms for staff, visitors,
and 125 students, Kassel Haus, as its occupants called it, functioned as
a reception and orientation center for volunteers, visitors, student
exchanges, and young men tending Heifer Project animals, and it host-
ed assemblies, conferences, and meetings.[22]

By 1949, four years after Germany's surrender, millions of refugees
still struggled despite the rebounding economy. A meeting of the
Brethren staff in Germany lamented the plight of those whom recovery
had bypassed.

The staff then engaged in considerable discussion concerning the
refugee problem. It was felt that although there was considerable
up-swing in the general economic condition of Europe and
Germany in particular, we nevertheless could not escape the fact
that eleven million people have been uprooted from their homes
and are now more or less [living] a miserable existence within

Germany. . . . These people have lost practically all of their positions; but more important than that, they are rapidly losing their feeling of hope for the future. Somehow or other, the conscience of the Christian church must be brought to face this situation. . . .

Byron [Royer] pointed out, however, that even at the present time, most of our work in Germany was definitely related to the refugee situation. Kaltenstein deals almost entirely with homeless and refugee boys. The heifers and our student [exchange] project of John Eberly are refugee projects. Mrs. [Cecile] Burke's progress in Bremen [i.e., distribution of relief supplies] is largely related to the refugee situation. Wilbur [Mullen], in his material aid distribution in Hamburg, has moved toward the alleviating of needs of refugees.

Brother [M. R.] Zigler, however, was quite concerned that even though in our day-to-day program we were doing our small bit for the refugees, we were nevertheless failing to bring the pitiful condition of these people to the attention of our own Church, as well as to the other Protestant bodies with whom we are cooperating. It was felt with Brother Zigler that at a time when the American folks were living in such abundance and luxury, it was not right that these eleven million people in Germany should be living in such desperate circumstances.[23]

Brethren Service also devoted considerable attention to Austria. In this German-speaking annex of the Third Reich, Ralph Smeltzer led a small but energetic Brethren Service team. Initially, Brethren Service wanted Smeltzer, who spent the war assisting Japanese Americans (see chapter 7), to locate in Japan after the conflict, and from November 1945 (Japan surrendered in August) until August 1946, he studied Japanese in California. But when the U. S. government repeatedly refused Smeltzer entry into Japan, M. R. Zigler asked him to head the Austrian project. Within a week, Smeltzer departed, leaving his wife and two small children in California. When Zigler and Smeltzer visited Washington, D. C., General Mark Clark, the commanding general in Austria, was coincidentally in town, and after a few phone calls, Smeltzer had Clark's blessing plus an unprecedented expedited issuance of his passport and entry permit.[24]

Once in Austria, however, Smeltzer grew frustrated. Although Brethren Service sent large amounts of material to Austria, all of it went through Church World Service (CWS) because the World Council of Churches favored national churches, i.e., the Protestant Churches of

Austria, over denominational programs like that of the Brethren. Smeltzer, therefore, had nothing to give away, and authorities threatened to expel the small Brethren staff. To justify the continuation of the Brethren in Austria, Smeltzer told army officials that between one-quarter and one-half of all CWS materials given to Austria came from his fellowship.

We are in the process of trying to determine what percentage of goods shipped to the RCPCA [Reconstruction Committee of the Protestant Churches of Austria] by CWS has been contributed by the Brethren Service Committee. We will supply you with this information as soon as we obtain it. At the moment our guess is that it has been between 25% and 50%. Included in our contribution to the RCPCA has been several hundred bales of used clothing, many tons of food, especially cereals, a large quantity of soap, and several cases of kitchen equipment. Some of these materials are still resting in the warehouses of the RCPCA for lack of transportation for distribution. We do not yet have full information as to how much goods are now on the way to the RCPCA shipped by our agency through CWS. However, we do know that within the past two months our U. S. headquarters has shipped at least two car loads of cereals and 400 bales of clothing which are yet enroute.

During February we have brought in six sewing machines and 1000 meters of work drill cloth. In cooperation with the RCPCA we are setting up a small clothing factory at Hamburgerstrasse 3. In addition to making new garments we will repair old ones.

Also during this month we have brought in two large trucks and the jeep. During the next two weeks we expect to bring in three more vehicles. In view of the fact that the RCPCA has no available trucks to distribute its supplies, we are using our trucks to effect its distribution throughout Austria and also to distribute goods to its six Vienna ausspeisungs [feeding stations]. . . .

Part II of our program is aid to a few selected children's homes. We are awaiting the arrival of food and clothing for this project. But in line with our proposal to also provide some recreational supplies to such homes, we have during February brought in the following list of such supplies:

92 deck tennis sets
100 checker sets
25 chess sets
50 ping pong sets
12 pairs of boxing gloves
10 footballs
36 handballs
30 softballs
20 skipping ropes
3 badminton sets
7 angles
1 case of horseshoes
20 bingo games
29 occarinas
2 flutes
2 button accordions
3 football pumps
40 pairs of football or soccer shin guards
50 dominoe sets
3 sets of other games
10 halma
6 ukeleles
3 violins . . .

At the suggestion of your Branch and the Education Division we have brought to Austria during February a quantity of supplies needed in Viennese Kindergartens and Schools. . . . They include:

10,000 toothbrushes
43,500 chalk sticks (blackboard)
60,000   "   "   "   (still en route from Belgium)
5,652 pencils
1,050 penholders
2,016 pen points
2,000 copy books
1,200 pads
6 foolscap
25 rulers[25]

Despite assurances from the Brethren Service Commission of forthcoming supplies, nothing came. Helena Kruger, now a Brethren

Service staffer in Austria, arranged for her home congregation, Spring Creek (Hershey, Pennsylvania), to send 1,440 hatching eggs and 65 sacks of feed, which arrived promptly. This was so well received that Brethren Service sent its own shipment of chicks and feed, which reached their destination in April and May 1947, the first supplies dispatched directly from BSC to its project in Austria.[26] But aside from this delivery, the staff had nothing to dispense except what they scrounged on their own, and idleness plagued them. Morale was low, as Smeltzer later recounted.

> Staff members felt as if they were on a raft in a sea of need without a cup of fresh water. This dissatisfaction and unrest expressed itself through emotional outbursts, unauthorized "side" projects, occasional irrational decisions by some members, and inter-staff tension. The task of the writer was to do everything possible in finding constructive outlets and service projects, and in counseling as best he could. However, to say the least, it was a hectic experience.[27]

Smeltzer complained to M. R. Zigler that "We have been so continually embarrassed by the lack of goods for the past few months that the Friends and Mennonites have laughed at us."[28]

Helena Kruger, Ralph Smeltzer (second from left), and Austrian officials examine newly arrived chicks. *Photo courtesy of Alexander Mack Memorial Library, Bridgewater College, Bridgewater, Virginia.*

Finally, in summer 1947, large quantities of materials arrived. Aid included heifers, bulls, baby chicks, farm implements, seeds, resettlement, and a shoe shop. Smeltzer used Heifer Project funds to purchase one hundred milk goats in Switzerland, and he personally rode the freight cars to tend the animals until their arrival on the outskirts of Vienna. Additionally, volunteers taught a variety of classes, including sewing, English, and vocational training courses for youth ineligible for the Austrian apprentice system.[29]

Brethren Service in Austria gave particular attention to the *Volksdeutsche*, ethnic Germans expelled from eastern Europe in the postwar settlement. Many relief organizations ignored these former enemies, who ranked among the neediest refugees in Austria. Smeltzer recalled that

> no relief agency was assisting this group and several agencies actually opposed helping *Volksdeutsche* because of their ancestral relationship to the ex-enemy country, Germany. In fact, the U. S. Army and most agencies designated this group of refugees as "ex-enemy refugees." In spite of the fact that this was the largest single group of refugees, neither the U. S. Army nor the UNRRA recognized the group as eligible for assistance. Similar discrimination was also practiced by some private agencies. Largely because of political reasons and post-war prejudice the most needy group in Austria was being denied help.[30]

Helena Kruger worked especially hard for these unfortunates. She had been a refugee after World War I, and she understood German and Russian. Although she was assigned to work with children, she was neither qualified nor interested in this. Instead she found passion for assisting the *Volksdeutsche*.[31] In Linz, Kruger wrangled permission to convert damaged railroad cars into shelter for refugees. In Thalham she organized a kindergarten. Many of the fathers of the children in this refugee camp were either dead, invalids, or prisoners in Russia, and the mothers worked on a brickpile, cleaning bricks from bombed out ruins. Kruger found several former teachers in the camp and cadged paint, windows, and scrap lumber, turning a "smoke-blackened room" into a classroom.[32]

Kruger's greatest success was the establishment of a tuberculosis hospital. Tuberculosis afflicted many refugees, but Kruger learned that Austrian hospitals refused to serve *Volksdeutsche* because they were not citizens. So she determined to turn a former Nazi labor camp into a facility for one hundred and twenty-five patients and persuaded the Austrian government to pay the staff and supply the food while she solicited miscellaneous supplies. The following is Ralph Smeltzer's account of Kruger's campaign to create the hospital.

> As she visited among the refugees and talked with government officials, Helena Kruger observed that refugees with tuberculosis could not be admitted to Austrian hospitals because they were not Austrian citizens and because the hospitals were over-crowded. During one of her conferences with Austrian officials the suggestion was made that perhaps BSC-ERC [Ecumenical Refugee Commission, a WCC agency] might cooperate with the Austrian government in establishing a TB hospital for refugees. The Austrian government agreed to make available a site at Thalham near St. Georgen. This was an old Nazi labor camp consisting of a half dozen old run-down wooden barracks. The government also agreed to pay the doctors and nurses and to supply the basic food ration. The refugees agreed to provide three doctors and nurses.
>
> Helena Kruger took the writer to the site. Then she proposed that BSC-ERC furnish the beds, bedside tables, mattresses, blankets, sheets, pillow cases, bed jackets, attendant's dresses and shoes, supplemental food, and gasoline for a hospital vehicle. This all seemed like a large order, but she convinced the writer that this project was the most valuable and significant one which BSC could engage in for refugees. . . .
>
> The writer does not know how Helena Kruger secured all of the hospital supplies needed, but she did. He knows she had some things made, others she bought, some she secured from the army, some she "scrounged." BSC Austria contributed a good many of the things it could, and the ERC supplied a few items. Anyway, by July the "hospital" was ready to open in a primitive way. It soon had 125 patients. As soon as possible Helena Kruger supplied additional needed items like paint, fever thermometers, wash basins, etc. The Thalham Hospital staff called Helena Kruger "our angel."[33]

Rosemary Block (Rose), a registered nurse who worked in the tuberculosis hospital and supervised public health in thirty-seven camps, gave Brethren back home a first-hand account of conditions among the *Volksdeutsche*.[34]

"*Danke vielmals! Auf Wiedersehen!*" These words of thanks and farewell come from a young Volksdeutsche refugee couple as they stand on the doorstep of their drab barrack in *Volksdeutsche* camp No. 53 near Linz, Austria, as our B. S. C. vehicle pulls away. In the father's arms is tiny Waltraud, their eight-day-old daughter, who with her mother has just arrived home from the welfare ward of the local city hospital. Had it not been for the B. S. C. jeep, Frau Mueller with her newborn daughter would have walked the three miles from the streetcar line to their home in the refugee camp just as many other refugee mothers do.

Herr and Frau Mueller were the son and daughter of industrious Rumanian farmers before they were forced to flee from their home in 1945 because of their German ancestry. Imagine, if you can, to have to flee suddenly from your own comfortable home and be able to take with you only what you can carry, traveling one weary mile after the other on foot, by oxcart or by cattle car transport, and not knowing where to go! This was the experience of not only Herr and Frau Mueller but of about 14,000,000 other *Volksdeutsche* refugees who were expelled from their homes in Rumania, Yugoslavia, Hungary and other eastern countries during the years 1945-47.

Since 1945 Herr and Frau Mueller have lived in Austrian refugee camps, where they often shared a room with as many as fifteen other people who represented several different families, both sexes and all ages. Also living with them are the two younger sisters of Frau Mueller. The last news from their home in Rumania was that their mother had died of starvation about six months ago. In the same forced labor camp where she died, their father is still working with only black bread and watery soup as his food. Such are the experiences of many other *Volksdeutsche* refugees. . . .

Yesterday afternoon I attended a mother's and baby's clinic in camp No. 121 that was being conducted by an unemployed *Volksdeutsche* lady doctor. In this small room where the clinic was held there were none of the usual facilities such as running water, white hospital linens or medical supplies. When the doctor would prescribe a medicine for one of the babies usually the mother would reply that the father was unemployed and that they could not buy it.

Such are the health problems and needs as they exist in the camps day after day. The need is vast. It is always greater than the amount of material assistance that we are able to give. However, our health work can be of assistance in other ways than just the material one. It is encouraging to those homeless people to know that their American Christian friends care about their plight and care enough to send them food, clothing, and medicine.

While we were visiting in the women's ward of the refugee tuberculosis hospital one day, a patient beckoned us to stop by her bed. This elderly lady had her worn German Bible open on her lap and was pointing to the following words: " 'Naked, and ye clothed me; I was sick, and ye visited me. . . .' The Brethren Service Commission is like that!" she said. As we humbly left that hospital ward we were more than ever impressed with our responsibility in attempting to keep this group of refugees in good health until they can have again a home and a country to call their own.[35]

In 1950, five years after the war ended, Smeltzer and Block still worried about tuberculosis and arranged to X-ray all twenty-two thousand *Volksdeutsche* in sixty-six Upper Austrian camps. The Swedish Red Cross supplied mobile equipment and a technician while Brethren Service paid for the film. Results revealed 4.1 percent of those tested had the disease.[36] After Block's period of service ended, grateful doctors named their laboratory in the tuberculosis hospital the "Rosemary *Zimmer*" (Rosemary Room) and hung her picture there.[37]

Overseas volunteers like Smeltzer, Kruger, and Block were the vanguard of the Brethren relief program, but thousands of stateside Brethren mobilized for their support. As the desperate situation of the Low Countries, France, Poland, Italy, Germany, Austria, and the rest of Europe became evident, Brethren at home responded in a variety of ways. A form letter to button manufacturers, for example, produced millions of out-of-style and surplus buttons, which filled large drums bound for Europe, where buttons were in short supply. Women in the "Purses for Peace" program crammed thousands of large handbags with buttons, needles, thread, and other small items and sent them to the New Windsor Service Center. Brethren poured kitchen grease into thousands of military surplus gas/water cans with "Grease for Peace" stenciled on them.[38] *The Gospel Messenger* asked every family kitchen in the denomination to donate its fats for soap-making.

A man connected with the relief program of New Windsor tells us that he saw some of the grease that had been donated the other day and that it looked like "lard good enough to eat." We suspect his enthusiasm for the soapmaking project led him into exaggeration, but we feel sure he wasn't a bit happier to see that grease than thousands overseas will be when they receive the soap made from it. The factory at Nappanee [Indiana] has turned out over seven and one-half tons of soap. To make that much soap it was necessary to purchase four tons of fat to add to the amount donated. Fat is costly. Soap made from donated fats costs less than half as much to produce per pound as that made from purchased fats. Has your church sent to New Windsor or Nappanee for a five-gallon container? Are you contributing your fats regularly? This country went all out to give grease for war; we have opportunity now to provide grease for peace.[39]

Relief materials arrived at New Windsor more quickly than they could be processed. Postal workers placed packages on the sidewalk, workers at the relief center stacked goods to the ceiling, and management rented boxcars from the railroad for temporary storage. To be sure, many Brethren rallied behind relief.[40]

The Christian Rural Overseas Program (CROP) and Heifer Project became especially popular pipelines for aid among rank-and-file Brethren. CROP quickly evolved from a spontaneous impulse of giving, especially among midwestern grain farmers. At one critical point in this movement's early days, M. R. Zigler attended an ecumenical meeting to discuss a cooperative national drive for grain. The participants decided to focus on ten major cities, but Zigler complained that this urban bias limited participation by the Brethren, who had few members in large urban areas. He suggested that Mennonites and Brethren take the rest of the country with emphasis on rural communities. Zigler left the meeting, made two phone calls, and returned saying that he had an organization, which developed into CROP. John D. Metzler, Sr., who directed the Brethren relief center at New Windsor, became CROP's director, and Ben Bushong, who already administered Heifer Project at New Windsor, headed the program there.[41] Metzler reflected on CROP's appeal.

Somehow one's crops are an extension of one's own self. There is a difference between giving actual produce resulting from the partnership of God and man working the soil, and selling that crop and writing a check on the cash received. It not only eliminates the middle man but seems to be a much more personal involvement.[42]

Among CROP's early ventures were several trains, including one sponsored by national columnist Drew Pearson, which traveled west to east through the grain belt picking up relief supplies. By late 1951 CROP had distributed 5,400 carloads of food to 32 countries; Brethren directly donated 45 of the freight cars. In 1952 Church World Service assumed control of CROP. Metzler, however, remained with it until 1954, and Brethren filled many other CROP staff positions.[43]

Heifer Project also appealed to postwar Brethren. When wartime transportation restrictions ended, Dan West's initiative to replenish farm animal populations became a natural cause for the Brethren, who still retained deep rural roots despite their gradual movement into towns and suburbs. Consequently, the Brethren Service Commission leased a farm in Maryland as a holding center and employed its owner as the manager. The first shipment, Guernsey and Holstein heifers for households with children, went to France, and another early delivery sent six Brown Swiss bulls to Greece. By the end of 1949, Heifer Project had provided eighteen bulls to Greece, who artificially inseminated over nineteen thousand cows.

Heifer Project quickly grew beyond Brethren boundaries. Other denominations joined its committee, including the Evangelical and Reformed (United Church of Christ), Northern Baptist Convention, Mennonite Central Committee, and the National Catholic Rural Life Society. The United Nations became a partner when UNRRA agreed to provide transportation for the animals and the young men who cared for them. Eventually, Heifer Project sent thousands of animals and poultry to postwar Europe.

In addition to material improvement, Dan West's program embodied reconciliation, exemplified by donations to former enemies. By September 1945, thirty different institutions in Germany, such as hospitals and orphanages, had already received heifers, and in 1949 Heifer Project received permission to give to individual families. For eight years thereafter, Heifer Project sent shipments of fifty to sixty-five animals at six-week intervals to West Germany. The cattle left from a processing center in Lancaster County, Pennsylvania, managed by Milton Hershey, an elder in the conservative White Oak congregation. Hershey accompanied each shipment to New York, where he customarily received an enthusiastic greeting from longshoreman. On the other side of the Atlantic, German families lavished extraordinary attention on their bovine gifts, often making pets of them and brushing their coats daily.[44]

The program obtained added energy from the seven thousand plus volunteers, called "sea-going cowboys," who accompanied the animals overseas and returned home as heroes. Some were experienced farmhands, but many were not.[45] One of the first was M. P. Coppock, from Ohio, who sailed on the first Heifer Project ship to Poland. He left Baltimore in January 1945.

I had 34 cows to care for on mid-deck, which is third down from the top, and the lowest on which there was livestock. We fed them ground feed before breakfast and supper (meals were at 7:00 a.m., 11:00 a.m., and 4:30 p.m.). We watered and fed them hay after our breakfast and supper, and during the day we cleaned stables and bedded and got our feed from the nearest storeroom. My feed was very handy, but because of being so low in the ship I could not always have my portholes open to clean stables, so I had to catch up with work on nice days. . . .

The cows would lay down at will and did lay down most of the time, especially when the water was rough. The horses had to stand all the time. The horses did not get so seasick standing up. They are much harder to ship than are cows and mules. The cows ate and drank less on rough days and seemed more droopy.

I do not know how many degrees the ship rolled, but I laid bales of hay down through my feedway lengthwise and put bales on top of them edgewise. The top ones would roll off on rough days. Also, we had to hold our dishes on the table while we ate. It was hard to wheel manure across the ship. Part of the time I had to set the handles down to keep the wheelbarrow from backing over me. And part of the time I had to set them down to keep the wheelbarrow from running away. . . .

I saw very little freezing weather in January and February, and I worked in my shirt sleeves. . . . We came in sight of the Azore Islands on Sunday, January 13, and learned by radio that we would not go through the English Channel because of mines, but would go north to Scotland instead, thus making the trip five days longer.

We arrived in Kirkwall, Scotland, on Sunday, January 20, and waited until Wednesday evening for a favorable weather report before crossing the North Sea. The sailors maintained a constant watch for mines. We did sight one early one morning but we were able to miss it by 20 feet by turning the ship as short as possible. We cattlemen did not know about it until later.

We arrived in Newport Harbor (suburb of Danzig) on Monday afternoon of January 28. On Tuesday and Wednesday the livestock was unloaded and then we were free to go and come when and where we pleased. One day we took a streetcar to Danzig which was four miles away. The city was all in ruins. One day we took a truck trip out to see where the cattle were being distributed. . . .

The ship moved from Newport to Gdynia on Sunday (about 10 miles) to finish unloading fertilizer. Gdynia was not damaged so much and was more like an American city. We went one day to a battlefield near Danzig where the Russians were chasing the Germans about one year before. I got a belt buckle from a German uniform, a helmet, and also a screwdriver from a disabled tank. . . .

The Polish people we saw had enough food and clothing (all relief stuff), but their morale was very low. They walked around like they were bewildered or in a fog. Families have been separated for so long, and they do not know if each other is alive or not. They act like they do not know where to start. They have been living with uncertainty so long, they seem half asleep. It is very pathetic.[46]

Harry Badorf, a sixteen-year-old cowboy, enjoyed smoother sailing and more sightseeing. In June 1946, Badorf and several other young men from the Lititz, Pennsylvania, congregation tended cattle aboard the *Cyrus Fields*, bound for Italy. His first day at sea became typical for the trip.

June 15, 1946
I got up at the usual time, 7:15, ate breakfast at 7:30, after which Ken [Dietrich] and I bedded, fed, and watered the heifers. Then I ate dinner, after which Jim [Dietrich], Ken, and I played 500 rum until 3:00 o'clock, then we fed the heifers again. At 5:00 I ate supper, then we finished our game of cards, but I lost. I went to bed about 10:30.

Arriving in port provided much adventure for the young sea-going cowboy. Italians came aboard to trade watches and cash for cigarettes until the captain "chased them off." From his ship Badorf observed a variety of sights.

July 1, 1946
From where our ship is docked, we can see Mt. Vesuvius and the
Governor's Palace. There are several wrecked and sunken ships in
the harbor. Some parts of the city are bombed up fairly bad. . . . It
is very hot and the flies are awful.

On July 4 Badorf and his colleagues set out for Rome where they
swam in Mussolini's private pool and miraculously stumbled upon a
friend from home.

Sixteen-year-old Harry Badorf with other sea-going cowboys in
Italy. *Photo courtesy of Harry Badorf.*

We got to Rome at 12:00. We saw the coliseum, the War Memorial of 1918, the balcony where Mussolini talked to the people, also the Forum, which is all in ruins. We could not see the Pope, so 11 of us cowboys got fixed up overnight at a U. S. Army Rest Center. It was originally Mussolini's private palace. I got supper free. It didn't take us long to look around, and low and behold we found a swimming pool, which we soon made use of. They gave us trunks free. It was 52 yds. by 25 yds. All the buildings were made of marble. They had Cokes, ping pong, books and magazines, bowling, tennis, track race. Some statues. We accidentally met Stanley Dietrich in the rest center. He had a 13 day furlough. He slept there at the center with us and showed us his pictures of Swiss [*sic*] and told us many army tales. Went to bed around 12:30.

On the return trip the ship reversed course to return a stowaway to Naples, and it also made an unexpected stop at Gibraltar to provide medical attention for an ill seaman. The *Cyrus Fields* docked at Jacksonville, Florida, and the sea-going cowboys had to arrange their own transportation home. They received $150 for their efforts.[47]

Cattle from the *Cyrus Fields* loaded onto trucks in Naples. *Photo courtesy of BHLA.*

A family milks a newly arrived cow on a farm in Poland. *Photo courtesy of BHLA.*

In 1947 UNRRA abruptly ended its cooperation with Heifer Project, leaving hundreds of cattle stranded in holding centers without transportation. Some of the cattle were sold, but the program continued, sending animals to a variety of suffering locations, including Japan, Ecuador, Ethiopia, and Eastern Europe. In 1953 Heifer Project became an ecumenical organization, Heifer Project International.[48] At this writing Heifer International remains a vigorous organization with headquarters in Little Rock, Arkansas, and boasts of its aid to "millions of people" around the world.[49]

Although the postwar growth in service enjoyed considerable support in the pews, there was quiet concern at higher levels over its impact. The Brethren Service Commission had blossomed into the largest program in the Church of the Brethren, and denominational leaders were uneasy with the free-wheeling style of the movement's managers, especially M. R. Zigler. In particular, Zigler's acquisition of the New Windsor facility and the financial risk of supporting CPS raised eyebrows. Older programs, especially mission, felt neglected and suspected that their fundraising had suffered because of popular service projects. By 1943 Brethren Service usually received two pages in *The Gospel Messenger,* giving it equal stature with mission, which always had its own space in the periodical. Some complained that the money raised to support conscientious objectors exceeded the remainder of denominational fundraising. Pressure built, then, to consolidate the denomination under one board that controlled all of its spending. This would give the Brethren a more rational process of fundraising that adequately support-ed less dramatic but no less vital programs than Brethren Service, so the argument ran. As a result, Annual Conference (1946) created a General Brotherhood Board of twenty-five members to coordinate the commis-sions. The board would budget for the entire denomination rather than having each agency raise its own funds. The single-sentence preamble to the committee's report left little doubt that this was a move toward effi-ciency.

> The commission believes that, for the sake of unity, efficiency, and economy in general brotherhood work, there should be one gen-eral board called the General Brotherhood Board of the Church of the Brethren.[50]

This integrated the Brethren Service Commission into the denomi-nation but also constructed a ceiling for it and added more administra-tive control. For the new executive post of General Secretary, the Board passed over M. R. Zigler and, instead, chose his former subordinate, Raymond R. Peters. In this the Board opted for efficiency and caution over charisma and aggressiveness. Board members feared that Zigler's passion for peace and relief coupled with his vigor would throw the denominational administration out of balance. Zigler accepted an assignment as the denomination's representative to the newly forming World Council of Churches and as supervisor of Brethren relief in Europe.[51]

Despite this bureaucratic restraint on Brethren Service, many Brethren considered relief work a high calling. Ambitious relief pro-grams in Germany and Austria, CROP, Heifer Project, purses and grease for peace, tractor boys, and sea-going cowboys testify to the ardor for an internationalized version of the Social Gospel among the Brethren. Although staffing projects in China, Germany, or Austria required rela-tively few people, boat after boat of heifers, thousands of young men to tend them, and copious amounts of supplies crossing oceans signify that this generation of Brethren pushed service to new levels.

The flourishing Brethren Service program was both a consequence and cause of modernization. Without the human need created by World War II, the existence of Brethren Service is hard to imagine. Prior to Pearl Harbor, Brethren relief consisted primarily of fundraising for

Armenians during World War I, local efforts for victims of the Depression, and the undertakings for Spain and China. The Brethren response to the largest modern war dwarfed these attempts. But if unprecedented relief was a legacy of modernity, it also contributed to this trend. The consolidated board system, created largely as a reaction to the growth of Brethren Service, rationalized the Brethren bureaucracy in a typically modern manner. Also, the globalized perspective of Brethren Service enhanced Brethren modernization. Admittedly, this followed a well-worn trail cleared by mission, but in the post-World War II world more Brethren volunteers and more Brethren dollars than ever crossed oceans. Thus, response to the destructiveness of modern war, a maturing bureaucracy, and a mounting global perspective indicate that Brethren Service and modernization walked together.

Fundamentalism

Brethren fundamentalists emerged from World War II just as energized as progressives. As before, they denounced modernist interpretations of the Bible, and as the denomination hoisted higher the flag of Social Gospel, fundamentalists grieved over what they considered a dangerous trend. But conservatives, immersed in the Cold War, focused less on cultural issues, such as evolution, popular culture, or bobbed hair, and more on the security of the nation.

World War II widened the breach between Protestant progressives and evangelicals. If the global conflict motivated liberals toward more involvement in service, it also provided a model of mission for conservatives. The war took many evangelical young men and women overseas, which they had always considered the mission field; there they witnessed poverty and found themselves at risk. Small wonder that some came home rededicated to mission as a wave of mission fervor swept over American evangelicals. The movement freely borrowed military imagery. In Youth for Christ rallies near American bases overseas, evangelicals asserted their desire to open "beachheads" that would lead to missionary "invasions."

Evangelicals, just like progressives, planned for the postwar world, except that they hoped to evangelize the world rather than bring it the Social Gospel. Led by organizations like Youth for Christ, Inter-Varsity, and Wycliffe Bible Translators, conservative mission boards increased their efforts as mainline agencies cut back. Conservatives were no less dedicated to evangelizing America, for without converting the home country, the grand goal of conquering the world within a generation was

unattainable. Fundamentalists were as zealous for mission as other conservatives, but aggressive anticommunism, especially among the most
militant fundamentalists, set them apart from the wider evangelical
movement.[52]

When Brethren fundamentalists, then, looked within their denomination, they were disappointed. They detected the postwar version of the
Social Gospel running full tilt, all but overwhelming soul-winning.
Furthermore, they remained infuriated over the denomination's 1942
decision to join the Federal Council of Churches. Fundamentalists still
objected to the Federal Council because they considered it saturated with
modernism, but now they also labeled it soft on communism, a new
emphasis. A pamphlet by Brethren fundamentalist Grant Mahan articulated this.

> We object to union with the Federal Council because it is not
> engaged in strictly religious work. We have a chart, furnished by
> the "Sunday School Times," in which are given the names of six-
> teen organizations with which sixty of the Federal Council's officers
> have also been connected. None are religious or have church
> names. Here are a few: "Socialist Party," "War Resisters League,"
> "Anti-Dies Committee Bloc,"* "League for Industrial Democracy,"
> and "People's Lobby."
>
> William Ward Ayer, Pastor of Calvary Baptist Church in New
> York City, says: The Federal Council of Churches very well repre-
> sents liberal Protestantism. "The Federal Council more often
> speaks for the Communistic shibboleth than the Gospel one—It
> has the backing of the extreme socialistic groups throughout the
> land."
>
> Sworn testimony before the Dies Committee: "The radical
> affiliation of the Federal Council of Churches of Christ is a subject
> of extensive discussion. Apparently, in lieu of primarily promoting
> Christianity among its several members, it more represents a huge
> political machine and appears to intermeddle with radical politics.
> Its directorate indicates that it interlocks with many of the most
> extreme radical organizations." . . .
>
> Whence did Modernism come? The answer: **Modernism
> was spawned in evil, originating in the mind of Satan**. It goes
> without saying that if Modernism is a system of false teaching, a tis-

---

*Martin Dies chaired the House Un-American Activities Committee, which in 1939
held hearings charging that Communists had infiltrated organized labor and several New
Deal agencies.

sue of lies—which it assuredly is—it must have originated in the mind of the devil, whom our Lord described as the father of lies. It is greatly to be regretted that the real Satanic origin and nature of Modernism are not more generally recognized and proclaimed by Christian people, **many of whom are most effectively aiding the anti-Christian campaign** by speaking softly about it and even flattering this Satanic system, if not actually fraternizing with it.[53]

I. N. H. Beahm repeated the charge that the Council promoted modernism but added that it divided the Brethren, that it would pull them from their traditions, especially prayer coverings for women, love feast, and feetwashing, and that it was too liberal on race relations.

I have a sermon given by a New York man on the Huntingdon [Pennsylvania] platform last June, which deprecates the Moses story of creation of Genesis One. He also tosses the Noah's Ark story over into the class of mere human stones. He would surely dispose of the Book of Jonah likewise. . . .

The preaching of the Mosaic story of creation and of the Noah story of the Ark and the Jonah story as mere human origin like the great New Yorker is rank modernism. Yet surely such preaching goes merrily on in the Federal Council. . . . Since modernism is making inroads among us, membership with the Federal Council will further tend in and to more of it. Brethren, it is time to withdraw. . . .

St. Paul . . . mentions three [ordinances]:

1. The order of appearance in religious service—the uncovered head of the man and the veiled head of the woman.
2. The Lord's supper, which was at night and eaten before the communion. In verse 20, one is taught that the bread and the cup were taken after the supper; hence not the supper as also Luke teaches in 22:20. John teaches feet washing before the supper. Luke and Paul teach the communion after supper. The Federal Council will train us away from the gospel order. Any how, we can still teach them the gospel on this after we cut loose from their membership. We should teach the whole world these sacred ordinances as among the climax things of our Savior's teachings that sleepless night, to which John devotes one third of his Gospel—

seven chapters—from Jno.13:1 to Jno 19:42. Further, there are
other N. T. ordinances. However, in the above mentioned three
ordinances Paul sought to correct the manner of observance. . . .

The Federal Council seeks to make all races and grades of
people one, which is purely communistic and for the mere physical welfare of society. If they win, what race will it be? . . . There
are generally speaking five particular races. God's way. The mixture of races socially rather guarantees interbreeding or amalga-
mation. The Federal Council way.[54]

Many of the most vocal opponents of the Federal Council came
from the Middle District of central Pennsylvania. They resembled sepa-
ratist fundamentalists, a growing segment of militant American fundamentalism that in the late forties urged the faithful to withdraw from
denominations contaminated by liberals and modernists lest they compromise with the devil. In 1945 Harold Snider, pastor of the Lewistown,
Pennsylvania, congregation, founded a monthly fundamentalist newsletter that attacked the Federal Council and eventually drifted into separatism. Initially Snider called his publication *The Gospel Trumpet*, but he
quickly changed its name to *The Brethren Fundamentalist*, and the mast-
head identified the periodical as "A Brethren Paper Protesting
Membership in the Federal Council." Donations supported *The Brethren
Fundamentalist*, and Snider mailed it to all ministers and elders in the
denomination, a list of three thousand.[55] The first issue of this self-
described "protest paper" listed three "needed changes" vital for the
denomination.

1—Dissolving relationship with the Federal Council of Churches.
2—Fewer editorials and articles savoring of the social-gospel, pacifism and politics, and more giving due prominence to God's Word,
Jesus Christ as Saviour, and the sin question.
3—More emphasis on evangelism as the first cause of the
church.[56]

In subsequent editions, Snider condemned denominational leadership with little restraint. He pointedly omitted Bethany from a list of
"reputable" seminaries, all notably fundamentalist, that he said agreed
with his rejection of pacifism. He compared the decision to join the
"modernistic Federal Council" to an illegal change in government and
accused denominational leaders of hiding their intentions; they "tell you

nothing, but continue to lead you farther and farther into modernism and false Christianity." He alleged that the "same autocratic leadership" responsible for membership in the Federal Council established the General Brotherhood Board through a "political finesse that would put to envy all the Hitlers, Stalins, and Francos the world has seen." To be sure, Snider belonged to fundamentalism's most militant wing.[57]

Offended denominational leaders responded, and in 1948 Standing Committee tapped district elders to request Snider to stop publication of *The Brethren Fundamentalist*. Snider predictably refused, and his eight-hundred-member congregation withdrew from the denomination. Snider promptly resigned from the Church of the Brethren,[58] and his letter identified two issues—pacifism and the Federal Council—as the cause of the rupture.

> The present leadership of the Church of the Brethren has indicated the test of loyalty to the church to be contingent on one's willingness to preach "pacifism" and approve the merger with the modernistic Federal Council of Churches of Christ (so-called) in America. . . .
>
> Inasmuch as the trend toward regimentation in the present leadership leads to the "unfrocking" of ministers who are not pacifistic and who do not approve our relationship with the aforementioned Federal Church, I am respectfully resigning my ministry of more than 20 years in the Church of the Brethren as of this date.
>
> I find it absolutely incompatible with my love for Jesus Christ and the whole Word of God to remain any longer in a fellowship which has become predominantly pacifistic and which has linked arms with bold deniers of the Bible.[59]

A minority of the Lewistown fellowship remained loyal to the Church of the Brethren, and difficult litigation ensued over which congregational faction got the church property. The denomination argued that the Church of the Brethren was not purely congregational and that upon schism property rights rested with the denomination, even if its supporters were a minority within the defecting congregation. The lower court agreed, and the State Supreme Court rejected the Lewistown congregation's appeal. The real estate remained with the Church of the Brethren. Undoubtedly, the denomination's courtroom victory deterred other fundamentalist congregations from seceding.[60]

In sum, the divisiveness of fundamentalism persisted. In part, the fundamentalist/modernist battleground shifted from culture wars to

Cold War. Fundamentalists continued to protect the Bible from modernism, but now they indicted opponents for unwillingness to defend the nation-state and complicity with its enemy. Moreover, as progressives encouraged a new round of the Social Gospel, fundamentalists saw another error. Finally, fundamentalists saw all of these problems—modernism, softness on communism, and the Social Gospel—in the Federal Council of Churches. The division between fundamentalists and progressives continued as wide as ever.

Brethren Volunteer Service

By the late forties, international relations, particularly the Cold War, influenced the Church of the Brethren more than ever. For Brethren pacifists this meant the likelihood of peacetime conscription. In 1947 President Harry S. Truman and Congress ended the draft, but Truman needed a strong military to back his belligerent foreign policy. In the same year that conscription lapsed, the president declared his intent to contain Communist expansion around the world. The Cold War intensified in the following years when Congress approved the Marshall Plan and Czechoslovakia joined the eastern block. Truman hoped for universal military training rather than a draft; he wanted every male to train for six months rather than a portion of the males serving a lengthier period. But in 1948 the President accepted restored conscription.[61] Meanwhile, the task of rebuilding postwar Europe persisted, as described earlier in the chapter. From these two stimuli—the draft and relief, both emanating from overseas developments—emerged a Brethren organization to coordinate youth service.

Much of the impetus for this new program of peace and volunteerism came from the youth themselves and their mentors. At the 1947 Annual Conference in Orlando, Florida, M. R. Zigler inspired a meeting of young people with his eyewitness description of devastation in Europe.[62] Almost every week *Our Young People*, a youth magazine, taught that war was wrong. One issue, for example, included the accounts of participants in the first Christian Citizenship Seminar, who lobbied their congressional representatives for peace.

> We tried to convince our congressman that there is a better way than war; that disarmament must come; that universal military training would be (1) a threat to international relations, (2) a threat to the moral life of the boys, (3) too costly, (4) a threat to religious liberty, and (5) a step in the direction of totalitarianism. . . . We

restated the historic peace position of the Church of the
Brethren.[63]

The Christian Citizenship Seminars, in which high school age students spent a week in New York and Washington, D. C., learning about
political power and social justice, themselves represented growing
Brethren Social Gospel in the postwar period.

In another issue of *Our Young People*, Martha Rittenhouse, winner
of a district peace oratorical contest, affirmed that peace is pragmatic.

> Experience also has proved that pacifism is a practical way of bring-
> ing peace. It has shown how impractical war has always been.
> Millions of lives have been lost for some ideal, such as world free-
> dom or peace, and then, several years later, millions more are lost
> for the same cause. Not only lives are lost. Happiness and hope
> are lost. Minds and souls are stunted by suffering. Is this practical?
> No. But is pacifism any more practical? Would it have been practi-
> cal to refuse to fight the Germans in the first World War? Would it
> have been practical to have let Napoleon march into the European
> countries? This would have cost neither more lives, nor more
> freedom than did war. If, back in history, nations had refused to
> fight for just one century of all time, refused to have war—for it
> takes two to make a quarrel and two to make a war—the thou-
> sands of wars since then would have been prevented. Billions of
> lives would have been saved, untold suffering prevented. But the
> nations did not make that sacrifice. Patrick Henry said, "Give me
> liberty or give me death." He did not say, "Give me liberty or let
> me take someone else's life." Many wars have been started on that
> basis.[64]

In addition to nonviolence, *Our Young People* blessed service. A
typical article reported that Brethren youth in Easton, Maryland, had
taken their relief campaign to a Halloween parade.

> The B. Y. P. D. [Brethren Young People's Department] of the two
> churches in the Peach Blossom congregation of Mardela District
> sponsored a Float for Relief in the annual Halloween parade in
> Easton on October 31.
> The float was built around the idea of the Statue of Liberty.
> One of the young women was dressed as the Statue of Liberty and

held aloft a light with the inscription, "Your gifts will make her light shine brighter." Large placards with the same words were also placed on the sides of the float. Around the feet of the Statue of Liberty were dozens of boxes of clothing, shoes, canned foods and other gifts which had been collected by the members of the B. Y. P. D. during the month of October. These had been donated by members and friends of the churches and other interested people in the communities. The members of the B. Y. P. D. worked hard at the task of collecting gifts. Collections were made at individual homes and at a central place in town. The local paper carried advertisements soliciting the giving of relief goods.[65]

Young Brethren peace activists took the message of peace and service to heart and organized. At the 1947 Annual Conference, the Brethren Service Commission sponsored a five-week combined work camp and peace institute at Salina, Kansas, for twenty-two youth. Out of this came the first year-round peace caravan with others pledging to raise money and participate in prayer vigils for the effort. In early June 1948, the National Youth Assembly, including the peace caravan, met in Chicago and departed determined to spread the peace message to other young people and to carry their cause to Annual Conference in Colorado Springs, Colorado.[66]

In Colorado Springs a small group of enthusiasts prayed together every morning in a park. They also developed a questionnaire to determine interest in a volunteer program among young people attending Conference. Of the 130 males and females who responded, almost all were favorable. Alma Moyers (Long), one of the organizers, recalled that they

sat around a table and counted all these ballots, all these papers, and we were so amazed that everybody—I think it was almost one hundred percent of young people agreed with us and a high percentage said they would take part in [a service program]. Well, then we knew we had something going.[67]

The leaders took their results to a youth meeting. According to Moyers, prior to Annual Conference none of the youth had anticipated requesting the formation of a volunteer service agency, although they had discussed the idea previously.

Nobody went to Conference thinking that we were going to do this. The whole church was concerned about conscription. But none of us went there saying we were going to pass BVS [Brethren Volunteer Service].[68]

Dan West helped the activists write a proposal. The young idealists faced a procedural obstacle because Standing Committee had already written the Conference's agenda, which delegates had approved at the opening of the gathering, and their proposal for a service agency was not on it. Never had an item appeared on the Conference floor without first going through Standing Committee. (Membership in the Federal Council of Churches had the approval of Standing Committee but not a district conference.) The young people, then, sought to break a long-standing precedent. (More than youthful distance from the levers of power may have been at work, because M. R. Zigler and Dan West thought that Standing Committee would have killed the proposal.)[69] Youth leaders decided that the Brethren Service report was an appropriate time for Conference to consider their proposal, and they delegated Alma Moyers to buttonhole the moderator, C. C. Ellis, between sessions and plead their case. She remembered that

since I was a delegate, they said, Alma, why don't you go see the moderator. Well, how you gonna get ahold of the moderator? I stayed backstage until he came in. Of course, he was a college president [Juniata], and I had only just graduated [from Bridgewater College] so I felt about this high. I knew I didn't have time to stand around and talk too long because he was ready to walk on stage. I just caught him as he was walking on, and so he was in a hurry and I didn't quite know what to say. I had this paper in my hand and said, "Do you think the youth could present this idea this afternoon." He said, "Well, Standing Committee isn't meeting any more. I don't know if we can do it or not. Everything has to go through Standing Committee."[70]

That quick conversation left the youthful envoy uncertain about its outcome. The afternoon session was about to begin, and Ellis took his seat with Moyers "stewing, wondering what was going to happen."

The moderator was ready to come on stage [to begin the session]. That's the way those guys do it; they come in at the last minute. I didn't know all the details. All I knew was that I talked to him, and he wasn't too excited about it. I didn't know if it worked or not. Paul Bowman was on stage with the moderator. He was at the front table. I didn't know this at the time, but when he went in to sit, he must have said to Paul Bowman—they kind of had a little get-together—he said what do you want to do about this thing that the young people want to do. I got the impression that Ellis wasn't too excited about doing something that Standing Committee hadn't approved because nobody does this. And, of course, Warren Bowman was the president of Bridgewater and he knew me.* I think the Lord put the right people together. Paul said, well, why not let them bring it up; that's all right. I think Paul Bowman gave kind of official approval. He told Ellis, what have we got to lose?[71]

Ellis asked the delegates for permission to suspend the rules and hear the proposal. With young Brethren sitting as a block in the balcony, Ted Chambers acted as their spokesperson. Chambers, so short that he brought an orange crate on which to stand, mounted his makeshift platform and introduced himself to the delegates.

I'm Ted Chambers, from Grand Rapids, Michigan, and believe it or not, I'm twenty-four years old.[72]

This drew a big laugh. Then Chambers read the request for a program to support volunteers, including those performing alternative service to the draft.

We, a group of young people at the 1948 Annual Conference, because of a concern for Brethren youth, in the event of conscription, wish to present to the delegate body this plan for immediate action.

We plead for a plan of definite action to implement the general statement of the Conference on the position and practices of the Church of the Brethren in relation to war.

2. We recommend that a broad plan of volunteer service be instituted for Brethren, especially those of conscription age, at once. We further recommend that this plan carry over into any crisis period as the core of our alternative service program. We are

*Moyers had just graduated from Bridgewater that spring.

willing and anxious to co-operate with the General Brotherhood
Board in constructing such a plan.

    3. Finally, we ask for the immediate and continuing support of
the entire brotherhood in the carrying out and financing of such a
program.[73]

Conference quickly approved the proposal and, according to Moyers,
"the young people sitting up in the balcony just cheered and nobody had
done that before or since. But it was just such a high moment that it was
like God cheering through them."[74]

    Brethren youth kept their word to support the program called
Brethren Volunteer Service (BVS), and in its first year, eighty eager volunteers enrolled. In September 1948, just months after Annual
Conference, the first recruits reported to orientation at New Windsor,
and another group went to Camp Harmony in Hooversville,
Pennsylvania. After their three-month orientation, these unpaid workers
received assignments in Falfurrias, Texas, and Puerto Rico, or on peace
caravans. (Alma Moyers was in the first BVS unit and became a peace
caravaner.) In the fall of 1949, the first volunteers went to Europe, and
throughout the fifties BVS trained four units of volunteers annually as
the norm.[75]

    With the birth of BVS, the Brethren completed their shift to service
as mission waned. The best and brightest young Dunkers—the late
forties spiritual descendants of Laura and Raymond Cottrell—undertook
a Social Gospel for the modern world rather than conversion of sinners.
Contributing to the postwar stage of this transformation were the afflic-
tion caused by modern war and conscription resulting from postwar,
superpower rivalry. Together both provided the primary motivation for
the founders of the Brethren's service agency.

CONCLUSION

Tom Brokaw's best-selling tribute to the World War II cohort hails it as
the Greatest Generation for its dedication and sacrifice.[76] Skeptics counter that Brokaw's favorite generation also harbored McCarthyism, abandoned the civil rights revolution to its children, and saddled them with
Vietnam and a nuclear arms race.

    So might the Brethren of this era be the Greatest Brethren
Generation, with all due respect to the founders. As with Brokaw's
beloved group, skeptics find fodder among this Brethren cohort.
Although the fundamentalist rebellion hardly began with them, it

worsened on their watch and foreshadowed what in the late twentieth century became a deeply divided fellowship. Also, after 1960, under this generation's leadership, denominational membership plummeted. Alexander Mack would not have been pleased. Yet this Greatest Brethren Generation, as it served the church, matched the dedication and sacrifice of Brokaw's subjects, who served the state. True, heightened Brethren interest in service began before the war. But, the stories of individuals within this group, such as Dan West, M. R. Zigler, Ralph Smeltzer, Helena Kruger, the plucky Alma Moyers Long, sea-going cowboys, and countless others, exemplified this period's vigor and suggest why the Church of the Brethren had more influence than its diminutive size merited. If nothing else, this generation was institutionally creative and left an impressive legacy of CROP, Heifer Project, and Brethren Volunteer Service. Alexander Mack would have been pleased.

No less than other generations during the age of World War, this Greatest Brethren Generation felt modernization, chiefly through the influence of modern war and modern nation-states. Though peace had returned, World War II cast a strong shadow over the postwar years; rebuilding war zones invigorated the denominational mainstream but caused a backlash among conservatives, who interpreted it as too much Social Gospel. The Cold War rivalry between the Soviet and American superpowers also shaped this period; conservatives elevated anticommunism to a priority, and the reinstitution of the draft generated the alternative service component of BVS. Modernization still made an impact on Brethrenism.

Some of modernity's effect was old; some was new. The Cold War, Brethren Volunteer Service, and heavy emphasis on overseas relief were unique to the period, but the Social Gospel, fundamentalism, and the mutual hostility of these two systems had prewar precedent. The post-World War II Brethren response to modernity had as much continuity as change.

⌘

For many Brethren, Kenneth I. Morse, editor of *Our Young People,* caught the spirit of the times with his stirring hymn "Move in our Midst." Written during World War II and set to a tune composed by Perry L. Huffaker, a Brethren pastor, the hymn quickly became part of the denomination's repertoire, and the new hymnal in 1951 included it. The opening verse captures the turmoil of the times in which Morse composed it and the ensuing distress of the Cold War.

Move in our midst, Thou Spirit of God;
Go with us down from Thy holy hill;
Walk with us through the storm and the calm;
Spirit of God, go Thou with us still.

But Morse's verse also shows this generation's optimism that the times would not overwhelm them.

Touch Thou our hands to lead us aright;
Guide us forever; show us Thy way.
Transform our darkness into Thy light;
Spirit of God, lead Thou us today.

And the final words intertwine social justice and spiritual life, as did so many at the end of the age of world war.

Kindle our hearts to burn with Thy flame;
Raise up Thy banners high in this hour.
Stir us to build new worlds in Thy name;
Spirit of God, O send us Thy power![77]

Notes

1. John W. Jeffries, *Wartime America: The World War II Home Front* (Chicago: Ivan R. Dee, 1996), 3-8. The theme of Tom Brokaw's popular accolade to this generation is dedication and sacrifice, but the book also prominently features the war-as-a-turning-point concept; see Brokaw, *The Greatest Generation* (New York: Random House, 1998), 19, 44, 65, 72, 336-37. See also Studs Terkel, *"The Good War": An Oral History of World War II* (New York: Pantheon Books, 1984), 7-16.
2. "Kingdom Gleanings," *The Gospel Messenger* (November 16, 1946): 17.
3. Wendell Flory, "A History of Brethren Involvement in China," *Brethren Life and Thought* (Autumn, 1966): 45.
4. Flory, "A History," 45-46.
5. Flory, "A History," 46.
6. Donald F. Durnbaugh, *Fruit of the Vine: A History of the Brethren, 1708-1995* (Elgin, Ill.: Brethren Press, 1997), 482; J. Kenneth Kreider, *A Cup of Cold Water: The Story of Brethren Service* (Elgin, Ill.: Brethren Press, 2001), 66-71.
7. "Home to Poland," *Our Young People* (April 11, 1948): 10-11.
8. Durnbaugh, *Fruit of the Vine*, 482; Kreider, *A Cup of Cold Water*, 66-77.
9. Kreider, *A Cup of Cold Water*, 171-181.
10. Russell Eisenbise, "Surely God has remembered me today . . . ," *The Gospel Messenger* (July 9, 1949): 19.
11. Durnbaugh, *Fruit of the Vine*, 483; Kreider, *A Cup of Cold Water*, 161-67, 179.
12. Howard E. Sollenberger, "The UNRRA Brethren Service Unit," in *To Serve the Present Age: The Brethren Service Story*, edited by Donald F. Durnbaugh (Elgin, Ill.: The Brethren Press, 1975), 155-60; Kreider, *A Cup of Cold Water*, 341-42.
13. Sollenberger, "The UNRRA," 159-60.
14. Sollenberger, "The UNRRA," 162; Kreider, *A Cup of Cold Water*, 342-45.
15. Donald F. Durnbaugh, *Pragmatic Prophet: The Life of Michael Robert Zigler (November 9, 1981-October 25, 1985)* (Elgin, Ill.: Brethren Press, 1989), 154-56; Kreider, *A Cup of Cold Water*, 137, 138, 147, 299-315.
16. John Evans, "Church Leader Tells of Plight of Low Countries," *Chicago Daily Tribune* (November 24, 1945): 12. Copyrighted November 24, 1945, Chicago Tribune Company. All rights reserved. Used with permission.
17. M. R. Zigler, "The Angels Sang, 'Peace . . . Goodwill,' " *The Gospel Messenger* (December 22, 1945): 6-7.
18. *The Gospel Messenger* (November 30, 1946): 17. Also quoted in Durnbaugh, *Pragmatic Prophet*, 161.
19. "The Pastor of the Schwarzenau Church Writes," *The Gospel Messenger* (March 8, 1947): 20.
20. Durnbaugh, *Pragmatic Pragmatic*, 161-62.

21. "Introducing *Das Jugenddorf*," *The Gospel Messenger* (August 27, 1949): 18-19.
22. Minutes of the German Staff Meeting, Frankfurt, June 5, 1949, Donald F. Durnbaugh Collection of M. R. Zigler Papers, Bridgewater College, Box 2, Folder 31; Kreider, *A Cup of Cold Water*, 217-43.
23. Minutes of the German Staff Meeting.
24. Ralph E. Smeltzer, "The History of Brethren Service in Austria: From Its Beginning (November, 1946) to July, 1949," unpublished term paper, Bethany Biblical Seminary, November 28,1949), Chapter I, 1-2, 8. See also Kreider, *A Cup of Cold Water*, 183-84.
25. Ralph E. Smeltzer to Dr. Karl Heiser, Chief, Public Welfare Branch of the U. S. Allied Control Administration (February 12, 1947), in Smeltzer, "The History of Brethren Service in Austria," Chapter III, 4-9. See also Smeltzer to [Eldon] Burke, et al (February 20, 1947), in Smeltzer, Chapter III, 8-9.
26. Smeltzer, "The History of Brethren Service in Austria," Chapter III, 10, 28; Smeltzer, "Brethren Service in Austria," in *To Serve the Present Age*, 177-78.
27. Smeltzer, "The History of Brethren Service in Austria," Chapter III, 29.
28. Ralph E. Smeltzer to M. R. Zigler (June 21, 1947), Durnbaugh Collection, Box 2, Folder 31; Smeltzer, "The History of Brethren Service in Austria," Chapter III, 26.
29. Smeltzer, "The History of Brethren Service in Austria," Chapter IV, 3; Smeltzer, "Brethren Service in Austria," in *To Serve the Present Age*, 178-79; Kreider, *A Cup of Cold Water*, 194-96. One of the first volunteers in Austria was Donald F. Durnbaugh, whose name graces this volume's endnotes so often. In 1949 he arrived in Austria as a volunteer and served a two-year term, supervising efforts to resettle *Volksdeutsche* families in the U. S. Between 1953 and 1956, he returned to direct Brethren work in Austria.
30. Smeltzer "The History of Brethren Service in Austria," Chapter II, 32-33. See also Smeltzer, "Brethren Service in Austria," in *To Serve the Present Age*, 175; and Kreider, *A Cup of Cold Water*, 186.
31. Smeltzer, "The History of Brethren Service in Austria," Chapter IV, 8-9 and Chapter II, 32-33.
32. Smeltzer, "The History of Brethren Service in Austria," Chapter IV, 10; Smeltzer, "Brethren Service in Austria," in *To Serve the Present Age*, 177; "Railroad Cars into Homes, *The Gospel Messenger* (July 3, 1948): 21.
33. Smeltzer, "The History of Brethren Service in Austria," Chapter IV, 13-14.
34. Kreider, *A Cup of Cold Water*, 189-90.
35. Rosemary Block, "I Was Sick and Ye Visited Me," *The Gospel Messenger* (August 13, 1949): 18-19.
36. Kreider, *A Cup of Cold Water*, 190. For a statement by Rosemary Block on the X-ray program, see Merlin G. Shull, "History of the Brethren Service Commission in Austria" (term paper, Bethany Theological Seminary, 1953), 33-35.

37. Shull, "History of the Brethren Service Commission in Austria," 30.
38. Kreider, *A Cup of Cold Water*, 84.
39. "Lard Good Enough to Eat," *The Gospel Messenger* (March 8, 1947): 21.
40. Kreider, *A Cup of Cold Water*, 82.
41. Durnbaugh, *Pragmatic Prophet*, 174-78; Kreider, *A Cup of Cold Water*, 94-98; John D. Metzler, Sr., "The CROP Idea," in *To Serve the Present Age*, 148-54.
42. Metzler, "The CROP Idea," 149.
43. Durnbaugh, *Pragmatic Prophet*, 177-78; Kreider, *A Cup of Cold Water*, 95-96; Metzler, "The CROP Idea," 148-49.
44. Durnbaugh, *Fruit of the Vine*, 464-65; Kreider, *A Cup of Cold Water*, 133-37; Thurl Metzger, "The Heifer Project," in *To Serve the Present Age,* 145.
45. Durnbaugh, *Fruit of the Vine*, 464.
46. Bill Beck and Mel West, eds., *Cowboy Memories: Published in Honor of the Seagoing Cowboys, Air Attendants, and Truckers of HPI Animals* (Heifer Project International, 1994), 39-40.
47. "Diary of Harry Badorf," unpublished manuscript. The manuscript remains in the possession of the diarist. For other accounts of sea-going cowboys, see Clara T. Johnson, *Milk for the World: The Heifer Project on the West Coast; A Story of Love in Action* (Elgin, Ill.: The Brethren Press 1981), 26-40.
48. Durnbaugh, *Fruit of the Vine*, 464-65; Kreider, *A Cup of Cold Water*, 137-147; Thurl Metzger, "The Heifer Project," 145-47. Hershey was not directly related to Milton S. Hershey, America's chocolate king. J. Kenneth Kreider was a Brethren Volunteer Service worker in Germany during the 1950s, and his book includes several of his photographs of Heifer Project cows.
49. www.heifer.org.
50. *Minutes of the Annual Conferences of the Church of the Brethren*, 1945-1954, compiled and edited by Ora W. Garber (Elgin, Ill. Brethren Publishing House, 1956), (1947) 52-80. See also (1946) 26-27.
51. Durnbaugh, *Pragmatic Prophet*, 180-83; Kreider, *A Cup of Cold Water*, 397-98.
52. Joel A. Carpenter, *Revive Us Again: The Reawakening of American Fundamentalism* (New York: Oxford University Press, 1997), 178-86; Gerald L. Sittser, *A Cautious Patriotism: The American Churches and the Second World War* (Chapel Hill: University of North Carolina Press, 1997), 204-05.
53. Grant Mahan, ed., *The Federal Council of the Churches of Christ in America and the Church of the Brethren* (pamphlet; n.p.; n.d.), 3, 8.
54. I. N. H. Beahm, *Twenty Reasons: A Prayer and Petition* (n.p., 1945), 7-8, 9, 11.
55. "We Put Out the Fleece!" *The Brethren Fundamentalist* (May 15, 1945): 1; Carpenter, *Revive Us Again*, 204-06; Donald F. Durnbaugh, "The Fundamentalist/Modernist Struggle Within the Church of the Brethren, 1910-1950," *Brethren Life and Thought* (Winter and Spring, 2002): 66-67.

56. "The 'Why' of the Paper," *The Gospel Trumpet* (January 30, 1945): 1.

57. "Non-Pacifism," *The Brethren Fundamentalist* (May 15, 1945): 8; "The 'New Look' in Brotherhood Autocracy: Congregational Government Gone with the Wind!" *The Brethren Fundamentalist* (April, 1948): 1.

58. Earl C. Kaylor, Jr., *Out of the Wilderness, 1780-1980: The Brethren and Two Centuries of Life in Central Pennsylvania* (New York: Cornwall Books, 1981), 266-74; Durnbaugh, "The Fundamentalist/Modernist Struggle," 67-71.

59. Harold Snider to Ministerial Board, Middle District of Pennsylvania (April 20, 1948) in "Elders Threaten Fundamentalist Leader," *The Brethren Fundamentalist* (May, 1948): 1.

60. Kaylor, *Out of the Wilderness*, 275-76; Durnbaugh, "The Fundamentalist/Modernist Struggle," 71-73.

61. George Q. Flynn, *The Draft, 1940-1973* (Lawrence: University of Kansas Press, 1993), 90-102.

62. Durnbaugh, *Pragmatic Prophet,* 199.

63. "They Went to Washington," *Our Young People* (November 1, 1947): 5. The article contains several reports filed by participants; Beatrice Zimmerman wrote the one quoted.

64. Martha Rittenhouse, "Is Peace Practical?: Martha Rittenhouse Says 'Yes,' " *Our Young People* (February 1, 1947): 3. See also 6.

65. "On a Float for Relief," *Our Young People* (February 14, 1948): 6. For examples of other articles on peace and relief in *Our Young People,* see Kenneth Morse, "Let's Face It . . . Conscription and You" (February 8, 1947): 2; Robert Root, "Working for Peace with Their Hands" (February 24, 1947): 4-6; Harry Elmore Hurd, "Not Considered at the Peace Table" (June 21, 1947): 8; "On the Prayer Vigil for Peace" (September 6, 1947): 6; "On a Young Pacifist" (May 23, 1948): 12.

66. Durnbaugh, *Pragmatic Prophet,* 199; Kreider, *A Cup of Cold Water*, 37-42.

67. Author interview with Alma Moyers Long (June 17, 2002).

68. Author interview with Alma Moyers Long.

69. Kreider, *A Cup of Cold Water*, 57-23.

70. Author interview with Alma Moyers Long.

71. Author interview with Alma Moyers Long.

72. Author interview with Alma Moyers Long.

73. *Minutes of the Annual Conferences, 1945-1954*, 103. The Minutes do not have a paragraph numbered 1, but the other paragraphs are numbered 2 and 3.

74. Author interview with Alma Moyers Long.

75. Durnbaugh, *Pragmatic Prophet,* 200; Kreider, *A Cup of Cold Water*, 45-46.

76. Brokaw, *The Greatest Generation*, xvii-xxx.

77. Kenneth I. Morse, "Move in Our Midst," No. 225 in *The Brethren Hymnal: Authorized by Annual Conference, Church of the Brethren* (Elgin, Ill.: House of the Church of the Brethren, 1951). Perry Huffaker named his tune "Pine Glen," after the congregation he served.

INDEX

evangelical, 24, 139, 141, 163, 319-20
evangelicalism, 88, 107
evangelists, 10, 59, 85-92, 103-08, 208
evolution, 155-63, 190, 319
family altars, 139-41
Faw, Chalmer, 226-27
Federal Bureau of Investigation, 42
Federal Council of Churches, 272-76, 284, 327; and fundamentalism, 275-76, 320-24
feetwashing, 321
Ferdinand, Franz, xv
First Church of the Brethren, Philadelphia, 30, 33
Flory, Rolland C., 259-60
Flory, Wendell, 292-93
France, 47, 54, 207, 213, 228, 240-41, 258, 271, 294-95, 310, 312
Frantz, Edward, 132-33, 242, 245
Friends, Society of, 47, 217, 224, 243-44, 266, 277, 306. *See also* Quakers
fundamentalism (fundamentalists), 152, 190, 203, 285, 330; and Brethren conservatives, 141-43, 189; and Dunkard Brethren, 186-87; and evolution, 155; and Federal Council of Churches, 275-76, 319-24; and modernization, 124, 150; and nonviolence, 226-27; and the Social Gospel, 147, 163-64, 319-21; after World War II, 319-24
Fundamentals, The, 141, 142
games, 170, 175-76, 304-05
garb. *See* dress
gender roles, 84, 108, 110-12, 116, 191. *See also* women
General Mission Board, 8, 21, 204-05, 263; and India, 205
General Service Committee, 71
General Welfare Committee, 110, 130
German Baptist Brethren, xxx, xxxiii
Germany, 6, 33, 42-45, 220-21, 228, 240-41, 258, 278, 307-10, 312, 318; and post-World War II relief, 298-303
Gish Fund Books, 17
Gist of the Church of the Brethren, 200
Good, Monroe, 280
Goshen, Indiana, 86

Goshen Conference, 71, 74. *See also* Goshen Statement; Goshen pamphlet
Goshen pamphlet, 72-74
Goshen Statement, 60-63, 71, 76
Great Depression, 195-96, 200, 204-11, 245, 292
Great War, 23, 31, 35-36, 38, 41
Greece, 312
hair, 115, 176, 200-01. *See also* bobbed hair
Harsh, Alva, 231
Harsh, Mary Hykes, 231
Harshbarger, Luther, 271
hats, xxx, 114, 169-70, 175, 187
Heifer Project, 269, 276, 307; after World War II, 298, 302, 307, 311-18, 330
Helser, Albert D., and Lola Bechtel, 92-94
Henry, J. M., 71-72
Hershey, Pa., 306; and 1918 Annual Conference, 63, 71-72, 76
Hertzler, Samuel H., 19, 189
higher criticism, 92, 141, 150-52, 163, 190; and Grant Mahan, 200-03
higher education, xxviii, 142, 150, 164, 187, 190-91. *See also individual colleges*
Holsinger, Henry, xxx
Holsopple, F. F., 150
holy kiss, xxv, 180, 185
Hoover, Herbert, 123, 133-34, 199-200
Hope, Christian, xxix, xxxi
Hope, Mary Katherine Nielson, xxix
Horning, Emma, 213-14
Huffaker, Perry, 330-31
India, xxxii, 3, 4, 5, 8-10, 205
individualism, 10, 30, 33, 170, 190-91, 284-85; and dress, 15, 22; and the ministry, 19, 22
Japan 211-12, 228, 231-32, 244-45, 267, 298, 303
jazz (Jazz Age), 83, 123-25, 128, 134-35, 139-42, 164, 190-91
Jesus, 7-8, 50, 62, 84, 89-92, 94-97, 111, 142, 147-50, 151-55, 163, 173, 219-21, 223, 301; and the Goshen Statement, 65-69
jewelry, xxx, 176, 180, 185, 200
Juniata College, xxviii, 22, 147, 150
Kassel, Germany, 302